MAKING
POLICY,
MAKING
LAW

AMERICAN GOVERNANCE AND PUBLIC POLICY SERIES
Series Editor: Barry Rabe, University of Michigan

Selected Titles:

After Disaster: Agenda Setting, Public Policy, and Focusing Events
THOMAS BIRKLAND

Ambiguity and Choice in Public Policy: Political Decision Making in Modern Democracies
NIKOLAOS ZAHARIADIS

Collaborative Public Management: New Strategies for Local Governments
ROBERT AGRANOFF AND MICHAEL MCGUIRE

Dam Politics: Restoring America's Rivers
WILLIAM R. LOWRY

Expert Advice for Policy Choice: Analysis and Discourse
DUNCAN MACRAE, JR. AND DALE WHITTINGTON

Federalism and Environmental Policy: Trust and the Politics of Implementation,
Second Edition
DENISE SCHEBERLE

Federalism in the Forest: National versus State Natural Resource Policy
TOMAS M. KOONTZ

Fenced Off: The Suburbanization of American Politics
JULIET F. GAINSBOROUGH

The Government Taketh Away: The Politics of Pain in the United States and Canada
LESLIE A. PAL AND R. KENT WEAVER, EDITORS

How Governments Privatize: The Politics of Divestment in the United States and Germany
MARK CASSELL

Improving Governance: A New Logic for Empirical Research
LAURENCE E. LYNN, JR., CAROLYN J. HEINRICH, AND CAROLYN J. HILL

Lobbying Together: Interest Group Coalitions in Legislative Politics
KEVIN HULA

Making Policy, Making Law: An Interbranch Perspective
MARK C. MILLER AND JEB BARNES, EDITORS

Metropolitan Governance: Conflict, Competition, and Cooperation
RICHARD C. FEIOCK, EDITOR

Pluralism by the Rules: Conflict and Cooperation in Environmental Regulation
EDWARD P. WEBER

Policy Entrepreneurs and School Choice
MICHAEL MINTROM

The Politics of Automobile Insurance Reform: Ideas, Institutions, and Public Policy in
North America
EDWARD L. LASCHER, JR.

The Politics of Ideas and the Spread of Enterprise Zones
KAREN MOSSBERGER

The Politics of Unfunded Mandates: Whither Federalism?
PAUL L. POSNER

Preserving Public Lands for the Future: The Politics of Intergenerational Goods
WILLIAM R. LOWRY

Terra Incognita: Vacant Land and Urban Strategies
ANN O'M. BOWMAN AND MICHAEL A. PAGANO

Transatlantic Policymaking in an Age of Austerity: Diversity and Drift
MARTIN A. LEVIN AND MARTIN SHAPIRO, EDITORS

Virtual Inequality: Beyond the Digital Divide
KAREN MOSSBERGER, CAROLINE J. TOLBERT, AND MARY STANSBURY

Welfare Policymaking in the States: The Devil in Devolution
PAMELA WINSTON

MAKING
POLICY,
MAKING
LAW

An Interbranch Perspective

MARK C. MILLER and JEB BARNES, Editors

GEORGETOWN UNIVERSITY PRESS
WASHINGTON, D.C.

Georgetown University Press, Washington, D.C.
© 2004 by Georgetown University Press. All rights reserved.
Printed in the United States of America

10 9 8 7 6 5 4 3 2 1 2004

Library of Congress Cataloging-in-Publication Data

Making policy, making law : an interbranch perspective /
Mark C. Miller and Jeb Barnes, editors.
    p.   cm. — (American governance and public policy series)
   Includes bibliographical references and index.
   ISBN 1-58901-025-6 (pbk. : alk. paper)
   1. Separation of powers—United States. 2. Judicial power—
United States. 3. Political questions and judicial power—United
States. 4. United States—Politics and government. 5. Policy
sciences. I. Miller, Mark C. (Mark Carlton), 1958–   II. Barnes,
Jeb. III. American governance and public policy.
JK305.M35 2004
320.6' 0973—dc22   2004004387

Contents

CONTRIBUTORS   vii

FOREWORD, JUDGE ROBERT A. KATZMANN   ix

ACKNOWLEDGMENTS   xi

PART I: SETTING THE STAGE: THEMES AND CONCEPTS

Putting the Pieces Together: American Lawmaking from an
Interbranch Perspective   3
JEB BARNES AND MARK C. MILLER

1   American Courts and the Policy Dialogue: The Role of
Adversarial Legalism   13
ROBERT A. KAGAN

2   Adversarial Legalism, the Rise of Judicial Policymaking, and
the Separation-of-Powers Doctrine   35
JEB BARNES

PART II: A CLOSER LOOK AT INTERBRANCH PERSPECTIVES

3   The View of the Courts from the Hill: A Neoinstitutional
Perspective   53
MARK C. MILLER

4   The View from the President   72
NANCY KASSOP

5   Courts and Agencies   89
R. SHEP MELNICK

PART III: STATUTORY CONSTRUCTION: THE INTERBRANCH PERSPECTIVE APPLIED

6   The Supreme Court and Congress: Reconsidering
the Relationship   107
LAWRENCE BAUM AND LORI HAUSEGGER

7 The Judicial Implementation of Statutes: Three Stories about
Courts and the Americans with Disabilities Act   123
THOMAS F. BURKE

8 The City of Boerne: Two Tales of One City   140
STEPHEN G. BRAGAW AND MARK C. MILLER

PART IV: CONSTITUTIONAL INTERPRETATION: THE INTERBRANCH PERSPECTIVE APPLIED

9 Judicial Finality or an Ongoing Colloquy?   153
LOUIS FISHER

10 Constitutional Interpretation from a Strategic Perspective   170
LEE EPSTEIN, JACK KNIGHT, AND ANDREW D. MARTIN

11 Is Judicial Policymaking Countermajoritarian?   189
NEAL DEVINS

12 Governance as Dialogue   202
JEB BARNES AND MARK C. MILLER

REFERENCES AND BIBLIOGRAPHY   209

COURT CASES   231

INDEX   236

Contributors

JEB BARNES, assistant professor of political science, University of Southern California, and Robert Wood Johnson Health Policy Research Fellow, University of California, Berkeley.

LAWRENCE BAUM, professor of political science, the Ohio State University, Columbus.

STEPHEN BRAGAW, associate professor of government, Sweet Briar College, Sweet Briar, Virginia.

THOMAS BURKE, associate professor of political science, Wellesley College, and former Robert Wood Johnson Health Policy Research Fellow, University of California, Berkeley.

NEAL DEVINS, Goodrich Professor of Law and professor of government, Marshall-Wythe School of Law, College of William and Mary, Williamsburg, Virginia.

LEE EPSTEIN, Edward Mallinckrodt Distinguished University Professor of Political Science and professor of law, Washington University of Saint Louis.

LOUIS FISHER, senior specialist in separation of powers, Congressional Research Service, Library of Congress, Washington, D.C.

LORI HAUSEGGER, assistant professor of political science, Louisiana State University, Baton Rouge.

ROBERT A. KAGAN, professor of political science and law, University of California, Berkeley.

NANCY KASSOP, professor of political science, State University of New York, New Paltz.

JUDGE ROBERT A. KATZMANN, U.S. Court of Appeals for the Second Circuit, New York.

JACK KNIGHT, Sidney W. Souers Professor of Government, Washington University of Saint Louis.

ANDREW D. MARTIN, associate professor of political science, Washington University of Saint Louis.

R. SHEP MELNICK, Thomas P. O'Neill Jr. Professor of American Politics, Boston College.

MARK C. MILLER, associate professor and chair of government, and director of the Law and Society Program, Clark University, Worcester, Massachusetts. Miller is a former Judicial Fellow at the Supreme Court of the United States and a former Congressional Fellow for the late U.S. Senator Paul Wellstone.

Foreword

The Framers of our Constitution, practicing the "science of politics," as Daniel Patrick Moynihan (1988, 301) put it, understood that our system of governance was grounded in interaction between the branches and levels of government. At the national perch, three institutions—legislative, executive and judicial—would act according to their own structures, workways, purposes, and interests. Yet, each branch would not be able to achieve its ends without the others. The Constitution, in Richard Neustadt's (1960, 33) celebrated phrase, created not separate institutions, but separated institutions sharing powers. This design would lead, the Framers believed, to a deliberative process, one in which the constructive tension among the branches contributed to decisions that were faithful to the needs of the people and respectful of their liberties. And these national institutions would function in the context of a federal system where the role of the states was to be secure. In the words of the *Federalist Paper No. 62*: "A good government implies two things: first, fidelity to the object of government, which is the happiness of the people; secondly, a knowledge of the means by which the object can be best attained."

Policymaking, as envisioned by the Framers, was to be dynamic; it is best viewed as a spectrum or continuum of institutional processes, sometimes acting independently, but seldom alone and usually interacting in subtle and often unconscious ways to influence the behavior of other processes (see Katzmann 1986, 9). As James Q. Wilson (1989) has taught us, it is the product of institutions and individuals with different incentives and professional norms, operating within and outside of government.

The literature of political institutions tends often to concentrate on particular ones—studies of Congress, or of the White House, or of the Courts. But such a selective focus, although useful, tends to obscure the interrelationships and interactions of those institutions that account for the ebb and flow of decision making in our federal system. Editors Mark C. Miller and Jeb Barnes capture the richness of interbranch relations by bringing together scholars who have much to say about the intricate web of policymaking. Their canvass is broad and richly textured, using both qualitative and quantitative approaches, analyzing the state of policymaking, applying an interbranch perspective to statutory construction and constitutional interpretation, and drawing lessons from the diversity of essays provided. This volume, a work about both institutions and policymaking, is an extraordinarily valuable resource for any student of government seeking to understand the ongoing American experiment.

Judge Robert A. Katzmann
U.S. Court of Appeals for the Second Circuit

Acknowledgments

This book began as a conversation in, of all places, Las Vegas. We had just finished presenting papers at the Western Political Science Association's annual conference in 2001, and we began chatting about our work. Before long, we realized that, although different in many ways, our research interests shared a common starting point: a conviction that American policymaking emanates from the interaction among the branches and could not be fully understood by focusing on any single branch of government. We also realized that we were not alone, and that a wide range of scholars were developing research that looked beyond the formal boundaries of the branches of government. Before long, we sketched out a rough outline of this project and began contacting the many wonderful contributors to this volume, who graciously agreed to participate. Above all, we would like to thank them for their professionalism and thoughtful essays.

We would like to give special thanks to several people who helped make this project possible. First, this project owes a special debt to Neal Devins and Mark Graber, who took the time early in the process to help sharpen the project's focus and improve our proposal. Second, we would like to thank Gail Grella and the staff at Georgetown University Press, whose dedication and enthusiasm maintained the momentum to bring this project to publication.

Jeb Barnes would also like to thank Howard Gillman and Gordon Silverstein for graciously responding to his requests for feedback on his chapter on the separation-of-powers doctrine. Any errors that remain are entirely his own. Jeb also acknowledges his loving family, Annie, Alexander, and Ryan, whose support, grace, and good humor made it possible for him to get through the relatively intense period of working on two books while learning the ropes as a brand new assistant professor. He dedicates this book to them.

Mark C. Miller would also like to thank the librarians, staff, and students at Clark University for their assistance with this project. Special thanks go to Cynthia Fenner, Mary Hartman, Bethany Williard, and Tony Iovieno for all their help. Mark also wants to thank his loving parents for all their support. He dedicates this book to them.

PART I

Setting the Stage:
Themes and Concepts

Putting the Pieces Together
American Lawmaking from an Interbranch Perspective

JEB BARNES AND
MARK C. MILLER

AMERICAN POLICYMAKING IS INHERENTLY COMPLEX. WHEREAS other industrialized democracies tend to feature centralized lawmaking processes, which channel policy disputes through national bureaucracies and strong political parties, the American system of checks and balances disperses federal lawmaking authority among multiple, overlapping political forums. As a result, federal policymaking power is shared: Congress is given the primary power to draft laws, subject to the president's veto and judicial review; the executive branch is given the primary power to implement laws, subject to congressional oversight and judicial review; and the courts have the primary power to interpret laws, subject to a variety of legislative and executive checks, including the appointment process, budgetary powers, and the passage of "overrides"—laws that explicitly reverse or materially modify existing judicial interpretations of statutes.

This complexity casts a long shadow over the teaching and studying of American politics and policymaking. In the classroom, because it is difficult to convey the tangled web of interactions among federal lawmakers—much less the interplay among federal, state, and local governments—that underlies the making of policy, students tend to learn about American politics piecemeal. Specifically, after a brief sojourn into the framing of the Constitution, many leading introductory texts turn to the major actors of American government, separately examining Congress, the courts, the presidency, agencies, the media, and so forth (see, e.g., Ginsberg, Lowi, and Weir 2003; Lasser 2000; Wilson and DiIulio 1995; Pfiffner 1995; and Nivola and Rosenbloom 1990).

Similarly, instead of attacking the complexity of American policymaking head-on, researchers have tended to specialize, focusing on specific governmental institutions, on distinct aspects of the policymaking process, or on particular methods of inquiry. This practice arguably reached a zenith during the behavioral revolution in political science, which challenged the existing focus on formal institutions and concentrated on the determinants of the behavior of individual political actors, such as how judges, members of Congress, and individual citizens vote. Despite inroads of so-called new institutionalism in bringing institutions and rules back into the study of policymaking, behavioralism remains a dominant perspective, especially in the field of judicial politics.[1]

Given the obvious classroom appeal of parsing the complexity of American policymaking into parts, and the ongoing scholarly contributions of specialized studies of political behavior, one might ask: Why put the pieces together? The immediate answer is that American policymaking does not result from the edicts of any single branch of government; it emanates from interactions among the branches. This is particularly true today, as the emergence of a modern, administrative state in the United States has blurred the already fuzzy lines between legislative, executive, and judicial functions. As a result, although often a useful starting point, studying the individual components of the American policymaking process often provides a superficial—and sometimes misleading—view of the policymaking process as well as the role of each branch in the making of policy.

Consider behavioralist accounts of the U.S. Supreme Court as a national policymaker. Overall, this approach tends to view the Supreme Court and Congress as rivals, and asks whether—and under what conditions—the Court uses its power of judicial review to thwart the preferences of the "dominant lawmaking coalition." Applying this approach, behavioralists have found that the Supreme Court generally does not challenge the other branches of government. Instead, the Court tends to rule consistently with the interests of the dominant coalition, and its most dramatic decisions seek to impose the policy agenda of the dominant national coalition on recalcitrant local and state officials (Dahl 1957). Moreover, to the extent the Supreme Court does confront the dominant coalition, it tends to fight rearguard actions, representing the old coalition's preferences against the emerging new coalition's preferences during periods of "critical realignment" in national politics (Funston 1975; Adamany 1980).

To reiterate: The behavioralist perspective has considerable merit. It offers a useful "first cut" at understanding the Supreme Court's role in the policymaking process, and helps to dispel naive assumptions that the Supreme Court is a "nonpolitical" branch of government that always champions the rights of unpopular political minorities. However, it is only scratches the surface of the Supreme Court's diverse relationships with the other branches of government (Casper 1976; Graber 1993; McCann 1999; Lovell 2003; see also Barnes 2004). For example, the Supreme Court and Congress are not always rivals. There are cases in which the dominant lawmaking coalition is either unwilling or unable to address issues, and the Court steps into the policymaking vacuum (Epstein and Walker 1995; see also Feeley and Rubin 1998). Indeed, as Graber (1993) has powerfully argued, members of the dominant lawmaking coalition may *invite* judicial policymaking to avoid issues that are politically too hot to handle. Under these conditions, independent judicial policymaking does not *thwart* the dominant lawmaking coalition; it *serves* the reigning coalition and party system by insulating the elected branches of government from divisive issues, such as slavery during the Jacksonian era, racial integration following World War II, and abortion during the 1970s (Graber 1993; McAdam 1982; see also McCann 1999, providing an insightful overview of the Supreme Court as a policymaker).

There is another, perhaps more subtle, reason for trying to put the pieces together through an interbranch perspective. As scholars have grown more specialized, the field has produced a growing number of "sects" that have become increasingly insular. To make matters worse, career pressures reinforce the drive to differentiate—as opposed to synthesize—insights and approaches (Heclo 1994). The result, in our judgment, is an unnecessary balkanization among scholars, which has identified a daunting array of causal factors relevant to policymaking and lost opportunities for fruitful dialogue within the discipline. A central irony follows: in the name of parsimony and simplification, specialization has produced a confusing clutter of studies and findings. Put differently, having let "one hundred flowers bloom," it is time to step back and look at the garden.

Accordingly, this volume seeks to put the pieces together on two levels. Substantively, we have collected original essays from some of the leading scholars who adopt an interbranch perspective on contemporary policymaking, with a special focus on the role of the federal courts in current policymaking. The goal is to offer students fresh perspectives on American policymaking, which challenge textbook descriptions of American government, especially the classic view that elected politicians are the "principals" in the making of policy and unelected judges should be their faithful "agents." Methodologically, we bring together diverse approaches to studying interbranch relations, especially relationships between the courts and the other branches. Some are quantitative; some are qualitative; and some are normative. Some chapters use a historical approach, some are behavioral, some are strategic, some are comparative, and some are institutional in nature. By collecting these diverse studies into a single volume, we hope to underscore the value of an eclectic approach to understanding American lawmaking, while pointing to significant common ground that lies beneath the surface of different methodological approaches.

We believe that this combination of contemporary policy analysis, an interbranch perspective, *and* diverse methodological approaches fills a gap in the literature, especially the literature on the role of the courts in the American policymaking process. For example, Cornell Clayton and Howard Gillman's superb edited volumes on the Supreme Court (Clayton and Gillman 1999; Gillman and Clayton 1999) focus on the Court and new institutionalist interpretive approaches, but do not focus on the policymaking process overall or highlight a range of methodologies. Lawrence Dodd and Calvin Jillison's (1994) thought-provoking collection of essays in *The Dynamics of American Politics: Approaches and Interpretations* consciously embraces diverse methodological approaches, but focuses on broad theoretical issues such as the nature of social change and the role of macro- versus microanalysis for studying politics. Other excellent edited volumes concentrate on specific institutions, such as Lawrence Dodd and Bruce Oppenheimer's (2000) *Congress Reconsidered*, Michael Nelson's (2000) *The Presidency and the Political System*, and Lee Epstein's (1995) *Contemplating Courts*, or on specific issues, such as David Ryden's (2000) *The U.S. Supreme Court and the Electoral Process*, but do not embrace an interbranch perspective. We hope that this collection of essays will find a place next to these volumes, providing a useful tool for teachers, who want to introduce students to the interactive nature of American policymaking, as well as for scholars, who are interested in building bridges across divisions in the field of political science.

PUTTING THE PIECES TOGETHER: AN OVERVIEW

The book is divided into four parts. Part I is titled "Setting the Stage: Themes and Concepts." It lays the book's foundation, providing context and introducing empirical and normative issues that are examined and reexamined throughout the book. To begin, in chapter 1, Robert Kagan offers a comparative perspective on interbranch relations in the United States. Kagan argues that the classic conception of interbranch relations envisages that the chief executive and legislature negotiate basic policy decisions, which are memorialized in legislation. Specialized regulatory agencies implement the law according to specific administrative rules. Courts then adjudicate disputes that arise under the statutes and regulatory rules and ensure that agencies do not act arbitrarily.

Although this idealized description may roughly capture the division of labor among lawmakers in other economically advanced democracies, Kagan argues it does not accurately reflect the current American experience. The reason is that, when compared cross-nationally, the United States has always featured greater levels of "adversarial legalism": a mode of dispute resolution, policymaking, and implementation in which public interest groups frequently place core policy and regulatory issues before the courts, and politically selected, independent judges not infrequently make policy under the guise of resolving legal disputes. Meanwhile, the groups that lose in court often "appeal" to the elected branches of government, demanding legislative relief from unfavorable court decisions. Throughout the process, the basic rules of the game are subject to constant litigation and political revision, in which legislative, executive, and judicial functions are often shared and sometimes reversed, in that the courts sometimes act as the lead policymakers and the elected branches intervene to resolve specific disputes among the contending interests.

In chapter 2, Jeb Barnes examines the implications of revved-up adversarial legalism and the related rise of judicial policymaking for the separation-of-powers doctrine. He argues that adversarial legalism's blurring of legislative, executive, and judicial functions clearly violates the standard view of the separation of powers, which holds that elected politicians should be the principal lawmakers and nonelected judges should serve as faithful agents. However, instead of criticizing heightened adversarial legalism and judicial policymaking, Barnes argues that the standard view of the separation-of-powers doctrine should be rejected, because it rests on questionable formal, functional, and normative arguments. In place of the standard view, Barnes proposes that the separation-of-powers doctrine is best understood as creating a general arrangement of primary powers among the branches of government that differentiates American policymaking from other systems, such as parliamentary systems, as opposed to delineating rigid policymaking roles. From this perspective, the issue is not whether current interbranch relations adhere to neatly defined roles, but whether—and under what conditions—interbranch relations promote core democratic values, such as broad political participation and mutual accommodation.

Part II, titled "A Closer Look at Interbranch Perspectives," presents interbranch lawmaking from the perspectives of Congress, the president, and the federal agencies. All the chapters recognize that policymaking and lawmaking often involve an intricate dance among various governmental institutions. Several themes emerge. First, similar to the Supreme Court, each branch of government looks beyond their own turf and considers the actions and reactions of other actors when formulating policy. Second, each branch has a unique institutional context. Third, regardless of the methodological approach taken, these chapters underscore that policymaking and lawmaking require negotiation and compromise among individual actors located in the various institutions. These chapters thus reinforce the theme that no governmental institution functions in a vacuum, but must act to accommodate other influences and actors in the policymaking process.

Chapter 3, by Mark C. Miller, serves two purposes. It starts by defining some of the key components of the historical strain of neoinstitutional analysis, including the concepts of institutional culture and institutional will. The rest of the chapter then describes the role of Congress in the policymaking process with particular emphasis on court–Congress relations. Miller argues that overall tension between Congress and the courts is on the rise in large part because of their different institutional cultures. Members on both sides of the aisle in Congress charge courts with trespassing on their lawmaking domain, while courts complain that Congress has largely fallen down on the job by writing inherently vague or flawed statutes, which then pass the buck to the courts.

This overall antipathy, however, masks a more complex reality in which court–Congress relations—and the underlying division of labor in the policymaking process between the branches—vary across types of committees. Thus the Judiciary Committees, which traditionally have been the committees of lawyers in Congress, show higher degrees of deference to the courts, whereas the Commerce Committees tend to treat courts as just another political actor, whose input is considered but is not entitled to special weight. The implication is that American policymaking not only features shared lawmaking power, but also that courts and Congress share lawmaking power differently in different institutional and issue contexts.

Nancy Kassop offers a similar analysis of the presidency in chapter 4, describing how the modern presidency and its relationship to the other branches of government defy its traditional role of implementing the law. Specifically, she views the policymaking role of the president through several lenses: (1) president as unilateral lawmaker, (2) president as negotiator in the legislative process, (3) president as administrator who selects officials to either perform independent responsibilities (judges) or implement his policies (executive officers), and (4) president as litigant, whose actions are reviewed and sometimes rebuffed by the courts. The common thread is that a few strong presidents have taken the largely undefined role of the chief executive under the Constitution and forged a place in the policymaking process that is far more complex, differentiated, and powerful than envisaged by the Framers.

In chapter 5, Shep Melnick views agencies from an interbranch perspective. He begins by detailing the rise of a powerful federal bureaucracy in the United States, which reflects two, inter-related factors. First, federal programs and bureaucracy were vastly expanded since the beginning of the New Deal. As result, federal programs now reach into nearly every corner of American society. Second, American politics has become nationalized in that (1) the federal government has gained power at the expense of state and local governments and (2) differences in state programs have come under fire, especially in the South, where states combined paltry public spending with a long history of racial discrimination.

Melnick argues that the growth of federal programs alone did not result in heightened judicial power. Indeed, for a brief period following the constitutional revolution of 1937, power shifted to the president and expert agencies and not to the courts. However, the traditional American distrust of centralized power reasserted itself as reformers in the 1960s created a series of procedural and substantive mechanisms, which allowed them to haul federal agencies to court. The bottom line? Similar to Kagan, Melnick argues that the combination of increased federal programs and distrust of centralized authority has resulted in both an expanded federal bureaucracy and more assertive courts in the United States.

Parts I and II offer a fresh look at the current state of policymaking in the United States. The crux of these chapters is that present-day American policymaking is not only more comprehensive and active, but also its structure is more complex and protean. This political reality, in turn, casts doubt on textbook accounts of the role of each branch in the policymaking process and the separation-of-powers doctrine. The question remains: how can we translate these rich descriptions of interbranch relations into a useful optic for examining today's policymaking and the contributions of the competing actors?

Parts III and IV seek to answer this question by example, collecting essays that apply an interbranch perspective to both statutory construction and constitutional interpretation. Part III, titled "Statutory Construction: The Interbranch Perspective Applied," examines how interbranch relations shape—and reshape—the meaning of federal statutes; it explains how Congress sometimes attempts to use statutes to overturn or to modify Supreme Court decisions; and it suggests how political actors have adapted their political resources to shape interbranch relations.

Lawrence Baum and Lori Hausegger open the analysis in chapter 6. Their chapter does double duty. First, it provides a concise—and insightful—overview of strategic accounts of court–Congress interaction, and identifies three core assumptions underlying the standard strategic model: (1) Congress and the courts act on ideological bases; (2) courts adapt their decisions so as to avoid congressional reversals of their decisions; and (3) Congress has the last word on the meaning of statutes. Second, it puts these assumptions to the test, using data on the theoretically interesting cases of the Supreme Court inviting congressional overrides of their decisions. They find that, although the strategic model remains a powerful framework, its core assumptions need to be adjusted to reflect a subtler landscape of court–Congress relations in which (1) motivations include nonideological factors, (2) courts do not always seek to avoid congressional overrides but sometimes invite congressional intervention, and (3) Congress does not always have the final say in matters of statutory construction, but rather is only one voice in an ongoing colloquy among the branches.

Tom Burke in chapter 7 takes a closer look at this colloquy, examining the continuing interbranch struggle to define the Americans with Disabilities Act (ADA), an ambitious statute that aims to open American society to the disabled as fully as possible. Similar to Baum and Hausegger, Burke begins with concepts drawn from economics and the rational choice literature. Specifically, he frames the analysis using the principal–agent theory, which offers a language to describe a core problem of statutory construction and implementation; namely, how can Congress ensure that its general laws are interpreted and applied faithfully?

Burke then argues that principal–agent theory does not fully capture the complexity of today's policymaking. The reason is that American reliance on adversarial legalism radically decentralizes implementation power, placing it in the hands of overlapping agencies, judges, public interest groups, and individual citizens. Under these circumstances, there is no single principal or agent to provide a definitive reading of the law. As a result, the ADA has taken on multiple meanings in (1) the minds of the diverse coalition members in Congress that originally passed the law, (2) the competing agencies that share jurisdiction over the law, (3) the various courtrooms that have resolved disputes over the law's meaning, and (4) the minds of ordinary citizens whose lives have been touched by this statute. Thus, principal–agent theory fails to capture the complexity of modern American statutory constructions because there are not only too many principals in the American system of separated institutions sharing power but also too many agents.

In chapter 8, Stephen Bragaw and Mark Miller explore various lessons from the *City of Boerne v. Archbishop Flores,* 521 U.S. 507 (1997), decision of the U.S. Supreme Court. The authors examine how a small local zoning dispute came to become a landmark decision regarding the power of Congress to challenge Supreme Court rulings through statutory mechanisms. The rest of the chapter then turns to the question of how lawyers attempt to exploit the tensions between Congress and the Court. Subnational governments were once thought to have ill-prepared and inexperienced lawyers arguing for their interests at the U.S. Supreme Court. This chapter, which is based in large part on interviews with the key players in this case, concludes that subnational governments have learned from a period of many defeats at the Supreme Court, and are now hiring lawyers who possess the necessary abilities to put their concerns in the best possible light at the Court. The City of Boerne won its case in large part because of the quality of the network of lawyers who assisted it in this landmark decision. This point offers an interesting gloss on Miller's discussion of the clashing institutional cultures of Congress and the courts: namely, whereas Congress and the courts may still, at some level, cling to the fiction of separate spheres of influence, subnational governments are adapting to a system of overlapping federal lawmakers and adjusting their political resources accordingly.

By considering the effects of statutory challenges to the Supreme Court's constitutionally based decisions, the Bragaw and Miller chapter also serves as a bridge to part IV of the book, "Constitutional Interpretation: The Interbranch Perspective Applied," which develops two themes in the context of constitutional interpretation. First, each of the chapters emphasizes that the courts are part of a broader policymaking dialogue, and that the courts do not have the final word on matters of constitutional interpretation. Second, these studies collectively suggest the complexity of judicial motivations when rendering decisions as part of the ongoing process of American policymaking.

In chapter 9, Louis Fisher opens the discussion, and consistent with earlier chapters, challenges standard accounts of the constitutional interpretation process. Specifically, contrary to textbook definition of judicial review, which holds that the Supreme Court has the final word on the meaning of the Constitution, Fisher argues that constitutional interpretation is a continuing process. To illustrate this point, he discusses interbranch relations over a number of important contemporary constitutional issues, including the death penalty, abortion, the right to die, and gay rights. Each example underscores how the meaning of the Constitution is not determined by judicial pronouncements alone. Instead, constitutional meanings are politically constructed over time with the involvement of all the branches, whose actions are tempered—and enriched—by each branch's strategic anticipation of the other branches' reactions as well as their need to preserve institutional legitimacy.

In chapter 10, Lee Epstein, Jack Knight, and Andrew Martin build on this strategic account of constitutional interpretation. They begin by sketching out a strategic model of court–Congress relations, which has been widely applied to statutory construction. The twist is that they extend this model to constitutional interpretation, hypothesizing that Supreme Court justices will vote their sincere preferences when they hold views similar to members of the other branches, but will strategically adjust their constitutional rulings when their preferences conflict with the other branches. They then test these hypotheses, using data on Supreme Court votes in constitutional cases and various measures of the underlying preferences of members of Congress, the president, and individual justices. Overall, they find moderate justices adapt their decisions to the other branches of government, whereas more ideological justices damn the torpedoes and vote their sincere preferences, regardless of the other branches' anticipated reactions.

In chapter 11, Neal Devins applies an interbranch perspective to constitutional interpretation in an entirely different way. Instead of looking at the determinants of judicial decision making, Devins uses an interbranch perspective to assess the claim that the Rehnquist Court's striking down state and federal statutes is "arrogant, self-aggrandizing, and unduly activist." As with earlier chapters, Devins begins with a standard principal–agent account of interbranch relations, which holds that elected officials represent the principal lawmakers in American democracy and should make all major policy decisions. By contrast, unelected officials, such as judges and civil servants, should serve as agents for elected officials, faithfully applying the law as written (as long as it is constitutional). From this perspective, the Court's striking down of statutes can lead to the "countermajoritarian difficulty": decisions by unelected officials that are contrary to the will of the majority.

Devins then dissects this classic account. He argues that judicial invalidation of statutes is often *majoritarian* in that they are consistent with legislative signals and public opinion. By calling attention to the majoritarian nature of judicial activism, moreover, Devins explains how the Supreme Court is embedded in a larger political context, which requires a careful balance between its impulses to demonstrate its independence and need to garner the support of elected officials. He also demonstrates, once again, that applying an interbranch perspective can force us to re-think standard accounts of interbranch relations.

PUTTING THE PIECES TOGETHER: FOUR LESSONS

In the concluding chapter, titled "Governance as Dialogue," we argue that the chapters collectively underscore the value of an eclectic approach to understanding American lawmaking and reveal significant common ground among different methodological approaches represented in this book. For example, the authors all stress that policymaking is best understood as a continuous dialogue among the institutions of government. The authors all recognize that the motivations of policymakers are complex, including ideology, strategic considerations, and the desire to preserve institutional legitimacy. And almost all the authors question standard analytic frameworks and normative baselines for evaluating interbranch relations, especially principal–agent theory and the so-called countermajoritarian difficulty. More specifically, the authors suggest the following four lessons about contemporary American policymaking:

First, the already weak divisions among legislative, executive, and judicial functions in the United States further eroded following the rise of a modern American administrative state, which places courts at the center of executive agency rulemaking and decisions. Or, as Barnes writes, "contemporary American policymaking does not feature branches of government. . . . It features a bramble of overlapping policymaking forums that share and compete for lawmaking, law-interpreting, and law-administering power."

Second, no branch of government has the final say on the meaning of federal statutes or the U.S. Constitution. Instead, policymaking is best understood as an ongoing, interbranch dialogue, which is shaped by institutional, political, and strategic contexts.

Third, the motivations of the various actors are complex, reflecting a mix of ideological, institutional, legal, and strategic factors. For example, following legal precedent may serve a variety of motivations for members of the Supreme Court. Ideologically, precedent may coincide with the justices' underlying preferences; legally, judges may believe in "good faith" that precedent requires a result; and strategically, appearing to follow precedent may help maintain the Court's institutional legitimacy—and political standing—by preserving the appearance of neutrality.

Fourth, taking an interbranch perspective challenges traditional baselines for conceptualizing and evaluating the role of each branch of government in the policymaking process. For example, the often-used framework of principal–agent theory becomes unwieldy, because an interbranch perspective underscores that there is no hierarchy of lawmakers in the American system of separated institutions sharing power and there are a welter of competing agents empowered to give laws meaning in the decentralized American administrative state.

We believe that this convergence on the idea that policymaking represents patterns of discourse shaped by institutional, political, and strategic contexts roughly parallels a similar convergence in other fields (see also Rubin 1996). For example, in the field of organizational theory, scholars have moved towards seeing organizations as information flows shaped by networks and environmental factors, which permeate formal institutional boundaries (see, generally, Scott 1992). In economics, there has been a surge of interest in how institutional contexts—formalized as rules of games—shape iterated, strategic interaction (see, generally, Ordeshook 1986). In political science, there has been an emergence of a new institutionalism, which encompasses formal, quantitative, and qualitative approaches for studying how institutional and ideational constraints shape political behavior (Smith 1988; see also Gillman and Clayton 1999; and Clayton and Gillman 1999). In legal circles, there is interest in understanding law as an "autopoietic" discourse, which unfolds according to its own logic and norms (see, generally, Teubner and Febbrajo 1992). Such convergence hints at a broader meeting of the minds, which could not only help us fit new pieces of the American policymaking process together but may also provide the basis for a broader coming together across disciplines and methodological camps.

NOTE

1. For leading examples of behavioralist studies of the Supreme Court, see Segal and Spaeth 1993; and Spaeth and Segal 1999. For more on new institutionalism and the courts, see Smith 1988; Gillman and Clayton 1999; and Clayton and Gillman 1999.

1

American Courts and the Policy Dialogue
The Role of Adversarial Legalism

ROBERT A. KAGAN

THE CONVENTIONAL IMAGE OF GOVERNMENTAL POLICYMAK-
ing and implementation in the American system of separation
of powers is something like this: Fundamental policy decisions are negotiated between the chief executive and the legislature and embodied in legislation. Implementation of those
statutes, including the elaboration of general policies through
more specific administrative regulations, is entrusted to specialized administrative and regulatory agencies. The courts
are available to adjudicate disputes between agencies and citizens or businesses about the meaning and application of the
regulations in particular cases, and to impose legal sanctions
on individuals and organizations that are found to have violated the regulations. The courts also have an important
boundary-setting role, ensuring that statutes and administrative regulations do not violate basic constitutional rights, and
that the agencies follow basic rules of nonarbitrariness and
procedural fairness in making and enforcing regulations.

That functional division of powers model prevails in
most other economically advanced democracies as well, and
for understandable reasons. Democratic theory suggests that
basic policy decisions be made by elected representatives,
identifiable by political parties, who can be held to account
at the polls. Yet the details of policymaking and implementation sensibly should be entrusted to specialized administrators, trained to tailor policies to particular contexts. And the
courts, as politically independent experts in the interpretation of statutes and regulations, are responsible for hearing
and adjudicating claims that the administrators have acted
contrary to their legal obligations, thereby guarding against
administrative corruption, arbitrariness, fecklessness, and
political bias. But in terms of policy issues, the elected politicians are the "principals" and the unelected judges should be
their faithful "agents."

In many democracies, that ideal-typical model, while
rarely completely effective, does reflect the relative institutional relationships among the legislature, the administrative
state, and the courts. But not in the contemporary United
States. There the lines between, and relationships among,

legislatures, administrators, and courts have become blurred. Organized advocacy groups, by filing lawsuits and appeals, pressure judges to act as policymakers themselves, and the judges not infrequently do so. Organized interests that lose in court often seek to grab the policy ball and toss it back to the legislature, demanding that the courts be overruled. Even then, policy issues frequently return to the courts. And courts often issue conflicting decisions, for Republican judges not infrequently decide differently from Democratic judges. Throughout the process, the basic rules of the game are perpetually subject to legal contestation and political revision.

I call this mode of governance *"adversarial legalism"*—a mode of policymaking, implementation, and dispute resolution characterized by frequent resort to highly adversarial legal contestation (Kagan 2001). In this chapter, I will first demonstrate the prevalence of adversarial legalism in the American governmental system, while emphasizing its distinctiveness compared to policymaking, implementation, and dispute resolution in other democracies. Second, I will discuss why adversarial legalism has come to occupy such a prominent and seemingly permanent position in American life. Let me begin, however, by making the phenomenon under discussion more vivid by telling a story of adversarial legalism in action.

ADVERSARIAL LEGALISM IN ACTION: THE PACIFIC NORTHWEST FORESTS–SPOTTED OWL CONTROVERSY

The U.S. Forest Service (USFS) and the Bureau of Land Management (BLM) administer huge tracts of federal forest land. Agency officials and forestry experts are guided, in that regard, by the National Forest Management Act, the Federal Land Policy and Management Act, and the National Environmental Protection Act. These laws require the agencies to seek a balance among competing land uses (including timber production, recreation, and conservation). But the laws do not insist on any particular balance among those uses. Rather, they instruct the agencies to conduct a decentralized planning process for each stretch of forest land, complete with environmental impact statements that outline alternative plans for scrutiny by other agencies and the public, and public hearings that invite comments by all affected interests. In addition, the agencies must abide by the Endangered Species Act (ESA) by protecting habitat needed by species that have been designated "threatened" or "endangered" by the U.S. Fish and Wildlife Service (USFWS).

Environmentalists have long sought to exempt broader swaths of forest from the usual "multiple-use" planning, prohibiting all logging there. One strategy is to persuade Congress to designate portions of national forest "Wilderness Areas," and Congress often has been willing to do so for higher elevation areas that are low in timber value. But congressional representatives from timber-dependent communities in the Pacific Northwest usually have blocked environmentalists' demands for further set-asides in forests with high timber value. Moreover, in the 1980s, Republican presidents and administrative agency heads were increasing rather than slowing timber harvest in the Pacific Northwest. To environmental advocates like the Sierra Club Legal Defense Fund (SCLDF), the federal courts, particularly the politically liberal Ninth Circuit Court of Appeals, looked like a more favorable forum for achieving their policy goals.

In the mid-1980s, SCLDF discerned an unwitting ally in the northern spotted owl, whose range extends from Northern California to Canada. A marked decline in owl populations, some scientists speculated, was signaling a decline in the extent and health of so-called old-growth forests. If USFWS would put the spotted owl on the official list of endangered species, then the USFS and BLM would be obliged to preserve most remaining stands of old-growth forest as necessary habitat. But considerable uncertainty prevailed concerning how much owl populations had declined, what their habitat needs actually are, and how much of the remaining Northwest forests were "ancient" old-growth forests as opposed to mature second growth. Hence, in 1987 the USFWS declined to "list" the spotted owl.[1]

LITIGATION AGAINST THE U.S. FISH AND WILDLIFE SERVICE

The SCLDF challenged USFWS's decision in federal court, and in 1988, U.S. District Court judge Thomas Zilly, responding to expert witnesses called by SCLDF, held the USFWS decision lacked a "rational basis."[2] The agency then listed the owl as threatened, but maintained that it lacked sufficient information to designate its "critical habitat" exempt from logging. SCLDF challenged that decision as well, and Judge Zilly again overrode the USFWS judgment. The agency then adopted an interagency report that, despite considerable scientific ambiguity concerning the owls' needs, recommended that millions of acres be exempted from logging.

Next, logging communities and timber interests sued the USFWS, challenging its owl protection plans as unnecessarily broad.[3] Other timber interests appealed the USFWS's plans for extensive logging-free zones on grounds that harm to *habitat* was not specifically covered by the ESA's prohibition of "takings" of endangered species. That issue was not resolved until the U.S. Supreme Court upheld the USFWS's broad interpretation of "takings" (to include habitat preservation) in June 1995.

LITIGATION AGAINST THE BUREAU OF LAND MANAGEMENT

Meanwhile, litigation had been proceeding on another front. In October 1987, SCLDF sued the Bureau of Land Management, claiming that BLM scientists, in approving timber sales covering certain old-growth forests, had neglected environmental evidence about logging's adverse effects on the spotted owl, thereby violating the National Environmental Policy Act's demand for full, updated analysis. (BLM had decided that the allegedly relevant evidence was not significant.) Timber interests, taking no chances, persuaded Congress to enact a rider to an appropriations act for fiscal 1988, ostensibly blocking lawsuits against BLM's timber sales based on new information. U.S. District Court judge Helen Frye, accordingly, dismissed the suit. SCLDF appealed. The Court of Appeals for the Ninth Circuit reversed, reinstating the suit, *Portland Audubon Society v. Hodel*, 866 F.2d 302 (9th Cir. 1989).

In May 1989, after a hearing that pitted the SCLDF's forestry and owl experts against BLM experts, Judge Frye held that BLM should have prepared a new environmental impact analysis, but she again dismissed the suit based on her reading of the litigation-barring congressional appropriations act. In December 1989, the Ninth Circuit agreed in part, but held that Judge Frye erred in dismissing certain *other* legal claims in SCLDF's suit, sending the case back to her court again.

Just before that Ninth Circuit decision, however, in October 1989, timber interests and the agencies had secured an even more explicit appropriations rider from Congress which (1) required USFS and BLM to sell specific amounts of timber from

Northwest forests, (2) exempted from logging spotted owl habitat identified in the agencies' planning documents, (3) directed the agencies to develop an owl conservation strategy, and (4) forbade judicial review of the current agency decisions. But in September 1990, the Ninth Circuit held that law an unconstitutional violation of separation of powers principles and remanded the case to Judge Frye. The government and industry appealed to the U.S. Supreme Court, which on March 25, 1992, unanimously reversed the Ninth Circuit's ruling that Congress had acted unconstitutionally.

By then, however, the congressional rider's ban on judicial review of BLM decisions had expired. Judge Frye reinstated SCLDF's suit, and she issued a sixty-day injunction of timber sales and a demand for a new environmental analysis. BLM appealed, but the Ninth Circuit affirmed the injunction in July 1993, reading ambiguous evidence in SCLDF's favor.

In a separate line of cases, in late 1990 environmentalists sued BLM after it authorized certain timber sales. The claim was that BLM consultations with FWS over the preservation of critical habitat for the spotted owl had been inadequate. In September 1991, U.S. District Court judge Robert Jones agreed and enjoined further logging and timber sales. BLM appealed to the Ninth Circuit, which affirmed, continuing the injunction. The agency also asked the secretary of the interior to convene the Endangered Species Commission (dubbed the "God Squad"), which can authorize exemptions from the ESA, to consider exempting the forty-four proposed sales. The commission exempted thirteen. But in February 1991, the Ninth Circuit granted environmentalists' request for an evidentiary hearing on whether members of President George H. W. Bush's staff had engaged in ex parte contacts with members of the Endangered Species Commission. In April 1993, with President Bill Clinton now in office, BLM abandoned its petition for the ESA exemptions.

LITIGATING AGAINST THE FOREST SERVICE

Most significant of all, in March 1991, responding to an SCLDF suit, U.S. District judge William Dwyer held that the USFS had failed to promulgate standards for the protection of the spotted owl on USFS lands, in violation of the National Forest Management Act (NFMA). (USFS had argued that following the listing of the owl, its obligations under NFMA had been superseded by its obligations under ESA, and that it had adopted a conservation strategy under that law.) Judge Dwyer held that USFS was obligated under NFMA to protect not only the spotted owl but "the entire biological community."

In May 1991, Judge Dwyer issued a sweeping preliminary injunction against further USFS timber sales within a much larger area than that called for by the agency's owl protection plan, and he ordered the USFS to prepare a new environmental plan that would protect not only the owl but entire biological communities. The injunction was based in part on the judge's finding that the owl "is now threatened with extinction" (a contested claim) and another finding that minimized concerns about the adverse economic effects of an injunction. In 1992, Dwyer made the injunction permanent. In July 1993, the Ninth Circuit upheld his order, rejecting the agency's scientific and legal counterarguments and leaving the injunction in effect in the national forests throughout the owl's entire range.

THE STRUGGLE CONTINUES

As of April 1993, judicial injunctions had reduced timber production and employment in the Pacific Northwest by perhaps one-half. Responding to the consequent political pressure, President Clinton, Vice President Al Gore, and Secretary of the Interior Bruce Babbitt presided over a Forest Conference in Portland, Oregon. Based on recommendations by a carefully selected team of ecologists and forest biologists, the Clinton administration produced a plan calling for large protected areas and sharply decreased timber yields over a ten-year period, but with some "front loading" of harvests to ease the economic blow to logging communities.

In June 1994, Judge Dwyer approved an environmental impact statement based on the administration plan and lifted his injunction. Nevertheless, the adverse economic impact on many timber-dependent communities was very great. So when a Republican Congress swept into office in early 1995, timber interests successfully lobbied for a "salvage logging rider," ostensibly aimed at clearing dead and dying trees from protected old-growth stands, but also providing exceptions that authorized harvesting of certain healthy trees (see Axline 1996, 613).

In subsequent court cases, environmental groups challenged the government's interpretation of provisions in the salvage logging legislation that concerned protection of owls and murrelets. On balance, though legal and practical uncertainty persisted, the repeated clashes between environmentalists and courts on the one hand and Congress on the other ended up tilting forestry policy strongly toward the "ecosystem management" concept favored by many environmentalists.

THE HALLMARKS OF ADVERSARIAL LEGALISM

In the Northwest forests–spotted owl saga, federal judges were not simply policing the boundaries of administrative decision making, that is, by ruling that the agencies had exceeded their legal powers. Rather, the judges repeatedly second-guessed administrative experts and policymakers, challenging their scientific models, their data analysis, their policy decisions, and their priorities—all in a context of scientific uncertainty and large economic consequences.

More fundamentally, the courts served as an alternative political forum for environmental interests who faced political obstacles in the elective branches of government. For all the complexity and legal detail of the National Forest Planning Act, the National Environmental Protection Act, and the ESA, the requirements of "the law" were far from clear. Different judges (with different policy preferences) regularly decided key issues differently. Moreover, judicial decisions failed to impose any legal finality on the controversy. Logging interests repeatedly sought and obtained congressional legislation that overrode judicial decisions on an ad hoc basis. Policy emerged from an ongoing adversarial struggle between environmentalists and timber interests—a struggle that lurched from forum to forum like an endless barroom brawl, generating what might be called a reluctant dialogue between courts, Congress, and the presidency. In sum, the hallmarks of this process were:

1. the organized use of courts by interest groups as an alternative political forum for seeking policy goals,

2. judicial boldness in scrutinizing and reversing governmental scientific and policy decisions, and
3. persistent legal uncertainty and political controversy surrounding judicial decisions.

These features are not unique to the Northwest forests–spotted owl controversy. During the 1980s, virtually every USFS plan for a particular forest was held up by legal challenge and appellate review, either in administrative forums or in the courts or both (*The Economist* 1990, 28). A database search in 1989 revealed 123 reported court cases, in federal courts alone, concerning government plans to dredge harbors (McCreary 1989, 43). Litigation has often reshaped the dredging and sediment-disposal plans designed by the Corps of Engineers, the lead agency for that process. The mere threat of litigation has had the same effect in many other cases (National Research Council 1986, 89–90; Kagan 1991). Similarly, governmentally approved plans for new highways, from the Century Freeway in Los Angeles (Detlefsen 1995) to the Boston artery and tunnel project (Palmer 1994), frequently are reshaped by litigation—sometimes because judges find fault with the relevant agency's decisions, more often because governments become desperate to forestall the extraordinary delays, costs, and unpredictability of adversarial litigation. The same is true with respect to many large infrastructural or industrial projects, such as building factories (Harris 1995), housing developments (Frieden 1979), waste disposal facilities (O'Hare and Bacow 1983; Welles and Engel 2000), and oil or mineral exploration projects (Lester 1992).

Adversarial legalism is common in other policymaking contexts as well. Litigation and judicial policymaking permeate the process for redrawing electoral district lines. Under the federal antitrust laws, federal judges have been the key policymakers for momentous decisions concerning the structure of the telecommunications industry (the AT&T case) and computer software (the Microsoft case). In the late 1980s and early 1990s, more than half of all new major regulations promulgated by the U.S. Environmental Protection Agency were appealed to court, either by environmental or business groups (Coglianese 1997). By critically assessing (and sometimes reversing) the scientific basis or policy reasoning of regulations made by the Environmental Protection Agency (Dwyer 1990), the Occupational Safety and Health Administration (Mendeloff 1987), and the National Highway Traffic Safety Administration (Mashaw and Harfst 1991), U.S. Courts of Appeals have profoundly reshaped the character and pace of policymaking by those agencies. It has been reported that in the hours before a new regulation is announced by some agencies, lawyers for contending interest groups (regulated enterprises or proregulation advocacy groups) wait in the hallways of different circuit courts of appeals, hoping to file their appeal first—because different circuit courts have reputations for being more or less proregulation.

In a flurry of decisions beginning in the late 1960s, federal judges transformed the Aid for Dependent Children program (AFDC), enacted by Congress in 1935, from a program grounded in state and local discretion in setting eligibility and benefit policies into a system of entitlements subject to federal legal guidelines and supervision (Melnick 1994, chaps. 4 and 5).[4] Millions of poor children, especially those subject to racially biased or simply stingy local rules, were added to the welfare rolls (Davis 1993, 68).

As in the Northwest forests–spotted owl story, however, if welfare advocates could appeal to courts, state governments could respond by appealing to Congress, and Congress eventually amended the AFDC law to rein the courts in. And hence by the mid-1980s, the Supreme Court, by then with a more conservative majority, routinely ordered the lower federal courts to defer to state administrators' judgments, as in the days before the welfare rights lawyers' campaign (Melnick 1996, 346–47).

This kind of court–legislature policy dialogue is far from unusual. Between 1967 and 1990, Congress passed statutes directly reversing or modifying at least 220 lower court and over 100 Supreme Court decisions (Eskridge 1991a). Yet, as in the forestry disputes, Barnes (2004) finds that such congressional "override" statutes end up "settling the law" only about half the time, because determined interest groups often continue to push for policy advantages through renewed litigation, and liberal and conservative judges interpret the override statute in different ways. A cross-national comparison of judicial styles of statutory interpretation labeled the American judiciary the most freewheeling and creative (Summers and Taruffo 1991). But a "creative" (and politically selected) judiciary is not likely to yield legal or policy stability.

The complex and often interdeterminate policy dialogue between courts and legislatures is much less common in the parliamentary political systems of other economically advanced democracies—Australia, Canada, Japan, and the countries of Western Europe. In comparative studies of regulatory policymaking and administration on particular topics—such as setting standards to reduce exposure to carcinogenic chemicals (Badaracco 1985; Brickman, Jasanoff, and Ilgen 1985), improving environmental protection (Vogel 1986; Kagan and Axelrad 2000; Verweij 2000), or cleaning up hazardous waste sites (Church and Nakamura 1994)—scholars consistently have found that the American method is uniquely legalistic and adversarial, and that courts and lawyers play a uniquely salient role.

In the Northwest forests saga and in most of the other policy spheres just mentioned, the basic direction of national policy had been set by one or more congressional statutes. The particular controversies arose from decisions (or nondecisions) by regulatory or administrative agencies. The courts' policymaking efforts took the form of interpretations and applications of those statutes or of general principles of administrative law. But in the United States, the courts' role in joining the policymaking dialogue also reflects two other sources of legal authority—the common law and the constitutions of the U.S. and state governments.

THE COMMON LAW AND THE POLICY DIALOGUE

In the wake of the American Revolution, the states decided to continue the British common law tradition, in which judges drew upon and adapted prior court decisions to articulate the governing principles of law (Friedman 1973). From the start, therefore, American state courts had license to make, not merely apply, the law. Because nineteenth-century state legislatures met only for short periods each year and were quite unprofessional, state court judges became the primary policymakers for broad swaths of property, contract, family, and tort law.

In the first half of the nineteenth century, judges amended British precedents to facilitate the growth of an investment-friendly, market-oriented economy (Horwitz 1977). The judges, however, sometimes became embroiled in a policymaking dialogue with politicians. State lawmakers could and often did enact statutes to change or reverse judicial precedent. And the growth of the regulatory state, beginning in the late nineteenth century, has seen statutory law (and accompanying administrative regulations) override and displace judicial common law policymaking in one field of public policy after another, from securities law and consumer protection to environmental and product safety regulation.

Nevertheless, at the beginning of the twenty-first century, common law adjudication remains alive and well. State courts have continued to be important policymakers in several significant spheres, including the protection of intellectual property, the contract law that is central to the multitudinous transactions of a free market, corporate law, and many issues of corporate governance.[5] In recent decades, tort law has been the most politically controversial realm of common law policymaking. Beginning in the 1960s, reform-minded state supreme court judges dramatically expanded the coverage and potency of tort law. They modified the common-law rule that tort claimants are barred from recovery by their own contributory negligence (Ursin 1981, 243–44), abolished governmental and charitable institutions' legal immunity from tort liability, changed evidentiary rules to facilitate medical malpractice cases, and imposed "strict liability" for product defects—all making it far easier for plaintiffs to win. Judges also expanded the right to recover compensation for accident-related emotional distress (Ursin 1981, 244) and enabled entrepreneurial lawyers to aggregate the claims of large numbers of injured persons into massive class action suits (Coffee 1995, 1356–58; Priest 1985, 461).

The changes in tort doctrine energized the plaintiffs' bar, as did other court decisions that invalidated state regulations forbidding advertising by lawyers. Entrepreneurial lawyers soon made tort litigation a much larger and more formidable presence in American life. Medical malpractice claims increased from 1 per 100 American physicians in 1960 (when malpractice suits, even when justified, were very difficult to win) to 10.6 per 100 in 1980 and then to 17 per 100 in 1986. (By way of comparison, there were only 1.8 malpractice claims for every 100 Canadian physicians in 1986, and the average American physician's medical malpractice insurance bill was eleven times that of her Canadian counterpart) (Dewees, Trebilock, and Coyte 1991, 219, 221; Nutter and Bateman 1989). Tort claims against officials of municipal and county governments in the United States grew dramatically (Tort Policy Working Group 1986). In many states, new judicial rulings on "unjust dismissal" shifted millions of jobs from the traditional employment-at-will arrangement to a legal regime that required dismissal only for "just cause." The result of these new doctrines has been that state court judges (and randomly selected lay juries) regularly make policy concerning the standards that define acceptable medical practice, the proper design of school playground equipment and traffic signs, the improper use of force by police, corporate personnel practices, and many other details of social and professional life.

As in the Northwest forests–spotted owl story, interests that lose policy battles in court often turn to legislatures for relief. Business, insurance, and medical groups have persistently lobbied legislatures, federal and state, to override judicially constructed tort doctrines or to limit the amount of damages (Burke 2002; Sanders and Joyce 1990). In 1986, about 800 civil justice reform bills were introduced in state legislatures, followed by 1,000 in 1987 and 1,400 in 1988 (Nutter and Bateman 1989, 16). In 1994, after lawsuits had virtually put a stop to domestic manufacture of small aircraft, Congress passed a law prohibiting lawsuits against makers of older piston-powered small planes. Yet plaintiffs' lawyers have been formidable, big-spending lobbyists for the court-constructed status quo. Moreover, in many states they have persuaded courts to hold statutory limitations on tort damages unconstitutional. And they have helped block congressional legislation designed to provide a government-administered fund to provide swift and automatic (but moderate) compensation to victims of workplace exposure to asbestos, even as asbestos cases have climbed to more than 750,000, driven sixty-seven corporations into bankruptcy (Warren 2003a, 2003b), and provided only erratic and long-delayed compensation to claimants.

In other economically advanced democracies, tort litigation and courts have not played such a large role in regulating the hazards generated by modern technologies, or in establishing compensation policies for the victims of accidents. In Western Europe, for example, product liability and medical malpractice suits are much less common—mostly because taxpayer-funded national health care and disability programs take care of victims' medical expenses and lost wages (Schwartz 1991).[6] Most disputes concerning compensation for injury are decided not by courts but by bureaucratic agencies and panels of medical and occupational experts.

In the United States, however, the regulation of hazards and the establishment of compensation standards have been in large part the province of adversarial legalism, with the characteristic features noted above: (1) the organized use of courts by interest groups as an alternative political forum for seeking policy goals; (2) judicial boldness in making scientific and policy decisions; and (3) persistent legal uncertainty and political controversy surrounding public policy, as warring interest groups seek to reverse judicial losses in the legislature and vice versa.

CONSTITUTIONAL ADJUDICATION AND THE POLICY DIALOGUE

The most famous form of judicial policymaking in the United States arises from the courts' power of judicial review—the authority to hold legislative statutes and executive branch decisions and actions unconstitutional. In engaging in constitutional adjudication, judges often make policy because the broad phrases of the Constitution—"due process of law," "equal protection of the laws," and so on—have no self-evident meaning. Hence, as was stated in 1907 by Charles Evans Hughes, later to become chief justice of the U.S. Supreme Court, "We are under a Constitution, but the Constitution is what the judges say it is" (quoted in Lockhart et al. 1991, 8). Since the early decades of the republic, therefore, both the U.S. Supreme Court and the state supreme courts, by interpreting the federal and state constitutions, have profoundly shaped and reshaped the boundaries of federal and state governmental power, invalidated policies made by the other branches, and defined individual and economic rights.

In the nineteenth and early twentieth centuries, the U.S. Supreme Court exercised its powers of judicial review mostly by saying "no" to state legislatures. The Court struck down state regulatory laws that in the judges' opinions unjustifiably interfered with the free flow of interstate commerce, or with the principles of economic liberty that the justices discerned in the Fourteenth Amendment's "due process" clause. The Court thus slowed the development of the modern regulatory state (although it also upheld a good deal of new regulation) (Friedman 1973; Novak 2002).

The Supreme Court also successfully flexed its policy muscles against the federal government, saying "no" to some expansions of federal power. In the *Civil Rights Cases*, 109 U.S. 3 (1883), the Court held that the Civil Rights Act of 1875, which forbade not only governmental but also private racial discrimination in public accommodations, exceeded Congress's constitutional powers. In *Pollock v. Farmers' Loan and Trust Co.*, 158 U.S. 601 (1895), the Court struck down a federal progressive income tax law as unconstitutional. Most dramatically, in the 1930s, a conservative U.S. Supreme Court majority held unconstitutional President Franklin D. Roosevelt's National Recovery Act and several other pieces of New Deal legislation.

Notwithstanding the quotation by Chief Justice Hughes given above, even in constitutional cases the courts do not necessarily have the last policy word. The interest groups and political leaders who lose in court often find ways to circumvent the court decisions. They also lobby for the appointment of more congenial new judges. In the late nineteenth century, when a state supreme court held regulatory legislation invalid, the state legislature frequently reenacted the same policy, clothing it in slightly different legal garb (Lindgren 1983). In 1913, a constitutional amendment explicitly authorizing Congress to impose an income tax overrode the Supreme Court's *Pollock* decision. In the 1930s, Congress reenacted New Deal policies in different form, and although President Roosevelt had to abandon his plan to expand the Supreme Court and "pack" it with supportive Democrats, the Court backed down and upheld the subsequent New Deal laws.

More generally, Roosevelt, followed by President Harry Truman, reshaped the federal judiciary. They appointed federal judges who believed in judicial deference to federal and state regulatory legislation and to the decisions of federal administrative agencies. Since then, the constitutional and administrative-law doctrines forged by the late New Deal Court have for the most part deterred the courts from using constitutional adjudication to reshape regulatory or tax policies.

But beginning in the 1950s, the courts leapt back into the policymaking process, evolving new constitutional doctrines concerning equality and individual rights. What is more, the courts used constitutional adjudication to take on a new, more affirmative policymaking role. They not only said "no" to new legislation or executive branch decisions, but also demanded proactive social change. In numerous cases, the courts' constitutional rulings obligated governments to make far reaching reforms in existing patterns of administration, and sometimes to take on new governmental responsibilities.

Most dramatic were the U.S. Supreme Court's decisions concerning school desegregation. Beginning with *Brown v. Board of Education*, 347 U.S. 483 (1954), the Court, abandoning a long-standing precedent, held that legally segregated schools violated the equal protection clause and ordered hundreds of school districts to dismantle the deliberate governmental apartheid that had long prevailed in southern and border state schools. *Brown* eventually led to litigation throughout the country in which judges assumed a primary policymaking role concerning school attendance and management plans, including the busing of school children to achieve more racial balance.

The courts became deeply involved in other aspects of educational policy as well. In *Abington School District v. Schempp*, 374 U.S. 203 (1963), the Supreme Court banned prayer in the public schools. In 1972, two U.S. District Courts found that the exclusion of costly-to-educate handicapped children from public schools was unconstitutional. Fearing a flood of similar litigation, state governments pressured Congress to enact legislation establishing (and partially funding), a nationwide right to an "appropriate education" for all children (Neal and Kirp 1986; Melnick 1995). And more than twenty state supreme courts held that the long-standing system of funding schools through local property taxes violated state constitutional provisions concerning equal education, thereby compelling legislatures to adopt new school funding schemes (Reed 1998; Heise 1998).

The "due process revolution" in criminal procedure of the 1960s was just as far reaching. During Chief Justice Earl Warren's tenure, the Supreme Court held that most of the specific Bill of Rights provisions relating to the criminal process were binding on state and local courts and police departments. Then, by offering new interpretations of the Bill of Rights, the Court articulated new nationwide rules regulating pretrial detention, interrogation of suspects, police searches for evidence, and jury selection. In addition, the Court interpreted the Constitution to require local governments to provide free defense counsel for indigent defendants—in effect mandating the creation and funding of public defenders' offices through the country. Defense lawyers' motions to suppress illegally obtained evidence and confessions became a routine practice in local criminal prosecutions. Appellate courts, not state legislatures, laid down the principles for determining when cops need a warrant, when they can search a suspect's car trunk, and so on.

The list could go on and on. Beginning in the 1960s, federal court judges began to hold that oppressive, dangerous, and overcrowded conditions in state and local prisons and jails were unconstitutional. By 1990, state prisons in 41 states were operating under court remedial orders, as were nearly one-third of large county jails (U.S. Bureau of Justice Statistics 1991). In effect, the federal courts ended up promulgating a comprehensive code for prison management, covering such diverse matters as residence facilities, sanitation, food, clothing, medical care, discipline, staff hiring, libraries, work, and education (Feeley and Rubin 1998). And the Warren Court's voting rights decisions in *Wesberry v. Sanders*, 376 U.S. 1 (1964), and *Reynolds v. Sims*, 377 U.S. 533 (1964), by ruling that unequal legislative districts violated the Constitution, compelled state after state to end the malapportionment that traditionally had given rural areas disproportionate political weight in state legislatures and delegations to the U.S. House of Representatives.

As in earlier eras, interests who lose in the courts, even on constitutional grounds, continue to fight in other political bodies for policies that skirt judicial precedents, and they lobby the president and the Senate for the appointment of judges who might shift constitutional doctrine in a more congenial direction. In the wake of the Supreme Court's invalidation of long-entrenched state laws forbidding abortion, virtually every proposed appointment to the Court has been the focus of intense lobbying by "prolife" and opposing "prochoice" advocacy groups, based on the candidate's presumed willingness to support, limit or overrule *Roe v. Wade*, 410 U.S. 113 (1973). Expansive state supreme court rulings on housing policy (Kirp, Dwyer, and Rosenthal 1995) and school funding (Yudof 1991; Goodnough 1997) often trigger repeated rounds of litigation and legislation, as state legislatures, responding to suburban constituencies that dislike the judge-mandated policies, resist or seek to modify the court rulings. Thus also in the realm of constitutional adjudication, American politics is marked by the same characteristics noted above: (1) the organized use of courts by interest groups as an alternative political forum for seeking policy goals; (2) judicial boldness in scrutinizing and reversing governmental policy decisions; and (3) persistent legal uncertainty and political controversy surrounding judicial decisions.

In recent decades, many other nations have established or strengthened constitutional courts. In many countries—from Germany (Currie 1990) and France (Stone 1994) to Hungary, Canada (Epp 1998), Russia (Epstein, Knight, and Shvetsova 2001), South Africa, and Taiwan (Ginsburg 2003)—constitutional courts have taken a more active role in national policymaking. The European Court of Justice has expanded the policymaking reach of the European Union (Shapiro and Stone 1994). Yet no governmental system approaches the United States in the extent to which constitutional adjudication and the judicial policymaking it engenders are woven into day-to-day adjudication by ordinary courts. The United States also remains unique in the extent to which courts, by wielding constitutional powers, have become intimately engaged in ongoing institutional reform efforts. In no other country has systematic litigation become such a recurrent form of political goal seeking. In few countries, if any, have political struggles over the selection of judges been so intense, or have the outcomes of those struggles had such a strong impact on the normative direction of judicial policymaking.

EXPLAINING AMERICAN ADVERSARIAL LEGALISM

Why is adversarial legalism such a prominent aspect of American policymaking, and more salient in the United States than in other economically advanced democracies? Legal scholars might look for explanations in the *legal philosophy* of American judges and the conceptions of law and judging encouraged by American legal education. Comparing the United States with the United Kingdom, Atiyah and Summers (1987, 404) observe that in American (but not British) law schools, the dominant general theory of law is "instrumentalism," which "conceives of law essentially as a pragmatic instrument of social improvement." "Instrumentalism" presumably encourages judicial problem solving, creativity, and boldness.

Many political scientists, in contrast, would look not to legal ideas but to the *governmental structures* of the United States and the distinctive set of *political incentives* they engender. Thus the fragmentation of power in the United States—between the national government and the states, among the branches of government at all levels, within legislatures and political parties—draws the courts into the role of umpire and makes it more difficult to mobilize legislatures to override judicial decisions. In contrast to judges in unitary parliamentary governments, therefore, American judges—such as the federal judges who dealt with the Northwest forests–spotted owl controversy—have more political space in which to make policy, and interest groups are quick to try to persuade them to do so.

Yet there is a deeper puzzle. Why do these particular governmental structures arise and persist? And if governmental structure is the key to American adversarial legalism, why has adversarial legalism been so much more pervasive in the past fifty years than it was in earlier decades, even though the basic structures of government remain about the same? The answer, some scholars might say, lies in the broader *political culture* of the society—the ideas and changing expectations or demands of the citizenry.

Although parsimonious explanations are much to be desired, complex political phenomena such as American adversarial legalism are most likely the product of a number of explanatory variables. That, at least, is the nature of the explanatory theory to be advanced here, which emphasizes the interplay of American political culture, America's fragmented structure of authority, and the distinctive qualities of American legal thought. This explanatory theory will be set out in two phases, the first focusing on traditions extending back to the founding of the nation, the second on the notable intensification of adversarial legalism that began in the 1960s.

THE ROOTS OF AMERICAN ADVERSARIAL LEGALISM

Judges have always been prominent policymakers in the United States. Early in the nation's history, two basic engines of adversarial legalism were already in place: a politically selected judiciary, with powers to make policy through common law and constitutional adjudication, and a highly entrepreneurial, politically engaged legal profession. One of the most quoted observations about American politics is Alexis de Tocqueville's remark in *Democracy in America* that in the United States of the 1820s and 1830s, most major political issues became judicial issues. The Supreme Court's *Dred Scott* decision, upsetting a congressional compromise, helped precipitate the Civil War (*Dred Scott v. Sandford*, 60 U.S. 393 [1857]). In the late nineteenth century and the first third of the twentieth, business interests often resorted to adversarial legalism, urging the courts to strike down prolabor statutes and to issue injunctions against striking workers.

Judicial policymaking in nineteenth-century America was rooted in the political liberalism that animated the American Revolution and the constitutional founding (Hartz 1955).[7] In that liberal vision, governmental power must be limited and restrained by law, invoked and applied by rights-bearing citizens. American political culture has also harbored a turbulent "populist" strain, deeply mistrustful of concentrated political or economic power (Goodwyn 1978). If powerful men cannot be trusted, power should be fragmented and decentralized, made accountable to local electorates. And the rule of law—invoked and applied in courts staffed by ordinary people serving as judges and jurors—provided another mechanism for controlling power. In addition, at least since Daniel Shays's 1786 agrarian rebellion (and post-Revolution state legislatures' inclination to side with debtors), American business interests have been mistrustful of the motives and competence of democratically elected politicians. Hence business also has favored legal controls on government, enforceable in the courts.

These basic political attitudes were embodied in constitutions, state as well as federal, that splintered governmental authority among separate branches and levels of government, establishing legal constraints on each. Both federal and state constitutions included a government-limiting Bill of Rights, enforceable in local courts at the behest of ordinary citizens.

With a mandate for limited, decentralized government, nineteenth-century American policymaking was dominated not by legislatures and national bureaucracies, as in Western Europe, but by decentralized political parties and courts (Skowronek 1982; Shefter 1994). Judges were selected by county-level political processes; political responsiveness, not professional uniformity, was the reigning ideal. American judges, in contrast to their legalistic European counterparts, adopted a pragmatic, problem-solving approach to legal decision making (Hurst 1956; Selznick 1976).

State legislatures met for limited terms and for limited pay, and that too encouraged judges, who heard cases throughout the year, to become active policymakers (Horwitz 1977). State and city governments often were corrupt and distrusted, and state constitutions were amended frequently to check governmental action (Friedman 1973), thereby throwing many significant issues into the courts.

Fragmentation of power in the economic realm also encouraged an important judicial policymaking role. In comparison with Western Europe, economic life in the United States—not only in the nineteenth century but in the twentieth as well—was more fully the province of private business firms and local banks, less subject to governmental financing, control, and guidance or to the influence of national banks and industrial cartels. Throughout the nineteenth century, business relationships, labor relations, and business–government interactions were policed primarily by litigation and by judge-made rules that favored entrepreneurial energy, freedom of contract, and private property (Hurst 1956; Horwitz 1977). Beginning in the 1870s, proponents of "economic nationalism" worked to expand federal courts' jurisdiction and capacity, so that new national policies could be enforced more effectively by private litigation (Gillman 2002). And as was noted above, in the late nineteenth century and early in the twentieth, business interests turned to the courts for constitutional decisions striking down "unreasonable" regulation of business and employment practices.

All in all, although comparative data is hard to find, it seems likely that at any point between 1800 and 1960, a comparativist would have found that American judges played a significantly more prominent policymaking role than their counterparts in Western Europe.

THE INTENSIFICATION OF ADVERSARIAL LEGALISM

The adversarial legalism that has pervaded the United States in the last few decades is both more extensive and more intense than that of the nineteenth-century and the first half of the twentieth. As recently as 1960, massive class actions against business corporations were rare, as were damage suits against police departments. Before the late 1960s, American administrative agencies, school boards, highway planners, and zoning commissions were much less likely than their contemporary counterparts to be challenged in court. Nominations to the federal courts did not unleash intensely partisan interest-group conflicts—partly because the Supreme Court had not yet issued rulings establishing, and then threatening to restrict, women's constitutional right to abortion. Between 1960 and 1987, expenditures on lawyers in the United States grew sixfold, from $9 billion annually to $54 billion (in constant 1983 dollars), almost tripling the share of gross national product consumed by legal services (Sander and Williams 1989, 434–35). Between 1960 and 1980, federal court appellate cases involving constitutional issues increased sevenfold (Kagan 2002). The volume and rate of state appellate and federal court cases involving public schools, roughly stable from 1920 through 1960, doubled in the 1967–81 period (Tyack and Benavot 1985).

What stimulated this intensification of adversarial legalism? The first important element, in my view, was a fundamental change in American political culture—widespread demands for a more active government, one that would enforce nationwide standards of justice and of security from harm. The most striking manifestations of these attitudes were the powerful political movements that swept the United States in the 1960s—the civil rights movement, the anti–Vietnam War movement, environmentalism, and feminism. The attitudinal changes also were reflected in the flowering of "public-interest groups" to demonstrate and/or lobby on behalf of Latinos, consumer interests, the aged, tenants, children, disabled persons, welfare recipients, and so on. Cumulatively, all these movements demanded major transformations in established social and economic patterns, and a major expansion of the regulatory role of the federal government.

To the legal historian Lawrence Friedman (1985), the new political ethos reflects a rising expectation of "total justice"—the notion that because governments and corporations now have the means (technological and financial) to make technologies safer, reduce pollution, compensate the injured, anticipate and prevent harms, provide better and more equal working conditions and education, and so on, then it is unjust for governments and corporations not to take such actions. The law, therefore, should require them to do so, whether through legislation, regulation, or litigation in the courts.

These changes in political and legal culture, however, are not quite enough to explain the intensification of adversarial legalism. After all, popular demands for governmental social engineering and for "total justice" are not unique to the United States. In the 1960s, Western European democracies extended preexisting governmental protections against misfortune and added new regulations to limit environmental degradation and unfair treatment. Like the United States, they liberalized divorce laws, created women's rights to obtain abortions (Glendon 1987), banned discrimination in employment, and expanded long-standing national social insurance and health care schemes well beyond American levels (Wilensky 2002). European "Greens" battled successfully for pollution controls, restrictions on nuclear power, and limits on hazardous chemicals that are comparable to parallel rules in the United States (Vogel 1986; Brickman, Jasanoff, and Ilgen 1985; Lundqvist 1980). In Western Europe, laws protecting employees from arbitrary termination, guaranteeing them a substantial minimum wage, and providing many other benefits are much more generous than those U.S. labor laws.

The expansion of entitlements and regulation in Western Europe, however, did not produce American-style adversarial legalism. There, national governmental bureaucracies and corporatist bodies implement ambitious regulations and welfare-state entitlements without much reliance on—and hence without much interference from—courts and lawyers. American-style securities class actions, mass "toxic tort" cases, and court-ordered institutional reform plans are virtually unknown. Regulatory policy decisions rarely are reviewed and reversed in court. Political movements are much less likely to seek their goals via litigation campaigns.

In sum, during the 1960s and 1970s, rather similar basic policy norms emerged on both sides of the Atlantic, but the national methods of establishing and implementing those norms were markedly different. Why? In the United States, I have argued (Kagan 2001), the growth of adversarial legalism arose from the tension between (1) a changing political culture that demanded the sweeping exercise of authority by a more powerful and activist government, and (2) an inherited political culture and governmental structure that distrusted centralized political authority and was more comfortable keeping authority fragmented and constrained through legal accountability mechanisms. American proponents of regulatory change and social justice, therefore, fought for new federal norms and programs but also fought for citizens' rights to employ litigation to supervise the implementation of those norms. A few examples should illustrate the point.

"TOTAL JUSTICE" AND CONSTITUTIONAL ADJUDICATION

By the 1950s, partly because of the claims to democratic virtue engendered by the Cold War, American national political elites and a good deal of the public in the north and west had become acutely uncomfortable about the contradiction between the egalitarian "American creed" and the ugly reality of Southern apartheid (Dudziak 1988). Pressures for change mounted. But the inherited political structure meant that neither Congress nor the president could displace local democratic control of public school policy and law enforcement. There was no national minister of education or minister of justice who could give instructions to segregationist local school officials or racist sheriffs, or replace them if they were recalcitrant. Because American political parties were not hierarchically controlled, Southern Democrats in the Senate repeatedly blocked congressional civil rights legislation.

Civil rights lawyers argued that if legislatures, federal and state, had persistently failed to act against a nationally recognized injustice, then it was incumbent on the courts to assert responsibility for policy change. Such an argument might not have swayed an apolitical judiciary, such as those of France or the United Kingdom, committed to legal formality and disinclined to engage in social problem solving. But the American judiciary, staffed with ex-politicians,[8] was open to arguments based on substantive justice. In 1954, the Supreme Court held that legally segregated schools violated the Equal Protection clause (*Brown v. Board of Education*, 347 U.S. 483 [1954]).

In addition, in a series of cases during the 1960s, the U.S. Supreme Court, as was noted above, extended the Bill of Rights to govern state criminal justice practices and elaborated nationwide rules regulating police evidence-gathering methods and criminal procedure in state courts. Moreover, the Court mandated *adversarial* enforcement mechanisms for those new legal standards—free counsel for indigent defendants and an "exclusionary rule" for evidence obtained in violation of the Supreme Court's rules. Thus in both school segregation and criminal justice, adversarial legalism filled an organizational void for reformers and their political supporters. It was the only politically viable way to impose national norms of justice on a fragmented political system.

FRAGMENTED GOVERNMENT AND THE POLITICS OF RIGHTS

Congress was just as active as the federal courts in promoting adversarial legalism. Between 1965 and 1977, in an extraordinary surge of activity, Congress passed twenty-five major environmental and civil rights acts, plus far-reaching statutes regulating workplace safety, consumer lending, product safety, private pension funds, and local public education.[9] At the same time, Congress was reluctant—for political, fiscal, and constitutional reasons—to create huge federal bureaucracies, with offices in every metropolitan area to enforce all these demanding regulatory programs. To many members of Congress, it seemed more expedient to assign primary enforcement responsibility to state and local governmental officials. But then how could reformers and their congressional allies be sure that the new federal norms would be faithfully implemented?

Adversarial legalism provided one answer. Regulatory reformers couched their goals in the form of sweeping legal rights—to equal treatment, a safe workplace, clean water, clean air (Melnick 1995). Armed with those rights, individual victims of injustice and energetic reform lawyers could act as "private attorneys general," bringing lawsuits against state and local governments for half-hearted implementation of federal laws, or they could sue regulated businesses directly. To energize the private attorneys general, Congress enacted scores of one-way fee-shifting statutes, which enabled successful plaintiffs to recover lawyers' fees from governmental and corporate defendants but did not require them, if they lost, to pay the defendants' lawyers' bills (Greve 1989a; O'Connor and Epstein 1985). In sum, whereas European polities generally rely on national bureaucracies to hold local officials accountable to national policies, the U.S. Congress, facing a more decentralized political system, added a new army of enforcers—a decentralized array of private advocacy groups and lawyers.

Congress also invited private attorneys general to police policy implementation by *federal* agencies. The public-interest movement of the 1960s and 1970s, as McCann (1986) has shown, wanted to expand the regulatory power of the federal government, but remained deeply suspicious of centralized power, fearing that regulatory agencies were all too easily "captured" by powerful regulated businesses and their allies in government. The reformers' solution was to subject the more powerful federal regulatory state to the checks of adversarial legalism. In McCann's phrase, they sought to institutionalize a "judicial model of the state."

The national legislature was sympathetic. Especially after 1968, when the executive branch was controlled by Republicans, a Democratic Congress willingly gave citizen watchdog groups and courts more leverage over administrative policymaking and policy enforcement. In contrast to New Deal regulatory statutes, which granted administrative agencies a great deal of discretion, the regulatory statutes of the late 1960s and 1970s set forth ambitious standards and strict deadlines. This legislative specificity enabled advocacy groups to challenge administrative leniency or inaction as illegal, and legislative specificity gave courts grounds to reverse agency decisions (Melnick 1992). Regulations promulgated by administrative agencies, the new statutes also said, had to be made through formal, adversarial procedures reviewable in court. No more backroom deals with regulated businesses. The courts policed that norm by reversing agency decisions that did not articulate persuasive justifications for the regulatory standards chosen or failed to respond adequately to criticisms of draft regulations (Shapiro 1988). Lawsuits against the federal government and appeals of governmental decisions, not surprisingly, increased apace.

During the late 1960s and early 1970s, even as the reach and power of the federal government were expanding, the American electorate, according to a variety of measures, became more mistrustful of government (Griffin 1991, 701–9), and political leaders seemingly became more mistrustful of each other. Voters more often elected legislatures and chief executives of different parties (Fiorina 1996; Thurber 1991, 653–57). The civil rights and anti–Vietnam War movements splintered the Democratic Party, instigating a new political primary and fund-raising system that weakened party leaders' control over individual candidates and legislators (Polsby 1983). The power of congressional committee chairs was redistributed among a multiplicity of subcommittees. Campaign finance reforms intensified each legislator's search for independent sources of funding and support. Taking all these changes together, political party leaders were stripped of a considerable measure of control over policy formulation (Polsby 1983; Ranney 1983).

The resulting "hyperpluralism" further promoted adversarial legalism. In political systems without "dominant disciplined political parties," it makes sense for interest groups and momentarily strong political coalitions to demand enactment of highly detailed laws, enforceable in court, for that will help insulate today's policy victories from reversal following tomorrow's electoral loss (Moe 1989; Cooter and Ginsburg 1996, 305). Thus in the United States, beginning in the late 1960s, politically divided government and fragmented political parties encouraged and enabled organized interest groups to win detailed statutory provisions that would help them exert influence on subsequent policy implementation and to challenge unsympathetic administrative officials in court (Moe 1989). In a politically fragmented Congress, statutes had to be painfully stitched together by shifting, issue-specific coalitions. Legislative proponents and presidents could gather support for their bills only by adding statutory loopholes and supplementary provisions demanded by a multitude of stakeholders. Individual senators and House subcommittee chairs often added hastily drafted last-minute amendments (Smith 1989).

Divided government, therefore, did not block congressional lawmaking (Mayhew 1991), but it made legislation more complex, lengthy, and confusing. American environmental statutes and regulations became much longer than their counterparts in other democracies (Cooter and Ginsburg 1996; Kagan 2001, 187–88). Multisubject omnibus acts, the impenetrable Employee Retirement Income Security Act, the 400-page 1990 Clean Air Act, and their ilk resembled incoherent patchwork quilts, laden with legally contradictory or incomprehensible provisions (Schuck 1992, 27–30). This style of legislation magnified legal uncertainty, inviting subsequent litigation and judicial reconstruction of congressional policy. The Northwest forests–spotted owl controversy is a perfect example.

POLITICAL CONSERVATIVES AND ADVERSARIAL LEGALISM

For all their criticism of "excessive litigation," Republican presidents and legislators also have been active supporters of measures that increase adversarial legalism, which helps explain its persistence even in the more conservative 1980s and 1990s. Just as the liberal "public-interest movement" feared that the federal agencies created in the 1960s and 1970s might be "captured" by business interests and betray reformist goals, political conservatives feared that the bureaucrats would be hostile to business and economic growth. Again, political uncertainty bred adversarial legalism. Republicans also fought for legislative provisions that restricted administrative discretion and subjected it to legal challenge. Unable to block regulatory legislation, they tried to ensure that regulatory statutes demanded from administrators high standards of economic and technological rationality. This gave business firms leverage for attacking regulatory decisions in court, which they did with considerable regularity.

Similarly, conservatives exploited the populist strain in American political culture—eager for the benefits of "total justice" perhaps, but also mistrustful of "big government" and hostile to tax increases. Thus Republicans helped craft regulatory schemes that called for private litigation, rather than public expenditure, to accom-

plish collective goals. For example, conservative senators' reluctance to fund a federal enforcement bureaucracy led liberal sponsors of the 1968 Truth-in-Lending Act
to enact an enforcement system that relies primarily on private lawsuits against
lenders (Rubin 1991). Similarly, in 1991, as case backlogs swelled at the under-
staffed Equal Employment Opportunity Commission, Republican president George
H. W. Bush's (and a Democratic Congress's) response was not to beef up the commission but to encourage more private lawsuits to implement antidiscrimination
laws: the Civil Rights Restoration Act empowered plaintiffs to obtain higher money
penalties, including punitive damages, in lawsuits against employers—a strategy that
requires few new federal bureaucrats and no new taxes (Potter and Reesman 1992).

Even the conservative "tort-reform movement" has done relatively little to displace adversarial legalism as a method of compensating accident victims. Rather
than seeking to supplant the adversarial tort and jury system with social insurance
plans and administrative tribunals, conservative reformers have simply tried to make
it harder for plaintiffs to obtain large damages (which tends to disadvantage the
most severely injured accident victims). Meanwhile, Democrats (and their trial
lawyer political allies), concerned that proposed administrative injury-compensation
plans might fall under the sway of stingy conservatives, also have shied away from
fundamental reforms. Thus the basic structure of the woefully inefficient and often
unjust tort-liability system (Kagan 2001), characterized by adversarial legalism and
shaped by judicial decision making, has remained intact.

LAWYERS, LEGAL CULTURE, AND ADVERSARIAL LEGALISM

One further contributing cause of American adversarial legalism must be mentioned:
the legal profession and the legal culture it generates. Beginning in the 1960s, the
advent of a distinctively American brand of activist government—one that seeks
"total justice" through decentralized governmental and economic institutions, legalistic regulation, adversarial legal challenge, and citizen-initiated lawsuits—vastly
increased the numbers, political influence, and entrepreneurial character of American lawyers. Lawyers have not been the primary cause of the expanding domain of
adversarial legalism. Broader political currents and interest groups, as suggested earlier, were the sorcerers that called forth adversarial legalism—thereby generating demands for more legally trained apprentices.

The sorcerers' apprentices, however, soon became richer, better organized, more
energetic, and harder to rein in. Although many judges and lawyers strive to *dampen*
adversarial legalism (Kagan 1994; Suchman and Cahill 1996), organized networks
of activist lawyers—such as the environmental lawyers who pursued the Northwest
forests–spotted owl cases, or plaintiff's lawyers who focus on particular hazardous
products (asbestos, tobacco, breast implants, etc.), or conservative organizations opposed to affirmative action—systematically push courts to *extend* the realm of adversarial legalism. The American Trial Lawyers Association and lawyers who bring
securities' class actions assiduously lobby legislatures and mobilize very large campaign contributions to block reforms that would reduce adversarial legalism (Kagan
1994; Heymann and Liebman 1988, 309).

Perhaps most important, American law professors, judges, and lawyers have elaborated legal theories that actively promote adversarial legalism—not as a necessary
evil but as a desirable mode of governance. The opinions and judges highlighted in law

school case books are those of judicial innovators such as Supreme Court justices Earl Warren and William J. Brennan, or California Supreme Court judge Roger Traynor, who played a leading role in reshaping tort law. This heroic view of the judiciary's role in government has not been uncontested in the law schools or in the judiciary. But on balance, in the last few decades American legal scholars and judges have become more supportive of a "social engineering" or even a political vision of law and the judicial role. Compare, for example, the views of German legal scholars and judges, as revealed by Greve's comparative study of "public-interest" litigation to shape public policy:

> In the United States, there has been a broad consensus for public interest litigation among legal scholars, judges, and the legal establishment in general. In the Federal Republic [of Germany], there is a similarly broad consensus against it. Judges on the Federal Constitutional Court and the Federal Administrative Court voiced their opposition to association lawsuits not only on the bench but in legal periodicals and in public. (Greve 1989a, 231)

Whereas European legal scholars speak of law as a logically coherent set of authoritative principles and rules, American legal scholars often speak of law as a manifestation of the ongoing struggle among groups and classes for political and economic advantage, or as a manipulable set of tools for achieving better government (Kagan 1988, 728–30; 1994, 24–27). As was noted above, Atiyah and Summers (1987, 404), comparing American law schools to those of the United Kingdom, see the former as inculcating a uniquely "instrumentalist" (rather than legally formalist) notion of law. The dominant strain in American academic legal culture supports easy access to courts, along with policy solutions that take the form of judicially enforceable individual rights, harsh penalties for torts and regulatory violations, and tight legal controls on official discretion. As law school graduates move on to legislative staff positions, governmental policymaking jobs, bar association committees, advocacy organizations, and the judiciary, they tend to be supporters of adversarial legalism as a mode of governance. Thus American judges have encouraged adversarial legalism by finding "implied" private rights of action in statutes and constitutional provisions, from the National Environmental Protection Act to the Fourth Amendment, thereby opening up new spheres of litigation against government officials by citizens and advocacy groups.[10]

American legal culture is far from monolithic in its endorsement of adversarial legalism. In recent years, U.S. Supreme Court rulings have called for greater judicial deference to administrative agency decisions, put some limits on standing to sue government agencies, and made it significantly harder for criminal defendants to overturn their convictions on constitutional grounds. Legislatures in many states have enacted restrictions on tort litigation. Congress enacted restrictions on class-action securities litigation. But these restrictions have not *substantially* changed the basic structures or curtailed the incidence of adversarial legalism in the United States. The basic causes of adversarial legalism—popular demands for fair treatment, recompense, and protection, combined with mistrust of government and fragmentation of political and economic power—remain unchanged and perhaps unchangeable. Indeed, three decades of expanded adversarial legalism have deeply imprinted the ideas of America's adversarial *legal* culture on the country's *political* culture as a whole.

CONCLUSION

In the last half of the twentieth century, all economically advanced democracies have experienced political demands for governmental action to enhance economic security, promote equal opportunity, provide for the injured, reduce the risk of harm, improve the natural environment, and protect human rights. The United States is unique, however, in the extent to which the governmental response has resulted in increased levels of adversarial legalism. The fundamental reason, this chapter argues, lies in the collision between demands for more active government and some enduring features of the American political system—political structures that fragment governmental power, a political culture that mistrusts "big government," an increasingly competitive but disaggregated business system, and a legal culture that promotes and validates adversarial legalism.

The catalytic reaction of these seemingly incompatible progovernmental and antigovernmental elements has produced an approach to governance that is active but decentralized, legally constrained, and litigious. Political and economic factions, fearing that their adversaries will have too much influence on federal bureaucracies and local governments, have insisted that regulatory and law-enforcement agencies, as well as large corporations, should be held accountable via detailed laws and procedures, lawsuits, and courts. In addition, an entrepreneurial, politically active legal profession, professoriat, and judiciary all have promoted the desirability of adversarial legalism as a response to policy problems and injury compensation, successfully foreclosing attempts to seriously curtail the powers of judges, lawyers, and juries in governance and dispute resolution. In consequence, as new demands for governmental problem-solving are pressed onto the American political agenda, adversarial legalism tends to spread and intensify, entrenching the courts' role in the ongoing policy dialogue with other government bodies.

NOTES

1. This account draws extensively on Swedlow's (2003) detailed analysis of the Northwest forests–spotted owl litigation.
2. *Northern Spotted Owl v. Hodel*, 716 F. Supp. 479 (W.D. Wash, 1988). Separately, a 1989 report by the General Accounting Office (GAO) claimed that USFWS, during the Reagan administration, had for political reasons changed its analysis from one that emphasized the dangers facing the spotted owl to one that supported the lack of adequate evidence to make a meaningful decision (Swedlow 2003, 263).
3. A suit by Douglas County, Oregon, challenged the USFWS crucial habitat designation. In December 1992, a U.S. District Court set that designation aside until USFWS prepared a new environmental impact analysis that took into account the extensive adverse effects on the human environment that huge reserves for the spotted owl would have (*Douglas County v. Lujan*, 810 F. Supp. 1470 [D. Ore. 1992]).
4. E.g., in *King v. Smith*, 392 U.S. 309 (1968), the Supreme Court, reinterpreting the Social Security Act, invalidated an Alabama regulation that provided that if a single mother had a "regular boyfriend," she was ineligible for AFDC assistance. In 1972, the Court ruled against the U.S. Department of Health, Education, and Welfare's policy of allowing state AFDC eligibility policies to vary from federal standards (*Carleson v. Remillard*, 406 U.S. 598 [1972]). That decision stimulated a flood of litigation in which the lower courts invalidated restrictive state rules on issues such as verification procedures, methods for determining applicants' income, and failure to register for welfare-to-work programs.

5. State court decisions developing corporate law are technically matters of statutory interpretation, based on corporation codes enacted by state legislatures. In fact, however, those codes have been relatively static, and a good deal of legal and/or policy development has been the product of state supreme court rulings, developing in a precedent-based, common law manner. The importance of courts in corporate governance policy stems in large part from judicial decisions that, in contrast with the company law of Western Europe, invite entrepreneurial lawyers to aggregate shareholders' claims in class actions.

6. In the 1970s and 1980s, the incidence of asbestos-related diseases among Dutch workers was five to ten times as high as in the United States. Dutch law authorizes tort claims against employers. As of 1991, almost 200,000 asbestos-based tort cases had been filed in the United States. Fewer than *ten* had been filed in The Netherlands because Dutch "employees get reasonable benefits in a non-confrontational way"—through the social security system. Disabled Dutch workers are entitled to all needed medical care and lifelong benefits equal to 70 or 80 percent of their lost earnings, without having to prove an employer or product manufacturer did anything wrong (Vinke and Witthagen 1992, 12, 17).

7. Some scholars have argued that Hartz and others have neglected the extent to which profoundly illiberal political ideas, such as nativism, sexism, and racism, have contended with liberalism in American political culture and law (e.g., see Smith 1993). Still, viewed comparatively, liberalism is what best distinguishes the American political culture from that of most other economically advanced democracies.

8. Goldman (1967) found that four-fifths of federal appellate court judges had been "political activists" at some point in their careers (see also Kagan, Detlefsen, and Infelise 1984).

9. Among these major enactments were the Civil Rights Act (1964), the National Environmental Protection Act (1969), the Clean Air Act (1970), the Occupational Safety and Health Act (1970), the Clean Water Act (1972), the Employees Retirement Income Security Act (1974), the Equal Employment Opportunity Act (1972), the National Highway Traffic and Motor Safety Act (1966), and the Surface Mining and Reclamation Act (1977) (see, generally, Sunstein 1990). In addition, congressional regulation of state and local government bodies reached new heights, sometimes through direct regulations, such as the Voting Rights Act, sometimes by means of conditions attached to federal laws providing funding for housing and welfare programs, mass transit, etc. (Mayhew 1991).

10. See Schuck 1983. See also Rabkin 1989 (implied private rights to sue Office of Civil Rights concerning enforcement priorities); and Taylor 1984 (implied rights to sue for enforcement of the National Environmental Protection Act).

2

Adversarial Legalism, the Rise of Judicial Policymaking, and the Separation-of-Powers Doctrine

JEB BARNES

ADVERSARIAL LEGALISM AND THE RISE OF JUDICIAL POLICYMAKING

Judicial policymaking is nothing new to American politics. Many traditional features of American government—such as fragmented political authority, the doctrine of judicial review, and the common law tradition—have placed courts at the center of important political and policy disputes almost since its founding. Hence Alexis de Tocqueville's observation in the 1830s that important political questions in the United States often become judicial questions (1835), and Skowronek's characterization of early American government as a "state of courts and [political] parties" (1982, 24, 24–35). Indeed, when compared cross-nationally, the United States has probably always featured greater "adversarial legalism": a mode of dispute resolution and policymaking characterized by high levels of "formal legal contestation," in which contending interests invoke preexisting legal rights and procedures backed by the threat of litigation (Kagan 2001; and Kagan, this volume).

The pervasiveness and intensity of contemporary judicial policymaking and adversarial legalism, however, is something new. Part of the difference lies in the sheer volume of today's legislation and statutory litigation. The patterns are striking. In the 1950s, Congress typically passed about 1,900 pages of new laws each session. In the 1990s, that number jumped to about 6,750 pages per session. Perhaps not surprisingly, this flood of statutes has coincided with a rising tide of litigation. In 1961, about 13,500 statutory claims were filed in U.S. District Courts. In 2002, that figure had climbed to 167,000, representing more than a twelvefold increase from 1961.[1]

More subtly, as Robert Kagan argues in the previous chapter, revved-up adversarial legalism and judicial policymaking reflect changes in the scope and structure of governmental programs and administrative law. To reiterate: Beginning in late 1960s and 1970s, American reformers successfully pushed for new programs that sought to address widespread social problems, such as discrimination, environmental degradation, and consumer safety. In contrast to European activists, who built on existing national bureaucracies to implement their ambitious agendas and thus created *centralized, bureaucratic* administrative states, American reformers built on previously fragmented policymaking structures and created an alphabet soup of federal agencies that often overlap with one another and state agencies. In addition, because American reformers feared powerful interest groups would capture the new agencies, they created a series of procedural mechanisms, such as public comment periods and citizen suits, which give the public—and public-interest groups—a voice in administrative decision making and direct means to hold agencies accountable. The result was a comparatively *decentralized, rights-based* administrative state, which often places courts at the center of complex—and contested—regulatory disputes (Kagan 1994; Burke 2002; Melnick, this volume).

During the same period, judicial innovations in administrative law enhanced the courts' role in reviewing agency procedures and decisions. For example, the landmark Supreme Court decision of *Goldberg v. Kelly*, 397 U.S. 254 (1970)—which required hearings for those facing the loss of welfare benefits—touched off the modern "due process revolution." The due process revolution, in turn, led to the creation of a myriad of administrative hearings that could be appealed to the courts as well as a constitutional basis for objecting to the fairness of agency procedures (Burke 2002; Melnick, this volume). Meanwhile, federal judges relaxed traditional limitations to bringing private actions against agencies, which facilitated public interest-group litigation (see, generally, Stewart and Sunstein 1982).

These changes have had a predictable and profound effect on judicial power in the United States. Put simply, today's federal judges not only serve their traditional role of resolving politically important constitutional disputes, but also play a significant role in administering conflicts among competing agencies over the meaning of statutes and considering public challenges to regulatory procedures and decisions under the "hard look" doctrine, which can serve as a doctrine of judicial second-guessing (Melnick, this volume).[2] As a result, federal judges shape issues far beyond the reach of their counterparts abroad, such as coal mine safety (Braithewaite 1985), nursing home care (Day and Klein 1987), corporate insolvency (Reich 1985), educational opportunity (Kirp 1979), labor relations (Bok 1971), new drugs (Teff 1987), air pollution (Lundqvist 1980), the use of polyvinyl chlorides (Badaracco 1985), and the list goes on and on (Kagan 2001).[3]

Some would undoubtedly criticize these developments as violating the traditional doctrine of the separation of powers, which holds that federal courts—as a nonelected branch of government—should avoid making policy and apply the law as written (see, e.g., Scalia 1997; Glazer 1975). In addition, the Supreme Court clearly takes the tripartite division of labor in the U.S. Constitution seriously, although the Court's separation-of-powers jurisprudence is admittedly muddled (Krent 1988; Chemerinski 1987; Elliott 1989; Gwyn 1989). For example, the Court has voided portions of important legislation on the grounds that the law improperly blurred legislative, executive, and judicial functions, including *Bowsher v. Synar*, 478 U.S. 714 (1986), which struck down portions of the Gramm-Rudman Act of 1985; *INS v. Chadha*, 462 U.S. 919 (1983), which reversed legislative vetoes in hundreds of statutes; *Northern Pipeline Construction Co. v. Marathon Pipe Line Co.*, 458 U.S. 50 (1982), which negated portions of the Bankruptcy Reform Act of 1978; and *Buckley v. Valeo*, 424 U.S.1 (1976), which overturned aspects of the Federal Elections Campaign Act of 1972.

This chapter takes a different tack. Instead of challenging heightened judicial policymaking and adversarial legalism on separation-of-powers grounds, it questions the separation-of-powers doctrine as traditionally applied to the policymaking process. Specifically, this chapter argues that the U.S. Constitution does *not* assign mutually exclusive policymaking roles to each branch of government; instead, it creates overlapping branches of government that are designed to respond to different constituencies and approach policymaking differently. The goals of this system of redundant and diversely representative lawmakers are to (1) hinder any single branch or interest group from dominating the process and (2) encourage broad participation in the making of policy. From this perspective, the crucial issue in evaluating contemporary interbranch relations is not whether Congress, agencies, and courts adhere to neatly defined roles, but whether—and under what conditions—interbranch relations promote important democratic outcomes, such as open deliberation and coalition-building among varied interests.

To develop this argument, this chapter proceeds in three stages. First, it defines what I call the "standard view of the separation of powers" as applied to the policymaking process. Second, it considers the rationales underlying the standard view and why these rationales—including the classic argument that judicial policymaking is countermajoritarian—are problematic at best. Third, it points to an alternative, and, in my judgment, more viable conception of the separation-of-powers doctrine in the constitutional design of American government.

THE STANDARD VIEW OF THE SEPARATION OF POWERS AS APPLIED TO THE POLICYMAKING PROCESS

Over time, the separation-of-powers doctrine as applied to policymaking has become entangled in overlapping formal, functional, and normative arguments, which arguably obscure the doctrine's significance (Feeley and Rubin 1998).[4] Specifically, some view the separation of powers as a legal principle, which delineates the proper role of each branch of government in policymaking (Calibresi and Rhodes 1992; Leiberman 1989; Fitzgerald 1986). Others associate the separation of powers with the functional principle of specialization, suggesting that each branch has adapted specific tools for addressing discrete aspects of policymaking and should avoid the tasks of the other branches (Rosenberg 1992; Fuller 1978; Horowitz 1977; Scheingold 1974). And some tend to view the separation of powers in terms of core democratic values, especially a commitment to majority rule, which requires that elected officials play the dominant role in policymaking (Bickel 1962).

Despite their differences, these views share several common themes that allow their synthesis into the standard conception of the separation of powers. First, and most importantly, the formal, functional, and normative perspectives hold that the separation-of-powers doctrine creates specific niches for each branch of government in the policymaking process. Thus Congress should write the law; the executive branch should implement the law; and courts should apply the law as written (provided that it is constitutional). Second, and related, these perspectives converge on the ideal of legislative supremacy in the construction of statutes, which holds that members of Congress, as elected officials in the national legislature, should be the principal policymaker and federal judges, who are appointed for life, should be Congress's faithful agents.

To its credit, the standard conception of the separation of powers provides clear guidelines for evaluating interbranch relations: namely, each branch should stick to their knitting. Accordingly, Congress should enact clear statutes that send strong and effective signals to the courts and agencies. In implementing and applying the law, agencies and courts should adhere to the letter of the law. Under the most extreme versions of this argument, even if a law produces absurd results, agencies and courts should apply the law as written, warn Congress of any unanticipated consequences, and force Congress back to the drawing board (Scalia 1997). Conversely, Congress should not pass vague statutes that send weak or unclear signals, and agencies and courts should avoid making policy under the guise of implementing or applying the law.

CRITIQUING THE STANDARD VIEW OF THE SEPARATION OF POWERS

If we take the standard view of the separation of powers seriously, the rise of judicial policymaking in an era of heightened adversarial legalism is deeply troubling, because it plainly violates the ideals of interbranch specialization and legislative supremacy in the policymaking process. As was noted above, however, there is another possibility. Instead of rejecting judicial policymaking, which is deeply entrenched in traditional features of American government as well as the structure of the modern American administrative state (Kagan 2001, and Kagan, this volume; Melnick, this volume; Burke 2002; see also Barnes 1997), we might reject the standard view of the separation of powers. To consider this possibility, we must delve beneath the standard view's surface and consider its underlying formal, functional, and normative rationales.

THE FORMAL RATIONALE OF THE STANDARD VIEW OF THE SEPARATION OF POWERS

It is beyond the scope of this brief chapter to canvas the vast legal literature on the separation-of-powers doctrine (see, generally, Krent 1988; Feeley and Rubin 1998, 323–26, collecting authority) or review the many detailed and nuanced textual arguments about its construction (see, e.g., Calabresi and Rhodes 1992; Fitzgerald 1986). Suffice it to say that the formal rationale of the separation-of-powers doctrine mainly rests on two separate grounds: (1) arguments about the text of the U.S. Constitution and (2) arguments about the intent of the Framers. Both are contestable.

With respect to the language of the Constitution, formalists point to references to "legislative," "executive," and "judicial" powers, and argue these references embody three ideal categories of authority, which in turn are given to the legislative, executive, and judicial branches, respectively. Thus, Chief Justice Burger in *INS v. Chadha* confidently states that the "Constitution sought to divide the delegated powers of the new Federal Government into three defined categories, Legislative, Executive, and Judicial, to assure, as nearly as possible, that each branch would confine itself to its assigned responsibility" (462 U.S. at 951). Former attorney general Edwin Meese echoed these sentiments, when he declared that the "founding Fathers . . . created a federal government with three well-defined branches. And they carefully enumerated the powers and responsibilities of each" (address to the Federal Bar Association, September 13, 1985, 2–3, on file at *Cornell Law Review*).

The references to legislative, executive, and judicial powers do establish a general arrangement of primary powers that distinguishes American policymaking from other policymaking systems, such as parliamentary systems that feature unified executive and legislative powers. These references do not, however, necessarily delineate mutually exclusive roles for each branch of government in the policymaking process (Strauss 1987). Indeed, the Constitution explicitly combines this general arrangement with a detailed system of checks and balances, which ensures a system of "separated institutions sharing power" (Neustadt 1990, 32).

Specifically, Congress is given the primary responsibility for drafting statutes, but its statutory handiwork is subject to presidential veto. In addition, the executive branch and the courts have considerable power to shape the meaning of statutes. Specifically, the executive branch has the power to "take care" that the law is properly executed, which includes the power to draft interpretive rules and regulations that flesh out the details of the governing statutes. Similarly, the courts are empowered to adjudicate cases and controversies arising under statutes, which invariably involves legislating "interstitially": filling gaps that appear when general laws are applied to specific cases (Cardozo 1921; Shapiro 1966). Of course, if members of Congress are not satisfied with agency interpretative rules or judicial statutory interpretation decisions, they can pass new laws in response. These new laws are typically subject to another round of agency and judicial construction. In short, policymaking power is not vested in a single branch; it is shared among the branches, each of which plays an important role in defining and refining the meaning of statutes (see also the chapters by Miller, Kassop, and Melnick in this volume).

One might counter that the Constitution erects some explicit barriers among the branches. Article I, Section 6, provides an obvious example. It prohibits members of Congress from serving in executive offices. This provision, however, does not establish separate and distinct spheres of influence for each branch of government in the policymaking process. It creates a bar against the branches of government sharing *personnel* (Nourse 1996), which is quite different from a prohibition against sharing *powers*. It also suggests that, when the Framers wanted to create exceptions to the general rule of overlapping branches of government, they did so explicitly.

In addition, although divining the Framers' intent is always speculative and the historical texts are admittedly open to more than one interpretation, a strong case can be made that the Framers did not intend mutually exclusive branches of government. Instead, they seemed to favor overlapping branches of government. After all, if the Farmers wanted to create wholly separate spheres of influence, they could have adopted language from a number of state constitutions, including James Madison's home state of Virginia, which explicitly provided for distinct branches of government. The Framers did not. They adopted a system of checks and balances, which expressly created shared—or mixed—powers.

Moreover, at least in the *Federalist Papers*, Madison appears to reject the argument that the legislative, executive, and judicial branches can or should be wholly separate in a republican government.[5] For example, in *Federalist Paper No. 37* (1788), Madison explains that "no skill in the science of government has yet been able to discriminate and define, with sufficient certainty, its three great provinces—the legislative, executive, and judiciary" (244). He adds in *Federalist Paper No. 47* (1788) that the separation of powers does not mean that "departments ought to have no *partial agency* in, or *no control* over, the acts of the other. [Rather,] where the *whole* of power of one department is exercised by the same hands which possess the *whole* power of another department, the fundamental principles of a free constitution are subverted" (304, emphasis in the original).[6] In *Federalist Paper No. 48* (1788), Madison further explains that, if the branches were "separate and distinct," no check would exist against any single branch, especially the "impetuous" legislative branch (309), from using its exclusive powers to "mask, under complicated and indirect measures, the encroachments which it makes on the co-ordinate departments" (310). Thus, during ratification, Madison argued against the *accumulation of power* in the hands of a single branch and not the *sharing of powers* among the branches.

One might counter that Madison abandoned this view, when he proposed an amendment to the Constitution in the first Congress that would have created mutually exclusive branches of government. His peers in the Senate, however, did not. They rejected his amendment and preserved a system of overlapping governmental functions (Kay 1988).

In sum, as a formal matter, it seems questionable to criticize Congress, agencies, or courts for violating one another's constitutionally prescribed turf, because the Framers did not create separate and distinct domains for each branch of government. Indeed, one can argue that the Framers knew how to create such a system but they (1) argued against it, (2) refused to adopt it, and (3) declined to change their minds when Madison provided them the opportunity to do so.

THE FUNCTIONAL RATIONALE OF THE STANDARD VIEW

The functional rationale for the separation-of-powers doctrine rests on the concept of specialization, which holds that each branch of government is designed to fulfill a distinct policymaking role and has developed tools for carrying out its function. To the extent any branch impinges on another's functions, it will result in ineffective or inefficient policy outcomes (Rosenberg 1992; Fuller 1978; Horowitz 1977; Scheingold 1974).

In "Forms and Limits of Adjudication," Lon Fuller (1978) offers a classic version of this argument, which identifies three forms of social ordering: contracts, in which parties make the rules themselves; elections, in which citizens vote for their lawmakers; and adjudication, in which parties present reasoned arguments. According to Fuller, courts must decide disputes according to reasoned arguments, and hence are limited to adjudication. Adjudication, in turn, is well suited for resolving "dyadic disputes," or well-defined conflicts among discrete numbers of parties that fall under preexisting principles, such as negligence suits or breach of contract claims. According to Fuller, adjudication is not apt for "polycentric disputes" that tend to dominate legislative agendas: controversies that are open-ended, affect a wide range of parties, and defy preexisting rules, such as the regulation of air pollution. Following this logic, Fuller concludes that judicial policymaking will tend to be ineffective, because polycentric policy disputes defy adjudication.

From the perspective of *evaluating* interbranch relations, this argument has a number of limitations. Most obviously, to the extent that the functional rationale rests on an assertion that judges are inefficient policymakers, it is not a normative argument at all; it is an empirical claim about the relative efficacy of judicial policymaking (Feeley and Rubin 1998, 314). The validity of this assertion, moreover, is both theoretically and empirically dubious. As a theoretical matter, transaction cost economists argue that human beings are highly resourceful and can adapt a variety of institutional mechanisms to solve problems effectively and efficiently (Williamson 1995). As a result, institutional competence is not a blanket concept, which can be asserted based on formal categories of legislative, executive, and judicial functions (Feeley and Rubin 1998). Instead, it is a relative and probabalistic concept that must be assessed on a case-by-case basis (Williamson 1995; Komesar 1994; Rubin 1996).

As an empirical matter, scholars have questioned whether the division of labor envisaged by the standard view of the separation of powers, and endorsed by the functional rationale, is always the most prudent and effective mode of policymaking. For example, legal scholars have argued that judges' strict adherence to the letter of the law may place unreasonable burdens on Congress, which must use its limited resources to correct patently absurd outcomes under overly literal readings of the rules (Bussel 2000; Brudney 1994).

Similarly, strict congressional adherence to a role as the principal policymaker may be problematic. For instance, it may make sense for Congress to delegate the lead policymaking role to the courts when issues involve fact-intensive inquiries or when technology, markets, or science are in flux (Douglas and Wildavsky 1982; Thompson and Tuden 1959). Consider court–Congress relations over how to balance protection of trademarks against monopolization of generic terms like "aspirin," "thermos," or "cellophane" (see, generally, Osoba 1985). Because there is no obvious bright line rule for balancing these concerns, Congress has allowed courts to develop the definition of genericness on a case-by-case basis. Although some dissensus exists over the specific formulation of the genericness test, the law traditionally has focused on whether the relevant purchasing public understands the term to be generic.[7]

In the late 1970s and early 1980s, the Ninth Circuit departed from this standard approach in litigation known as the "Anti-Monopoly case." In that case, a company developed a board game titled "Anti-Monopoly: The Bust the Trusts Game," and sought a judicial declaration that "Monopoly" had become a generic term. In response, General Mills, the maker of the popular board game "Monopoly," sued for trademark infringement. Instead of looking at public perceptions of the term "Monopoly," the Ninth Circuit adopted a novel test. It examined whether purchasers were motivated to buy the product *solely* because of its name.[8] If not, the term would be deemed generic.

The Anti-Monopoly case was highly controversial. Business groups lobbied Congress for a new statute, which would reverse the purchaser motivation test and greatly limit the courts' discretion in determining whether a term had become generic. Ultimately, Congress refused. Instead, it passed a narrow statute, which overrode the Anti-Monopoly case and invited courts to continue adapting the law on a case-by-case basis. Although experts disagreed on the specific merits of the bill, they approved Congress's refusal to reduce "genericness" to a narrow statutory formula, because courts needed some discretion to adapt the standard for genericness as well as flexibility to consider what should count as evidence of genericness at trial (Barnes 2004). In short, in this case, judicial discretion seemed the better part of policymaking valor.

To reiterate: The point is *not* that case-by-case adjudication by judges is always preferable when issues require fact-intensive inquiries or when technology, markets, or science are changing. Incrementalism—whether through Congress, agencies, or the courts—has its limitations, especially when policy solutions require bold strokes at the outset and when decisions have irreversible threshold effects or latent adverse consequences (see, generally, Dror 1964; McCurdy 1990; Hayes 1992; and Weiss and Woodhouse 1992).[9] The point is that the procrustean bed of interbranch relations underlying the standard view of the separation of powers is not always appropriate, and that a period of flexible rulemaking by the courts may be a sensible and efficient mode of policymaking, at least for a period of time.

In their brilliant account of judicial policymaking in the prison reform cases, Malcolm Feeley and Edward Rubin offer a more fundamental critique of the functional rationale of the separation-of-powers doctrine, maintaining that it rests on a flawed conception of specialization. Specifically, Feeley and Rubin argue that specialization is an organizational principle that seeks to *increase* inputs into problem solving as opposed to placing barriers to participation. Thus, in medicine, specialization increases the number of doctors who contribute to a patient's diagnosis and treatment, which is quite different from compartmentalizing roles as prescribed by the functional rationale. As Feeley and Rubin explain (1998, 321), such compartmentalization "certainly occurs—in fact, it is the familiar 'that's-not-my-department-syndrome'—but most people regard it as a defect to be avoided, not a guiding principle to be respected."

To summarize: The functional rationale seems flawed as a standard for evaluating interbranch relations. Indeed, it is not a normative argument at all; it is an empirical argument about the competence of judicial policymaking, which rests on theoretically and empirically questionable assumptions about the relative efficacy of legislation versus adjudication. Moreover, the functional rationale arguably relies on an odd notion of specialization, which calls for a type of organizational pigeonholing that is hard to defend as a functional strategy, much less as an ideal division of labor among the branches.

THE NORMATIVE RATIONALE FOR THE STANDARD VIEW

Unlike the formal and functional arguments, some defenses of the standard view of the separation of powers are truly normative, drawing on the ideal of majority rule to justify legislative supremacy in the policymaking process. Alexander Bickel's work, *The Least Dangerous Branch* (1962), provides the seminal text. He argues that the promise of majority rule lies at the heart of American democracy and requires that lawmakers be publicly accountable via elections. Accordingly, elected officials represent the principal lawmakers, and should make all major policy decisions. By contrast, unelected officials, such as judges and civil servants, should serve as agents for elected officials and faithfully apply the law as written (as long as it is constitutional).

Bickel concedes that members of Congress cannot fully achieve this ideal in practice; they simply lack the time and resources to make every decision or micromanage the courts or agencies. Consequently, Congress inevitably delegates some decisions to judges and civil servants, who enjoy significant opportunities to make policy under the guise of statutory interpretation or implementation. Because delegation provides courts and agencies significant policymaking opportunities, it can lead to what Bickel calls the "counter-majoritarian difficulty": decisions by unelected officials that are contrary to the will of the majority (Bickel 1962, 16–23). Such countermajoritarian decision making is objectionable in Bickel's view on at least two grounds: It violates the core value of majority rule and it erodes the courts' institutional legitimacy as a neutral arbiter of the law.

This argument is subject to a variety of attacks (see Friedman 1993, 2001; Whittington 2001a; Peretti 1999; Feeley and Rubin 1998; Mishler and Sheehan 1993; Klarman 1996; Graber 1993, 1995; and Rosenberg 1992). First, if one accepts majority rule as the benchmark for American democracy, it is not clear that Congress and legislation are necessarily more majoritarian than courts and judicial decisions, because (1) elections do not guarantee majoritarian lawmakers and (2) even if members of Congress are perfectly representative of their constituents, taking votes among elected members of Congress does not guarantee majoritarian legislation. Second, it is far from clear that majority rule is the proper benchmark for evaluating interbranch relations. Indeed, the Framers saw unchecked majority rule as a potential *threat* to the republic. Each argument is discussed in the following sections.

ARE MEMBERS OF CONGRESS MAJORITARIAN LAWMAKERS?

Bickel assumes that Congress is more majoritarian and hence more democratic than courts and agencies, because its members are elected whereas judges and civil servants are appointed. Although this argument has strong intuitive appeal, a wide range of scholars have challenged it. Public choice scholars, for instance, have strongly questioned whether elections provide a meaningful voice to the public. Specifically, public choice scholars work within a rational choice framework and assume that voters are self-interested and seek to maximize their wealth. As such, rational voters would never elect officials that systematically fail to represent their interests in direct and informed elections. But congressional elections are seldom direct and informed. Instead, congressional elections are indirect, because, unlike single-issue referenda, citizens vote for candidates who fight over a variety of policy stands. Thus, it is extremely difficult to untangle voter preferences on the issues from their single vote for a candidate. Congressional elections are uninformed because they include a broad subset of citizens, regardless of whether they take the time to weigh the candidates thoughtfully. Under these circumstances, elections send static-filled signals to elected officials.

The limits on elections as signals to representatives, in turn, make elected officials more likely to respond to other more direct and costly forms of political communication, especially lobbying and campaign contributions. Public choice scholars assert that the costs of these forms of participation are not evenly distributed. Instead, they are said to fall disproportionately on broad, diffuse groups, which lack the resources, determination, and allies to organize for political action and press their agendas through the policymaking obstacle course on Capitol Hill. The result, it is argued, is skewed laws that systematically favor well-organized interests (Olsen 1971; Stigler 1971).

Under this logic, federal judges may be *more likely* to act in accordance with broad public interest than members of Congress. Why? Federal judges are insulated from lobbyists and enjoy lifetime tenure and hence may be better situated to resist political pressure from narrow, well-organized groups than Congress and congressional committees (Shapiro 1966). It should be added that an impressive body of literature shows that federal judges are in fact responsive to broad public opinion, even though they are not elected (see, e.g., Mishler and Sheehan 1993; Marshall 1989; and Peretti 1999, 178–80, collecting authority; and Devins, this volume).

Working in an entirely different tradition, postmodernists also challenge the assumption that elected officials are representative of their constituents. Instead of attacking the limits of elections, however, these scholars attack the very notion of political representation. They argue no one can truly step into the shoes of another and represent their interests. Instead, politicians filter the demands of voters through their own orthodox views, and thus fundamentally change the demands of their constituents, especially when the demands emanate from groups outside the mainstream (Aronowitz 1988).

Of course, one can—and probably should—question whether public choice and postmodernist attacks on elections and political representation tell the whole story. Surely elections count for something. It seems obvious that members of Congress, who stand for reelection, are likely to be responsive to their constituents, even at a time when the number of competitive—or marginal—seats in Congress is declining (Mayhew 1974; Brady 1988; Jacobson 1996, 1997; Mann 1981). The reason is that, despite "vanishing marginals," as Mayhew calls this phenomenon, incumbents often perceive their advantage is soft, reflecting highly personal and fickle voter sentiment and not enduring party loyalty.

As a result, members of Congress feel obligated to staff large district offices dedicated to constituent service, cultivate local ties carefully, and raise large war chests to dissuade viable challengers (Fenno 1978). Thus, while incumbents seem hard to beat on paper, they may be running scared on the ground (Mann 1981). And if members are running scared, it seems reasonable to assume that members will think twice before running roughshod over the clear preferences of a majority of voters, even if elections send imperfect signals and members of Congress cannot perfectly step into the shoes of their constituents.

At the same time, one need not adopt the most extreme versions of public choice theory and postmodernism to question whether Congress's elected status automatically renders it more majoritarian than other branches of government. Instead, the most reasonable approach—it seems to me—is to concede that elections are an important ingredient in American democracy, while recognizing that elections do not *guarantee* majoritarian representation. This middle ground still offers a substantial challenge to the normative rationale for the standard view of the separation of powers because it implies that elections—like all mechanisms for democratic accountability—have their strengths and weaknesses. Accordingly, Congress's electoral status should not entitle it to a place of honor in American democracy. Instead, Congress as the elected, national legislature should be seen as only one part of an American democratic regime, which features diversely representative policymaking forums.

The converse is also true. Federal courts and agencies should not be seen as exceptions to democratic rule in the United States, simply because their members are not elected. Instead, appointed federal judges and bureaucrats are part of the accepted fabric of American democracy that includes a wide range of policy forums, each of which is designed to give voice to different types of factions and respond to different types of political resources (Feeley and Rubin 1998; Leiter 1996; Perreti 1999; Shapiro 1966). Of course, accepting that agencies and courts are part of an American democratic regime does not mean that they should be seen as somehow better or more important than the elected branches. All the branches are integral to American democracy, even though each provides imperfect channels for participation in the policymaking process. Under this perspective, the issue is not how policymakers are selected, but whether they *use* their power to advance substantive democratic values.

IS LEGISLATION NECESSARILY MORE MAJORITARIAN THAN COURT DECISIONS?

Putting aside the problematic assumption that elections render Congress more majoritarian than courts as an institution, social choice—or Arrovian Public Choice—theorists question whether legislation is majoritarian. In general, social choice theory implies that legislation may not reflect the views of a majority, even if individual members of Congress faithfully represent their constituents' interests. Specifically, building on the work of Kenneth Arrow, social choice scholars argue that, as long as legislators' preferences cannot be arrayed along a single dimension with a median voter, cycling preferences naturally emerge (Arrow 1963; McKelvey 1976; and Shepsle 1992). Under these circumstances, the collective decisions of Congress may not reflect the preferences of a clear majority of lawmakers, but the process by which decisions are made.

A simple hypothetical should illustrate the point. Assume a legislature consists of three representatives—1, 2, and 3—who must choose among three budget proposals—A, B, and C. Further assume that Representative 1 is the speaker, who has the power to determine the pairing and order of votes. Finally, suppose the representatives' preferences cycle, meaning there is no clear majority choice—Proposal A beats B; B beats C; and C beats A. Table 2.1 depicts this scenario.

In this case, there is no clear majority preference; however, Representative 1 can manipulate the votes to assure his preferred outcome, Proposal A, is approved. How? Representative 1—as speaker—calls for a vote on Proposals B and C. Under majority rule, B would pass on the strength of votes from Representatives 1 and 2, both of whom prefer B to C. Representative 1 then calls for a vote on Proposals A and B. Under majority rule, A would win, receiving votes from 1 and 3, even though a majority in the legislature would prefer C to A. In short, under these conditions, legislation does not embody a clear majority view among the representatives; it is a product of Representative 1's strategic manipulation of the process. It should be added that strategically pairing and ordering the votes can ensure victory for *any* of the budget proposals, even though none commands a clear majority over the others.

The implications are troubling. Taken to its limit, social choice theory implies that legislation may be random or the product of procedural legerdemain by agenda setters in Congress (Shepsle 1992; Mashaw 1989; Riker 1986). Of course, one can fairly question whether social theory should be taken to its limit; it seems unlikely that the legislative process is as random or chaotic as the most extreme versions of social choice theory suggest. Indeed, a large body of positive political theory shows how political parties, caucuses, committees, rules of recognition and agenda setting, and well-defined status quos produce stable and predictable legislative outcomes (see, generally, Schwartz, Spiller, and Urbiztondo 1994; Farber 1989; and Panning 1985, collecting authority). Moreover, experimental data and a variety of formal models show that voting outcomes are fairly stable around balanced compromise,

Table 2.1   Cycling Preferences

Representatives	Preferences by Rank
1	A > B > C
2	B > C > A
3	C > A > B

even when the individual voter preferences cycle (Farber 1989, 169, collecting authority). Finding that legislative outcomes are often stable and predictable, however, does not obviate social choice theory's basic critique of the normative rationale of the standard view of the separation of powers: Taking votes among elected officials does not *necessarily* produce majoritarian outcomes.

The upshot is straightforward: just as elections are not a fail-safe formula for majoritarian representation, taking votes among elected officials is not a foolproof recipe for majoritarian legislation. Equally, appointing judges and bureaucrats does not guarantee countermajoritarian outcomes. Indeed, as Graber has powerfully argued (1993, 37), judicial policymaking may not reflect the countermajoritarian difficulty at all, but the "nonmajoritarian difficulty"—when the problem lies in clashes within the dominant coalition in Congress—or the "clashing majority difficulty"— when stalemate exists among majorities in different chambers of Congress. Once these points are conceded, the assumption that Congress always produces more majoritarian outcomes than the other branches seems doubtful at best.

SHOULD MAJORITY RULE BE THE BENCHMARK?

One can also question whether majority rule is the proper touchstone for evaluating interbranch relations. Certainly, if one takes the Framers' design seriously, as many advocates of the standard conception of the separation of powers urge, there is little reason to place majority rule above other democratic values or, for that matter, place Congress above other branches of government. Indeed, the Framers saw unchecked majority rule as a threat to the republic and often described the Congress as the most dangerous branch.[10] It should not be surprising then that the Framers incorporated a host of institutional mechanisms in the Constitution that may thwart the ideal of majority rule, including the Electoral College, presidential veto, apportionment rules, and so on.

That is not to say that majority rule and elections do not have a place in American democracy. Obviously, they do. But the role of elections and majority rule in the Framers' design is qualified. To elaborate, the Framers feared the "mischief of faction": the natural tendency of individual citizens to form groups—either majority or minority groups—that pursue narrow self-interests, which are inimical to others or the aggregate interests of the community (*Federalist Paper No. 10*, 1788). Given this definition of the problem, the challenge was creating a system of governance that would tame the threat of minority and majority faction without extinguishing the spirit of popular sovereignty or restricting individual liberty unduly.

With respect to tyranny of the minority, the solution was straightforward. The Framers provided regular elections, which offer a majority of citizens ample opportunity to remove corrupt or biased representatives from office. Accordingly, the ideal of majority rule and elections are an important aspect of the Framers' design. They are not, however, the only important aspects. Why? The Framers also feared the tyranny of the majority, and elections cannot overcome this threat because a majority faction, by definition, cannot be voted out of office.

To address the problem of majority tyranny, the Framers designed a system of government that resists domination by any single majority faction. Specifically, they employed a twofold strategy. First, they fragmented lawmaking authority at the federal level among separate but overlapping legislative, executive, and judicial branches of government. Moreover, because they believed Congress was the most susceptible to majority faction, they took the extra step of bifurcating legislative power between the House of Representatives and the Senate. As a result, even if a faction managed to capture one branch of government or a single chamber of Congress, it could not unilaterally impose its preferences on others. Instead, the faction would have to persuade the other branches to endorse its preferences.

Second, to reduce the likelihood a single faction would gain simultaneous control of all branches of government, each branch of government and chamber of Congress is made accountable to different political constituencies. Thus members of the House of Representatives answer directly to voters in congressional districts; senators were initially accountable to state representatives (and now are accountable to voters in statewide elections); the president is selected by the Electoral College, whose members represent all the states; and federal judges are insulated from the electoral process as political appointees with lifetime tenure and salary protection. As a further safeguard against a tyrannical majority sweeping into office on a wave of popular sentiment, the Constitution staggers the terms of the Senate, House, and presidency, and provides that the Senate be a continuing body, in that only one-third of its members run for reelection at a time.

Under this system of checks and balances, no single branch should be seen as the principal policymaker, because a hallmark of American government is the dispersal of power among *overlapping* and *diversely representative* political forums. It should be added that, although this combination of fragmented power and diverse modes of representation may run counter to majority rule, it has the potential to promote other values. Specifically, the U.S. system of checks and balances is consistent with the modern managerial principle of redundancy, which is a viable organizational strategy for enhancing interaction as well as increasing inputs and information flows into decision-making processes (Feeley and Rubin 1998). Such interaction, in turn, promises to (1) provide multiple access points to policymaking that should encourage a wide range of interests to participate in the process; (2) reduce opportunities for unilateral action by any single branch of government—or majority or minority faction—which should protect individual liberty; and (3) promote iterative policymaking among the branches of government, which should generate interbranch feedback, lead to revision of poorly drafted or outmoded laws, and, over time, foster policy consensus and legal certainty (Barnes 2004; Peretti 1999; Sunstein 1993; Dahl 1956; *Federalist Papers No. 10* and *No. 51*, 1788).

In short, the Constitution does not place its faith in elections and majority rule alone; instead, it creates a system that features multiple modes of representation that would encourage interbranch interaction and discourage tyranny of the minority and majority. The implicit goal was to create dynamic tension among redundant branches facing countervailing political pressures and not an orderly division of labor between elected principals and appointed agents. Accordingly, the normative argument that Congress enjoys a privileged position in American policymaking may overstate the role of majority rule and elections in the Framers' design.

WHITHER THE SEPARATION-OF-POWERS DOCTRINE?

The gist of the argument thus far is that the standard view of the separation of powers seems a house of cards, resting on a series of shaky formal, functional, and normative foundations. Thus, we should consider toppling the standard view and no longer hold the branches of government to formal categories of legislative, executive, and judicial functions. It should be added that rejecting the standard view of the separation of powers as applied to the policymaking process does *not* require the wholesale rejection of the separation-of-powers doctrine. As was alluded to above, we can accept the concept of the separation of powers as creating a general arrangement of primary powers that is distinct from other forms of democratic governance, such as parliamentary systems, while we jettison the concept of the separation of powers as creating rigid and static policymaking roles for the branches of government.

The rejection of the standard view of the separation of powers as applied to policymaking, however, does raise the following concern: what standards should we use to evaluate interbranch interaction? A systematic development of such criteria is beyond the scope of this brief chapter. Instead, democracy and policymaking can be evaluated from a range of values, and those values should be subject to rigorous examination and reexamination. There are, however, values that many would agree are important, even if one could disagree as to how to prioritize them or whether these values are realized in practice. For example, many scholars—ranging from pluralists to capture theorists—share a commitment to the value of broad interest-group participation and mutual accommodation, despite their obvious disagreements as to whether the American policymaking process, in fact, serves these values.

Accordingly, as policy analysts, we may profitably ask whether—and under what conditions—interbranch relations engender broad participation and compromise. As court watchers, we may urge judges to evaluate specific legislative mechanisms governing interbranch relations in light of whether they might preserve a balance of power among the institutions as well as promote deliberation among diverse interests within and across the branches (see, generally, Silverstein 1994; and Sunstein 1993, 1996). Following this line of reasoning, line-item vetoes may be seen as unconstitutional not only because they may run afoul of the formal requirements of the presentment clause but also because they encourage members of Congress to throw up their hands and pass the buck to the president on budgetary issues. Why? Under a system with a line-item veto, members of Congress can enact exorbitant budgets, claim credit for securing programmatic benefits for their constituents, and blame the president if the benefits are denied in the end. Of course, some may complain that such evaluations are, by nature, highly contextual and hence may have limited generalizability; however, as was noted above, assessing whether institutions and formal structures are likely to produce desired outcomes *requires* careful case-by-case analysis because institutional competence is inherently a relative—not absolute—concept (Williamson 1995; Komesar 1994; Rubin 1996).

What is the bottom line? Contemporary American policymaking does not feature branches of government that adhere to well-defined judicial, legislative, and executive functions; it features a bramble of overlapping policymaking forums that share and compete for lawmaking, law-interpreting, and law-administering power (Feeley and Rubin 1998; Shapiro 1964; Resnick 2000; and the chapters by Kagan, Miller, Kassop, and Melnick in this volume). Instead of rejecting this state of affairs as violating the standard view of the separation of powers, we should consider rejecting the idea that the branches of government should adhere to preassigned, narrow roles when making policy, and examine the more pressing issue of whether—and under what conditions—the complex American system of separate institutions sharing power promotes core democratic values, such as encouraging diverse voices to participate in the shaping and reshaping of national policy.

NOTES

1. These figures were taken from the *Statistical Abstract of the United States* (U.S. Department of Commerce) for 1962 and 2003.
2. Circuit judge Harold Leventhal coined this phrase in *Greater Boston Television Corp. v. FCC*, 444 F.2d 841, 851 (D.C. Cir. 1970). For more on these lawsuits, see Shapiro 1988; Rabkin 1989; and Melnick 1983. For interesting glimpses into the world of public interest lawyers, see Seager 1991 and Derthick 2002. For a penetrating—and critical—analysis of how the changing role of the courts in the policymaking process has changed the practice of judging and the culture of the judiciary, see Resnick 2000.
3. Of course, this discussion of federal courts puts aside the enormous role of state courts in stretching traditional legal doctrines, such as tort and family law, to address complex policy issues. These innovations have provided public and private interests with an avenue to bypass federal legislative and regulatory processes altogether and have given the courts another powerful platform for affecting issues beyond the reach of judges abroad. See, e.g., Schwartz 1991; and Glendon 1987.
4. It should be emphasized that the following discussion focuses on the separation of powers *as applied to the American policymaking process*. The separation of powers often takes on a different meaning in the context of comparative politics, referring to the strengths and weaknesses of presidential versus parliamentary systems of government. See Ceaser 1986; Ackerman 2000.
5. No claim is being made as to Madison's "true" beliefs based on his arguments in the *Federalist Papers*. Indeed, the *Federalist Papers* are probably best understood as an attempt to justify a series of compromises and logrolls made at the Constitutional Convention as opposed to a treatise on Madison's theory of constitutional design (Kernell 2003). Moreover, Madison's views evolved over the course of his lifetime (Dahl 2001; Ferejohn 2003). Nevertheless, the *Federalist Papers* do offer insight into how Madison viewed the Constitution and presented it during ratification. Or, as Samuel Kernell argues (2003, 120), although the combination of factional competition and checks and balances portrayed in the *Federalist Papers* does not represent Madison's "political science, [it] does describe the Constitution."
6. I thank Howard Gillman for bringing these passages in the *Federalist Papers* to my attention.
7. Some courts adopt Learned Hand's standard: "the single question . . . is merely one of fact: What do the buyers understand by the word for whose use the parties are contending?" *Bayer Drug Co. v. United Drug Co.*, 272 F. 505, 509 (S.D.N.Y. 1921). Others have adopted the Supreme Court's *dicta* in *Kellog Co. v. National Biscuit Co.*, which provides that the manufacturer "must show that the primary significance of the term in the minds of the consuming public is not the product but the producer"; 305 U.S. 111, 118 (1938). Other courts ask whether the trademark refers to a "genus" of products or a group of products that consumers can reasonably interchange. See, e.g., *Surgicenters of America, Inc. v. Medical Dental Surgeries Co.*, 601 F.2d 1011, 1014 (9th Cir. 1979); and *Abercrombie and Fitch Co. v. Hunting World, Inc.*, 537 F.2d 4, 9 (2d Cir. 1976). See, generally, Osoba 1985, 201–2, describing these and other standards.
8. *Anti-Monopoly, Inc. v. General Mills Fun Group, Inc.*, 611 F.2d 296, 302 (9th Cir. 1979) (remanding for consideration of purchaser's motivations in buying the product); *Anti-Monopoly, Inc. v. General Mills Fun Group, Inc.*, 684 F.2d 1316, 1319 (9th Cir. 1982) (reversing the district court decision after remand and holding the district court's rejection

of the purchaser motivation survey was clearly erroneous) *certiorari denied* 459 U.S. 1227 (1983).

9. For more on incrementalism, see Charles Lindblom's famous articles, "The Science of 'Muddling Through'" (Lindblom 1959) and "Still Muddling, Not Yet Through" (Lindblom 1979).

10. As Nancy Kassop argues in chapter 4 below, the idea that the legislative branch is the most powerful branch of government may now seem quaint, given the extraordinary growth of executive and judicial power since the Founding. Nevertheless, on the basis of the *Federalist Papers*, there is little doubt that the *Framers*—or at least the Federalists— believed that the legislative branch was the most susceptible to tyranny of the majority and hence the most dangerous branch of government (Ferejohn 2003).

PART II

A Closer Look at Interbranch Perspectives

3

The View of the Courts from the Hill
A Neoinstitutional Perspective

MARK C. MILLER

THE INTERACTIONS BETWEEN THE U.S. CONGRESS AND THE federal courts are a vital part of the lawmaking process in the United States. As political scientist and now Judge Robert A. Katzmann notes, "Governance . . . is premised on each institution's respect for and knowledge of the others and on a continuing dialogue that produces shared understanding and comity" (Katzmann 1997, 1). Resnik of course reminds us that interactions between legislatures and the courts can be both cooperative and conflictual (see Resnik 2000; Resnik, Boggs, and Berman 2004). However, institutional misunderstandings more often seem to be the norm, especially when one studies the interactions between Congress and the federal courts. These potential conflicts are often due to different institutional cultures and different institutional wills. As Davidson and Oleszek argue, "Communications between Congress and the federal courts are less than perfect. Neither branch understands the workings of the other very well" (Davidson and Oleszek 2002, 343). Thus, I believe that some of the difficulties in court–legislative interactions arise from each institution misunderstanding the needs, views, and institutional realities of the other.

This chapter will explore the relationship and interactions between the federal, legislative, and judicial branches from the perspective of Congress. These interactions are at times strained, with each institution of government having its own unique perspective as well as its own duties and responsibilities. The interactions between and among governmental institutions are complicated and at the same time not well understood. As Fisher states, "The boundaries between the three branches of government are strongly affected by the role of custom and acquiescence" (Fisher 2003, 164). And of course each branch in our separation of powers system has "checks" over the other branches in order to "balance" their powers (see, e.g., Fisher 1988). For example, Congress controls the annual appropriations for the federal courts (see Murphy, Pritchett, and Epstein 2002, 317), the Senate confirms judicial appointments (see Goldman 1997), and Congress can fairly easily overturn the statutory interpretation decisions of the courts by merely passing another statute (see Eskridge 1991a; Barnes 2004). When Congress is unhappy with the courts, it can also attack the courts in a variety of other ways to be discussed below.

NEOINSTITUTIONALISM

In order to understand better the institutional differences that lead to potential mis-understandings between Congress and the federal courts, this chapter will use a neoinstitutional approach. Beginning in the 1980s, many political scientists began to use what has become known as the neoinstitutionalist or new institutionalism analysis for studying the U.S. government (see, e.g., March and Olsen 1984, 1989; Smith 1988). Although there are now at least three approaches that come under the neoinstitutionalist umbrella (see Hall and Taylor 1996; Clayton and Gillman 1999, 1–12), it is now generally agreed that the neoinstitutional analysis examines how in-stitutional features constrict the actions of individual political actors (see, e.g., Gill-man 1999, 67). As Smith argues, neoinstitutionalists focus on the "interrelationship between human 'institutions' or 'structures' and the decisions and actions of politi-cal actors" (Smith 1988, 91). Thus, the neoinstitutional approach attempts to com-bine the traditionalist scholar's interest in understanding governmental bodies as institutions with the behavioralist's emphasis on empirical, individual-level research (see, e.g., Epstein, Walker, and Dixon 1989).

The three main approaches to neoinstitutionalist analysis have been termed ra-tional choice institutionalism, historical-interpretative institutionalism, and socio-logical institutionalism (see Hall and Taylor 1996). Rational choice institutionalism is rooted in formal theory, mathematical modeling, positive political theory, and the economic theory of the firm (see Weingast 2002). In general, it attempts to add in-stitutional variables to previously developed formal models of individual political behavior. Sociological institutionalism arose in the late 1970s, primarily from soci-ology's subfield of organizational theory. Sociological institutionalists tend to argue that institutional forms and procedures are culturally driven as opposed to being in-herently rational. Thus, according to the sociological institutionalists, "even the most seemingly bureaucratic of practices have to be explained in cultural terms" (Hall and Taylor 1996).

The particular approach taken by this chapter, however, draws most heavily from the third approach, the historical-interpretive stream of neoinstitutionalist analysis (see Smith 1988), although it does borrow somewhat the concept of insti-tutional culture from the sociological approach. The definitions of institutions used by the three neoinstitutional schools of thought help to highlight the differences among the three approaches. According to Hall and Taylor, historical institutional-ists define institutions "as the formal or informal procedures, routines, norms, and conventions embedded in the organizational structure of the polity" (Hall and Tay-lor 1996, 938). Rational choice institutionalists define institutions as organizations where individual actors assemble for a series of collective action dilemmas. In insti-tutions, "the relevant actors have a fixed set of preferences or tastes, behave entirely instrumentally so as to maximize the attainment of these preferences, and do so in a highly strategic manner that presumes extensive calculation" (Hall and Taylor 1996, 944–45). Conversely, the sociological or cultural approach "stresses the de-gree to which behavior is not fully strategic but bounded by an individual's world-view" (Hall and Taylor 1996, 939).

Therefore, it is important to repeat that historical institutionalists define institutions broadly, while stressing the institutional processes and procedures that constrain the behavior of individual political actors over time. Contrasting the historical-interpretative strain of neoinstitutionalism with both behavioralism and with rational-choice modeling, Pierson and Skocpol explain that "historical institutionalists analyze organizational and institutional configurations where others look at particular settings in isolation; and they pay attention to critical junctures and long-term processes where others look only at slices of time or short-term maneuvers" (Pierson and Skocpol 2002, 693). Historical institutionalists see the relationship between individuals and institutions as being quite complicated and eclectic, and as developing over time. As Hall and Taylor conclude, "Historical institutionalists rarely insist that institutions are the only causal force in politics. . . . In this respect, they posit a world that is more complex than the world of tastes and institutions often postulated by rational-choice institutionalists" (Hall and Taylor 1996, 942). Therefore, historical institutional analysis conceptualizes the relationship between the behavior of individual political actors and the institution in very broad and complex terms. It examines power differences among members of the institution, while still emphasizing that this relationship can produce many unintended consequences. Historical institutionalists also stress the power of intellectual arguments and ideas to help shape the perspectives of the individual members of the institution, the institutional culture, and eventually the collective institutional will (see Hall and Taylor 1996, 938).

A very important aspect of the new institutionalist approach is attempting to understand the so-called institutional will of the institution (see Dodd 1981, 391). Institutions are more than just mere automatically functioning organizations or systems, in large part because of the importance that ideas play in molding their institutional cultures and institutional wills. Smith explains that institutions "have a kind of life of their own. They influence the self-conception of those who occupy roles defined by them in ways that can give those persons distinctly 'institutional perspectives'" (Smith 1988, 95). The institutional will of an institution then comes from a combination of the collective perspectives of the individuals who make up the institution and the institutional culture of the organization. As Hall and Taylor conclude, "Not only do institutions provide strategically-useful information, they also affect the very identities, self-images, and preferences of the actors" (1996, 939). And as Brigham argues, "Institutions are not simply robes and marble, nor are they contained in codes or documents" (1987, 21). Or as Rawls conceptionalizes institutions, they are "an abstract object" realized in "thought and conduct" (1971, 11). A neoinstitutional analysis can help provide more clarity in this area by examining the institutional constraints facing both Congress and the federal courts, constraints that can have a profound effect on how these two institutions interact.

The neoinstitutionalist approach also allows shifts in the levels of analysis employed (see Miller 1995, 12). Traditionally, behavioralist political scientists looked only at the lowest level of analysis, often relying solely on statistical studies of how individual members of Congress voted on the floor or on studies of how individual judges voted on case opinions. But the interactions between Congress and the federal courts take place in a variety of ways, in a variety of contexts, and at a variety of levels. Each institution has a unique institutional culture that constrains behavior of the political actors located in that institution. Each institution also has a unique institutional will that can be shaped by the actions of the individual political actors, by the actions of component parts such as committees or political parties, and by the actions of the institution as a whole. In order to understand better the institutional will of Congress in its interactions with the federal courts, it is important to examine the reactions of individual members of Congress, of the party caucuses, of congressional committees, and of each house of Congress.

STRAINED INSTITUTIONAL PERSPECTIVES BETWEEN CONGRESS AND THE COURTS

The relationship between Congress and the federal courts as institutions is clearly complicated and often strained. Political scientist and now Judge Robert Katzmann has consistently argued that the two institutions need a better understanding of how the other institution functions (see Katzmann 1988, 1997). Judges clearly see themselves as part of a coequal third branch of government that deserves proper funding and respect. For example, the federal courts think that their current lack of an adequate number of judges to handle their ever increasing workload should be the top priority in Congress. Congress, on the other hand, is more concerned that the courts do justice in individual cases and that they uphold congressional policy decisions. Legislators may also view judges as offering just one more political input into highly complex political decisions. As Michael H. Armacost, then president of the Brookings Institution, has noted, "The judiciary seeks an environment respectful of its independence. Congress seeks a judicial system that faithfully construes the laws of the legislative branch and efficiently discharges justice" (quoted in Katzmann 1997, vii).

A historical institutional perspective also argues that the interactions between Congress and the courts should be viewed over a long period of time. Tensions between the legislative branch and the judicial branch have been a common feature of the American system of government since our founding (see, e.g., Canon and Johnson 1999, 117; and O'Brien 2003, 356–65). As Fisher and Devins note, "Volleys between the elected branches and the courts take place on a regular basis" (2001, v). These conflicts were especially strong in the early 1800s through the Civil War. After the Civil War, the Radical Republicans in Congress passed various statutes designed to prevent the Supreme Court from declaring the Reconstruction Acts to be unconstitutional. The House of Representatives also passed legislation to require a two-thirds majority of the Court before the justices could strike down any federal statute as unconstitutional. Some members even advocated abolishing the Supreme Court altogether (see Fisher 2003, 474–78). In the 1910s and 1920s, Progressives attacked the federal courts for their conservative activism in promoting laissez-faire economic policies. In the 1930s, the New Dealers and President Roosevelt severely criticized the federal courts for failing to uphold FDR's anti-Depression programs (see, e.g., Murphy 1962, 57). Since the 1950s, conservative members of Congress have frequently attacked decisions of the federal courts that they felt were too liberal. In the 1980s, President Reagan was a vocal critic of what he termed liberal activist federal judges.

Recently, however, the tensions between the two institutions seem to have increased greatly, in part because the institutional cultures of the two institutions produce such different institutional perspectives and institutional wills. In the past few years, several justices serving on the U.S. Supreme Court have been quite critical of Congress. For example, in the recent past, Chief Justice William Rehnquist has strongly criticized Congress for delaying the confirmation of federal judges (see

Rehnquist 2002), for federalizing too many crimes he feels are better left to state law (quoted in Davidson and Oleszek 2002, 342), for refusing to provide adequate salaries for federal judges (see Havemen 1989; Rehnquist 2000), for monitoring how individual federal judges deviate from the federal sentencing guidelines (see Rehnquist, 2003), and for holding the judiciary's budget hostage because of disputes over the 2000 census (Biskupic 1999, A27).

Other justices have complained that Congress should take better care in the drafting of statutes. For example, Justice Ruth Bader Ginsburg has written, "The national legislature expresses itself too often in commands that are unclear, imprecise, or gap-ridden" (Ginsburg and Huber 1987, 1421). Agreeing with this criticism, Chief Justice Rehnquist has written, "The effort to determine congressional intent . . . might better be entrusted to a detective than to a judge" (*Harrison v. PPG Industries*, 446 U.S. 578, at 595 [1980], Rehnquist, J., dissenting).

Other recent judicial criticisms of Congress have been more pointed and highlight the different institutional perspectives of these two bodies. For example, Justice Antonin Scalia said in an April 2000 speech that Congress is "increasingly abdicating its independent responsibility to be sure that it is being faithful to the Constitution" (quoted in *Washington Post* 2000, A2). Justice Scalia continued, "My Court is fond of saying that acts of Congress come to the Court with the presumption of constitutionality. But if Congress is going to take the attitude that it will do anything it can get away with and let the Supreme Court worry about the Constitution, . . . then perhaps that presumption is unwarranted" (quoted in Mauro 2000a, 8). Justice Scalia has also been a vocal critic of using legislative history materials such as floor statements, committee reports, or conference reports to help courts determine the intent of Congress when interpreting congressional statutes (see Davidson and Oleszek 2002, 343–45). Many in Congress[1] and on the Supreme Court[2] argue that Justice Scalia's views reveal a lack of understanding of the institutional culture of Congress.[3] For example, Justice Stephen Breyer has argued that the use of legislative history "seems likely to promote fair and workable results" (see Breyer 1992, 861). Other judges and academics have been quick to criticize Justice Scalia's textualist approach to the use of legislative history. For example, Judge Patricia Wald has stated that she is concerned that the refusal to use legislative history could disrupt the balance among the three branches.[4]

INDIVIDUAL ATTACKS ON THE COURTS

These institutional misunderstandings clearly go both ways. In addition to these institutional attacks on Congress coming from Supreme Court Justices, individual members of Congress have long felt little constraint about criticizing the federal courts in general and especially specific judicial decisions with which they disagree. The institutional will of Congress and its institutional culture are clearly shaped by the reactions of individual legislators to the decisions of the federal courts.

For individual politicians, verbal attacks against court decisions and the courts in general are an easy and relatively cost-free method for gaining political points with their constituents (see Baum 2001, 247). Thus, politicians have verbally attacked the courts since the early days of the Republic following the ratification of the Constitution (see, e.g., Berger 1969). Politicians often attacked federal court decisions in the early 1800s, in the 1820s and 1830s, and in the period before the Civil War (see, e.g.,

Nagel 1965). During the Reconstruction Period, the Radical Republicans were extremely vocal in their attacks on the courts. At the beginning of the twentieth century, Progressives attacked the Supreme Court because of its laissez-faire policies (O'Brien 2003, 357–58). For example, Senator Robert M. LaFollette was said to characterize all federal judges as "petty tyrants and arrogant despots" (quoted in McDowell 1988, 1). In the 1930s, the New Dealers and President Roosevelt attacked the Court for failing to uphold FDR's anti-Depression New Deal programs (see, e.g., Murphy 1962, 57). In the 1950s and 1960s, conservative legislators frequently attacked decisions of the federal courts that they felt were too liberal (see, e.g., Pritchett 1961; Breckenridge 1970; and Schmidhauser and Berg 1972). For example, during debate on a bill that would have attempted to overturn a variety of Supreme Court decisions concerning the rights of criminal defendants, Senator McClellan charged that the Supreme Court wanted to "protect and liberate guilty and confirmed criminals to pursue and repeat their nefarious crimes" (quoted in Schmidhauser and Berg 1972, 165). In 1980, Ronald Reagan ran for president in part on a platform that he would never appoint liberal activist judges to the federal bench. Many of the conservatives Reagan brought with him to Congress clearly agreed with that goal.

In the late 1990s, the tide changed as liberals became unhappy with a growing series of 5–4 Supreme Court decisions that placed radical new limits on various constitutional powers of Congress, especially its power to regulate interstate commerce. Just as they did in the 1930s, liberals are now complaining about the evils of "conservative judicial activism" (see, e.g., Schwartz 2002). This new judicial activism has certainly created disdain for the federal courts among many in Congress, and has led to claims that the Supreme Court does not understand the institutional needs of Congress nor its constitutional responsibilities. As Fisher and Devins described the situation in 2001, "The Rehnquist Court may be poised to enter into a battle royale with Congress" (2001, 92). Thus some commentators have said that this line of rulings "has roots, in part, in the Court's mistrust of the national legislative process and its sense of institutional competition with Congress" (Jackson 2001, 145). Many legislators were outraged at the Court's conservative decisions. In 2000, the reporter Tony Mauro offered his opinion that "the Supreme Court has declared constitutional war on Congress" (Mauro 2000b, 1).

This lack of institutional understanding between the Supreme Court and Congress appears to be escalating, with liberal politicians now quite willing to attack these new conservative Supreme Court federalism decisions (see, e.g., Carney 1998). Responding to a U.S. Supreme Court opinion that exempted state employees from coverage under the federal Americans with Disabilities Act, *Board of Trustees of the University of Alabama v. Garrett*, 531 U.S. 356 (2001), U.S. senator Tom Harkin (D-Iowa) said the decision "undermines every citizen's constitutional right to be protected against irrational and unfair discrimination" (quoted in Rosenbaum 2001, A20). U.S. senator Patrick Leahy (D-Vt.) stated, "The court today continued its assault on the powers of the people. The court's 'federalism' crusade now adds those with disabilities to its growing list of victims" (quoted in Biskupic 2001, 3A).

When the Supreme Court in *U.S. v. Morrison*, 120 S.Ct. 1740 (2000), declared parts of the federal Violence Against Women Act to be unconstitutional because the majority felt that the provisions in question violated federalism principles, not surprisingly *Congressional Quarterly Weekly Report* reported that many federal lawmakers "blasted the ruling" (Palmer 2000, 1188). For example, U.S. senator Charles E. Schumer (D-N.Y.), responded to the Court's decision by complaining, "Just at a time when the economic and social conditions of the world demand that we be treated as one country and not as 50 states, the Supreme Court seems poised to undo decades and decades of a consensus that the federal government has an active role to play" (quoted in Greenhouse 2000, A14). U.S. senator Joseph Biden (D-Del.) said after the decision, "This decision is really all about power: Who has the power, the court or Congress?" (quoted in Greenhouse 2000, A14). Asked what would be required to fix the legislation the Court had just struck down, Senator Biden responded, "Two new justices" (quoted in Palmer 2000, 1188). These comments clearly reveal the differences in institutional perspectives among the branches.

But liberals are not the only ones unhappy with contemporary decisions of the federal courts. When in the summer of 2002 the Ninth Circuit in *Newdow v. U.S. Congress*, 292 F.3d 597 (2002), declared the phrase "under God" in the Pledge of Allegiance to be unconstitutional, politicians from all across the ideological spectrum quickly lined up to criticize that decision. Representative Linder (R-Ga.), a conservative, called the decision "inexplicable" and complained that "some clown from the Ninth Circus, as it has been called, decides that Congress did not know what it was doing in 1954" (*Congressional Record*, June 27, 2002, H4121). Representative Jim McGovern (D-Mass.), a staunch liberal, called the decision "just plain dumb" (*Congressional Record*, June 27, 2002, H4121). Conservative Senator Orrin Hatch (R-Utah), chair of the Senate Judiciary Committee, called the decision "outrageous" (Weinstein 2003, 1). Representative Darrell Issa (R-Calif.), a conservative, reacted to the decision by stating, "As a Californian, I want to make it very clear that when we are called the 'left coast,' they are only speaking about our courts; they are only speaking about the insane actions that often come from our judiciary" (*Congressional Record*, June 27, 2002, H4074). Representative James Sensenbrenner, Jr. (R-Wisc.), a member of the House Judiciary Committee, stated, "The Ninth Circuit ruling treated the word God as a poison pill. Rarely has any court, even the notoriously liberal Ninth Circuit, shown such disdain for the will of the people, an act of Congress, and our American traditions" (*Congressional Record*, June 27, 2002, H4125). Majority Whip Tom DeLay (R-Tex.), never a friend of the federal courts, said of the decision, "Congress is going to stand up in this particular case and fight the judiciary of this country and stop them from running amuck" (*Congressional Record*, June 27, 2002, H4126). Representative John Conyers Jr. (D-Mich.), a liberal member of the Black Caucus, stated that he opposed the Ninth Circuit's "radical secularist decision" (*Congressional Record*, June 27, 2002, H4129). However, he tempered his criticism of the decision when he went on to say, "Lost in today's debate and in the resolution before us is the value of our judicial system, the crown jewel of our democracy. . . . It is no surprise over the years that the judiciary has ultimately been the greatest protector of our rights and our liberties" (*Congressional Record*, June 27, 2002, H4121).

By a vote of 416–3 in the House and 99–0 in the Senate, Congress passed a resolution condemning the Ninth Circuit's decision on the Pledge of Allegiance. Conservatives were even able to get an amendment passed in the House of Representatives to prevent any federal funds from being used to enforce the court's decision in this case. This was a clear indication on many levels of the institutional will of Congress on this issue. In March 2003, the Ninth Circuit en banc upheld a revised ruling that narrowed the effects of the opinion, stating that the Pledge of Allegiance is unconstitutional if required to be recited by children in a public school setting (see Lane 2003, A1; Denniston 2003, A3). The Ninth Circuit responded to the political attacks on this decision by modifying the decision somewhat, but nevertheless asserting its institutional will on this issue.

Congressional reaction to this court decision regarding the Pledge of Allegiance has renewed efforts by many conservative legislators to split the huge Ninth Circuit into several circuits (see, e.g., statement of Senator Murkowski, *Congressional Record*, July 15, 2002, S6731). The Ninth Circuit currently covers nine Western states and two U.S. Pacific territories. Part of the push for this effort to split the Circuit is to reduce the influence of the current Ninth Circuit, which is seen by conservatives as being far too liberal in its decisions (see Kasindorf 2003, 3A). The threats to split up the Ninth Circuit may also be an attempt to influence that court's future rulings.

Conservative legislators are also clearly upset with what they perceive to be other liberal activist court decisions, such as the U.S. Supreme Court's decision in *Lawrence v. Texas*, 123 S. Ct. 2472 (2003), striking down state antisodomy laws, or the Massachusetts State Supreme Court decision in *Goodridge v. Department of Public Health*, 440 Mass. 309, 798 N.E. 2d 941 (2003), declaring same-sex marriage to be a constitutional right in that state. President George W. Bush has also been a vocal critic of what he sees as these liberal activist decisions, calling for a federal constitutional amendment to overturn the *Goodridge* decision, among others (see, e.g., Melady 2004; Perine 2004b). Some conservative Republicans in the U.S. House were so angry with liberal activist judges that in 2003 that they created a new House caucus on judicial accountability. According to a press release issued by the new caucus, the House Working Group on Judicial Accountability planned to educate members of Congress and the public about liberal judicial activism and abuses. On the basis of early meetings of the group, House Majority Leader Tom DeLay (R-Tex.) stated that "when it comes to judicial abuses, they're going to take no prisoners" (quoted in U.S. Courts Office of Public Affairs, Administrative Office 2003, 1). Some members of this group were also highly critical of the fact that various federal courts have begun citing international precedents in cases such as *Lawrence v. Texas* and in death penalty cases and other types of cases. In March 2004, Representatives Tom Feeney (R-Fla.) and Bob Goodlatte (R-Va.) even introduced a resolution in the House along with more than fifty cosponsors that would require that federal courts could not cite foreign laws, foreign court decisions, or pronouncements of foreign governments without the express prior approval of a majority of Congress.

Individual legislators or party groups in Congress may also attempt to influence court decisions in more traditional, legalistic ways. For example, in 2003 the U.S. Supreme Court heard *Grutter v. Bollinger*, 123 S.Ct. 2325 (2003), a case that challenged the constitutionality of affirmative action programs at the University of Michigan. The case attracted a very large number of amicus curiae briefs. Three separate amicus curiae briefs from members of Congress were filed in that case. One amicus brief was signed by more than 100 Democratic members of the House, one brief was signed by former House Minority Leader Richard Gephardt (D-Mo.) and six House colleagues, and the third brief was signed by twelve Democratic members of the U.S. Senate (Schmidt 2003, A25). Obviously, members of the Democratic Party were attempting to sway the Supreme Court's decision in this case.

ADVICE AND CONSENT IN THE PARTY CAUCUSES

A new institutionalist approach will also examine more specific processes that require interaction between Congress and the federal courts. Another way that individual legislators and party caucuses may attempt to influence court decisions is through the Senate confirmation process for federal judicial appointees. During the Clinton and George W. Bush administrations, judicial confirmation fights have polarized the two parties in the Senate, with Republicans doing everything they could to stall or defeat many Clinton nominees while the Democrats have balked at many Bush judicial appointees. As one reporter described the situation, "Increasingly, Democrats and Republicans have come to view the fight over federal judges as another powerful way to mobilize their base on Election Day—drawing a clear connection between the ideological balance of the courts and the balance of power on such hot-button issues as abortion and gun control. Neither party wants to compromise" (Dlouhy 2002, 2722). Congress now see judicial confirmations as highly partisan decision points, but the federal courts just want more judges to help reduce their growing backlogs of cases.

The Constitution, of course, gives the Senate the power of advise and consent over judicial nominees. Throughout our history there has been a debate about how the Senate should exercise that power. In recent history, the Senate has rejected nominees to the U.S. Supreme Court appointed by Presidents Lyndon Johnson, Nixon, and Reagan, and almost rejected President George H. W. Bush's nomination of Clarence Thomas to the Court (see Maltese 1998). Although filibusters of judicial nominees are certainly rare, in 1968 Republicans and conservative Democrats filibustered and eventually killed LBJ's nomination of Justice Abe Fortas to become chief justice (Maltese 1998, 71). The filibuster occurred at the end of Johnson's presidency, allowing President Nixon to appoint Warren Burger as chief justice.

What has changed over time is that today the parties are fighting more and more over lower federal judicial nominees (see, e.g., Campbell and Stack 2001, 11; Perine 2003b, 2431). In the past, controversial nominees have often been stalled in the Senate Judiciary Committee, but in 2003 Senate Democrats filibustered on the floor of the Senate or threatened to filibuster a variety of judicial nominees, including the nomination of Miguel A. Estrada, a George W. Bush appointee for the D.C. Circuit Court of Appeals (see Dlouhy 2003a; Lewis 2003). The Senate Democrats publicly claimed that they did not have enough information to vote on the Estrada nomination. Some commentators felt that the Democratic filibuster was a clear statement that liberals would not accept a highly conservative nomination to the U.S. Supreme Court should an opening occur on that court (see Dlouhy 2003b). After months of fighting over the Estrada nomination, President Bush eventually withdrew the Estrada nomination in September of 2003 at the request of the nominee. The Senate had failed on seven attempts to cut off debate and thus end the filibuster (Perine 2003b, 2431).

The partisan stalemate over judicial nominations continued throughout 2003 and into 2004, with the Democrats objecting to at least seven nominations and filibustering at least three of them. As one commentator observed in October of 2003, "The Senate standoff on judicial nominations has settled into a predictable, carefully choreographed struggle, that probably will not end before the 2004 elections" (Perine 2003b, 2431). To combat the Democratic filibusters, the Republicans have proposed a rules change in the Senate that would prohibit filibusters on judicial nominations. Senate Democrats are likely to filibuster that proposed rules change if the Republican leadership actually brings it to the floor for consideration (see Perine 2003b, 2431). In an extraordinary move, in early 2004 President Bush employed the rarely used procedure of recess appointments to put at least two of the contested nominees onto the federal bench. These recess appointments allow the judges to sit on the federal bench for a maximum of two years (Perine 2004a). The Democrats in the Senate expressed their outrage over this maneuver. Both parties seem to be benefiting from their particular strategies, and it seems unlikely that either party will capitulate on this issue any time soon. The lesson from this latest round of fights over judicial nominations is that the neoinstitutional approach points out that the reactions of parties and of individual legislators are critically important in order to understand the interactions between the two branches.

CONGRESSIONAL COMMITTEES

Moving from the individual level of analysis to a higher level of analysis, it is also important for scholars to understand how congressional committees vary in their reactions and approaches to federal court decisions (see, e.g., Henschen 1983; Miller 1992, 1993). Solimine and Walker note that "both the House and the Senate are decentralized institutions, and the actions of individual committees in both institutions may well have an impact on the interaction between the Court and Congress" (Solimine and Walker 1992, 438). Committees may vary in their reactions to court decisions depending on the primary goal orientation of the committee (see Deering and Smith 1997, 58–86; Fenno 1973) or by the number of lawyer-legislators who serve on the committee (see Miller 1995). For example, the House Judiciary Committee has traditionally been the committee of lawyers in the House. Until fairly recently, almost all the members of the committee were lawyers, and the committee showed a great deal of respect for the federal courts and their decisions. The House Commerce Committee, on the other hand, tends to approach the courts as just one more routine source of political inputs. Thus, the Commerce Committee treats court decisions in much the same way that it treats federal agency decisions (see Miller 1993). Constituency based committees (also called reelection committees) such as Resources or Agriculture only react to federal court decisions when constituents or interest groups demand that the committee react.

Two cases will illustrate the point that specific committees vary in their reactions to court decisions. Before the House Judiciary Committee in 1989 endorsed legislation to overturn the Supreme Court's constitutionally based decision that flag burning is protected political speech, the committee held four solid days of exhaustive hearings on the issue. When the Commerce Committee endorsed legislation to circumvent the Supreme Court's ruling in 1989 that congressional legislation to combat the so-called dial-a-porn industry violated the First Amendment, the committee inserted the language into pending legislation without even debating the issue. Thus, congressional committees can vary widely in how they react to federal court decisions.

DIFFERENT INSTITUTIONAL WILLS

The new institutionalist approach also considers how the two institutions as a whole react to each other's decisions. Moving to the highest level of analysis in this chapter, Congress as a whole can certainly take action when a majority of its members disagree with specific decisions or trends in the federal courts. The U.S. Supreme Court and other federal courts generally hand down two main types of decisions: statutory interpretation decisions and constitutionally based decisions. When Con-

gress disagrees with a constitutionally based court decision, in theory the main op-
tion available to Congress is to approve an amendment to the Constitution by a two-
thirds vote in both houses, which must then be ratified by three-fourths of the states.
The Eleventh, Fourteenth, Sixteenth, and Twenty-Sixth Amendments were all enacted in direct response to U.S. Supreme Court decisions.[5]

However, Congress can also attempt to enact a statute in order to overturn or
to modify substantially the effects of a constitutionally based court decision. Many
of these attempts are later declared unconstitutional by the U.S. Supreme Court. Examples of such statutes invalidated by the U.S. Supreme Court include parts of the
Crime Control and Safe Streets Act of 1968, declared unconstitutional by *Dickerson v. U.S.*, 530 U.S. 428 (2000); the Flag Protection Act of 1989, declared unconstitutional by *U.S. v. Eichman*, 496 U.S. 310 (1990); and the Religious Freedom
Restoration Act of 1993, declared unconstitutional by *City of Boerne v. Archbishop
Flores*, 521 U.S. 507 (1997) (see also chapter 8 in this volume by Bragaw and
Miller). Congress will often express its opposition to court decisions in whatever
fashion it can. Depending on the specifics of the case, even the passage of a statute
can have an impact on the implementation of constitutionally based court decisions
(see also Murphy, Pritchett, and Epstein 2002, 318–19). Fisher therefore argues that
Congress and the courts have coordinate responsibility over constitutional interpretation duties (see chapter 9 in this volume by Fisher).

If Congress disagrees with a specific statutory interpretation decision of the federal courts, then Congress must merely enact a new statute in order to overturn the
court ruling. This action is fairly commonplace because "Congress is supreme in
statutory law" (Baum 2001, 242). In his comprehensive study of when Congress
overturns judicial statutory interpretation decisions, Eskridge found that Congress
overrode or significantly modified the Supreme Court's interpretation 121 times between 1967 and 1990 (Eskridge 1991a). Congress has certainly been willing to overturn more recent statutory interpretation decisions as well. For example, the Civil
Rights Act of 1991 overturned at least twelve more civil rights decisions handed
down by the U.S. Supreme Court (see Davidson and Oleszek 2002, 344). Therefore,
it is fairly routine for Congress to overturn statutory interpretation decisions from
the federal courts. The politics surrounding attempts to overturn statutory interpretation rulings closely resemble other votes on the floor of the House and the Senate.
As Baum concludes, "The success of efforts to overturn statutory decisions depends
on the same broad array of factors that influence the fates of other bills in Congress"
(Baum 2001, 243).

Sometimes the institutional will of Congress, its members, and its committees
leads the legislative branch to ignore completely a federal court decision, especially
one that directly affects the internal workings of Congress (see Baum 2001, 246–47).
For example, in *Immigration and Naturalization Service v. Chahda*, 462 U.S. 919
(1983), the Supreme Court ruled that congressional tradition of one-house legislative
vetoes of administrative actions was unconstitutional because it violated separation
of powers principles (see Cooper 1985). Congress responded by basically ignoring
the Court's decision. After Chahda, Congress has continued to enact numerous pieces
of legislation that have included legislative vetoes. In fact, at the end of the 106th
Congress in 2000, the list of new legislative vetoes since Chahda had increased to
over 400 (see Fisher 2003, 221–23). Fisher says that the fact that Congress has ignored this Supreme Court decision is not surprising. He concludes his analysis of the

legislative veto decision by stating, "Through its misreading of history, congressional procedures, and executive–legislative relations, the Supreme Court has commanded the political branches to follow a lawmaking process that is impracticable and unworkable" (Fisher 2003, 223).

THE POWER OF THE PURSE

A major point of conflict between the institutional cultures of Congress and the courts occurs over congressional funding for the judiciary. Thus Congress may also take out its frustration with the courts through the annual appropriations process. Congress, of course, must approve the annual budgets for all federal agencies, including the federal courts. The federal courts have given the Administrative Office of the United States Courts the responsibility to lobby Congress for adequate overall budgets, adequate staffing levels, and especially for salary increases for federal judges (McCarthy and Treacy 2000, 151–59). The Constitution prohibits Congress from lowering the salaries of federal judges, but nothing in the Constitution requires Congress to increase judicial salaries or to give the courts more money to spend on staff, facilities, or equipment. Thus, a major point of contention between the two institutions has always been the budgets for the judiciary, including judicial salaries. For example, in 1964 Congress increased the salaries for lower federal judges by $7,500 per year, but increased the salaries for Justices of the Supreme Court by only $4,500 per year. As Schmidhauser and Berg explain, "The $3,000 differential clearly reflected a direct Congressional reprimand to the Supreme Court. This crude rebuff clearly stemmed from Congressional dissatisfaction with several controversial decisions rendered by the Court" (Schmidhauser and Berg 1972, 9).

The annual appropriations process provides a clear avenue to see the different institutional perspectives of the Supreme Court and of Congress. The courts rightly see themselves as an independent third branch, and many judges seem to resent Congress's interference with their budget requests. For example, in March 1969, Chief Justice Earl Warren publicly criticized Congress for ignoring the budgetary needs of the federal courts. The chief justice stated, "It is next to impossible for the courts to get something from Congress" (Warren 1969, A4). Chief Justice Rehnquist has used many of his annual year-end reports on the state of the federal judiciary to scold Congress for not approving sufficient funds for the federal courts. The fiscal year 2004 annual budget process was an especially difficult one for the federal courts. Congress missed its October 2003 deadline for enacting the budget for the judicial branch, and when it did finally pass a budget the courts were faced with severe spending cuts. As Chief Justice Rehnquist described the situation in his 2003 year-end report on the federal judiciary, "The continuing uncertainties and delays in the funding process have necessitated substantial effort on the part of judges and judiciary managers and staff to modify budget systems, develop contingency plans, cancel activities, and attempt to cut costs. Many courts may face hiring freezes, furloughs, or reductions in force" (Rehnquist 2003, 1).

Congress, on the other hand, often tends to see the courts as just another federal agency begging for money (see, e.g., Resnik 2000, 1011). As former representative Neal Smith, a longtime chair of the House Appropriations subcommittee with jurisdiction over the judiciary's budget, explained, "The courts do not have many advocates in Congress. They do not have a constituency. Congress continues to pass more and more laws that require the courts to assume jurisdiction of more cases and add to their workload. Congress is eager to authorize more judges, but when it comes to paying for them, the members of Congress do not think that is a very high priority" (Smith 1996, 177).

This difference in institutional cultures and perspectives can become especially visible during the annual journey that Supreme Court justices make across the street when they testify before the House and Senate Appropriations Committees' Subcommittees on Commerce, Justice, State, and the Judiciary (see Perry 1999, 114–15). This annual trek began in 1943 (see Rishikof and Perry 1995, 676). The testimony of the justices before the House Subcommittee is one clear avenue for public communication between the two institutions.

During the fiscal 2000 budget cycle, the frustration level of the federal courts toward Congress reached a peak. In an early vote, the Senate cut $280 million from the $4.3 billion that the federal judiciary had requested that year. The Supreme Court decided to pull out all the stops in an attempt to get Congress to restore the requested funds. In an extraordinary August 9, 1999, letter to then Senate Majority Leader Trent Lott (R-Miss.), Chief Justice Rehnquist called the Senate's proposed cuts "unjustified and impractical" (see Carelli 1999). The chief justice continued by arguing, "The courts do not control their workload, but rather must respond to filings created in large part by Congress' expansion of the federal courts' jurisdiction" (quoted in Johnson 1999, A2). Upon the urging of federal judges, many newspapers around the country condemned the proposed budget cuts. Eventually most but not all of the potential budget cuts were eventually restored.

INSTITUTIONAL ATTACKS ON THE COURTS

When the conflicts between the federal courts and Congress become especially fierce, there are times when Congress considers more serious attacks on the courts. Congress determines the size of the Supreme Court, and of the lower federal courts. Frustrated that the Supreme Court was declaring his New Deal programs to be unconstitutional, FDR proposed his infamous court-packing plan (see Segal 1991, 384). This plan would have allowed the president to appoint an extra justice for every justice who was then over the age of seventy years, thus temporarily increasing the size of the Court to fifteen members and allowing FDR to appoint a practical voting majority of the justices. Congress refused to enact this plan, but the Court eventually began to uphold the constitutionality of the New Deal legislation when Justice Roberts switched his position and started voting to uphold the president's programs (see Canon and Johnson 1999, 123).

Congress also has the constitutional power of removing federal judges through impeachment, although that power is almost never used for purely ideological reasons (see Volcansek 2001). In 1803, Supreme Court justice Samuel Chase was impeached by the House, but the Senate narrowly failed to remove him from office. After the Supreme Court decided *Brown v. Board of Education* in 1954, bumper stickers throughout the South proclaimed "Impeach Earl Warren." But Congress never took action on these threats. Because of opposition to his strong liberal ideology, conservatives in the late 1960s and early 1970s advocated impeaching Justice William Douglas. The impeachment effort was privately encouraged by President Nixon (see Ehrlichman 1982, 122). But that impeachment effort also failed. Several lower federal judges were removed from office in the 1980s, but none for ideological reasons. In 1997, House Majority Whip Tom DeLay (R-Tex.) called for the impeachment of federal judges who upheld affirmative action programs (see Baum 2001, 248), and in 2004 Representative Tom Feeney (R-Fla.) called for the impeachment of federal judges who cite non-American or international precedents in their decisions. However, it appears unlikely that Congress would actually use impeachment today to try to change the ideological direction of the federal courts. As O'Brien concludes, "Removal from office has never been a serious threat" (2003, 101).

A final method for Congress to attack the federal courts would be through removing certain types of cases from their jurisdiction. Although there have been many calls for these so-called "court stripping" actions, Congress has actually enacted very few of them.[6] In 1868, fearing that the Supreme Court would declare the Reconstruction Acts to be unconstitutional, Congress withdrew the Court's jurisdiction over habeas corpus actions. In *Ex Parte McCardle*, 74 U.S. 506 (1869), the Supreme Court acquiesced and dismissed the case for lack of jurisdiction. After the Supreme Court's decision in *United States v. Klein*, 80 U.S. 128 (1872), however, it is not clear whether the Court would still agree that Congress still has the ability to limit the appellate jurisdiction of the Supreme Court. It now appears that the Court would resist legislative efforts to prevent it from hearing specific types of cases. The legal community seems to be in agreement that the powers of Congress to restrict the appellate jurisdiction of the federal courts are limited. In a 1981 report titled "Jurisdiction-Stripping Proposals in Congress: The Threat to Judicial Constitutional Review," the Association of the Bar of the City of New York argued that court stripping proposals would probably not be constitutional. The report concludes, "We conclude that this radical departure from the system of checks and balances that has served our nation well for the past two centuries is unwise and probably unconstitutional" (quoted in Fisher 2003, 1088–89).

One area where Congress has been quite willing to restrict the powers of the federal courts, however, is in the realm of criminal sentencing. Feeling the need to be seen as "tough on crime" and concerned about wide discrepancies in the criminal sentences handed down by federal judges throughout the nation, Congress enacted the Sentencing Reform Act of 1984. This act severely limited the sentencing discretion of federal judges by creating federal sentencing guidelines that were legally binding on the judges. It also established the Federal Sentencing Commission to advise Congress on future amendments to the guidelines. At least three of the seven members of the commission had to be federal judges, and no more than four members could be from the same political party. Although more than 150 lower federal judges declared the new scheme to be unconstitutional (see Epstein and Walker 2004, 268), the U.S. Supreme Court in *Mistretta v. U.S.*, 488 U.S. 361 (1989), upheld its constitutionality by a vote of 8–1.

Although most federal judges were quite unhappy with their reduced discretion in sentencing and with the Federal Sentencing Commission's intrusion into their judicial decisionmaking, they generally adapted to their new environment. In the period after 1984, Congress tinkered with the sentencing guidelines, but the legislature had made no radical changes in the overall scheme. However, that all changed in 2003 when Congress adopted the so-called Feeney Amendment to legislation creating new federal crimes for offenses against children and to create a federal alert system for finding missing children (see Perine 2003a). The new legislation is also known as the PROTECT Act.

Without prior hearings and without seeking the views of the judiciary on the issue, both houses of Congress approved an amendment by Representative Tom Feeney (R-Fla.) to alter the sentencing guidelines system. The so-called Feeney Amendment greatly further reduced the discretion of federal judges in sentencing crimes involving children, reduced the presence of federal judges on the Federal Sentencing Commission by requiring that no more than three of the seven members be federal judges instead of "at least three," language used the 1984 act, and required the monitoring of how individual federal judges deviated from all of the sentencing guidelines. Federal judges often reacted in outrage to the idea that the government would be gathering statistics on their individual sentencing patterns, in part because they feared that Congress might attempt to impeach judges who consistently deviated from the guidelines. For example, in appearing before the House Appropriations Committee during the yearly trek of Supreme Court justices across the street to discuss the annual budget for the judicial branch, Justice Anthony Kennedy told Congress that he thought judges who gave sentences that were lower than the federal sentencing guidelines were "courageous" and he believed that federal judges should not have to "follow, blindly, these unjust guidelines" (quoted in Holland 2004, A2). Chief Justice Rehnquist scolded Congress for its failure to consult with the judicial branch prior to enacting such important changes to the federal sentencing system. In his year-end report on the federal judiciary, the Chief Justice stated:

> During the last year, it seems that the traditional interchange between the Congress and the Judiciary broke down when Congress enacted what is known as the PROTECT Act, making some rather dramatic changes to the laws governing the federal sentencing process. . . . The PROTECT Act was enacted without any consideration of the views of the Judiciary. It is, of course, the prerogative of Congress to determine what to consider in enacting a statute. But it surely improves the legislative process at least to ask the Judiciary its views on such a significant piece of legislation. It is Congress's job to legislate; but each branch of our government has a unique perspective, and taking into account these diverse perspectives improves the process. (Rehnquist 2003, 2)

After expressing his discontent with the problems in the communications between the branches on this issue, the chief justice continued by raising concerns about the specific provisions that required the monitoring of how specific federal judges deviate from the guidelines. He continued:

> Among the provisions in the Act that many find troubling is that requiring the collection of downward departure information on an individual judge-by-judge basis. Congress may, of course, change the rules under which judges operate. And there can be no doubt that collecting information about how the Sentencing Guidelines, including downward departures, are applied in practice could aid Congress in making decisions about whether to legislate on these issues. Collecting downward departure information on a judge-by-

judge basis, however, seems to me somewhat troubling. For side-by-side with the broad authority of Congress to legislate and gather information in this area is the principle that federal judges are not to be removed from office for their judicial acts. The subject matter of the questions Congress may pose about judges' decisions, and whether they target the judicial decisions of individual federal judges, could appear to be an unwarranted and ill-considered effort to intimidate individual judges in the performance of their judicial duties. (Rehnquist 2003, 2)

Although the relationship between Congress and the federal courts is often strained, it rarely leads to full-scale attacks on the courts in general or the Supreme Court in particular. Individual members of Congress certainly hurl verbal attacks at the courts, and Congress will use its institutional will to attempt to overturn specific decisions with which a majority in Congress disagrees. And clearly Congress will limit the discretion of federal judges when it comes to criminal sentencing decisions. But attacks on the integrity of the institution, such as impeachment of judges for ideological reasons or court-stripping proposals, almost never seem to survive in the legislative process.

REVERENCE FOR THE COURTS

In the 1960s, the conventional wisdom among political scientists came to be that the federal courts in general and the U.S. Supreme Court in particular are protected from the most deadly of congressional attacks by the high respect and reverence that the American public extends to the judicial branch. In the early 1960s, Murphy and Pritchett argued that "courts are protected by their magic; only rarely can a hand be laid on a judge without a public outcry of sacrilege" (Murphy and Pritchett 1961, 554–55). In the late 1960s, Nagel continued this theme when he argued that milder forms of attacks on specific decisions of the Supreme Court had more chance of passing in Congress than did more frontal attacks (Nagel 1969, 277). Others argue that many in Congress actually prefer that the federal courts hand down decisions on extremely divisive issues (see, e.g., Dahl 1957; Bickel 1962; Graber 1993). As Graber explains this line of reasoning, "Mainstream politicians may facilitate judicial policymaking in part because they have good reason to believe that the courts will announce those policies they privately favor but cannot openly endorse without endangering their political support" (1993, 43). Schubert (1960) and Miller (1995) have argued that the presence of so many lawyers in Congress also protects the courts from serious institutional attacks. Harry Stumpf summarizes this line of scholarship when he writes, "The prestige or sacrosanctity argument in Congress is used and used with some effectiveness in protecting the judiciary against anti-Court legislative reaction" (Stumpf 1965, 394).

In their important work on the interactions between Congress and the Supreme Court, Schmidhauser and Berg, however, questioned the conventional wisdom that the Supreme Court, and by implication the lower federal courts, are protected from institutional attacks by an "aura of reverence" (Schmidhauser and Berg 1972, 1). These scholars found that on a variety of occasions in the 1950s and 1960s one House of Congress would pass legislation to impose serious damage to the institutional power of the federal courts. However, very few of these institutional attacks were enacted into law because they usually died by a close vote in one of the chambers. From a long-term perspective from the beginning of the twenty-first century, it appears that Murphy and Pritchett, and their colleagues, seem to be correct. Congress will certainly attack specific decisions of the federal courts, but members of Congress seem extremely hesitant to endanger the institutional integrity of the judicial branch. In other words, Congress will attack specific decisions of the federal courts but in general the legislative branch refuses to take steps that would hinder the constitutional responsibilities and duties of the judiciary.

CONCLUSION

The historical institutional perspective employed by this chapter helps to explain the often strained relationship between Congress and the federal courts. The historical institutionalists are very interested in the interrelationships among various governmental institutions. They stress the effects that time can have on these institutional interactions. And they ask the big picture questions that are of interest to political scientists and to the public at large. As Pierson and Skocpol conclude, "Historical institutionalists address big, substantive questions that are inherently of interest to broad publics as well as to fellow scholars. . . . Historical institutionalists [also] take time seriously" (Pierson and Skocpol 2002, 695). Historical institutionalists pay attention to institutional contexts and interactions in an attempt to understand better how our governmental institutions actually work. They also pay attention to the unintended consequences that occur when institutional interactions are strained because of the different institutional perspectives that drive each governmental body. Thus, Congress and the federal courts have very different institutional cultures and institutional wills, and scholars must attempt to understand better these institutional differences.

Thus, it should now be clear that the three branches of the federal government cannot be studied in isolation from each other, nor can the interactions among the three branches be understood without examining the traditional role each institution plays in our overall system of government. As Katzmann has stated, "Governance in the United States is a process or interaction among institutions—legislative, executive, and judicial—with separate and sometimes clashing structures, purposes, and interests. The Founders envisioned that constructive tension among those governmental institutions would not only preserve liberty but would also promote the public good" (1997, 1). As Neustadt has argued, in reality in our system of government we have "separated institutions sharing powers" (1980, 26). And as the concluding chapter of this volume demonstrates, in the United States we have a process of governance as dialogue. These colloquies between and among the institutions of government are not always properly appreciated by either institution, nor by the scholars who study them.

NOTES

1. This assault on the use of legislative history in statutory interpretation cases has even led some members of Congress to defend the practice. (See, e.g., Statutory Interpretation and the Uses of Legislative History, Hearings before the House Subcommittee on Courts, Intellectual Property, and the Administration of Justice, April 19, 1990.)

2. Justice Scalia also attacked Justice Souter's use of legislative history in *Johnson v. United States*, 529 U.S. 694 (2000). Here the dispute was over the meaning of the term "revoke" in a criminal statute. The majority opinion examined the legislative history behind the statute and concluded that Congress had intended the term to have an unconventional meaning. Justice Scalia's dissent argued that the term should have a more common meaning. Justice Scalia's dissent actually stated, "Of course the acid test of whether a word can reasonably bear a particular meaning is whether you could use the word in that sense at a cocktail party without having people look at you funny." In a footnote in the majority opinion, Justice Souter responded, "When text implies that a word is used in a secondary sense and clear legislative purpose is at stake, Justice Scalia's cocktail party textualism . . . must yield to the Congress of the United States" (*Johnson v. United States*, n. 9).

3. The demand from some justices that the courts refuse to consider legislative history places a totally unrealistic burden on Congress. As Davidson and Oleszek note, "Judges often are unaware that ambiguity, imprecision, or inconsistency may be the price for winning enactment of legislative measures. The more members try to define a bill, the more they may divide or dissipate congressional support for it" (Davidson and Oleszek 2002, 331). Members of Congress have also expressed their frustrations that the courts misunderstand how Congress actually functions. As U.S. Representative Carlos Moorhead argued in 1990, "Sometimes, I think it would be helpful if more of the judges had had legislative experience because it is very difficult when you deal with 435 people in the House and 100 people in the Senate, to get a feeling of legislative intent unless you look to the reports and to the debates" (Statement of Representative Carlos Moorhead, in Statutory Interpretation and the Uses of Legislative History, Hearings before the House Subcommittee on Courts, Intellectual Property, and the Administration of Justice, April 19, 1990, at 2).

In addition, members of Congress enact legislation with the assumption that the courts will read the legislative history in cases where the statute needs further interpretation (see Greenawalt 1999, 200). As Representative Kastenmeier, then chair of the House Subcommittee on Courts, Intellectual Property, and the Administration of Justice, explained during 1990 hearings on the subject, "It is probably safe to say that most of us in Congress assume committee reports, colloquies on the floor and other sources of legislative history can explain and amplify statutory language in ways that are instructive to the courts. If that assumption is incorrect, that is to say if the courts will not or should not ordinarily look beyond the text of the statute in divining the meaning of legislative language, it may have a profound effect on the way Congress should be drafting legislation" (Statement of Chairman Kastenmeier, in Statutory Interpretation and the Uses of Legislative History, Hearings before the House Subcommittee on Courts, Intellectual Property, and the Administration of Justice, April 19, 1990, at 2).

Thus Justice Scalia's attacks on the use of legislative history reveal a grave misunderstanding of the institutional needs of Congress.

4. Judge Wald has written, "While certainly not yet triumphant, the textualists are beginning to have a very definite impact on the manner in which the Supreme Court and lower courts decide cases. . . . From my perspective, this trend has important implications for the balance of power in an ever ongoing tug-of-war among the three branches in our constitutional system. I personally resist the trend because in my view it needlessly disrupts that balance" (Statement of Judge Patricia Wald, Statutory Interpretation and the Uses of Legislative History, Hearings before the House Subcommittee on Courts, Intellectual Property, and the Administration of Justice, April 19, 1990, at 6).

5. The Eleventh Amendment negated *Chisholm v. Georgia*, 2 U.S. 419 (1793), the Fourteenth Amendment negated *Dred Scott v. Sandford*, 60 U.S. 393 (1857), the Sixteenth Amendment negated *Pollock v. Farmers' Loan and Trust Company*, 158 U.S. 601 (1895), and the Twenty-Sixth Amendment negated *Oregon v. Mitchell*, 400 U.S. 112 (1970).

6. Resnik, Boggs, and Berman (2004, 20) discusses several recent examples of what she sees as potentially serious court stripping proposals that Congress has actually enacted into law. These include restrictions on the jurisdiction of federal courts over some cases involving aliens and prisoners, as well as in some securities cases. She also cites the fact that President George W. Bush has attempted to bypass both the regular federal courts and the traditional military justice system by creating new military commissions to try those suspected of promoting terrorism. It is unclear if Congress will continue this trend of restricting the jurisdiction of the federal courts.

4

The View from the President

NANCY KASSOP

[T]he president's power
to see that the laws are
faithfully executed refutes
the idea that he is to be a
lawmaker.

> —*Youngstown Sheet
> and Tube Company v.
> Sawyer*, 343 U.S. 579
> (1952)

WITH DUE RESPECT TO JUSTICE BLACK'S OPINION FOR THE court in *Youngstown*, the modern president *does*, in fact, make law—every day. Presidents make law unilaterally, on their own authority, and jointly, when their actions intersect with those of Congress and the courts. This assertion of lawmaking authority has contributed to the most significant development in interbranch relations since the writing of the Constitution—the increased influence of the presidency far beyond the imagination of the Framers. James Madison's self-assured statement in *Federalist Paper No. 51* that, "In republican government, the legislative authority necessarily predominates," sounds quaint and archaic in a twenty-first-century world where power has flowed into the executive branch in an almost unbroken stream for the last seventy years (Hamilton, Madison, and Jay 1961, 322). The story is one of the growth of the institution of the presidency in all aspects—its numbers, the scope of its powers, its increasing specialization, and its technical expertise.

Today, the Executive Office of the President is composed of approximately twelve units, in which the White House Office alone contains about 450 staff members. This expansion of resources, along with the near-constant condition of divided government in recent decades, has heightened the competition with Congress for policy ownership, and has contributed to the centralization of policymaking in the White House. Consequently, contemporary presidents possess enhanced ability to seek (and to seize) all available opportunities to "make law" to ensure their imprint and to advance their agendas.

Although these developments provide the president with an institutional advantage over the other two branches, no part of government exists in a vacuum, and each must calculate the reactions of the others when contemplating its own policymaking efforts. It is the fluidity and the interactions among all three that ultimately produce identifiable outcomes, and those exchanges will be the focus of examination here.

The view of lawmaking from inside the White House can be analyzed from various angles: (1) What types of "law" can a president make on his own constitutional authority? (2) What reactions can a president reasonably anticipate from Congress and the courts to unilateral lawmaking, and how can a president devise a strategy to address those possible reactions, in order to maximize his chances of success? (3) What is the president's role in the legislative process, and what are the presidential–congressional interactions that occur during that process? (4) What impact can a president have on the federal judiciary as an institution and on the decisions that emanate from it? and (5) What is the legacy from cases where a president's action has been challenged in the courts? This last inquiry is the quintessential one that characterizes the "president–court" relationship—the record that demonstrates those presidential claims to power that the courts will and will not accept.

UNILATERAL LAWMAKING

Article II of the Constitution provides the president with one source of absolute, exclusive power (to grant pardons), and, over time, presidents have found other tools to assert independent lawmaking power from either the "silences" or the undefined grants of authority in the Constitution. These other types of unilateral lawmaking include executive orders and executive agreements, as well as the lesser-known but similar actions, such as memoranda, proclamations, directives, findings and determinations. Each of these varies slightly in definition, but they all serve the same purpose, ultimately, of executive lawmaking. Executive orders and executive agreements have been the subject of challenges by Congress and in the courts, but both have survived and prospered, and have created precedents for the future that are not easily undone. The enlargement of the presidency owes much to this pattern of behavior.

PARDON POWER

The pardon power in Article II, Section 8, Clause 1, provides that "The President . . . shall have Power to grant Reprieves and Pardons for Offences against the United States, except in Cases of Impeachment." The only expressed limitation is that of impeachment; in all other cases, the president may exercise this power to correct judicial errors by commuting, or reducing, a sentence or by exempting from punishment individuals who have been or might be convicted of a crime.

A few Supreme Court rulings have provided guidance on this power. The 1866 case of *Ex parte Garland*, 71 U.S. 333 (1866), struck down statutory restrictions on the pardon power. However, in *Ex parte Grossman*, 267 U.S. 107 (1925), and *Shick v. Reed*, 419 U.S. 256 (1974), the Court held out the prospect that presidential pardons could be subject, under certain circumstances, to judicial review, although neither case, in fact, resulted in such a ruling (see, generally, Adler 1989, 209–35).

Of far greater likelihood is the ever-present possibility of a political challenge to a president's use of *any* power, exclusive and absolute, or otherwise. Congress and the voters have effective means to register their disapproval and to hold a president accountable for his actions. President Gerald Ford's full and unconditional pardon in September 1974 of former president Richard Nixon for "all offenses against the United States which he, Richard Nixon, has committed or may have committed" during his tenure in office resulted in a series of political repercussions: an extraordinary appearance by President Ford before the House Judiciary Committee to explain the pardon, a precipitous drop in his public approval rating from 71 to 49 percent within a week of his issuance of it, and the sense that, ultimately, the pardon was a likely contributor to Ford's reelection defeat in 1976 (see U.S. House of Representatives 1974, 87–158; Kutler 1990, 564, 566).

Similarly, President George H. W. Bush's December 24, 1992, pardon of six of the Iran-Contra defendants, occurring even after Bush's reelection defeat, elicited an adverse political reaction that clouded his departure from office. President Bill Clinton's 140 controversial last-minute pardons and 36 commutations of prison sentences just prior to his departure in January 2001 created a firestorm of disapproval and provoked hearings by the House Government Reform Committee, after he had left office, to investigate for improprieties (see, generally, Fisher 2002c, 586–99). Beyond besmirching a president's legacy, however, it is unclear what more Congress could have accomplished at that point, although a sitting president could, ultimately, be subject to impeachment for abuse of his pardon power.

EXECUTIVE ORDERS AND EXECUTIVE AGREEMENTS

Presidents have found sources of lawmaking authority in their implied powers, in congressionally delegated powers, or from inherent executive authority (prerogative). They may issue executive orders that bind officials and agencies in the executive branch, and they may conclude executive agreements in the foreign policy sphere, which provide a vehicle, in addition to treaties, to negotiate and formulate accords with other nations. Both of these tools offer a chief executive far greater latitude, flexibility, and influence for policymaking than either the routine legislative process with both houses of Congress or the formal treaty process that requires ratification by a two-thirds vote of the Senate.

The Supreme Court has ruled that executive orders and executive agreements, though not authorized expressly in the Constitution, are, nevertheless, constitutionally based, and that both are binding law. An executive order must not conflict with existing statutory law, and must be implied or inferred from some grant of authority, but it may "make" law, applicable to and controlling the executive branch, in areas where statutes have left a void. Executive agreements are not treaties, although scholars have struggled mightily and in vain to explain any substantial difference between the two, other than offering the unhelpful and circular logic that the *only* distinction is the requirement of a two-thirds vote in the Senate for treaties.

The use of executive orders was upheld by the Supreme Court in *In re Neagle*, 135 U.S. 1 (1890), where the Court said that "any obligation that is fairly and properly inferable" from the Constitution is equal in weight and status to a law. Presidents have used executive orders or other types of unilateral lawmaking in specific policy areas, such as civil rights, environmental policy, labor and trade issues, and foreign intelligence matters.

Executive agreements were reviewed by the Supreme Court in three cases, and were declared valid lawmaking instruments as the "law of the land" that require neither congressional nor Senate approval, but that were sufficiently justified by the president's authority in foreign affairs and, more specifically, as an auxiliary to his Article II power "to receive ambassadors and other public ministers"; see *Altman and Co. v. U.S.*, 224 U.S. 583 (1912); *U.S. v. Belmont*, 301 U.S. 324 (1936); and *U.S. v. Pink*, 315 U.S. 203 (1941).

But the substance of executive orders and agreements is not immune from congressional oversight or judicial review, and both tools can be overturned by the courts or superseded by subsequent congressional action. President Harry Truman's order to his secretary of commerce, Charles S. Sawyer, in the Steel Seizure Case, *Youngstown Sheet and Tube Company v. Sawyer*, 343 U.S. 579 (1952), is a classic example of a president whose "overreaching" resulted in a severe rebuke by the Court, where it ruled that Truman had exceeded his constitutional authority in the face of a congressional rejection of presidential power to seize private property during emergencies. President Nixon felt the sting of a congressional overturning in 1972, when Congress prohibited the expenditure of funds to carry out his Executive Order 11605, which tried to revive the McCarthy-era Subversive Activities Control Board (Mayer 2001, 28). Many examples abound of presidents who backed down or chose not to proceed with executive orders when congressional opposition was apparent.

Executive agreements have also been the subject of congressional concern, prompted by the dramatic increase in their number in the post–World War II era and the corresponding decline in the number of treaties. In acknowledging the shifting of authority in this area to the president and the loss of Senate influence, Congress passed the Case-Zablocki Act in 1972, which required submission of any executive agreement to Congress within sixty days (later amended to twenty days). As an effort to reassert some congressional control over the president's expanded foreign affairs powers and to restrict the use of executive agreements, this act was not very effective. Instead of curbing the president's use of this tool, it actually legitimated it, requiring only that Congress be informed when agreements are used. Evidence since 1972 indicates that the rate at which executive agreements are concluded has not slowed, relative to treaties, and that they are growing at a steady rate (Farrar-Myers 2002, 16).

For both executive orders and agreements, presidential communication and negotiation with Congress during the policy development stage facilitates a better chance of success, fostering open deliberation and providing opportunities to clear up disagreements and promote satisfactory compromises early in the process. However, executive orders and agreements are often used by presidents for the precise reason that they *are* an independent source of authority, and, as such, can be employed as a strategic tool where a president may be uncertain of winning congressional approval of legislation or Senate ratification of a treaty. But where the possibility exists of sufficient political strength in Congress to overturn executive lawmaking efforts, a president proceeds at his peril, despite his constitutional authority to do so.

THE PRESIDENT AND CONGRESS

The common perception is that the legislative branch makes the laws and the executive branch implements them. But government is neither so watertight nor so compartmentalized, and at least beginning with the administrations of Theodore Roosevelt and Woodrow Wilson and from Franklin Roosevelt's presidency forward, the legislative process was no longer, if it ever was, the exclusive province of Congress (Pika, Maltese, and Thomas 2002, 176). Presidents not only participate fully in its unfolding, but would be regarded as negligent if they refrained. Precedents and public expectations have engrafted this power of legislative leadership onto the presidency: it is a weak president who comes into office today without having articulated a vision of an ambitious agenda during his campaign, and without "hitting the ground running" to get his legislative priorities into the congressional pipeline early in the "honeymoon" phase of his administration.

There is no better explanation of the shared role that both Congress and the president play in lawmaking than the quote attributed to President Dwight Eisenhower at his July 22, 1959, press conference that "I am part of the legislative process" (as quoted in Neustadt 1964, 42). Equally, Peterson emphasizes that Congress and the president are "tandem institutions" that must "legislate together" as a genuine partnership, if they expect to produce policy outcomes (Peterson 1990, 8). The president's role has expanded from one of simply recommending legislation to Congress, as provided for in Article II, and signing or vetoing it, as authorized in Article I. Today, the modern chief executive, through his White House staff in the public and congressional liaison offices, monitors every step of the process, and actively engages in it when necessary to preserve and advance his preferences.

As the president's role as legislative leader grew in the last half of the twentieth century, new institutional structures were needed to assist him. President Eisenhower created the Office of Congressional Relations (OCR) in 1953, described by Bradley Patterson, a White House staff member in the Eisenhower, Nixon, and Ford years, as "an ambulatory bridge across a constitutional gulf" (Patterson 2000, 114). This office's responsibility is to monitor legislation and to lobby members of Congress to support the president's priorities and to prevent enactment of proposals he opposes. The "bridging" function consists of the president's personal outreach to members, assisted by a daily list from the OCR staff of the names of members of Congress the president will call (Patterson 2000, 115). Other lobbying efforts might include OCR staff discussions with liaison staffs of executive branch departments, or meetings between members of Congress and the president, or invitations extended to members to attend presidential events (Warshaw 2000, 275–77). "Bargaining, arm-twisting and confrontation" are typical tactics used by the White House staff to build legislative coalitions and votes, according to Pika, Maltese, and Thomas (2002, 193).

Other units in the executive branch play critical roles in the legislative process. "Central clearance" is an essential function performed by the Legislative Reference Office within the Office of Management and Budget (OMB). It consists of the review of all bills that have passed both houses and all legislative proposals submitted from the departments. OMB's most basic job is to ensure coordination of all legislative proposals from departments to prevent duplication and to monitor these for congruence with the president's priorities and goals (Warshaw 2000, 278).

Truman was the first president to employ a central clearance function under the predecessor of OMB, the Bureau of the Budget, and Nixon expanded the role of the Legislative Reference Office in 1970. The key job here is to track legislation as it wends its way through both houses, and to provide an analysis for the president of the final version of the bill. OMB offers the president its recommendation as to whether he should sign or veto it. When bills are controversial, the White House counsel's office provides a recommendation, as well. The director of OMB acts as a manager of the executive branch's participation in the legislative process, reviewing program requests carefully for consistency with the president's objectives, as well as for the budgetary impacts of these proposals (Warshaw 2000, 278).

The final conclusion to passage of a bill into law is the president's signature, but along with that signature comes a signing statement by the president that has taken on increased significance and visibility in recent administrations. The practice of issuing a written statement as to the president's understanding of the bill he is signing into law is, generally, an unremarkable one that has existed at least since the time of Andrew Jackson. It took on added interest, however, during Ronald Reagan's administration when Attorney General Edwin Meese announced that these statements would be included in the "Legislative History" section of the *United States Code Congressional and Administrative News* (USSCAN), and he suggested that they should be considered as "presidential intent," similar to the "congressional intent" that courts refer to when interpreting statutes (Kelley 2002, 3). President Reagan began this process, followed by all of his successors in office, of using signing statements to direct departments and agencies on how to implement the law, and more specifically, to single out parts of the law that he directed them to *decline* to enforce because of constitutional infirmities. In effect, this practice of designating certain provisions for non-enforcement amounted to the equivalent of a line-item veto, a tool the Constitution does not give to the president (Fisher 1997, 135; see also Dellinger 1993, 131–41; 1994, 199–211; Garber and Wimmer 1987, 363). Understandably, Congress did not look favorably upon such action, as it directly undermined the law agreed to by both houses. The courts also weighed in against President Reagan, when litigation ensued in the mid-1980s over a case of his non-enforcement directive in a signing statement for the Competition in Contracting Act. The courts emphatically rejected the administration's position, calling it "utterly at odds with the texture and plain language of the Constitution, and with nearly two hundred years of judicial precedent" (*Lear Siegler, Inc. v. Lehman*, 842 F. 2d 1102 [9th Cir. 1988], at 1121) and "the constitutional equivalent of an abuse of the judicial process" (842 F. 2d, at 1125–26).

Yet, Presidents George H. W. Bush, Clinton, and George W. Bush have continued to use and defend this practice, largely as a consequence of the polarized political environment prompted by entrenched, divided government. Thus, the practice survives—and flourishes, by one count, which notes that Bush and Clinton each issued more signing statements in their separate administrations than Reagan did in his (Kelley 2002, 35).[1] In effect, this tool gives a president the true "last word" in the legislative process, contrary to the expectations of the Framers, and indicative of the extent to which the president's role has seeped into all phases of that process.

THE PRESIDENT AND THE COURTS

A president's relationship with the federal courts is multifaceted, in at least four ways. First, he has the constitutional responsibility from Article II to nominate all federal judges, subject to the Senate's duty to advise and consent to those nominations. These life tenure appointments are the longest lasting legacy of any president, and, thus, provide him with a potential opportunity to shape the judiciary—and its decisions—for decades to come, dependent upon the vacancies that arise during his administration and on his success rate in the Senate, which has become increasingly more muscular and combative in the confirmation process.

Second, the president can profoundly affect the work of the courts through the selection of cases that the administration brings to them, largely as a result of the solicitor general's choices of lower court decisions to appeal, and the substantive arguments he makes to the court in those cases. The president's selection of a solicitor general is, also, a cue that may suggest whether the president tends to see this office more as a political rather than the strictly legal one that it has traditionally been, but has been less so in recent administrations.

Third, the president's choice of an attorney general has significant implications for the direction of Justice Department policies throughout the legal system.

Fourth, two less visible offices, one in the Justice Department and one in the White House, wield enormous influence in determining the constitutional contours of the institution of the presidency, based on the specific issues that arise for each occupant of the Oval Office. The Office of Legal Counsel in the Justice Department and the Office of Counsel to the President, as part of the White House staff, both labor "under the radar screen" much of the time, and from different vantage points that sometimes lead to conflicting conclusions between them. But, their importance and function are central to any discussion of the "view of the law" from the president's perspective, since they are responsible for interpreting the president's powers under the Constitution.

JUDICIAL SELECTION

Presidents consider their power to appoint federal judges as one of the "plums" of the office: with considerable luck in timing—and sufficient and strategic judicial vacancies during a president's term of office—this power affords a president the chance to influence the direction of federal law for decades to come in ways that are more far-reaching than most legislation from Congress. Some presidents, such as Presidents Franklin Roosevelt, Nixon, and Reagan, are able to appoint one or more Supreme Court justices, and can change the course of that court's rulings by "tipping" it, ideologically, in either a liberal or conservative direction. Other presidents, such as President Jimmy Carter, may not be presented with Supreme Court vacancies during their tenure, but may have a large number of district court and circuit courts of appeals positions to fill (President Carter benefited from passage by Congress of the Omnibus Judgeship Act of 1978, which created 117 new district court judgeships and thirty-five new appeals court judgeships) (Goldman 1997, 241–42). Those appointments can have a substantial impact on decisions at these lower levels, where, in essence, the effect across the legal system reaches a larger number of litigants than those few who make it to the Supreme Court. Some presidents, such as Clinton, are afforded the opportunity to appoint at *both* the Supreme Court and lower court levels in such numbers as to make a considerable imprint.

The appointment process for all three levels is similar, although local considerations figure more prominently at the district court level. The practice of "senatorial courtesy" obligates a president to consult, in advance, any senators of his party from the home state of a potential nominee to assure the acceptability of that nominee to those senators. Rejection at this early stage by any of these senators usually prevents the nominee's name from moving forward. Deference is given to senators, generally, throughout the entire process, as even a senator of the opposite party from the president may register disapproval of a candidate at the Judiciary Committee stage through an objection on the "blue slip." Traditionally, such objection signals the demise of a nomination, and the committee declines to schedule a hearing.

The selection process occurs in two steps: (1) the generating of a short list of the top candidates, produced through the joint efforts of officials in the Justice Department and the White House counsel's office, and presented to the president for his ultimate selection of a nominee; and (2) confirmation in the Senate, consisting of hearings and a personal appearance of the nominee for questioning before the Judiciary Committee, and, finally, an up-or-down vote on the Senate floor.

Other players in this process include the American Bar Association (ABA) and the Federal Bureau of Investigation. Beginning in the 1950s, the ABA's Standing Committee on Federal Judiciary evaluated federal judicial candidates to determine if they were "exceptionally well-qualified," "well-qualified," "qualified," or "not qualified," and these assessments were forwarded to the Justice Department. Favorable evaluations from the ABA result in sending candidate names to the Federal Bureau of Investigation, which then conducts an exhaustive background check of all potential candidates at this stage and provides its reports to the Justice Department and White House officials for use in their extensive "vetting" and interviewing of candidates. However, political tensions over ABA ratings of some judicial nominees from recent Republican presidents prompted President George W. Bush to suspend the executive branch's use of these ratings in 2001, although Democrats on the Senate Judiciary Committee continue to receive them.

The Senate approaches its role in the appointment of federal judges differently than in the appointment of executive branch officials. It is willing to permit a president wide latitude in his choice of those subordinates, including Cabinet officials and their deputies, who assist the president in policy development and are responsible for carrying out his decisions. Confirmation of federal judicial nominees, however, represents a different plane of authority and influence, and the specter of a thirty- or forty-year tenure for each judge, with full independence and little accountability once on the bench, compels the Senate to scrutinize these appointees with considerably more care and far less deference than those for the executive branch.

Historically, the Senate rejection rate for Supreme Court nominees has been about 20 percent, or twenty-seven unsuccessful candidates, though most of those occurred in the nineteenth century (Baum 2001, 50). However, the increasingly raw tensions over the confirmation process that have surfaced over the last few administrations and that continue unabated signal that an unusually high level of testiness and confrontation now characterizes the relationship between the president and the Senate over this function. A few high-profile Supreme Court confirmation hearings, such as the rejection of Robert Bork in 1986 and the dramatic and explosive confirmation of Clarence Thomas in 1990, fueled this interbranch conflict, but it has spread far beyond that to infect lower court confirmation proceedings, as well. Not a single appeals court judge was confirmed by the Senate in 1996, and it took four years, from January 1996 to March 2000, for the Senate to confirm Clinton appointee Richard Paez to the Ninth Circuit (Kassop 2002, 10). In the period 1996–97, the Republican Senate engaged in a strategy termed "court-blocking" by Goldman and Slotnick (1997, 271), where the confirmation process ground to a virtual halt. The Senate will often slow down the process late in a president's term, awaiting the election outcome and the new possibilities it might bring. But this slowdown continued into 1997, and this pattern of holding judicial nominations hostage to partisan politics in the Senate not only remains unabated to the present day, but has intensified, as the Senate has resorted to the procedural hurdle of a filibuster, and has made extensive use of it with six appeals court nominees of George W. Bush. One nominee, Miguel Estrada, withdrew his name from further consideration for the D.C. Circuit Court of Appeals in September 2003, after multiple Senate filibusters. Two others, Charles Pickering Jr. and William Pryor Jr., received recess appointments from Bush in early 2004 for the Fifth Circuit and the Eleventh Circuit Courts of Appeals, respectively. Three others, Priscilla Owen for the Fifth Circuit, Carolyn Kuhl for the Ninth Circuit, and Janice Rogers Brown for the D.C. Circuit, are still awaiting floor votes, as of March 2004, after their Senate supporters failed to muster sixty votes for cloture (Dewar 2003, A06; Simon 2004, A1; U.S. Department of Justice, Office of Legal Policy, "Nominations," http://www.usdoj.gov/olp/nominations.htm).

Presidential influence over the courts, and, by extension, over the subsequent decisions generated by presidential appointments, varies widely, and is often unpredictable. History is replete with presidents who hope to influence the direction of the Supreme Court with their appointments, only to be disappointed and surprised at the decisions their appointees make. President Eisenhower's eventual dismay at the liberal jurisprudence of two of his Supreme Court appointees, Earl Warren and William Brennan, was illustrated by his response when asked if he had made any mistakes as president. He answered, "Yes, two, and they are both sitting on the Supreme Court" (quoted in Abraham 1985, 263). President Nixon thought he was appointing a strict constructionist conservative in Harry Blackmun, who turned out to be one of the most liberal justices on the Burger Court. Still, Franklin Roosevelt, despite the failure of his Court-packing plan in 1937, *was* able to engineer the desired change in course of the Court's decisions, prompted by the switch of Justice Roberts in *West Coast Hotel v. Parrish*, 300 U.S. 379 (1937), and the eventual retirements that soon followed. President Reagan's three appointees and elevation of Rehnquist to chief justice *are* bearing full fruit in the string of ten federalism decisions throughout the 1990s, and the narrowing of earlier expansive civil liberties rulings. President Carter's lower court appointments changed the face of the federal judiciary, adding more women and minority judges than those appointed by all previous presidents combined. By the end of the Clinton administration, roughly 45 percent of the approximately 800 federal judges were Clinton appointees, and a similar percentage were those holdovers from the combined Reagan/Bush era (Berman and Murphy 2003, 215–16). Thus, a president's impact on the judiciary is dependent on timing, vacancies, and success rate in the Senate, while his impact on the substantive *law* that emanates from those courts is much less predictable, though that unpredictability is tempered by the sizable role played by political party, ideology, and judicial philosophy in the modern confirmation process.

THE SOLICITOR GENERAL

In considering the president's influence on the judiciary, second only to his power to appoint federal judges would be his selection of a solicitor general, who is entrusted with the responsibility to serve as the attorney for the United States government in cases before the courts. Primary among the solicitor general's functions are: (1) authorizing the civil cases to be appealed from the district courts to the circuit courts, and deciding which cases to appeal to the Supreme Court, when the federal government is a losing party in either of the two lower court levels; (2) representing the federal government, through legal briefs and oral argument, in all cases where it is a party; and (3) submitting amicus curiae briefs in those cases where the United States is not a party but has an interest (Salokar 1992, 12–13).

The office of the solicitor general was created by Congress in the Justice Department Act of 1870. Today, it is the third-ranking position in that department, following the attorney general and deputy attorney general. In contrast to the attorney general—who serves as the chief law enforcement officer in the nation, the administrator of a vast legal bureaucracy, and a cabinet member who generates and implements legal policy—the solicitor general's job is more narrowly focused with its sole concentration on litigation on behalf of its only client, the federal government. Yet, even an office that appears to have a clear line of accountability and a single-minded attention to matters of law has found that it is never very far removed from the vagaries of politics, and its position at the intersection of both provides challenging and sometimes controversial choices for its occupant to make.

The solicitor general is a presidential appointee, confirmed by the Senate, and serves at the chief executive's pleasure. At the same time, the statute that created the office requires that its holder be "learned in the law," establishing a high standard of integrity and independence for it that has characterized much of its history (Salokar 1995, 63). However, a constant debate has swirled around whether its nature is truly independent of politics as a servant of the law, or whether, as an appointed official of the administration in power, it operates as a policy advocate for those under whose authority it serves. Reconciling these two conflicting expectations is a delicate task for any solicitor general, although some scholars have suggested that the "either–or" quality of this debate is misguided; rather, the propensity for a solicitor general to become a policy advocate for the administration depends largely on the political context and atmospherics of the time in which he serves, on the perspective of the appointing president, and on his relationship with the attorney general (Salokar 1995, 78–79). The position requires that the solicitor general employ his or her best legal judgment on the issues before him, but if the attorney general to whom he or she reports disagrees, the attorney general possesses the authority to overrule the subordinate. In this way, the solicitor general has remained faithful to providing independent legal advice, but the reality of policy considerations may still play a role (Clayton 1992, 59).

Although there are many examples of conflicts between the legal position of a solicitor general and the policy preferences of an administration, *Bob Jones University v. U.S.*, 461 U.S. 595 (1983), in the Reagan administration provides a dramatic episode where the acting solicitor general, Lawrence Wallace, a career attorney in the office, disagreed with the brief submitted by his office under pressure from White House counselor Edwin Meese, and Wallace appended a footnote, indicating his disassociation from the legal position advanced in the brief (Clayton 1992, 55).

The solicitor general plays a distinctive and unusually important role in determining key cases on the agendas of the federal courts, in general, and on the Supreme Court, in particular. Its significance is measured by the extraordinary weight it carries as a "repeat player" in the courts, and this is best illustrated by the high success rate it has garnered at the Supreme Court. Scholars have determined that, over a thirty-year period between 1959 and 1989, the Court granted review to approximately 70 to 80 percent of the petitions for certiorari from the solicitor general's office, and that the office prevailed on the merits in about 70 percent of its cases heard by the Court during that period (Salokar 1992, 25–29). Thus, not only does the federal government succeed mightily in its efforts to get its cases before the Court for review, its lopsided win-loss record makes it a formidable, if not almost unbeatable, foe for its opponents. To the degree that the solicitor general's legal positions represent the administration's positions, the connection to the president is a direct one.

Finally, a president's choice of a solicitor general can be a cue to how politicized the office may be under that administration. Presidents are entitled to select executive branch officials who share their ideological and political predispositions, although the specific emphasis here on professional credentials, along with the special relationship the Solicitor General enjoys with the Supreme Court as an adviser on the law, give this position a slightly different cast to it than most others. President George W. Bush's selection of Theodore Olson as his solicitor general added a unique new twist to the mix of legal and political factors that bear on presidential choice here: Olson was the private attorney who argued successfully on behalf of candidate Bush in *Bush v. Gore*, 531 U.S. 98 (2000), the December 2000 Supreme Court case that ended the presidential election in Bush's favor. Shortly thereafter, President Bush nominated Olson to be solicitor general.

THE ATTORNEY GENERAL

As a member of the inner cabinet, along with the secretaries of state, defense, and treasury, the attorney general is one of the president's closest advisers. The position is among the oldest in the executive branch, dating back to 1790 when Edmund Randolph served in that capacity to George Washington. The office was established in the Judiciary Act of 1789, with the chief functions of arguing federal cases before the Supreme Court and advising the president and executive departments on questions of law (Baker 1995, 39). The solicitor general, originally authorized in 1870 to assist the attorney general with litigation, has, in fact, assumed most of the litigating role, although the attorney general still maintains final approval over any legal positions the department takes (Clayton 1992, 26). Alternatively, the attorney general has added more functions to the job description. With the creation of the Department of Justice in 1870, the attorney general took on administrative and supervisory roles, and now commands an entire bureaucracy, including six divisions that handle legal cases, maintain policy offices, and comprise a number of vital law enforcement agencies and units, including the Federal Bureau of Investigation, the Immigration and Naturalization Service, federal prisons, and the network of U.S. attorneys (Baker 1995, 31–32).

Thus, the purview of the attorney general has expanded considerably from its inception with this increased oversight responsibility. The attorney general also provides advice to the president, appears before Congress as the representative for the administration's legal policies or to request new laws, plays a major role in the judicial selection process, and participates as a member of the National Security Council (Baker 1995, 33).

As with the solicitor general, the attorney general faces the comparable dilemma of trying to reconcile both legal and political responsibilities. The president depends on this official for sound legal advice, yet as a political appointee of an administration that has policy priorities it wishes to advance, the attorney general may find that the law may not always accommodate the president's preferences. A classic example was the discomfort that Attorney General Francis Biddle felt at Franklin Roosevelt's plan for the internment of Japanese Americans during World War II, in direct conflict with Biddle's strong support of civil liberties. Biddle did not prevent Roosevelt from pursuing the plan, but expressed his remorse years later for not exerting more pressure on Roosevelt to abandon the idea (Baker 1995, 34).

Considerations that affect a president's choice of attorney general vary greatly. Some presidents view the attorney general as a position for one of their closest confidantes, and appoint personal associates in whom they have implicit trust. President John Kennedy appointed his brother, Robert, who had had no legal experience and saw the job as a purely political one, and President Reagan appointed William French Smith, his personal attorney, and then, Edwin Meese, a long-time political confidante (Baker 1995, 49). Other presidents have placed priority on selecting skilled legal professionals, with less attention to political or personal relationships. Presidents Ford and Carter chose highly regarded individuals, Edward Levi and Griffin Bell, respectively, especially, in the wake of the Watergate scandal and its tainting of the attorney general's office by the involvement of former Nixon attorney general John Mitchell (Clayton 1992, 5).

The attorney general has a competitive relationship with the White House counsel, as both vie for the president's attention on legal issues, but the source of authority for the two offices is vastly different. The attorney general is a statutory office with clearly defined authority and is appointed under the constitutional process of presidential nomination and Senate confirmation. The White House counsel is a staff position, needing no Senate approval, and the services it provides to the president are more wide-ranging, less predictable, and include monitoring all of the president's actions. Moreover, the counsel's office is in the West Wing, steps away from the Oval Office, with all of the perks that come with physical proximity to the president, while the attorney general is blocks away at the Justice Department, managing a bureaucracy of 10,000 people. The attorney general's office may have the stronger claim to legitimacy and longevity within the federal government, but the counsel's office benefits from more informality and flexibility. As a personal aide to the president, political considerations may trump legal ones for the counsel, while the attorney general feels obliged to offer legal judgments based on precedent and with the acknowledgement that any *new* interpretations or policies emanating from the Department of Justice will establish executive branch precedents for the future.

Presidents usually signal with their selection whether they will have a closer relationship with the attorney general or a White House counsel. A president with a large judicial agenda will select an attorney general with whom he has long-term ties and personal knowledge of that person's abilities (Borrelli, Hult, and Kassop 2001, 570–71). Conversely, when a president chooses as White House counsel someone with whom he is well-acquainted, that suggests that the attorney general's influence on the president may be eclipsed by the White House aide. The selections of Philip Buchen, C. Boyden Gray, and Bernard Nussbaum as White House counsels exemplify this tendency in the Ford, Bush, and Clinton administrations, respectively (Baker 1995, 45).

THE OFFICE OF LEGAL COUNSEL AND THE OFFICE OF COUNSEL TO THE PRESIDENT

The Office of Legal Counsel in the Justice Department (OLC) and the Office of Counsel to the President in the White House are, perhaps, the president's most intimate connections (or, more accurately, *connectors*) to the law, broadly defined. Both have the primary responsibility of providing legal advice to the presidency as an institution, and, consequently, competition between these two offices can be intense. They share this overlapping function, although there are differences between them, as well.

Both offices originated in the Roosevelt administration. The OLC was established in 1935 under Attorney General Homer Cummings, with the responsibility of "assisting the Attorney General in his role as legal advisor to the President and the executive branch" (*Annual Report of the Attorney General*, 1936, quoted in Clayton 1992, 125). Additionally, the office received some of the functions that had previously been lodged in the solicitor general: the drafting of the opinions of the attorney general, offering legal advice to executive branch officials, and reviewing executive orders (Clayton 1992, 34).

The Office of Counsel to the President, known also as the White House counsel's office, began when President Franklin Roosevelt assigned the title of counsel to the president to Samuel Rosenman, whose functions were more as a speechwriter and policy adviser than a legal advisor. The office took on a greater legal role under John Dean in the 1970s. The real story of the counsel's office is its expansion into and oversight over every facet of presidential activity. It still retains its role as legal adviser to the president, but also carries out many routine tasks, such as vetting all presidential appointments, directing the judicial nominations process, reviewing legislative proposals and recommending signatures or vetoes, editing and clearing presidential speeches, writing executive orders, and determining the applicability of executive privilege. The office takes on heightened responsibility when scandals or crises strike. In sum, the counsel's office "monitors and coordinates the presidency's interactions with other players in and out of government" (Borrelli, Hult, and Kassop 2001, 561).

The source of tension between these two offices lies in the "advising" function. As an established office within an executive branch department, OLC maintains an "institutional memory" that the counsel's office lacks, because all counsel office files are removed after each president leaves office and are subject to the Presidential Records Act, and, ultimately, are deposited in presidential libraries. Thus, the established practice is for the counsel's office to go to OLC for authoritative legal decisions regarding the chief executive's powers before the counsel makes any recommendation to the president involving a legal question.

Both C. Boyden Gray, counsel for President George H. W. Bush, and Lloyd Cutler, counsel for both Presidents Carter and Clinton, recognized the service that OLC provides for the counsel's office. Cutler commented, "They [OLC staffers] are where . . . the President's counsel has to go to get an opinion on whether something may properly be done or not" (Borrelli, Hult, and Kassop 2001, 3).

Gray noted, "The White House doesn't go to court without the department. . . . We were free to ignore their advice but you knew so you did so at your peril because if you got into trouble you wouldn't have them there backing you up, you wouldn't have the institution backing you up. . . . When in doubt, ask them and they'll tell you where the landmines are" (Borrelli, Hult, and Kassop 2001, 571).

Still, the counsel's office approaches OLC warily and sees it as a "brake," as the one to tell them "no," although OLC has also developed a reputation for rather permissive interpretations of presidential power. One of its more infamous decisions upholding a generous view of power was the one in December 1986 by Charles Cooper, interpreting broadly the president's compliance with the "timely notification" requirement of the National Security Act, the provision that was at the heart of the Iran-Contra affair during the Reagan administration (Cooper 1986, 159).

There is, however, an inherent tension, if not rivalry, between the two offices: OLC has seen its function duplicated by the counsel's office, and considers the counsel's office driven more by politics than law, while the counsel's office may resent the theoretically "pure" opinions emanating from OLC that may give little attention to political realities. Charles Cooper, assistant attorney general in charge of OLC in the Reagan administration, explains that, for the White House counsel's office, "Preserving presidential prerogatives, protecting the office itself, was not viewed as that important. Far more important was getting a good political result and avoiding a bad one" (as quoted in Eastland 1992, 330 n. 24). But OLC has, also, at times, been very responsive to politics, especially during the Reagan administration, where Attorney General Edwin Meese filled OLC with young lawyers, such as Cooper, who were "New Right" activists who asserted aggressive positions on behalf of the president (Clayton 1992, 151). In a similar way, the counsel's office under Boyden Gray in the Bush administration developed a reputation as a legal shop with a single-minded focus on protecting the president's prerogatives and powers vis-à-vis Congress (Lund 1995, 218–19).

What has become increasingly clear is that, with the polarization of contemporary Washington, the White House counsel's office has found itself more embroiled in raw politics, as it was, for example, during the Clinton administration when it was in the center of numerous investigations, such as Vince Foster's suicide, the Travel Office firings, and improper contacts with Treasury Department officials regarding the Whitewater inquiry, in addition to the role that Counsel Charles Ruff played as the president's primary defense attorney in the Senate impeachment trial in February 1999. Responding to numerous congressional requests for information has also added to the weight of the demands on this office, especially during periods of divided government. Moreover, the heightened political stakes over judicial nominations, and the central role that the counsel's office has come to play in that process, has been and continues to be another arena where the office has made itself vulnerable to partisan politics. Finally, the counsel's office under Alberto Gonzales in the George W. Bush administration was blindsided after the terrorist attacks of September 11, 2001, when it found itself overwhelmed by the unprecedented issues that were now on its plate: this office, in conjunction with the attorney general, had central responsibility for generating all parts of the administration's policies in the war on terrorism, including new law enforcement practices, indefinite detention of aliens, military tribunals, and defending the president's emergency powers and war powers. Events have forced this office into the forefront of politics, far from where Louis Brownlow had contemplated White House staff should be, when he advocated in the Brownlow Committee report in 1936 that these aides to the president should have "a passion for anonymity."

THE PRESIDENT'S LEGACY IN THE COURTS

In the grand scheme of the system of separated governmental powers established by Madison in the Constitution, it was inevitable that clashes would eventually occur between the president and the courts. From as early as *Marbury v. Madison*, 5 U.S. 137 (1803), there was little question that the federal courts would have the power to review and determine the scope of the president's constitutional authority. That the courts would approach this delicate task with a sense of humility was understandable, though it may seem surprising that such deference has translated into so very few real conflicts between them. Moreover, the specific issues fall into a few defined categories: war and emergency powers, treaties, executive agreements, executive orders, executive privilege, presidential immunity from civil liability, appointment and removal power, and aspects of the veto power.

Those rare cases where presidential assertions of power *were* challenged and ultimately decided by the Supreme Court come from both the foreign and domestic affairs realms, although the win–loss record for the president tips greatly in his favor in the foreign affairs category, and especially in the twentieth century. Some early cases on war powers (*Bas v. Tingy*, 4 U.S. 37 [1800]; *Talbot v. Seeman*, 5 U.S. 1 [1801]; *Little v. Barreme*, 6 U.S. 170 [1804]) made clear the Court's understanding that the Framers gave the lion's share of this authority to Congress, and, similarly, it rebuked Lincoln in the postwar case of *Ex parte Milligan*, 71 U.S. 2 (1866), for his unilateral suspension of habeas corpus without Congress's participation during the Civil War and his use of military commissions where civil courts were functioning. But the result was different for Lincoln in *The Prize Cases*, 67 U.S. 635 (1863), where the Court upheld his power in 1863 in the midst of war to defend the nation against attack, and in the twentieth century foreign affairs powers cases where the Court ruled broadly in the president's favor in *U.S. v. Curtiss-Wright Export Corporation*, 299 U.S. 304 (1936), and *U.S. v. Belmont*, 301 U.S. 324 (1937). The ruling in *Goldwater v. Carter*, 444 U.S. 996 (1979), was far less expansive in its substance, and was reached only with Justice Powell's swing vote, but it provided a pragmatic, though not a constitutionally authoritative, victory for President Carter on the undefined issue of treaty termination.

The ledger registers mostly in the opposite direction when it comes to cases defining the parameters of the president's powers in the domestic sphere, but there are some qualifications even here that might give a president some reason for optimism under only slightly different circumstances. There are a few cases, however, that defy the norm among domestic powers rulings. Two that provide a president with expansive and conceivably unlimited power to act independently in the national interest are *In re Neagle*, 135 U.S. 1 (1890) and *In re Debs*, 158 U.S. 564 (1895), where the Court upheld presidential actions taken without any statutory authorization. Presidents also won big in *Myers v. U.S.*, 272 U.S. 52 (1926), in the Court's extending to them the unlimited right to remove executive officers performing executive duties, although this ruling was clarified and qualified subsequently in *Humphrey's Executor v. U.S.*, 295 U.S. 602 (1935). Presidential control over the appointment and removal of officers exercising executive functions was limited considerably in *Morrison v. Olson*, 487 U.S. 654 (1988), by a rather robust decision by Chief Justice William Rehnquist that upheld the constitutionality of the independent counsel provision in the Ethics in Government Act of 1978, permitting judicial appointment of independent counsels who exercise prosecutorial power and limiting their removal only for "good cause" by the Attorney General.

In practical political terms, this decision was a blow to presidents, since it permitted the continuation of the controversial practice of investigation of executive branch wrongdoing by special prosecutors, a practice that aimed uncomfortably at presidents and that could subject their actions to intense political scrutiny under a relatively light trigger. The criticism of this practice reached such a fever pitch after its use against President Clinton that the provision authorizing the appointment of independent counsels was allowed by Congress to lapse in 2000, despite the Court's validation of it twelve years earlier. Thus, presidents "won" in the public arena what they had been unable to secure in the judicial arena.

The cases most often cited as those that sharply rebuked presidents who tried to stretch their powers beyond acceptable constitutional limits are *Youngstown Sheet and Tube Company v. Sawyer*, 343 U.S. 579 (1952); *New York Times v. U.S.*, 403 U.S. 713 (1971); and *U.S. v. Nixon*, 418 U.S. 683 (1974). However, careful readings of the decisions in all three cases, and of the concurrences in *Youngstown* and *New York Times*, reveal much less certainty in the doctrinal outcome of these cases. All of them, in fact, suggest strongly that the Court issued narrow decisions here, striking down a president's claim in each instance to exclusive and absolute power—to seize private property in an emergency in *Youngstown*, to impose prior restraint of publication on government documents that might affect national security in *New York Times*, and to assert an unqualified right of confidentiality of all Oval Office communications in *Nixon*—but, again, in each instance, qualifying the decisions to reflect that, under certain circumstances, such presidential claims might survive judicial scrutiny. In all three cases, the *president* lost the battle, but the *presidency* may have won the war.

The final meeting between the president and the Court, though not a determination of presidential powers but an encounter that cemented the relationship between these two institutions more than any other in history had ever done, was the *Bush v. Gore* decision that ended the 2000 presidential election (see Gillman 2001). This case was an extraordinary anomaly that even wild dreams could never have predicted. But the simple fact is that it *did* happen, amid considerable speculation that the Court's decision was politically driven for a variety of unseemly motives that would benefit the five conservative justices who voted in the majority to halt the electoral recount in Florida and, in effect, to hand the election victory to George W. Bush.

CONCLUSIONS

Presidential intersection with the other branches in lawmaking can be viewed through many lenses: president as unilateral lawmaker, as negotiator in the legislative process, as administrator who selects officials who either perform independent responsibilities (judges) or implement his policies (executive officers), and as a player who is answerable to the courts for his own actions. What ties all these elements together is the recognition of just how much larger and more differentiated a role the president plays in lawmaking today than when the Framers conceptualized the office more than 200 years ago. The powers in Article II were few and most were undefined, although the potential for growth and expansive interpretation was certainly evident. But it took a few strong presidents at specific points in history to set precedents by pushing the boundaries of executive power a little further, and to increase the size, complexity, and available resources of the institution. Madison's concern for balance among the branches was countered by Alexander Hamilton's desire for "energy in the executive," and, while Madison may have emerged victorious on paper, Hamilton has prevailed in practice.

NOTE

1. Kelley (2002) classifies signing statements as constitutional, political, or rhetorical. Of the constitutional signing statements, Kelley determined that Reagan issued 71 (in eight years), G. H. W. Bush issued 146 (in four years), and Clinton issued 105 (in eight years).

5

Courts and Agencies

R. SHEP MELNICK

WE OFTEN THINK OF A LAWSUIT AS A CASE PITTING ONE PRIvate individual or group against another. Most of the important federal court decisions over the past half century, though, have come in cases that revolve around the authority, duties, and performance of public bureaucracies. Ever since *Brown v. Board of Education* in 1954, federal courts have been deeply involved in evaluating the practices of school systems throughout the nation. One of the most important consequences of the Warren Court's incorporation of the Bill of Rights into the Fourteenth Amendment was that federal judges became enmeshed in the difficult job of supervising the behavior of thousands of police officers and public prosecutors. Since the early 1970s, federal courts have restructured scores of state prisons, housing authorities, institutions for the mentally ill, and social service agencies. At about the same time federal judges intensified their oversight of old regulatory agencies such as the Federal Communications Commission (FCC) and the Atomic Energy Commission (AEC); started to give a "hard look" at the thousands of rules issued by new "social regulation" agencies such as the Environmental Protection Agency (EPA), the Occupational Safety and Health Administration (OSHA), and the Equal Economic Opportunity Commission (EEOC); demanded that development and natural resources bureaucracies such as the Corps of Engineers, the Federal Highway Administration, and the Forest Service pay more attention to environmental values; and scrutinized the procedures and policies of state and federal agencies that distribute health and welfare benefits. Today federal judges spend much of their time regulating the behavior of government bureaucrats, and virtually all government agencies must deal with courts on a regular basis.

These extensive judicial efforts to supervise, reform, and second-guess administrative agencies are the result of three major features of American politics since the New Deal. First and most obvious is the vast expansion of government programs and bureaucracy. Most of the programs listed above did not exist before the presidency of Franklin Roosevelt.

Government agencies now touch the lives of average citizens in ways unimaginable before 1932.

Second is the nationalization of American politics. Not only has the federal government expanded its power at the expense of state and local governments, but many differences among the states—the way they educate their children, care for the needy, or handle those accused of crimes—have become suspect. This has been particularly true for the often-peculiar practices of Southern states, which combine extremely low levels of public spending with a long history of racial discrimination. Judicial review has become a key mechanism for imposing national standards on state and local agencies.

Third is the revival of confidence in judges' ability to engage in extensive social engineering. After the constitutional revolution of 1937, many people expected the federal courts to play only a minor role in policymaking. The triumphant New Deal exalted executive power—presidential leadership combined with administrative expertise. It seemed quite possible that American courts would become as meek in their dealings with administrative agencies as the courts of Great Britain. But this was not to be. The traditional American distrust of bureaucracy and insistence upon having a "day in court" reasserted themselves. The more powerful public bureaucracy became, the more assertive the judicial response.

The sweeping nature of judicial oversight of public bureaucracy coupled with the amazing diversity of administrative agencies makes generalizing about court-agency relationships particularly perilous. After all, we are dealing not just with local, state, and national agencies but also with bodies charged with everything from teaching children to spying on foreign countries, from maintaining law and order to setting safety standards for nuclear power plants, from managing forests to establishing eligibility standards for food stamps, from building sewage treatment plants to treating mental illness. Not surprisingly, judges have handled some of these agencies well, and some poorly.

This chapter attempts to bring some order to this huge universe of controversies by examining three streams of cases: (1) federal court review of *federal* agencies; (2) federal court review of *state and local* agencies on the bases of judges' interpretation of the U.S. *Constitution*; and (3) federal court review of *state and local* agencies on the basis of judges' reading of *federal laws and regulations*.[1] These three streams have distinctive histories, rationales, and political characteristics.

STREAM ONE: THE MANY REFORMATIONS OF AMERICAN ADMINISTRATIVE LAW

In 1937, the decades-long battle between progressive reformers and conservative judges culminated in the triumph of the New Deal. The Supreme Court granted Congress the power to regulate virtually any form of commerce and to spend public monies for virtually any purpose. Henceforth, economic regulation and spending programs would survive judicial review if the Court could conceive of some plausible rationale for the policies in question—hardly a demanding standard.

Nearly as dramatic as this shift in constitutional law was the Court's new attitude toward administrative discretion and statutory interpretation. For years, indeed since the founding of the Republic, the Court had insisted that determining the meaning of federal laws was the job of federal judges, not administrators. This meant that judges would show little deference to the rules and interpretations issued by administrative agencies or even, in many cases, to their findings of fact. Protecting individual liberty and private property, judges maintained, required that administrative agencies be treated simply as another private litigant, granted no more authority and entitled to no more deference than an individual or corporation (Shapiro 1988, 36–37). To the extent judges recognized that agencies were part of government, they treated them not as essential components of a coequal branch of government but as subordinate, inferior courts—subordinate to the Supreme Court, and inferior to "real" courts.

To make regulatory agencies acceptable to federal judges, Congress often gave them the form of appellate courts. The Interstate Commerce Commission, the Federal Trade Commission, and many other "independent" regulatory commissions were multimember bodies that operated through adjudication, reviewing decisions made "on the record" by "hearing examiners." Yet this was seldom enough to placate judges hostile to administrative power. In the 1890s, for example, "the ICC suffered disastrous defeats at the hands of the Supreme Court" that "emasculated" its regulation of the railroads (Hoogenboom and Hoogenboom 1976, 35, 37). Institutional rivalry reinforced the dominant judicial understanding of the constitution of limited government.

In the years immediately following 1937, the Court's newfound deference to Congress was nearly matched by its deference to administrative agencies. Never again would the Court object to excessive delegation of legislative power to administrators. They tacitly conceded that running government programs required a substantial amount of administrative interpretation of broadly written federal statutes. They also recognized agency authority to issue general rules that have the full force of law.

Because both the jurisdiction of the federal courts and the authority of federal agencies are controlled by statutes enacted by Congress, part of the battle over judicial review of agency action took place in the legislative arena. To make a very long story short, the Roosevelt Administration wanted to give agencies broad rulemaking power subject to lenient judicial review, while Republicans, business, and their toadies in the American Bar Association wanted to require agencies to use time-consuming case-by-case adjudication subject to rigorous judicial review. After years of debate, Congress approved a compromise called the Administrative Procedures Act (APA) of 1946. The APA laid out two forms of agency action: "notice-and-comment rulemaking" in which agencies act like a legislature announcing general rules; and "formal adjudication" in which agencies act like a court deciding a particular case. A court must approve regulations produced by notice-and-comment rulemaking unless it finds them "arbitrary and capricious." Formal adjudication is subject to the somewhat more restrictive "substantial evidence" test. Congress retains authority not only to determine whether an agency must use rulemaking or adjudication, but also to invent various forms of hybrid rulemaking. Federal judges remained free to determine whether "arbitrary and capricious" means (1) a policy that is completely crazy, (2) a policy they do not particularly like, or (3) something in between (see Shapiro 1988, chap. 2).

If the APA largely codified existing practices, judicial review under it reflected the New Deal consensus. By the 1950s, federal regulators and regulated industries had reached a modus vivendi, which the courts generally accepted (Bernstein 1955). Regulation of labor–management relations by the National Labor Relations Board remained contentious, but even there the courts' role remained secondary (Shapiro 1964, chap. 3). Agencies tended to avoid ambitious rulemaking, favoring narrow adjudication and incremental change based on negotiations with representatives of the industries most directly affected. As long as agencies followed established procedures, did not expand their authority too rapidly, and avoided unethical practices, the courts were willing to go along.

Two sets of developments transformed administrative law in the late 1960s and early 1970s. The first and most obvious was the vast expansion of "social regulation"—health, safety, consumer, civil rights, and environmental regulation—enacted between 1964 and 1978. By any measure, the programs administered by the newly created EPA, OSHA, EEOC, National Highway Traffic Safety Administration, and Consumer Product Safety Commission dwarfed those of the New Deal. Their rules affected not just one or two industries, but the entire national economy. Compliance costs for a single rule could run into the billions of dollars. Some (but not all) of these statutes required administrators to balance regulatory benefits against economic costs. Some also contained "citizen suit" provisions allowing anyone, not just those directly affected by the regulation, to sue the agency for failing to perform a "non-discretionary duty." The laws of the 1970s established strict deadlines for agencies to issue hundreds of new rules. During this period, Congress also passed the National Environmental Policy Act (NEPA), which requires all federal agencies to document and to take into consideration the environmental consequences of their actions.

Never before had the stakes of regulation or judicial review of agency action been so high. Courts reviewing agency rules wanted to make sure that regulators had adequate justification for imposing billions of dollars of costs on consumers. They also insisted that the new "social regulation" agencies meet the many duties and deadlines that had been rapidly thrust upon them, and that older development-oriented agencies give greater weight to environmental protection. In the words of Judge Harold Leventhal, a principal author of what became known as the "hard look" doctrine of judicial review,

> The rule of administrative law, as applied to the congressional mandate for a clean environment, ensures that mission-oriented agencies . . . will take due cognizance of environmental matters. It ensures at the same time that environmental protection agencies will take into account the congressional mandate that environmental concerns be reconciled with other social and economic objectives of our society. (Leventhal 1974, 555)

With so much at stake, the judiciary became the governor of the governors, preventing them from going too fast or too slow, requiring them to listen to a variety of voices and to give "adequate consideration" to all "relevant factors." Given the administrative and technical complexity of the new regulation and the large number of groups engaged in these controversies, this was no easy task.

Congress encouraged the courts to conduct this augmented oversight. Those members of Congress and lobbyists who worried about the cost of regulation saw judicial review as a mechanism for blocking or at least braking agency action. Environmentalists and their congressional allies often saw judicial review as a way to prevent Republicans in the White House from subverting legislative intent, which they equated with a demand for aggressive regulation. For decades, program advocates on congressional committees (usually, but not always, Democrats) battled with the White House and with economists and political executives within the agencies. Many of these conflicts ended up in court (see Melnick 1999b, 167–74).

A second and equally important cause of the "Reformation of American Administrative Law"[2] during the late 1960s and early 1970s was a profound shift in judges' understanding of public bureaucracy and government regulation. During the New Deal, attacks on regulation and bureaucracy came primarily from business and defenders of laissez-faire economics. They maintained that unless courts constantly looked over their shoulders, regulatory bureaucracies would run roughshod over private property and individual liberty, creating massive inefficiencies along the way. Three decades later, the attack on regulation and bureaucracy came primarily from the left; government agencies, advocates of stringent regulation argued, tend to be too slow and too wedded to the status quo. Rather than threatening the hegemony of business, government regulators all too often served business interests by stabilizing and dividing up markets. In the past, regulators had failed to serve the public interest because they had been "captured" by the private interests they dealt with day after day. These timid bureaucrats resisted innovation, ignored the broader consequences of their policies, and refused to listen to the many new "public interest" groups that suddenly appeared in the second half of the 1960s. Many of these groups turned to the courts to "open up" agency deliberations to a new set of players, new issues, and new values (Stewart 1975, 1713–15; Shapiro 1988, 62–73; Melnick 1983, 9–13).

Although the arguments of these new "public-interest" litigants resonated with the egalitarianism of the Warren Court, most of the "reformation" of administrative law was the work of the lower federal courts, especially the D.C. Circuit, which by statute hears an unusually large number of important administrative law cases. One of the first signs of change came in a case challenging a decision by the Federal Power Commission (FPC) to approve a large hydroelectric project on the Hudson River. The Second Circuit ruled that the FPC could not limit its analysis to energy issues; it had to demonstrate that it had given "adequate consideration" to countervailing values, especially environmental protection. This, in turn, required the FPC to allow environmental groups to intervene in licensing proceedings (*Scenic Hudson Preservation Conference v. FPC*, 354 F.2d 608 [2d Circuit, 1965]). The next year the D.C. Circuit ruled that a national church group could speak on behalf of the potential listeners reached by a radio station in Jackson, Mississippi. The Court warned that "unless the listeners—the broadcast consumers—can be heard, there may be no one to bring programming deficiencies or offensive overcommercialization to the attention of the [FCC] Commissioners in an effective manner." By limiting participation in licensing hearings to broadcasters, the FCC had "elected to post the Wolf to guard the Sheep" (*Office of Communications, United Church of Christ v. FCC*, 359 F.2d 994, at 1004-5 and 1008 [D.C. Circuit, 1966]). The author of this opinion was future Supreme Court chief justice Warren Burger.

The manifesto of the "new administrative law" appeared in a 1971 D.C. Circuit decision ordering the fledgling EPA to regulate the pesticide DDT. This is fitting because publication of Rachel Carson's famous article on the dangers of DDT is widely viewed as the beginning of the modern environmental movement. In the words of Judge David Bazelon,

> We stand on the threshold of a new era in the history of the long and fruitful collaboration of administrative agencies and reviewing courts. For many years, courts have treated administrative policy decisions with great deference, confining judicial attention primarily to matters of procedure. On

matters of substance, the courts regularly upheld agency action, with a nod in the direction of the "substantial evidence" test, and a bow to the mysteries of administrative expertise. . . . Gradually, however, that power has come into more frequent use, and with it, the requirement that administrators articulate the factors on which they base their decisions. Strict adherence to that requirement is especially important now that the character of administrative litigation is changing. . . . [C]ourts are increasingly asked to review administrative action that touches on fundamental personal interests in life, health, and liberty. These interests have always had a special claim to judicial protection, in comparison with the economic interests at stake in ratemaking or licensing proceedings. (*EDF v. Ruckelshaus*, 439 F.2d 584, at 597–98 [D.C. Circuit, 1971]; internal footnotes omitted)

Bazelon's stirring rhetoric disguised the fact that he had his history backwards: in the past the economic interests of regulated industries had "always had a special claim to judicial protection"; protecting the health of the public was the special job of expert agencies. In the bad old days judges worried about administrative overzealousness. Now they worried about bureaucratic timidity and capture. It was indeed a "new era."

The first phase of the "reformation" of administrative law focused on participation. Courts would ensure "adequate consideration" of "all relevant factors" by opening up the decisionmaking process to a wider array of interest groups. In the words of Richard Stewart,

Faced with the seemingly intractable problem of agency discretion, courts have changed the focus of judicial review . . . so that its dominant purpose is no longer the prevention of unauthorized intrusions on private autonomy, but the assurance of fair representation for all affected interests in the exercise of the legislative power delegated to agencies. . . . If agencies were to function as a forum for all interests affected by agency decisionmaking, bargaining leading to compromises generally acceptable to all might result, thus replicating the process of legislation. (Stewart 1975, 1712)

The courts not only broadened participation rights but also required agencies to respond fully to all reasonable criticisms of its proposals (Stewart 1975, 1717–60; Shapiro 1988, 44–49).

In the second phase, the courts slowly and subtly transformed the demand for greater pluralism into a demand for what Shapiro has called "synopticism"—"a process that gathers all the facts, considers all alternatives and all the possible consequences of each, and chooses those policies with the highest probability of achieving agreed goals at least cost" (Shapiro 1988, 15). Agencies need to do more than listen to everyone; they need to come up with the most rational, most comprehensive answer. This in turn requires judges to divine exactly what it is that Congress expects the agency to do. Judge Leventhal explained that "the courts are in a kind of partnership for the purpose of effectuating the *legislative* mandates" (*Portland Cement Association v. Ruckelshaus*, 486 F. 2d 375, at 394 [D.C. Circuit, 1973]). His colleague on the D.C. Circuit, Skelly Wright, added, "our duty, in short, is to see that the legislative purposes heralded in the halls of Congress are not lost in the vast halls of the federal bureaucracy" (*Calvert Cliffs Coordinating Committee v. AEC*, 449 F.2d 1109, at 1111 [D.C. Circuit, 1971]). Judges took on the task of reading between the lines of ambiguous legislation to discover a standard for establishing how a "rational" administrator would act. Frequently they resolved controversies by emphasizing that the central purpose of a newly minted statute was to protect public health and the environment. These underlying goals trumped all other concerns (see, e.g., the cases discussed in Melnick 1983, 76–80, 129–35, 157–62, 261–69).

One consequence of these new judicial demands was that the rulemaking process, once short and simple, became extremely complex and protracted. The courts told agencies to consider all "relevant" evidence, respond to all "significant" comments, and weigh all "reasonable" alternatives without giving them much guidance on what "relevant," "significant," and "reasonable" mean. Because agencies do not like losing big court cases, they reacted defensively, accumulating more and more information, responding to all comments, and covering all their bets. As a result, Pierce reports, "The time to make policy through rulemaking has been stretched to nearly a decade" (Pierce 1988, 302; see also Melnick 1992). Little wonder that agencies looked for ways to avoid the rulemaking quagmire. Some decided it would be easier to use adjudication to establish agency policy. Others set policy through interpretive rulings, internal enforcement policies, and recall orders (Mashaw and Harfst 1991, chaps. 5, 8; Pierce 1991).

A second consequence was that agencies were subject to a plethora of "action-forcing" suits based on the multiple demands and deadlines included in the new regulatory statutes. According to a 1985 study, the EPA alone was subject to 328 statutory deadlines. Among the other findings of this report were the following:

1. Very few statutory deadlines (14 percent) have been met. . . .
2. Congress imposes more deadlines on EPA than it can possibly meet. . . .
3. Court-ordered deadlines almost always command top management attention at EPA. . . .
4. The multiplicity of deadlines reduces EPA's ability to assign priority to anything not subject to a deadline. (Environmental Law Institute and Environmental and Energy Study Institute 1985, 11, ii, iii, v, iv; see also Rabkin 1989)

In effect, this form of policymaking transfers responsibility for setting agency priorities from top administrators to interest groups, some of which use attorneys' fees won in relatively easy "action-forcing" cases to cross-subsidize other activities.

A third consequence was that the White House, the Office of Management and Budget, and political executives in the departments and agencies lost power to congressional committees and to technical personnel within the agencies. In searching for "congressional intent," courts paid much more attention to the statements and reports of the congressional sponsors, subcommittee leaders, and committee staff who shaped the legislation than to the views of the president who signed it. Agency leaders faced strong incentives to hide political judgments behind mountains of technical data and analysis, which strengthened the bargaining position of technical personnel (and lawyers) within the bureaucracy. After all, if policymaking is to be synoptic, then the outcome cannot depend on the accident of who won the last presidential election (Shapiro 1988, chap. 5; Melnick 1985, 653).

A fourth consequence was judicial exhaustion. The rulemaking record grew longer and longer, far beyond any judge's ability to review in its entirety. Statutes, committee reports, and floor statements grew as well, with all participants in the legislative process giving the courts an earful about their "intent." Most major rules were challenged by both industry—which claimed they were too stringent—and public interest groups—who claimed they were too lenient. The issues before the court were often of mind-numbing complexity.[3] Not infrequently, the result was stalemate.

Despite the importance of these developments, the Supreme Court played a peripheral role in administrative law during most of the 1960s and 1970s. As the then–law professor Antonin Scalia put it, "As a practical matter, the D.C. Circuit is something of a resident manager, and the Supreme Court an absentee landlord" in administrative law (Scalia 1978, 371). But the high court was obviously uneasy with what it saw going on below. In a 1978 opinion, it reprimanded the D.C. Circuit for imposing on the Nuclear Regulatory Commission procedural requirements that the Supreme Court described as "judicial intervention run riot" and "border[ing] on the Kafkaesque" (*Vermont Yankee Nuclear Power Corp. v. NRDC*, 435 U.S. 519, at 557 [1978]). But the D.C Circuit quickly found new legal justifications for its previous practices (see Pierce 1989).

In 1984, the Supreme Court took a more significant step. In *Chevron v. NRDC*, 467 U.S. 837 (1984), the Court instructed the lower courts to show greater deference to administrators' interpretations of the statutes they are charged with implementing:

> If the statute is silent or ambiguous with respect to the specific issue, the question for the court is whether the agency's answer is based on a *permissible* construction of the statute. . . . [A] court may not substitute its own construction of a statutory provision for a reasonable interpretation made by the administrator of an agency. (467 U.S. 843–44)

Studies of lower court response to *Chevron* indicate that deference increased for a few years, but then returned nearly to pre-*Chevron* levels (Schuck and Elliott 1990; Avila 2000). Part of the problem is that the Supreme Court has not been giving the lower courts consistent signals. On a number of occasions the Court has departed from *Chevron* without explaining why.[4] But the problem of hierarchical control goes much deeper than this: almost all general rules about judicial review leave lower courts with substantial discretion to review the adequacy of an agency's evidence and its interpretation of innumerable statutory phrases.

Whether judges appointed by Republican presidents vote differently in administrative law case than judges appointed by Democratic presidents is a topic of considerable debate. On the one hand, most administrative law decisions, even in the contentious D.C. Circuit, are unanimous. On the other hand, in a significant number of highly contentious cases, judges appointed by Democrats tend to be more sympathetic to challenges brought by "public-interest" groups, and Republicans tend to be more sympathetic to challenges brought by industry (Revesz 1997; Cross and Tiller 1998; Edwards 1998; Avila 2000). This is not surprising given the fact that many of these cases in the end come down to how much trust one has in the agency before the court, how much damage one thinks the agency might do to the economy, and how inclined one is to believe that existing business practices threaten public health and safety.

Administrative law doctrine tends to focus more on regulatory programs than on spending programs. But federal agencies that distribute such entitlements as Social Security benefits, unemployment compensation, food stamps, and health care also experienced a substantial increase in judicial scrutiny starting in the late 1960s and early 1970s. The federal courts held that those deprived of the so-called new property have a constitutional right to a "due process" hearing.[5] More important, the courts became much more willing to second-guess agencies' determination of what sorts of benefits have been promised to citizens by particular entitlement statutes (see Melnick 1994, chaps. 3, 5, 8, 10). The most dramatic example of this was the multiyear battle between the federal courts and the Reagan administration over eligibility for disability benefits (see Derthick 1990, chap. 7).

The administrative law decisions discussed in this section not only are far-reaching in their policy significance, but also play a major role in structuring relationships among the three branches of government. Yet few of them would be included in courses or books on "constitutional law." The courts try to avoid overt constitutional language when adjusting relations among the branches of the federal government. But when federal judges took on the huge task of reforming state and local bureaucracies, the constitutional dimension of the undertaking was evident to all.

STREAM TWO: CONSTITUTIONAL DUTIES

From shortly before the turn of the century until 1937, the federal courts sporadically engaged in a form of judicial activism commonly known as "Lochnerism."[6] Lochnerism placed multiple restrictions on the role of government. The Supreme Court adopted a definition of "interstate commerce" that left a considerable portion of the national economy outside the reach of Congress. Its reading of the due process, contract, and takings clauses limited the regulatory power of both the state and national governments. Somewhat haphazardly it distributed "Government Keep Out" and "No Public Trespassing" signs throughout the policy landscape.

The activism that began with *Brown v. Board of Education* in 1954 produced more complicated judicial orders. These commands took the form, "If and when you engage in governmental activity X, you must do it in the following way." For example, if a state or local government provides public education, it must do so in a racially nondiscriminatory fashion. When government seeks to imprison someone for committing a crime, it must follow judicially mandated rules of evidence. If it confines a mentally ill person to a state institution, it must abide by standards of care and habilitation laid out by the court. The Supreme Court has never unequivocally said that states must provide education, care for the mentally ill, or even law enforcement. It does not need to; with very rare exceptions, no state would ever consider withdrawing from these areas. As a result, the federal courts are frequently in the business of telling state and local agencies how and to whom they must provide a variety of goods, services, and protections.

A fundamental yet little noted feature of the most controversial decisions of the Warren Court is that they sought to change the behavior of the two largest and most decentralized sets of public bureaucracies in America: schools and police. Schools and police are decentralized not just in the sense that they tend to be locally run and financed but also in the sense that they are peculiarly resistant to centralized administrative direction. It is hard for managers either to measure the output of the patrolman and the classroom teacher, or to monitor in any meaningful way the activities in which they engage. James Q. Wilson has called these "coping" organizations—managers cannot hope to solve the core compliance problem, only cope with it as best they can (Wilson 1989, 168–71). This meant that the courts were engaged in a high-visibility, high-stakes effort to lay down general rules for those bureaucracies that are particularly resistant to control through rules.

As a consequence, judges have delved deeper and deeper into these organizations in a desperate effort to stop behavior they consider unacceptable. (It would go too far to say "to achieve their goals," because courts are seldom clear about what they want schools and police forces to do. They are much clearer about what they want them to avoid doing.) In desegregation cases, judges started with issues of school assignment. Before long, they were dealing with the hiring and placement of teachers, tracking and testing, language training, discipline, sports facilities, and, ultimately, the content of the curriculum. Judges selected sites for new schools and imposed taxes to pay for them. For example, in Kansas City, Missouri, a federal district court judge ordered the construction of seventeen new schools—including several state-of-the-art magnet schools—and major renovation of fifty-five others. The cost of the changes mandated by the court exceeded a billion and a half dollars (Wise and O'Leary 2003, 177–91). Some judges, justifiably worried about white flight, tried to desegregate public housing projects within the school district.

These extensive desegregation efforts produced innovative "structural injunctions," complex, evolving, negotiated judicial orders that "establish a long, continuing relationship between the parties and the tribunal" (Fiss 1972, 1). A prominent feature of these injunctions is their longevity: court supervision frequently persists for decades. Some desegregation cases begun in the 1960s and 1970s have yet to be terminated. Year after year the special masters and monitoring committees appointed by the court worked with plaintiff attorneys and school officials to establish educational policies and priorities (see, e.g., Sandler and Shoenbrod 2003, chap. 3). Before long, structural injunctions were being used to reform other state institutions—often by the same judge who was engaged in the desegregation of public schools.[7]

Judicial efforts to control the behavior of state and local police have relied heavily on a key element of judicial leverage: finding that the Fourteenth Amendment incorporates the Fourth and Fifth Amendments, federal judges have restricted the type of evidence police and prosecutors can use in state as well as federal court. Wielding the exclusionary rule, though, does not give judges control over those police practices that do not ordinarily culminate in a criminal prosecution. So judges have searched for other mechanisms for controlling police discretion. Starting in 1961 with *Monroe v. Pape*, the Supreme Court has allowed citizens alleging misconduct to file suit for damages in federal court against police departments.[8] In 1971, the Court authorized similar suits against federal law enforcement officials (*Bivens v. Six Unknown Agents of the Federal Narcotics Bureau*, 403 U.S. 388 [1971]).

Such tort suits give courts the opportunity to define acceptable official behavior and create incentives for compliance. In a few instances federal courts have also issued injunctions against city police departments, prohibiting them from engaging in specific practices.[9] The extent to which such remedies have actually changed police behavior for the better is, of course, the subject of considerable debate. Neither judges nor anyone else can effectively monitor what thousands of patrolman are doing on their beat each day.

In the early 1970s, a number of federal district court judges took on the difficult task of reforming two other types of public institutions: facilities for the mentally ill and retarded, and prisons. The reform effort began in the South, where the condition of those confined to these "total institutions" were particularly shocking. For state mental hospitals and facilities for the developmentally disabled, the seminal case was Judge Frank Johnson's opinion in *Wyatt v. Stickney*.[10] For prisons, the breakthrough came with Judge J. Smith Henley's decisions in Arkansas.[11] Other federal district court judges quickly followed suit. Six years after *Wyatt*, ten other states were operating under similar court orders (Frug 1978, 718 n. 15). By 1995, prisons in forty-one states plus the District of Columbia, Puerto Rico, and the Virgin Islands "had at one time or another been under comprehensive court orders, as had the entire correctional system of at least ten states" (Feeley and Rubin 1998, 13; see also DiIulio 1987, 73; 1990a).

In 2000, more than thirty state child welfare agencies were operating under court order (Sandler and Shoenbrod 2003, 122). The Supreme Court did little to initiate or even encourage such intervention. Its first decision on mental health facilities did not come until 1982, when it announced a relatively deferential standard for evaluating state practices (*Youngberg v. Romeo*, 457 U.S. 307 [1982]). In prison cases also, the Supreme Court urged district court judges to exercise caution and restraint.[12]

As was the case with school desegregation, judges in institutional reform cases issued detailed structural injunctions that lasted for years, even decades, and required constant modification. Judge Johnson's orders in *Wyatt v. Stickney*, for example, included the following:

- The patient must have bathroom privileges every hour and must be bathed every 12 hours. . . .There will be one toilet provided for each eight patients and one lavatory for every six patients.
- The number of patients in a multi-patient room shall not exceed six persons. There shall be allocated a minimum of 80 square feet of floor space per patient in a multi-patient room. . . . Single rooms must have a minimum of 100 square feet of floor space. The area of day rooms must be at least 40 square feet per patient, for dining rooms 10 square feet per patient.
- Room temperature must remain between 83 and 68 degrees. Hot tap water must be 110 degrees. (344 F.Supp. 373, at 380–82)

To monitor compliance, Judge Johnson appointed a Human Rights Committee for each institution. When Alabama failed to meet court deadlines, he put the facilities into receivership, where they remained for years.[13] This was a pattern that recurred in state after state.

Another key feature of these institutional reform cases is that judges frequently start off with broad support from professional groups, federal agencies, and even the state administrators being sued. Judge Johnson relied on the advice of the Department of Justice, the Department of Health, Education, and Welfare, the Food and Drug Administration, the Public Health Service, and professional groups such as the American Psychological Association and the Ortho-Psychiatric Association to write his implementation orders. The defendant in *Wyatt*, the marvelously named

Dr. Stonewall Stickney, agreed to 90 percent of the standards established by the court (Cooper 1988, 182). Usually, the administrators of these facilities have been battling with governors and state legislatures for years to increase funding and staffing levels. They are all too well aware of their institutions' deficiencies, and they recognize that a court order can help them get the money they so desperately need. Administrators who come to office after the initial round of litigation are particularly likely to "embrac[e] the court and its orders, using the court as justification for the reforms the new chief executive officer wants to bring about on his or her own initiative" (Wood 1990, 58).

Although "collusion" might be too strong a word to describe relations between the nominal plaintiffs and defendants, the real political struggle is almost always that between the plaintiffs and defendants on the one side and those who control the state's purse strings on the other. In their study of the Kansas City, Missouri, School District (KCMSD) desegregation case, Wise and O'Leary found that

> hundreds of small bureaucracies have formed around the issues of the case, from the purchasing of textbooks to infrastructure development. These networks of bureaucracies are not about to willingly fade away. In the end, with the KCMSD's dependence on court-driven funding has come a dependence on continued court supervision. The court has become a convenient scapegoat and a shield keeping the KCMSD from accepting responsibility. (Wise and O'Leary 2003, 187)

While judges initially intervene in order to bring about major change, over the years they inevitably become protectors of the bureaucratic status quo.

At the same time, administrators are likely to become frustrated and resentful at the resulting contraction of bureaucratic autonomy. They particularly object to what they see as the court's tendency to establish unrealistic guidelines for staff levels. Judge Johnson established staffing ratios for psychiatrists, nurses, aides, clerks, psychologists, social workers, cooks, repairmen, housekeepers, and even messengers. Administrators never came close to filling all these positions. Tension also frequently develops between advocates on court-appointed monitory committees, who wish to publicize the institution's shortcomings, and administrators, who are concerned about protecting agency morale and their own reputations. Moreover, the accumulation of court orders and consent decrees reduces the ability of incoming mayors and governors to set new priorities or to institute innovative programs (Sandler and Shoenbrod 2003, 67).

Court orders frequently include elaborate "due process" requirements to structure relations between lower level bureaucrats and clients. For the disabled, this has meant individualized treatment plans. While this can be time consuming, it is very much in tune with the professional norms of physicians, psychologists, teachers, and other social service professionals. In prisons, due process has meant an increase in the number of rules prison officials must follow, enhanced opportunities for appeal, and, as a result, significantly less autonomy for the guards who are in close daily contact with inmates. Of all the "street level bureaucrats" affected by court orders, prison guards—who spend their working hours in an unusually dangerous environment—are particularly resistant to (and angry about) judicial constraints on administrative discretion (DiIulio 1990b).

Whether or not judges have improved conditions in these state institutions is the subject of considerable debate (see the essays in DiIulio 1990a). The courts' greatest success has come in closing or sharply reducing the size of institutions for the mentally ill and retarded. Here the courts played a supporting role in the wider movement toward deinstitutionalization. Today, there is a broad political and professional consensus that only those with the most severe problems are best cared for in large, impersonal institutions. The courts helped dramatize the horrors of the "warehousing" of thousands and thousands of helpless people. Ironically, though, it is much harder for either public administrators or judges to monitor the care and treatment of those who have been deinstitutionalized. This is just the tip of a larger paradox: Judges frequently demand individualized treatment for agencies' clients. The more individualized the treatment, though, the more difficult it becomes for judges to control the behavior of street-level bureaucrats. Once judges take on the task of reforming complex bureaucratic institutions, they inevitably confront the same dilemmas that administrators face on a daily basis.

STREAM THREE: THE MANDATE STATE

Four years after *Wyatt v. Stickney*, Congress passed the Education for All Handicapped Children Act. All children with disabilities are now entitled by federal law to a "free appropriate education" as spelled out in an "individualized education program" (IEP) composed by teachers and administrators in consultation with parents. When parents disagree with an IEP, they can appeal first to an independent hearing officer and then to a federal judge. Federal funding provides less than 10 percent of the cost of this mandate; state and local governments must raise the remaining 90 percent. In 1975, Congress also passed the Developmentally Disabled Assistance and Bill of Rights Act, which included lengthy guidelines for the care and treatment of those confined to state institutions. In 1980, Congress enacted the Civil Rights of Institutionalized Persons Act, which authorized the Department of Justice to file suit against state institutions that violate the constitutional rights of patients. In short, Congress was not only actively encouraging suits such as *Wyatt v. Stickney* but was also providing judges with statutory standards to impose on state and local governments. Advocates for the disabled praised Congress for protecting human rights. State and local officials complained about a steady stream of "unfunded mandates."

Today, court orders against state and local agencies are much more likely to be based on statutory rather than constitutional claims. This reflects Congress's willingness to impose mandates on subnational governments and the lower courts' willingness to read these mandates broadly. Ironically, while state and local officials have often welcomed federal legislation as an alternative to the uncertainty of litigation, the passage of federal law has usually increased opportunities for judicial review of their activities (Melnick 1994, chap. 8). Few state or local agencies are exempt from some form of oversight by federal courts.

No federal mandate has been more important than Title VI of the Civil Rights Act of 1964. Title VI requires federal agencies to terminate funding to those who engage in racial discrimination. Title VI was originally viewed as a quick and effective administrative *alternative* to litigation: agencies could simply stop the flow of federal money rather than commence a lengthy court battle. Within a few years, though, Title VI became an important *source* of civil rights litigation. Federal courts declared that the rules issued by administrators under Title VI could be enforced through "private rights of action," that is, court suits filed by private citizens. As a result, federal administrators could write elaborate regulations defining discrimination but avoid the politically dangerous task of cutting off federal funds for state and local programs. Court enforcement usually meant injunctions specifying the steps subnational governments must take to eliminate discriminatory practices rather than termination of federal funding.

Title VI was thus transformed from an administrative enforcement mechanism for guaranteeing equal protection of the law into a judicial mechanism for enforcing federal administrative rules defining a wide variety of forms of prohibited discrimination. Because it is a rare state or local agency that does not receive some sort of federal funding, the reach of the federal courts' new authority was enormous.

What Hugh Davis Graham has called "the cloning of Title VI" soon followed (Graham 1999, 197–99). Congress, federal agencies, and federal courts forbade recipients of federal funds from discriminating on the basis of gender, disability, age, or language. In deciding the thousands of cases brought against state and local agencies, the courts spelled out the standards and procedures administrators must adopt in order to avoid judicial reprimands and large damage awards. For example, in a 1998 case involving Title IX of the Education Amendments of 1972, the Supreme Court established what the majority considered "a sensible remedial scheme" for dealing with sexual harassment of public school students by teachers (*Gebser v. Lago Vista Independent School District*, 524 U.S. 274 [1998]).

Because these mandate cases usually involve judicial enforcement of regulations issued by federal administrators, they combined the "new administrative law" doctrines described in the first section of this chapter with the effort to set national standards for the operation of state and local bureaucracies. A graphic illustration of this is the long-running civil rights case of *Adams v. Richardson*, 358 F.Supp. 97 (D.D.C. 1973). In 1973, Judge John Pratt, a federal district court judge in the District of Columbia, ruled that the federal Office of Civil Rights had failed to enforce Title VI with sufficient zeal. The original plaintiffs sought to increase efforts by the Nixon administration to desegregate southern schools. Litigants representing women's groups, Hispanic groups, and the disabled later joined the suit to demand more attention for their causes. Judge Pratt essentially placed the Office of Civil Rights in receivership, specifying how it was to divide up and utilize its enforcement resources. The federal court was thus attempting to restructure a federal agency whose job it was to restructure a large number of state and local agencies. Nearly two decade later, the *Adams* case was still going strong (see also Rabkin 1989; Halpern 1995).

Title VI and Title IX are often referred to as "cross-cutting" requirements. That is, they apply to a wide variety of state and local programs receiving federal funds. Another way federal courts supervise state and local agencies is by interpreting and enforcing the "strings" attached to individual spending programs. When Congress first started providing federal funding for such things as highway construction and public assistance, it imposed only a few restrictions on the use of federal money. Enforcement of these "strings" was lax since federal administrators hesitated to terminate funding for programs they believed were in the public interest.

Over time, the number and specificity of federal strings grew and grew. In the late 1960s the federal courts announced that they, too, had authority to enforce these statutory requirements. But they would not use the counterproductive funding cutoff. Rather, they would issue injunctions to state and local officials ordering them to comply with federal rules (Melnick 1994, 48–51, 245–49). Federal administrators frequently concluded that this was a wonderful idea, and they churned out hundreds of pages of interpretations of federal law for the courts to apply. The federal courts thus became deeply involved in the details of programs run by state welfare offices, social service departments, and natural resources agencies (see Melnick 1994; Kagan 2001, chaps. 8, 10).

In recent years, the Supreme Court has tried to reduce these forms of federal court oversight of state and local governments. It has been unwilling to find private rights of action in federal spending and civil rights laws unless Congress has made its intent explicit.[14] It has refused to enforce regulations issued by the Department of Justice under Title VI that go beyond the clear commands of the statute itself (*Alexander v. Sandoval*, 532 U.S. 275 [2001]). It has narrowed the conditions in which it will issue systemwide injunctions against state agencies (*Blessing v. Freestone*, 520 U.S. 329 [1997]). The extent to which these rules will result in a substantial decline in court supervision of state and local agencies depends both on the lower courts' willingness to follow the Supreme Court's lead and Congress's reaction to the new rules established by the judiciary.

In the cases cited in the previous paragraph, the Supreme Court established standards for lower courts in their oversight of federal agencies, which regulate state and local agencies, which in turn establish standards for the behavior of private individuals. Sound pretty convoluted? It is. Given the complexity of these chains of regulation and the immense variation among agencies and programs, it is nearly impossible to offer useful generalizations about "court–agency relations." What should be clear, though, is that this is a very strange way to run a government. It is highly unlikely that anyone who set out to design the machinery of government would ever come up with something that looks like this.

How, then, did we end up here? The best answer, I think, is that during the past fifty years public expectations of government have grown enormously, but the traditional American distrust of government and bureaucracy has become even more pronounced. On the one hand, we demand that the federal government protect the environment, expand government financed and mandated health care, maintain Social Security, promote an educational system that "leaves no child behind," ensure "homeland security," guarantee civil rights, keep inflation levels low and employment levels high, and fight poverty, crime, drug use, teen pregnancy, HIV/AIDS, and child pornography. On the other hand, most citizens believe the federal government "can't be trusted to do what is right most of the time" and even that "the federal government has become so large and powerful that it poses a threat to the rights and freedoms of ordinary citizens" (Melnick 1999a, 300–301). Trust in government continues to sink, yet demand for government services and protections continues to grow.

The result is the layer upon layer of review and litigation described in this chapter. We demand programs that require extensive bureaucracy. We distrust centralized bureaucracy, so we rely heavily on state and local agencies. But we expect these agencies to respect the basic rights of Americans and to meet minimum national standards. So we subject these agencies to substantial regulation by federal agencies. Because we do not trust these federal agencies either, we demand judicial oversight. But this often allows a single federal district court judge to try his hand at reconstructing complex institutions, which usually involves remaking the budgetary priorities of cities and states. Few people seem to like this either. So we grouse about excessive litigiousness and the fees collected by trial attorneys without doing anything serious to reduce adversarial legalism (Kagan 2001; Burke 2002). We dream of a helpful, equitable government without an intrusive, impersonal bureaucracy. But, alas, it is only a dream. When we wake up, we start suing.

NOTES

1. State courts engage in many of the forms of judicial review examined in this chapter. Most states have statutes similar to the Administrative Procedures Act, and state constitutions often contain detailed criteria for the provision of education, welfare, and social services. It would be interesting to compare state and federal courts' oversight of administrative agencies. But this is beyond the scope of this chapter or the competence of its author.
2. The phrase comes from the title of Stewart's (1975) article, which remains the most comprehensive examination of the changes in legal doctrine during this period.
3. A good example is the *Alabama Power* case described in Melnick 1983, 103–10. The initial litigation on this topic was relatively simple—or at least it seemed so at the time.
4. Leading examples include *Motor Vehicle Mfg. Association v. State Farm Mutual Auto Insurance Co.*, 463 U.S. 29 (1983); *INS v. Cardozo-Fonseca*, 480 U.S. 421 (1987); and *K-Mart v. Cartier*, 486 U.S. 281 (1988). See also Merrill 1992. In two recent cases, *Christensen v. Harris County*, 529 U.S. 576 (2000), and *United States v. Mead Corp.*, 533 U.S. 218 (2001), the Court seems to have backed away from Chevron in a more sustained manner.
5. *Goldberg v. Kelly*, 397 U.S. 254 (1970). The structure and timing of the hearing depend on the nature of the benefit. See, e.g., *Mathews v. Eldridge*, 425 U.S. 319 (1976). The term "new property" comes from an influential article by Reich (1964).
6. The name comes from the Supreme Court's decision in *Lochner v. New York*, 198 U.S. 45 (1905), in which it ruled that a state law restricting the number of hours bakers could work violated the workers' right to contract protected by the Fourteenth Amendment.
7. The leading example is Judge Frank Johnson of Alabama, who was simultaneously engaged in desegregating the schools of Montgomery, reforming state institutions for the mentally ill and retarded (see below), and restructuring Alabama state welfare department.
8. *Monroe v. Pape*, 365 US 167 (1961). The ruling was originally limited to state officials. It was extended to local officials in *Monnell v. New York City Department of Social Services*, 436 U.S. 658 (1978).
9. Cooper (1988) provides a detailed examination of litigation involving the Philadelphia police department in chapter 11.
10. 325 F. Supp. 582 (M.D. Al., 1972). Subsequent orders were announced at 334 F. Supp. 1341 (1971), 344 F. Supp. 373 (1972), and 344 F. Supp. 387 (1972).
11. *Holt v. Sarver*, 300 F. Supp. 825 (E.D. Ark., 1969); *Holt v. Sarver*, 309 F. Supp. 362 (1970); *Holt v. Hutto*, 363 F.Supp. 194 (1973); *Finney v. Hutto*, 410 F.Supp. 251 (1975). This litigation is examined in Cooper 1988, chap. 8.
12. E.g., *Pell v. Procunier*, 417 U.S. 817 (1974); *Wolfe v. McDonnell*, 418 U.S. 539 (1974); *Estelle v. Gamble*, 429 U.S. 97 (1976); and *Bell v. Wolfish*, 441 U.S. 520 (1979).
13. A number of studies have followed the long process of formulating and implementing the court's orders, including Cooper 1988, chap. 7; Note 1975; and Yarbrough 1981.
14. E.g., *Gonzaga University v. Doe*, 536 U.S. 273 (2002); *Gregory v. Ashcroft*, 501 U.S. 452 (1991); *Dellmuth v. Muth*, 491 U.S. 223 (1989); *Welch v. Texas Highways and Public Transportation Departments*, 483 U.S. 468 (1987); and *Pennhurst State School and Hospital v. Halderman*, 451 U.S. 1 (1981).

PART III

Statutory Construction:
The Interbranch Perspective Applied

6

The Supreme Court and Congress
Reconsidering the Relationship

**LAWRENCE BAUM AND
LORI HAUSEGGER**

IN THE COMPLICATED PROCESS THAT SHAPES NATIONAL POL-
icy, Congress and the Supreme Court interact regularly. The
largest share of the Court's work is interpretation of statutes
enacted by Congress, and the Court frequently determines
whether provisions of federal statutes violate the Constitution. For its part, Congress monitors the Court's decisions, it
considers responses to many of those decisions, and it often
seeks to overturn decisions through new legislation.

Scholars have long been interested in the interaction between the Court and Congress. In recent years many scholars
have adopted a particular approach to study this interaction, an approach that centers on the Court's anticipation of
congressional responses to its decisions. This approach has
brought new insights about the relationship between the legislative and judicial branches. However, inevitably, the assumptions on which it is based are not fully consistent with
what we have learned about the realities of that relationship.
In this chapter, we examine the differences between assumptions and reality in order to get a better understanding of the
interaction between Congress and the Court.

A FIRST LOOK AT THE ISSUES

Congress can respond to Supreme Court decisions in a variety
of ways. If the Court interprets a federal statute, Congress can
override the Court's interpretation by revising the statute. For
example, in *Gitlitz v. Commissioner*, 531 U.S. 206 (2001),
the Supreme Court interpreted a provision of the Internal
Revenue Code to mean that a company's stockholders could
deduct their share of the company's debts from their taxable
income under certain circumstances. A year later, the Job Creation and Worker Assistance Act of 2002 included a section in
which Congress reversed the Court's decision.

If the Court rules that a federal statute is unconstitutional,
Congress can propose a constitutional amendment to override
the Court's decision. Congress did so after *Oregon v. Mitchell*,
400 U.S. 112 (1970), in which the Court held that Congress
could not reduce the voting age to eighteen for elections to

state offices. Congress responded with a proposal to lower the voting age in all elections to eighteen, a proposal that quickly became the Twenty-Sixth Amendment when the states ratified it.

Alternatively (and more easily), it is sometimes possible for Congress to enact a new statute to advance the same goal as the old statute within the limitations established by the Court's decision. One example concerns congressional efforts to regulate campaign finance. The Federal Election Campaign Act, enacted in 1971 and amended in 1974, established a broad set of regulations for political contributions and expenditures related to federal elections. In *Buckley v. Valeo*, 424 U.S. 1 (1976), the Supreme Court struck down a large portion of the statute on the ground that it infringed on First Amendment rights. Over time, support grew for a new attempt to regulate campaign finance within the constraints of *Buckley*. In 2002, Congress enacted the McCain-Feingold law, formally titled the Bipartisan Campaign Reform Act, and a year later the Court ruled that the central features of the new law were constitutionally acceptable.[1] Congress can also act against the Court itself through mechanisms such as limiting the Court's jurisdiction over a disputed area of policy and denying pay increases to the justices.

Over the years, political scientists and other scholars have given considerable attention to the various forms of response to Supreme Court decisions. Some research has dealt with situations of high conflict. Examples include the frictions that resulted from the Court's decisions expanding certain civil liberties during the 1950s (Pritchett 1961; Murphy 1962) and from its 1989 and 1990 decisions striking down criminal laws against flag burning (Goldstein 1996). Other research has examined the more mundane responses of Congress to Court decisions in less conflictual times, with primary attention to decisions that interpret federal statutes (e.g., Henschen 1983; Miller 1992; Solimine and Walker 1992).

Scholars who study situations of high conflict have recognized that Supreme Court justices might try to minimize such conflict as a way of deterring congressional action against the Court. Many observers have concluded that one or two key justices responded to President Franklin Roosevelt's 1937 proposal to "pack" the Court with additional members by abandoning their opposition to his New Deal programs (but see Cushman 1998). And the studies of civil liberties in the 1950s suggest that some justices retreated under congressional pressure.

However, a recent wave of scholarship on the Court–Congress relationship gives much greater emphasis to the justices' anticipation of congressional action. This scholarship adopts the rational choice perspective developed originally by economists. According to the version of the rational choice perspective that scholars typically apply to the Court–Congress relationship, people act on the basis of certain goals, and they choose the actions that are the best means to achieve these goals.

Scholars who take this perspective posit that Supreme Court justices have the primary goal of achieving what they perceive to be good public policy through their decisions. Because congressional responses to Court decisions may detract from this goal, justices are expected to take possible responses into account in a systematic way when they reach decisions. In other words, they act strategically with regard to Congress.

A number of studies have considered how this kind of strategic behavior might affect the Court's interpretations of statutes (e.g., Gely and Spiller 1990; Eskridge 1991b; Spiller and Gely 1992; Schwartz, Spiller, and Urbiztondo 1994; Hettinger

2001). A smaller body of research has considered decisions that interpret the Constitution (Gely and Spiller 1992; Epstein and Walker 1995; Epstein, Knight, and Martin 2001; Martin 2001). In both areas, much of this new wave of Court-centered research is theoretical, analyzing the justices' behavior in formal or mathematical terms.

Although not all scholars take this perspective on the relationship between Congress and the Supreme Court, it has been highly influential. In fact, the conception that justices routinely take Congress into account in reaching decisions has become the predominant way of thinking about how the Court responds to congressional power. Thus, for the purposes of this chapter, we label it the "standard model" of the Court's interaction with Congress.

We have discussed the basic assumption about the justices' behavior that underlies the standard model: justices take the actions that best advance what they regard as good policy. Scholars who take this approach generally incorporate a set of more specific assumptions about the characteristics of interaction between Congress and the Court, though these assumptions are sometimes left implicit (Segal 1997, 31–33). The next section of the chapter explores these specific assumptions.

ASSUMPTIONS: CHARACTERIZING THE COURT AND CONGRESS

Of the assumptions that are reflected in the standard model of the Court–Congress relationship, three are especially important. The first is that the justices try to prevent Congress from overriding the Court's decisions. In other words, when justices act strategically, taking potential action by Congress into account, their specific aim is to avoid reaching decisions that Congress would overturn. In order to achieve this end, a justice might take a position in a case that differs from the justice's true policy preferences.

This behavior can be illustrated in the arena where it is most often studied, congressional overrides of statutory decisions. One frequent subject of the Court's decisions is the set of federal statutes that prohibit discrimination in areas such as voting and employment. Ordinarily, justices who interpret such a statute would adopt the interpretation that perfectly reflects their preferences concerning government policy on discrimination. But under some circumstances, that interpretation would displease members of Congress enough to trigger an override of the Court's decision through enactment of a new statute. Such a statute is likely to produce a policy on discrimination that is quite different from what the justices would prefer. If the Court has a strongly conservative majority on issues of discrimination and Congress is considerably more liberal, a narrow interpretation of the Voting Rights Act that reflects the Court's conservatism might well elicit an override that broadens the act considerably.

In that situation, the standard model posits, the justices will reach a decision that differs from their most preferred interpretation. In effect, they compromise with Congress by taking a position that is sufficiently acceptable to Congress as a whole to prevent an override but that is closer to the justices' preferences than a new civil rights statute would be.[2] Thus, if the Court is conservative on antidiscrimination policy and the House and Senate are liberal, the justices may temper their conservatism by taking relatively moderate positions in order to prevent overrides.

This discussion points to a second assumption of the standard model: Both Congress and the Court act on an ideological basis. Within any field of policy, the policy preferences of justices and members of Congress can be thought of as ideal points on an ideological scale (Schubert 1965; Coombs 1964). The points are ideal in the sense that justices and members prefer a policy at their ideal point to one that is more liberal or more conservative. Alternatively, this place on the scale can be considered an indifference point, in that a justice or member is neutral between alternative policies that lie an equal distance to the left or right of this point.

This ideological dimension can be illustrated with the issue of company mergers under antitrust law. Stronger limits on mergers are considered to be a liberal position, so the liberal end of the spectrum is one in which government establishes severe limits. At the conservative end of the spectrum, government places no constraints on mergers. Each justice and member of Congress has an ideal point somewhere on the spectrum. The Court's positions on mergers, as on other issues, are the ones that a majority of justices support. Thus, if the nine justices take individual positions on the basis of their ideological views, the "median" justice—the one in the ideological middle of the Court—determines where the majority stands. In turn, because the median justice occupies this pivotal position, the Court's decisions on mergers will coincide with that justice's ideal point. In the same way, congressional action on a bill concerning mergers will reflect the position of the median member of the decision-making body involved, such as a committee or the House as a whole.[3]

Because Congress acts on an ideological basis under this assumption, the justices analyze Congress in ideological terms. In considering potential policies on civil rights, the justices determine where the ideal points of the median members of the House and Senate are on the civil rights issue in question. In most versions of the standard model they go further, taking into account the president's position and the median positions of congressional committees and other potential "veto points" (points in the lawmaking process where a bill could be killed) in Congress. The Court's decision will be overridden if the needed majority at each stage of the legislative process prefers an alternative policy that could be adopted through an override to the policy established by the Court. If the justices calculate that their most preferred policy would create that situation, they will adjust their policy to avoid an override.

The final assumption of the standard model is that Congress has the last word (see Segal 1997, 32). More precisely, when Congress responds to a Supreme Court decision with new legislation, that legislation settles the issue. Both justices and members of Congress are assumed to act on this basis. As the justices see it, what Congress does in response to a Court decision establishes the ultimate policy on the issue in question. Thus it is quite important for them to prevent Congress from taking an action unfavorable to the Court's position. For their part, members of Congress need not worry about Court action in response to a new statute. Thus they have no reason to act strategically by departing from their own ideal points. In the standard model, Congress clearly is in the dominant position.

ASSUMPTIONS AND REALITY

If these assumptions are not fully consistent with reality, as they surely are not, models of Court–Congress interaction that incorporate them can still have considerable value. At the same time, however, substantial deviations of a model's assumptions from reality do provoke some rethinking of the model and the political processes that it depicts. In the standard model of the relationship between Congress and the Supreme Court, four types of deviations stand out.

THE FREQUENCY OF CONGRESSIONAL ACTION

In the first deviation, the assumption that justices try to avoid overrides of their decisions confronts a reality in which a significant number of overrides actually take place. It is surprisingly difficult even to catalogue congressional overrides of statutory decisions by federal courts. The task is difficult because many overrides receive little publicity and some are barely visible. (This difficulty in itself has important implications, which we will discuss below.) Thus, any catalogue is necessarily an underestimate. William Eskridge (1991a) did the most comprehensive research on overrides, for the period from 1967 to 1990. Updating his list of overrides through 1996, and comparing it with the Court's statutory decisions, we calculated that a minimum of 5.6 percent of the decisions in the 1978–89 terms were overridden altogether or in large part (Hausegger and Baum 1998, 228). The actual proportion is certainly somewhat higher.

This number of overrides is even more impressive when two factors are taken into account. First, because of the appointment process, the collective policy positions of the Supreme Court tend to be similar to those of Congress and the president (Dahl 1957; Segal 1997, 32–33). Second, override legislation is difficult to enact. Even when a Court decision is at some distance from the overall positions of the House and Senate, there is a good chance that at some veto point (including the president's decision to sign or veto a bill) there will be insufficient opposition to the decision for override legislation to pass. Therefore, it is likely that in a considerable proportion of cases, the Court's decision would be immune to an override no matter which way the Court ruled. Taken together, these two factors suggest that the realistic upper limit to the proportion of statutory decisions that Congress could be expected to override is far short of 100 percent. Indeed, that upper limit is probably a distinct minority of all statutory decisions. From that perspective, even a figure of 5.6 percent is fairly high.

Of course, Congress faces greater constraints in reacting to constitutional decisions. But the relative importance of constitutional decisions gives members greater incentives to reverse the Court's rulings, and it is often possible to use a new statute to achieve the same end. Studies of responses to constitutional decisions suggest that this kind of action is common. Robert Dahl (1957, 286–91) focused on the twenty-three decisions in which the Court had struck down what he classified as major federal statutes within four years of their enactment. Dahl calculated that after seventeen of the twenty-three decisions, Congress achieved "a reversal of the actual policy results of the Court's action" (p. 289). Using a conception of "reversal" similar to the one employed by Dahl,[4] Ignagni and Meernik (1994, 364–68) found that Congress reversed thirteen of the sixty-five decisions holding federal laws unconstitutional between 1954 and 1990. When the Court struck down state laws during the same period, Congress acted to reverse the decision about 5 percent of the time (Meernik and Ignagni 1995, 52). Classification of congressional response to a constitutional decision as a reversal can be uncertain, but the findings of these studies suggest that decisions striking down statutes are at least as likely to provoke congressional action as are those interpreting statutes.

The frequency with which Congress overturns Supreme Court decisions raises the question of why the Court suffers so many adverse results. Either the justices are not trying very hard to avoid overrides, they are not very effective in avoiding them, or both.

JUDICIAL INDIFFERENCE TO CONGRESSIONAL ACTION

A different body of evidence also raises questions about how high a priority the justices give to avoiding legislative reversals of their decisions. For one thing, the Court sometimes makes decisions that the justices must recognize have a high probability of leading to reversals in some form. The decisions striking down New Deal legislation and some of the Court's civil liberties decisions in the past half-century (such as the flag-burning decisions of 1989 and 1990) are examples.

More striking is the Court's practice of inviting reversals in its opinions (Hausegger and Baum 1999, 2001; Hettinger 2001). Such invitations can range widely in their content. What might be called weak invitations include off-handed suggestions to litigants that Congress is a more appropriate forum for their grievances and suggestions that Congress must make its intent clear if it wants to produce a different result. Moderately strong invitations include, among other forms, statements that the statute as interpreted by the Court creates a problem or saying that Congress can act if it disagrees with the Court. Very strong invitations directly say that there is a need for Congress to consider action in response to the decision. Leaving aside the weak invitations, we found that 7.8 percent of the Court's majority opinions in statutory decisions during the 1986–2000 terms included strong invitations in some form (Hausegger and Baum 2001, table 1, updated by the authors).

Very strong invitations are far less common than those that we characterize as moderately strong, but they raise the most serious questions about the justices' interest in avoiding overrides. In a 1989 decision on the rights of divorced spouses to a share of military retirement pay, Justice Thurgood Marshall wrote for the majority: "We realize that reading the statute literally may inflict economic harm on many former spouses. But we decline to misread the statute in order to reach a sympathetic result when such a reading requires us to do violence to the plain language of the statute and to ignore much of the legislative history. Congress chose the language that requires us to decide as we do, and Congress is free to change it" (*Mansell v. Mansell*, 490 U.S. 581, at 594 [1989]). These are not words calculated to discourage Congress from reversing the Court.

Invitations can also be included in decisions that strike down statutes on constitutional grounds. These invitations most often take the form of guidelines for reestablishing a legislative policy in a different form. For instance, *United States v. National Treasury Employees Union*, 513 U.S. 454 (1995), involved a federal law that prohibited federal employees from receiving payments for speeches or articles. The Court struck down the law on the ground that it violated employees' First Amendment rights, but it also offered general guidelines for a more limited prohibition on payments that would be consistent with the First Amendment. The frequency of constitutional invitations is uncertain, but such invitations are not rare (Ignagni and Meernik 1994, 362–63).

Invitations in both statutory and constitutional decisions are correlated with congressional action to reverse the Court's decision (Hausegger and Baum 1999,

166–67; Ignagni and Meernik 1994, 367); Congress is more likely to take such action when the Court has invited it. The direction of the causality underlying that correlation is uncertain: invitations might encourage reversals, or the Court might issue invitations when justices perceive that reversal is likely. But either direction raises questions about the justices' interest in avoiding reversal. If invitations encourage congressional action, the Court is acting with some effectiveness to subvert its own decisions. If invitations reflect the likelihood of congressional action, the justices are able to recognize when potential decisions are vulnerable to reversal but go ahead and make such decisions anyway.

NONIDEOLOGICAL FACTORS IN OVERRIDES

The Civil Rights Act of 1991 overrode nine Supreme Court decisions of the late 1980s and early 1990s. Each of the nine decisions had adopted a narrow interpretation of a federal statute prohibiting discrimination. During this period, the Court was considerably more conservative than Congress in its collective views on civil rights, and the mass override reflected that ideological difference. Indeed, Eskridge (1991b, 659–62) used the likely enactment of the 1991 statute to illustrate the ideological element in the standard model of relations between the Court and Congress. Thus this override seems to support the assumption that Congress reacts to Supreme Court decisions on an ideological basis.

Studies of congressional responses to statutory decisions suggest that the 1991 act was not unique in this respect; some evidence indicates that Congress is more likely to reverse decisions that are ideologically distant from congressional positions (Hausegger and Baum 1998; but see Hettinger and Zorn 2004). Further, some other variables that affect the likelihood of reversal can be interpreted in terms of ideological distance. In particular, the most consistent finding of quantitative studies is that unanimity in the Court makes it less likely that Congress will override a statutory decision (e.g., Eskridge 1991a; Solimine and Walker 1992; Hausegger and Baum 1998; Hettinger and Zorn 2004). Unanimity is a fairly good indicator of ideological moderation in a decision, and moderate decisions generally are close enough to the preferences of the median members of Congress and its subunits to avoid overrides. More generally, a great deal of what Congress does can be understood in ideological terms. For instance, members' roll-call votes tend to fall along a single ideological dimension (Poole and Rosenthal 1997), just as they do in the Supreme Court (Grofman and Brazill 2002).

Yet ideology is not the whole story of the Civil Rights Act of 1991, and a focus entirely on it misses some of the complexity of the override process. The enactment of this statute reflects both the ideological divergence between Court and Congress at that time and the role of interest groups in setting legislative agendas and influencing legislative action. The Rehnquist Court's civil rights decisions covered a wide range of issues. As a result, those decisions disturbed a large and diverse set of interest groups concerned with discrimination, among them the NAACP, the American Civil Liberties Union, and the Women's Legal Defense Center. Those groups mobilized to secure passage of an override bill in 1990. After President George Bush vetoed that bill, they built sufficient congressional support in 1991 to deter a second veto, and Bush signed the bill.

In this respect as well, the 1991 act was not unique. A number of studies have indicated the importance of interest groups in spurring congressional action. We found that, controlling for ideological distance and other factors, the number of amicus curiae briefs on the losing side in the Supreme Court was related to the likelihood of an override (Hausegger and Baum 1998; see also Ignagni and Meernik 1994). This finding makes sense, in that there is more likely to be interest-group pressure on Congress to override a decision when groups felt strongly enough about the issue in question to submit amicus briefs to the Court. Other studies have pointed to the importance of interest groups in the override process, especially in getting an issue on the congressional agenda (Note 1958; Henschen and Sidlow 1988; Eskridge 1991a, 359–67). Of course, interest groups play an integral role in shaping congressional agendas and decisions in general, and it would be surprising if they did not have considerable impact on responses to the Supreme Court's decisions.

There is a second and quite different reason to conclude that congressional response to Court decisions is not solely ideological. The Civil Rights Act of 1991 fits the image of statutory overrides in the standard model in several respects: it was designed specifically to reverse a set of Supreme Court decisions, its purpose was explicit and clear, and it worked through each stage of the legislative process. But only a minority of override bills share these characteristics.

More often, provisions that overturn decisions are parts of broader legislation. The 2002 override of the *Gitlitz* tax decision that we discussed earlier is an example; that override was one of several "miscellaneous provisions" in a statute that dealt with a variety of issues in tax law and other fields. For the period from 1991 through 1996, we identified twenty-two new statutes that overrode one or more statutory decisions. Only nine of the twenty-two had overrides as their primary subject (Hausegger and Baum 1998, 228–29). A study of overrides in an earlier period (Solimine and Walker 1992, 449) reported a similar pattern.

In nearly all the other thirteen statutes that we identified, the overrides were fairly minor provisions of legislation with other purposes, such as budget and omnibus bills. Melnick (1994, 263–64) found the same thing in welfare law. In some of these instances, it is doubtful that many of the members who supported the bill were aware of the override provision. Melnick (1994, 263) refers to one override as "a little-noted piece of a larger bill," and this instance was far from unique. An extreme example is the Oceans Act of 1992, which added one word, the word "any," to an existing statute. This seemingly innocuous change, buried in a bill dealing with a wide range of issues, overrode a 1991 Supreme Court decision by allowing passengers to sue an ocean cruise line for personal injuries in *any* federal district court rather than one specified by the line. But few members of Congress who voted for the Oceans Act had any way to know that they were voting for this override (see Franklin and Weldy 1993).

The difficulty of cataloguing overrides, which we mentioned earlier, results from the obscurity of so many override provisions. When an override is buried in a bill, undiscussed in committee reports (sometimes because it is added after committee action) or floor debates, even the most careful search may fail to locate it. Thus Eskridge's (1991a) extraordinarily thorough research missed some overrides of federal court decisions in welfare and environmental law that only close study of these fields could identify (Melnick 1994, 331 n. 13). Undoubtedly, the same was true of other policy areas. In turn, this means that the proportion of overrides that come in larger bills is higher than we calculated because we failed to locate some of the hidden overrides.

In contrast with statutory overrides, congressional responses to constitutional decisions are unlikely to go unnoticed—though a significant proportion of the decisions striking down federal laws are surprisingly obscure. But these responses too may be contained in broader legislation. For instance, the 1968 provision that purported to overturn *Miranda v. Arizona*, 384 U.S. 436 (1966), was one section of a massive anticrime bill.

The inclusion of a legislative provision in a bill that has a different primary purpose is a time-honored practice. This practice can reflect various motivations, but its effect (and usually its purpose) is to ease the path to enactment for the included provision. If the necessary majorities at each stage of the process are inclined to favor a bill because of its primary purpose, an unrelated provision grafted onto the bill obtains something of a free ride into the United States Code, when a ride on its own might not be successful.

In the case of the word inserted in the Oceans Act of 1992, in all likelihood a bill with that change alone would have failed to secure enactment. One reason is that the attention of members and affected interest groups would have been drawn to a proposal that escaped congressional debate as an obscure part of a broader bill. Even without serious opposition, however, such a bill probably would have died early in the legislative process for a different reason: a reluctance to use some of the limited congressional agenda for a matter of no great import and no urgency.

The 1968 anti-*Miranda* provision might have won enactment on its own; after all, *Miranda* was an unpopular decision. But it probably would have faced considerable opposition, abetted by doubts about whether Congress could override a constitutional decision by changing rules of federal criminal procedure. Indeed, when a lower court revived the provision after federal prosecutors had ignored it for three decades, the Supreme Court responded by striking it down.[5]

It should be reiterated that ideology does influence congressional overrides in substantial ways. Even if an override provision is buried in an omnibus bill, its inclusion is likely to reflect partisan control of the originating house and the ideological positions of leaders such as committee chairs. But a purely ideological conception of congressional response to Supreme Court decisions misses much of the reality of override legislation.

SUPREME COURT RESPONSES TO CONGRESSIONAL ACTION

When the Supreme Court struck down the statutory provision that was intended to overturn *Miranda*, it illustrated the final deviation of the standard model from reality: contrary to the model's last assumption, Congress does not necessarily have the last word (Segal 1997, 32). If Congress tries to restore a government practice that the Court has held to be unconstitutional, the Court can determine whether the restoration itself is acceptable under the Constitution. If Congress overrides the Court's interpretation of a statute, the Court can offer its interpretation of the overriding statute, an interpretation that lower federal courts must follow.

These responses to congressional action have not been studied systematically. As a result, it is impossible to assess the balance of power between the two branches in those situations when Congress intervenes. But it is clear that the Court often plays a substantial role after legislative intervention.

In the statutory arena, undoubtedly most overrides of decisions resolve the issue that Congress addressed by leaving no meaningful room for interpretation. Even so, the Court often can shape the impact of the override through its interpretations of related issues. A good example is the override contained within the Voting Rights Act of 1982. Congress overrode *City of Mobile v. Bolden*, 446 U.S. 55 (1980), by requiring that the Court determine whether an election rule discriminates on the basis of the rule's *impact* rather than the *intent* of the body that adopted it. The Court readily acceded to Congress, but it retained the power to determine when rules have discriminatory impact, and it has used that power in a series of cases to shape the effects of the 1982 override.

At least occasionally, an override leaves the Court with room to limit its effects directly. *Westfall v. Erwin*, 484 U.S. 292 (1988), made federal officials liable to lawsuits for personal injuries under some circumstances. Congress responded by allowing the U.S. Attorney General to certify that an employee was acting as a federal official, thereby shielding the employee from liability. But in *Gutierrez de Martinez v. Lamagno*, 515 U.S. 417 (1995), the Court ruled that the attorney general's certification was subject to challenge in court.

In the constitutional arena, the Court's ruling against the legislation to overturn *Miranda* was not unique. During the frictions over economic regulation in the early twentieth century, the Court twice struck down statutes intended to restore regulatory power that the Court had taken away—though Congress ultimately triumphed in each area with a third statute (Dahl 1957, 289–90). The classic case in recent years was the federal statute intended to reestablish criminal penalties for flag burning after the Court had struck down the Texas flag-burning statute in *Texas v. Johnson*, 491 U.S. 397 (1989). The Court quickly heard a challenge to the federal statute (*United States v. Eichman*, 496 U.S. 310, 1990) and declared it unconstitutional on the same ground as the Texas law.

A current example concerns congressional efforts to limit the exposure of children to sexually oriented material on the Internet. In 1997, the Court struck down one statute with that aim on the ground that it violated the First Amendment, so in 1998 Congress enacted a new statute intended to meet the Court's objections to the first one. The Court's final response to this statute is still pending. In 2002, a divided Court disagreed with the reason that a federal court of appeals had offered for declaring the statute unconstitutional. However, the Court sent the case back to the court of appeals to determine whether the statute was unconstitutional for other reasons. In 2003, the court of appeals did indeed strike down the new statute on a different ground. The Supreme Court agreed to review this decision and held oral argument in early 2004. At the time of this writing, the Court had not yet issued its decision in the case.[6]

In a more unusual situation, the Court struck down a statute designed to broaden rights that the Court had interpreted narrowly (see Long 2000). In *Employment Division v. Smith*, 494 U.S. 872 (1990), the Court adopted a doctrine that made it easier for government to regulate religious practices without violating religious freedom under the Constitution. In the Religious Freedom Restoration Act of 1993, Congress sought to use its power to enforce the Fourteenth Amendment to override the Court's doctrine with one that provided greater protection for religious freedom. But in *City of Boerne v. Archbishop Flores*, 521 U.S. 507 (1997), the Court struck down the 1993 law on the ground that Congress lacked the power to expand the meaning of Fourteenth Amendment rights in this way.

Such examples cannot substitute for more comprehensive analysis of Supreme Court action after congressional reversals of decisions. However, they do undermine the assumption that the Court's role ends when Congress intervenes. Of course, that is not surprising in a governmental system in which issues seldom get a definitive resolution in a single forum.

IMPLICATIONS OF THE DEVIATIONS

Thus the assumptions that underlie the standard model of relations between Court and Congress deviate substantially from reality in several respects. In turn, those deviations have important implications for analysis of those relations, and particularly of the justices' responses to potential action by Congress.

IDEOLOGY IN CONGRESS

The first of these implications relates to the assumption that the Supreme Court and Congress respond to each other on an ideological basis. Scholars have found it convenient and appropriate to incorporate this assumption into their analyses of Supreme Court behavior vis-à-vis Congress. If the justices act strategically to avoid overrides of decisions, they are expected to calculate the potential for overrides in terms of the ideological composition of Congress and of the subunits that would consider an override proposal.

However, as we have discussed, congressional responses to Supreme Court decisions are determined only in part by the ideological composition of Congress and its subunits. One reality is that interest groups are important to the initiation and success of override proposals. A second reality is that most successful overrides do not follow an orderly progression of direct consideration at each stage of the congressional process. Instead, they are grafted onto broader bills, and they are sometimes added to those bills at later stages of the process.

For justices who would like to avoid overrides, the second reality makes strategy considerably more complicated by introducing large elements of idiosyncrasy and quasi-idiosyncrasy into congressional action. If strategic justices study the override process carefully, they come to recognize that even the best efforts to anticipate Congress are inherently flawed, leading to two types of mistakes. First, the Court's decisions may trigger overrides that had seemed unlikely. Second, justices may deviate from their preferred positions to avoid overrides that would not have occurred in any event. One plausible response from strategic justices is to throw up their hands and simply take positions that coincide with their preferences.

The first reality is easier for strategic justices to deal with: in calculating the potential for adverse congressional action, they take into account the efforts that interest groups may undertake to secure an override. In the standard model of Court–Congress relations, justices must make complex calculations of the ideological stances of Congress and its subunits and predictions of those stances after the next election or two (once the justices have resolved for themselves how to make these calculations—a matter subject to disagreement among scholars). It seems unreasonable to think that they engage in this labor of heroic proportions yet ignore the evidence about interest group positions that is readily available from amicus briefs.

Of course, any model can only approximate the ways that strategic justices calculate prospective congressional action. But the appropriate starting point is the set of conditions that determines the likelihood of overrides, and models based on only one of those conditions probably do not depict justices' calculations especially well. For that reason, scholars who seek to determine whether justices take the potential for overrides into account should consider adopting models of congressional action that go beyond ideology. To put it another way, the findings of research on the determinants of overrides should be applied to research on the Court's actions in light of congressional power.

LONG-TERM STRATEGY

Because it assumes that Congress has the last word, the standard model has treated interaction between the Court and Congress as involving a single stage of action by each: the Court decides a case, and Congress decides whether to override the decision. Thus justices' strategic considerations are short term, and members of Congress have no need to act strategically in regard to the Court.

This conception of policymakers in the two branches depicts them as unduly short-sighted—in the term used by formal theorists, myopic. The reality is that interaction between Court and Congress over a policy issue can always extend beyond the two stages, and it frequently does. If justices and members of Congress are fully strategic, they must take into account choices that follow the first congressional reaction to a Supreme Court decision.

For members of Congress, calculations of Court responses to congressional action might have a variety of effects on that action. One task for designers of formal models is to analyze what those effects might be under various circumstances. In all likelihood, the dominant effect is to limit the range of options available to Congress.

This effect is quite clear in constitutional law. When the Supreme Court strikes down a statute, members of Congress who seek to reinstate the policy reflected in that statute must consider what alternatives the Court would accept. Depending on the Court's ruling, they may be left with a wide or narrow range of alternatives from which to choose. When the Supreme Court struck down existing death penalty statutes in *Furman v. Georgia*, 408 U.S. 238 (1972), both Congress and the state legislatures had considerable room to enact new statutes. But certain options were effectively ruled out: the Court would not accept any law that provided no standards for judges or juries to use in determining whether to impose a death sentence.

Of course, Congress is in a stronger position in statutory law, in that it can always undertake a second override if the Court's response to its initial action is unsatisfactory. Yet space on the congressional agenda is limited, and the membership of Congress changes over time. Thus if current members want to achieve a particular effect on the law, they have an incentive to obtain the best possible judicial response to their first override effort. In turn, this may mean adopting a position different from the one they most prefer.

For justices, the capacity to respond to congressional action widens the range of options that are available to the Court on a particular issue. Strategic justices may be willing to make a decision that might provoke a legislative override if they can continue to shape policy on that issue after an override as new cases come to them. To put it more simply, justices can accept the risk of an override more readily than the standard model would suggest.

Acceptance of risk is all the more important given the realities of congressional response to Supreme Court decisions. The standard model of response is deterministic: given a particular decision and a particular ideological composition of Congress, an override is either guaranteed or impossible. In the real world of Congress, in which responses to judicial policies are probabilistic, risk-averse justices frequently might shy away from potential decisions in fear of reversal. But if the Court can repair the damage after an override, justices can accept the possibility of a congressional override with greater equanimity. As a result, the constraints on their choices may be fairly loose.

SYMBIOTIC RELATIONSHIPS

The broadest implications of the differences between the standard model's assumptions and reality arise from the evidence that, contrary to one key assumption, Supreme Court justices do not do all they can to prevent overrides. The number of overrides raises questions about justices' commitment to avoid overrides, their capacity to do so, or both. And the Court's invitations to Congress indicate that the justices can accept overrides and even welcome them under some conditions.

In turn, these realities lead us to question the way that the standard model conceives of interaction between the Court and Congress. Institutional conflict is fundamental to that model. Policymakers in the two branches each want to move policy as close as possible to their preferred positions. Unless the positions of Congress and the Court coincide, the interaction between the two branches can be characterized as a zero-sum game: Whatever one side gains, the other side loses.

Within the assumptions of these models about policymakers' motivations, this characterization is perfectly appropriate—at least for the justices and members of Congress who determine the positions of their branch.[7] Once other motivations come into play, however, conflict becomes less important to the relationship between Court and Congress (see Lovell 2003).

In Congress, of course, considerations related to reelection affect incentives to override decisions. For one thing, there may be an incentive to undertake ineffective overrides as a means to take credit for a popular action. The members of Congress who voted for the 1989 flag burning statute after *Texas v. Johnson* knew that the Court was likely to strike down the statute. But voting for the statute and securing its adoption allowed members to demonstrate that they had done something to attack a highly unpopular decision. That demonstration was especially valuable for liberal Democrats who sought to avoid both a constitutional amendment to reverse the Court and Republican attacks for siding with flag burners (see Clark and McGuire 1996, 773 n. 3).

Further, the Court sometimes plays the valuable role of shielding Congress from difficult issues. So long as *Roe v. Wade* stands, federal and state legislators can take the positions on abortion that they think most appealing to their constituents without facing the political dangers that would confront them if legislatures could actually prohibit abortion.[8] The repeated failures of congressional resolutions for constitutional amendments to override highly unpopular Court decisions through constitutional amendments, on issues such as school religious practices and flag burning, are instructive. These resolutions allow some members to take positions and cast votes that are politically useful, but thus far none have received enough support to send to the states. (This does not mean that such resolutions never could get through Congress. Since 1995, the House regularly has voted for anti-flag-burning amendments, and it is quite possible that such an amendment will receive the requisite support from both houses in the next few years.) As a result, members are protected from actually having to make effectual policy on difficult issues.

For the Court, relaxing assumptions of the standard model about the motivations of Supreme Court justices changes expectations about their behavior in substantial ways. First of all, policy-minded justices do not necessarily have a strong aversion to congressional overrides. Rather, they may obtain satisfaction primarily from taking positions that reflect their policy preferences, from securing a Court decision that comes as close as possible to their preferences, or from a combination of the two. In none of these instances does an override detract from achievement of their primary aim. Further, they may view congressional overrides as involving no element of failure; Congress, after all, responds to different considerations from those relevant to the Court.

Second, justices may welcome congressional action rather than fearing it. Even strategic justices who seek to achieve good policy may advance that goal by securing legislative intervention. For instance, Walter Murphy (1964, 129–31) posited that justices could interpret a statute narrowly in order to evoke comprehensive legislation that is in line with the justices' policy preferences. Thus the Court might rule that existing law provides no remedy for a certain form of corporate fraud as a way of spurring Congress to act against corporate fraud as a general problem.

Congressional action may be especially attractive to justices who seek to make both good policy and good law (see Spiller and Tiller 1996; Eskridge 1991a, 388–89). The strongest Court invitations to Congress to override statutory decisions have a simple message: we are constrained by the law as it stands, but you have the power to change the law and thus achieve what we regard as the right policy. With good reason, scholars tend to assess judges' claims that they are constrained by the law with considerable skepticism. But it is not unreasonable to think that such constraints exert some impact on the justices. This is especially true on issues that are not highly salient to justices as policy (as is probably true of a high proportion of the statutory issues that the Court addresses).

Indeed, we found evidence to support this conception of the justices' motivations in one recent period (Hausegger and Baum 1999). During that period the Court was considerably more likely to invite congressional overrides of statutory decisions in policy areas that were of low salience to the justices, where presumably they did not feel a strong stake in the ultimate policies that emerged from government. Invitations were also more likely when the Court's decision was ideologically distant from the preferences of the justices in the majority opinion coalition. In that situation the justices may have adopted what they regarded as the appropriate interpretation of a statute while hoping that Congress would restore what they regarded as good policy on the issue.

Thus, when justices claim that congressional reversal of their decisions does not bother them (e.g., Atkinson 1974, 733), they are not necessarily dissembling. Nor are the strong and weak invitations to Congress that appear in many majority opinions always simply rhetorical. Overrides of Supreme Court decisions may detract little from the justices' achievement of the goals they care about, and under some circumstances overrides may actually help the justices get what they want.

CONCLUSIONS

The interaction between Congress and the Supreme Court is one key component of the process that shapes national policy. That interaction merits the considerable attention it has received from scholars. Indeed, there is a need for far more research to provide a more extensive picture of the relationship between the two branches.

The new wave of research on the behavior of Supreme Court justices with regard to Congress in recent years has expanded our understanding of the relationship between Court and Congress in substantial ways. In particular, rational choice approaches have illuminated aspects of the relationship that had not been considered and provided a framework for empirical analysis of the Court's part in the relationship.

As we have shown, however, there is a gap between the assumptions of the standard model in this research and what we know of the realities of the relationship. In light of this gap, we think that the standard model can be made even more useful if it is modified. Modification will allow it to encompass more of what we know (and what we continue to learn) about the Court and Congress. In particular, it will lead to more effective empirical tests of how and how much the justices take Congress into account when they cast votes and write opinions. In turn, the building and testing of refined models can give us a better understanding of the forces that shape judicial behavior as a whole.

NOTES

1. The decision was *McConnell v. Federal Election Commission*, 124 S. Ct. 619 (2003).
2. If justices are strategic, then they should act strategically in relation to their colleagues as well as Congress. In other words, they would take into account the effect of their own positions on their colleagues and thus on the Court's collective decision. Indeed, there is a large body of research that posits or identifies strategic behavior within the Court (e.g., Maltzman, Spriggs, and Wahlbeck 2000). But research on strategic behavior toward Congress typically ignores or rules out the possibility of intracourt strategy, probably to simplify analysis (e.g., Gely and Spiller 1990, 267).
3. This approach treats justices or members as having the freedom to choose the particular policy that coincides with their ideal. In practice, they are likely to be constrained to choose from a limited number of alternatives, often two. Indeed, a long line of research on judicial behavior explicitly or implicitly treats the justices as facing a dichotomous choice between the two alternatives represented by votes for the two sides in a case (e.g., Schubert 1965). But formal theorists who study the Court in relation to Congress see the justices as having a wider range of alternatives (e.g., Spiller and Gely 1992, 466).
4. Ignagni and Meernik employed the definition of reversal used by Stumpf (1965, 382), which includes legislation "to modify the legal result or impact, or perceived legal result or impact of a specific Supreme Court decision, or decisions."
5. The decision was *Dickerson v. United States*, 530 U.S. 428 (2000).
6. The decisions were, in chronological order, *Reno v. American Civil Liberties Union*, 521 U.S. 844 (1997); *Ashcroft v. American Civil Liberties Union*, 535 U.S. 564 (2002); and *American Civil Liberties Union v. Ashcroft*, 322 F.3d 240 (3d Cir. 2003). The case pending before the Supreme Court is *Ashcroft v. American Civil Liberties Union* (03-318).

7. Policymakers who lose out in their own branch might seek to induce help from the other branch. A straightforward example is pleas for congressional overrides in dissenting opinions (Hausegger and Baum 2001).

8. This situation is especially appealing to legislators who want to appeal to pro-life constituents without arousing the wrath of prochoice constituents. They can take something like the position that George W. Bush adopted in his first presidential campaign: "I would support a constitutional amendment with the exceptions of life, incest and rape. I want to tell you something, though: The country is not ready for a constitutional amendment" (Bruni 1999). Dean Lacy brought this example to our attention.

7

The Judicial Implementation of Statutes
Three Stories about Courts and the Americans with Disabilities Act

THOMAS F. BURKE

JEFFREY PRESSMAN AND AARON WILDAVSKY MEMORABLY GAVE their book *Implementation* a ridiculously long, old-fashioned subtitle: *How Great Expectations in Washington Are Dashed in Oakland; or, Why It's Amazing That Federal Programs Work at All, This Being a Saga of the Economic Development Administration as Told by Two Sympathetic Observers Who Seek to Build Morals on a Foundation of Ruined Hopes* (Pressman and Wildavsky 1984). Pressman and Wildavsky were concerned with the ways in which states and localities frustrated implementation of federal programs. But the nub of their problem should be familiar even to those unversed in federal–state relationships: When you give someone else a job to do, you cannot be sure they will do it the way you want.

Social scientists call this the "principal–agent" problem, and if one thinks about it, social life is filled with such difficulties. You pay your mechanic to overhaul your car, but how much do you know about what he actually has done, or whether the car needed the fix in the first place? You leave your investments in the hands of a broker, but can you be sure that all the trades she makes are aimed at improving your finances rather than generating more fees? In political science, principal–agent theory has most vigorously been applied to bureaucratic implementation. Political scientists have carefully explored the myriad ways in which bureaucrats frustrate or fulfill the wishes of legislators who, at least theoretically, give them their marching orders. (For a helpful review of this literature and a strong recent contribution to it, see Huber and Shipan 2002.)

Much less political science research has been done on implementation of statutes by courts. The bulk of the research on judicial implementation uses the principal agent perspective to analyze how actors within the two branches strategize to achieve their policy goals. In the court–Congress game, judges are driven by their policy preferences to interpret statutes in ways that sometimes depart from the wishes of the principal, Congress. This inclination on the part of judges is disciplined, however, by the threat of congressional override—Congress can enact new legislation that explicitly overturns the interpretation. Passing new legislation, though, is "costly" because putting a majority coalition together takes time and energy away from other goals that legislators might want to pursue. The costliness of legislating means judges can on occasion depart from the wishes of Congress without being overruled, because legislators may consider the trouble of correcting the deviation to outweigh the benefit. Through intensive analysis of these kinds of calculations, academics have developed models that attempt to predict how both judges and legislators will behave.[1]

As Barnes has noted, the game-theoretic approach's virtues—parsimony and hypothesis generation—are the flip side of its limitations. By focusing solely on judges and legislators, and thus ignoring the larger context in which statutory implementation occurs, strategic modelers can produce precise predictions about when judges will depart from the wishes of legislators. But if one wishes to see how law operates beyond the formal institutions of courts and legislatures, this literature is of limited use (Barnes 2004).

The richest work on statutory interpretation ventures further outward than the game-theoretic literature. Yet like game theory, it emphasizes the most dramatic moments of judicial policymaking—the points at which courts make particularly far-reaching interpretive decisions—rather than the everyday processes of judicial implementation. For example, Melnick's (1994) *Between the Lines: Interpreting Welfare Rights* demonstrates how welfare, food stamps, and disability education policies were reshaped by federal court decisions interpreting statutes. Melnick's book is filled with insights about the ways in which judges, bureaucrats, and legislators interact in producing policy, and the strategies this creates for interest groups. But because Melnick's book is concerned with high moments of policymaking, it necessarily ignores the seemingly more mundane aspects of judicial implementation—the daily grind of claims and counterclaims in court, and perhaps even more significant, the compliance that happens without court action.

Studying judicial implementation, as opposed to judicial policymaking, turns our attention to less-often explored aspects of the court–Congress game. It focuses us, for example, on the litigants who bring cases at least as much as on the judges who decide them. Judicial implementation, after all, is implementation by plaintiffs, who must press claims before courts even learn of them, and defendants, whose attempts to evade, comply with, or defend against claims determines which cases reach trial. Indeed, it is this reliance on private parties to bring and defend claims that separates judicial implementation from its main alternative, bureaucratic implementation. Thus if we want to understand what judicial implementation looks like, and particularly how it might look different from bureaucratic implementation, we must move beyond the formal institutions, courts and Congress. We must consider the perspectives of the interest groups who campaigned for the legislation, those who fought against it, those who seek to use the law to their advantage, and those on whom the law's commands fall. Indeed, for many statutes, we must even consider the attitudes of the mass public, who, though uninvolved in litigation, may have a decisive impact on processes of implementation. It is the behavior of this much larger cast—litigants, potential litigants, and seeming bystanders—that provides the context in which legislators and judges interact.

In this chapter, I analyze the court–Congress interaction in judicial implementation from this broader perspective. Principal–agent theory provides the starting point for my analysis, but not the endpoint: my purpose is to consider aspects of judicial implementation whose significance has been slighted in the political science literature. My interest in implementation outside the courts and legislatures reflects my grounding in the work of the Law and Society Association, whose members have produced the bulk of research on law outside of formal institutions. In this chapter, I draw extensively on law and society research to help analyze three ways of thinking, three "stories," about judicial implementation of the Americans with Disabilities Act (ADA). These three stories illustrate the complexities of judicial implementation.

THE CASE OF THE ADA

If my goal were simply to show what happens in the ordinary case of statutory implementation by courts, the ADA would not be a good choice. The ADA is an extraordinary statute, and the interaction that has created between the federal courts and Congress has been extraordinary as well. The ADA assigns enforcement to a bunch of federal agencies, but also gives individuals the right to sue to implement the law—and the resulting court decisions trump agency interpretations of the statute.[2] Enacted into law in 1990, the ADA has now had more than a decade of parsing in the federal courts, a process that has infuriated both the drafters of the law and the judges who are charged with interpreting it. A series of Supreme Court ADA decisions in 2001 so exasperated one of the chief congressional sponsors of the law, Representative Steny Hoyer (D-Md.), that he wrote an article titled "Not Exactly What We Intended, Justice O'Connor" (Hoyer 2002). A couple of months later, Supreme Court Justice Sandra Day O'Connor, the primary target of Hoyer's criticisms, complained to a group of business lawyers that the ADA's poor draftsmanship happens when "sponsors are so eager to get something passed that what passes hasn't been as carefully written as a group of law professors might put together" (quoted in Lane 2002). In a shot from the drafters' side, Chai Feldblum, a law professor who, as it happens, helped put together the ADA, summarized the Supreme Court's ADA jurisprudence with some frustration: "The outcomes of the cases have been unexpected and remarkable" (Feldblum 2000, 103).

As these comments suggest, the ADA has become one of the most disputed, most controversial statutes in the federal courts. This is reflected in the sheer number of ADA cases on which the Supreme Court has weighed in: between 1997 and 2004, the Court ruled on twenty ADA cases, and there is no sign that this stream of cases will let up. Justice O'Connor went so far as to predict that the 2000–1 term could be remembered as the "disabilities act term," a prediction that seemed justifiable on purely numerical grounds: Five of the Court's docket of eighty-one cases that term involved the ADA (Lane 2002).[3] And the Supreme Court is a relative island of calm next to what's going on in the lower courts, where an array of disputes over such matters as what counts as a disability, what is considered a "reasonable accommodation," and how much consultation employers must conduct with employees with disabilities continue to rage (see Edmonds 2002).[4]

Why has ADA implementation proved such a difficult, controversial enterprise? First, the ADA is a broad, ambitious statute. It aims to open up American society so as to fully include people with disabilities. It does this by barring discrimination against them in a vast array of social settings, from bars and bakeries to parks and zoos. The ADA's fifty pages of text cover a remarkable range of issues, from the accessibility of buses and subways, to medical screening of job applicants, to the operation of phone systems for deaf people. According to one estimate, the ADA regulates more than 600,000 businesses, 5 million places of public accommodation, and 80,000 units of state and local government (West 1994).

Second, many of the key terms in the ADA are general, vague, and so easily disputed. The main thrust of most civil rights statutes is to ensure that all are treated similarly. The drafters of the ADA realized, however, that because of the diversity of disabilities and individual experiences with those disabilities, ADA enforcement must be handled in a much more case-by-case matter. So rather than simple rules, the ADA provides a list of general standards that must be applied to individual cases. Employers must provide "reasonable accommodations" to people with disabilities, the ADA says, unless this results in "undue hardship." But what is "reasonable" and what "undue"? The ADA applies to "qualified individuals" who can perform a job's "essential functions." But what exactly makes one "qualified" and which parts of a job are really "essential"? The words provide a lot of room for argument, and this has made ADA jurisprudence a morass of adversarial exegesis.

But most important of all, the drafters of the ADA attempted to reshape the way Americans think about disability, a goal that makes interpretation of the statute part of a larger battle over the interpretation of disability in American culture. The dominant, familiar view of disability is that it is a tragedy for the individual, one that inevitably limits one's chances in life. Disability theorists label this the "medical model" of disability because, as with sickness, it locates the problem of disability in the individual. The ADA, by contrast, is premised on a "social model" or "rights model" of disability, in which disability is produced by society.

To see the world in this way requires a radical shift in perspective. In the social model, people with disabilities are disabled not by their impairments, but by structural barriers and prejudicial attitudes. The basic, taken-for-granted arrangements of society, in this vision, are discriminatory because they fail to take into account the full diversity of human beings—the fact, for example, that some of us get around on legs, others on wheelchairs. A building entrance that wheelchairs cannot fit into is, in this view, equivalent to a "no blacks allowed" sign on the door. An employer who refuses to alter workplace practices so as to accommodate an employee with a disability is not simply being unkind, but discriminatory. Traditional approaches to disability that segregate or institutionalize people with disabilities become tokens of an embarrassing past, like Jim Crow laws and white-only schools. Even many seemingly good-hearted organizations devoted to helping people with disabilities—most notoriously Jerry Lewis's Muscular Dystrophy Telethon—take on a sinister cast, because they treat people with disabilities as "childlike, helpless, hopeless, nonfunctioning and noncontributing members of society," as disability activist Evan Kemp put it (Kemp 1981, A19). (Several years after making his critique of the telethon, Kemp became chair of the Equal Employment Opportunity Commission, or EEOC, one of the main federal agencies charged with enforcing the ADA.)

This view of disability is not merely politically controversial; it is hard for many to grasp. As disability activist Bob Funk has written, "the general public does not associate the word 'discrimination' with the segregation and exclusion of disabled people. . . . Historically the inferior economic and social status of disabled people has been viewed as the inevitable consequence of the physical and mental differences imposed by disability" (Funk 1986, 7).

In the social model of disability, however, every sidewalk curb without a "cut," every subway without an elevator, and every elevator without Braille buttons is an act of discrimination. The disability activists who helped draft the ADA hoped it would inspire judges and the other implementers of the statute to redistribute resources, restructure institutions, and transform attitudes so as to achieve an inclusive society—a truly radical goal.

STORY ONE: BACKLASH

By 1999, these hopes had been deflated. It was in that year, as the tenth anniversary of the passage of the ADA neared, that a group of legal scholars and disability activists gathered at an academic conference in Berkeley, California, widely considered the birthplace of the disability rights movement, to analyze the "backlash" against the ADA. It was not a happy meeting. In the hands of federal judges the ADA had become a creature quite different from the one the participants thought had been created (Krieger 2000a, 2000b).

There was, for example, the issue of who is considered "disabled" under the statute. This had not seemed during the enactment of the ADA to be a concern. There were major controversies in Congress over the cost of accommodations, rules for the hiring of people with contagious diseases, and coverage of drug addicts. The disability definition matter was, in contrast, resolved rather easily. The drafters simply took the language from a statute, Section 504 of the 1973 Rehabilitation Act, which had barred discrimination against the "handicapped" (then the standard term) by entities receiving federal government funds. To be considered handicapped under Section 504, one had to be "substantially limited" in a "major life activity."[5] These terms were lifted out of 504 into the ADA, and were never seriously debated in Congress.

Section 504 had been litigated extensively, and the question of who counted as handicapped had not arisen as a major issue. In perhaps the most prominent Section 504 case, *School Board of Nassau v. Arline*, the Supreme Court ruled in favor of a teacher fired because she had bouts of tuberculosis. The Court concluded that the plaintiff was handicapped simply because her disease "was serious enough to require hospitalization, a fact more than sufficient to establish that one or more of her major life activities were substantially limited by her impairment" (*School Board of Nassau v. Arline*, 480 U.S. 273, at 280–81 [1987]). Given the Court's nonchalant handling of the "who counts as disabled" issue in *Arline*, the drafters of the ADA did not anticipate that it would arise much in ADA litigation (Feldblum 2000, 126–35).

But defendants in ADA cases saw an opportunity. Defending ADA employment claims on grounds of "reasonable accommodation" or "undue hardship" involved a close examination of employer practices—and a legal headache. Moreover, these were likely to be matters for a jury to decide, and defense lawyers would rather avoid the danger and cost of a jury trial. If, instead, defendants could convince a judge that the plaintiff was not disabled, the case would never get to trial; the plaintiff had no legal claim under the ADA. So defendants began arguing that plaintiffs in ADA cases were not really disabled.

They attacked the two prongs of the ADA's definition of disability, challenging both the claim that the plaintiff was "substantially limited" and that the limitation was in a "major life activity." The attack seemed to catch plaintiffs' attorneys off guard. In many cases, they simply used the plaintiff's own statement about his impairment as evidence for the "substantial limitation" prong. This was in line with the belief that the prong merely ruled out minor impairments, like an injured finger. But defense attorneys cited EEOC regulations specifying that "substantially limited" means "significantly restricted as to the condition, manner or duration" that a person can perform a major life activity as compared to the ability of "the average person in the general population."[6] Defendants won many cases on summary judgment—before a trial—when federal judges ruled that the plaintiff had not assembled sufficient expert evidence making this comparison (Van Detta and Gallipeau 2000, 515–23).

The "major life activity" prong proved even more troublesome for plaintiffs. The EEOC created a list of major life activities that was exemplary rather than exhaustive; it included very basic activities such as "caring for oneself." Plaintiffs who could not make a case that they were substantially limited in one of the EEOC's listed activities had to create their own. When they did, they were met with the argument that, for example "lifting," or "interacting with others" was not major enough, or was too poorly defined. Many plaintiffs, and many courts, focused on "working" as the life activity, but this created myriad problems for plaintiffs.[7] One problem is that, again according to EEOC regulations, plaintiffs have to show that they are limited not only at their particular job or employer but at a broad range of jobs in their region. Proving this involves assembling a convincing assessment of the regional economy, not an easy task for the typical plaintiff (Van Detta and Gallipeau 2000, 526–35).[8]

Given all these difficulties, it soon seemed almost impossible to be declared disabled under the ADA. Plaintiffs with breast cancer, stroke-induced paralysis, spastic colon aggravated by multiple sclerosis, brain tumor, epilepsy, hemophilia, heart disease, diabetes, cancer, ulcerative colitis, carpel tunnel syndrome, depression, paranoia, and bipolar syndrome all were declared nondisabled by federal courts (see Diller 2000, 24–26).

And there was more. The EEOC had declared that the assessment of whether a person is substantially limited in a major life activity should be made "without regard to mitigating measures such as medicines, or assistive or prosthetic devices"; 29 C.F.R. Pt. 1630, App. Section 1630.2(j); EEOC Compliance Manual Section 902.4(c)(1). Defendants successfully challenged this rule in a trio of Supreme Court cases in 1999. In *Sutton v. United Air Lines*, 527 U.S. 471 (1999), the Court concluded that two sisters with severe myopia who sought jobs as airline pilots were not disabled because their glasses mitigated their limitations. In *Murphy v. UPS*, 527 U.S. 516 (1999), the Court declared that a man fired because of his high blood pressure was not disabled because medication mitigated the effects of his condition. And in *Albertson's v. Kiringburg*, 527 U.S. 555 (1999), the Court reversed a lower court's finding that a truck driver fired because he had vision in only one eye was disabled. The Court concluded that the lower court had failed to consider whether the truck driver's impairment was mitigated by his brain's ability to compensate for the loss of vision. The Supreme Court's mitigating measures decisions have made it even more difficult for plaintiffs to get themselves considered disabled under the ADA.

There have, of course, been victories for plaintiffs in ADA cases at the Supreme Court.[9] The most famous is *PGA v. Martin*, in which the justices ruled that the use of a cart was a "reasonable accommodation" for mobility-impaired professional golfer Casey Martin. That case is by far the most well-known of all ADA decisions, receiving lots of front page coverage and media analysis, on both sports and news programs. Many other Supreme Court ADA cases can be considered draws.[10] But over-all, the record of ADA plaintiffs in federal courts has been lousy. In Colker's much-cited study of ADA employment litigation, defendants prevailed in 94 percent of cases at the trial court level. Losing plaintiffs who appealed lost 84 percent of the time. Of the 6 percent of cases in which plaintiffs won at the trial level, defendants won on an appeal 48 percent of the time (Colker 1999, 108). These remarkably one-sided statistics, more than anything else, have fueled claims of a backlash against the ADA.

Appellate opinions in ADA cases support the backlash narrative. One sees little evidence that the social model of disability, the transformative vision that animated the disability rights movement, is guiding the judges. Instead the dominant concern seems to be that the ADA could turn into a litigation nightmare if it is interpreted too broadly. In some cases federal judges voiced these fears, as in this passage in which an appellate judge approvingly cites a district judge's tirade against the ADA:

> This Court agrees with the *Pedigo* court's observation:
>
> that the ADA as it [is] being interpreted [has] the potential of being the greatest generator of litigation ever . . . [it is doubtful] whether Congress, in its wildest dreams or wildest nightmares, intended to turn every garden variety worker's compensation claim into a federal case.
>
> The court doubts that the ultimate result of this law will be to provide substantial assistance to persons for whom it was obviously intended. . . . One of the primary beneficiaries of [the ADA] will be trial lawyers who will ingeniously manipulate [the ADA's] ambiguities to consistently broaden its coverage so that federal courts may become mired in employment injury cases, becoming little more than glorified worker's compensation referees.[11]

This passage exemplifies another tendency commentators see in ADA opinions: judges simply ignore the difference between the conception of "disability" in the ADA as opposed to welfare and workers' compensation programs. In the disability welfare programs, disability means "inability to work" or, even more broadly, "helplessness." Those who are able to work are by this definition nondisabled and therefore ineligible for the ADA's protections (Feldblum 2000, 140). But this view turns ADA enforcement into an incomprehensible muddle. The vision behind the ADA, after all, is that people with disabilities are perfectly capable but hindered by prejudicial attitudes and structural barriers. According to this view, people with disabilities, with and without mitigating measures, should be expected to function in society, and the ADA's purpose is to eliminate barriers to their flourishing. If, instead, the ADA is interpreted to apply only to those so disabled that they cannot work or participate in society, it is hard to see what purpose the law serves—the statute only covers those who are not in a position to use it. In the backlash narrative, then, ADA implementation has been derailed by an outdated, inappropriate conception of disability (see O'Brien 2002).

If the backlash story is correct, why did not the disability groups who advocated the ADA get Congress to reverse the Supreme Court's interpretation of the law? There was talk about this, especially after the trio of mitigating measures cases. But as disabilities rights advocates explained, the dangers were great (*Successful Job*

Accommodations Strategies 1999). Opening up the law to amendment could wind up making it even weaker. Although research found that ADA plaintiffs were losing in droves, media reports suggested that disability rights litigation had run amok. It was not a favorable media climate for an expansion of the ADA (LaCheen 2000). Moreover, as principle-agent theory suggests, the bipartisan coalition that enacted the law could splinter depending on the amendments offered. So even we assume that a majority of the Congress, if given the chance, would vote against the Supreme Court's rulings (an assumption perused below), it might not be in the interest of disability rights supporters to bring up such legislation. Thus the backlash narrative highlights the power of courts in the principal–agent game, their ability to defect from the wishes of the agent, Congress and the president.

STORY TWO: SYMBOLIC POLITICS

The backlash story measures the vast distance between what the drafters of the ADA intended and what the federal courts have been doing. But, one might argue, does this not conflate the aspirations of the drafters with the wishes of Congress? After all, drafters do not make statutes into law—Congresses do, usually with the president's signature. Thus to understand intent we must find out what all the members of Congress who voted in favor of the measure and the president who signed it intended. This is one of the main problems of principal–agent theory as applied to the implementation of statutes in general, and American statutes in particular. The problem is that there is no single "principal," but instead many principals, the vast majority of whom have given no explicit indication of what they want their agent to do in a specific case.[12]

Take, for example, the definition of disability under the ADA. What was the intent of Congress? Feldblum, who helped draft the text, notes that the Supreme Court has made much out of the preamble of the ADA, which states that there are 43 million Americans with disabilities. Surely if that is true, Justice O'Connor reasons in her opinion in *Sutton v. United Airlines*, Congress could not possibly have intended the law to apply to people with eyeglasses.[13] But Feldblum argues that there was not much intent at all behind the number:

> I can attest that the decision to reference 43 million Americans with disabilities in the findings of the ADA was made by one staff person and endorsed by three disability rights advocates, that the decision took about ten minutes to make, and that its implications for the definition of disability were never considered by these individuals. Moreover, it was my sense during passage of the ADA that this finding was never considered by any Member of Congress, either on its own merits or as it related to the definition of disability. By contrast, I can attest that the statement in three separate committee reports that mitigating measures should *not* be taken into account in determining the existence of a disability was extensively discussed by Congressional staff members, disability rights advocates, and some Members of Congress. (Feldblum 2000, 154)

Following the conventions of statutory interpretation, Feldblum analyzes what participants in the legislative process *said* to demonstrate legislative intent. Statutory interpreters often quote from committee hearings, floor debates and other aspects of the legislative process to prove they have gotten intent right. But these bits of data simply cannot tell us what every member of Congress intended, because the vast majority never spoke up. As a matter of convention, one can *assume* that those who do not speak up consent to how others characterize legislation, but ultimately it is only the text that they agree to—a text that in this case includes 43 million estimate and excludes any language on the issue of mitigating measures. The text is the only way in which most of the principals in this principal–agent game spoke.

The fact that statutes have many (silent) principals undermines the backlash narrative about the ADA. Just because the drafters envisioned a fundamental transformation of American society, there is no reason to believe that this belief was widely shared among the members of Congress, many business-friendly Republicans and Democrats, who voted for the ADA, or George H. W. Bush, who signed it. Indeed there is an alternative narrative about the ADA that is at least equally plausible, though maddeningly cynical: the politicians who voted for the ADA did so because it was a low-cost vote-getter, a symbolic law. They are, according to this storyline, quite content with the federal courts' narrow interpretation of the ADA.

The symbolic story about the ADA gains credence when we consider the broader context of the ADA's passage. For politicians, the ADA was close to something for nothing, a statute that allowed them to stand for something that was noble and heroic-sounding at little cost. Unlike many other ways of improving the life chances of people with disabilities, supporting the ADA did not tap the federal budget; it merely created mandates against states and localities and nongovernmental organizations. Moreover, the ADA did not establish a federal agency to enforce the law; it simply added responsibilities to existing agencies, often without commensurate funding increases (see Moss et al. 2001). This shifted much of the burden for implementation away from the government to plaintiffs. For the politicians who sponsored it, then, the ADA was a low-cost law, requiring no great principled vision of social change. No surprise, then, that Congress has failed to react to the stream of prodefendant ADA rulings in the federal courts.

The political scientist Murray Edelman wrote extensively about the place of symbolism in politics generally and in statutory implementation specifically. Edelman argued that many regulatory statutes delivered symbolism to the mass public while failing to deliver material benefits. "Some of the most widely publicized administrative activities," he wrote, "convey a sense of well-being to the onlooker because they suggest vigorous activity while in fact signifying inactivity or protection of the 'regulated'" (Edelman 1974, 39). Bureaucratic agencies come into daily contact with the regulated; regulators often take jobs in the regulated industries. Thus agency personnel take on the attitudes and interests of the regulated. They become "captured." Yet the agency and the law that created it can still symbolically reassure the public that a social problem is being addressed.

Courts are not captured by powerful interests in exactly the way that Edelman and others suggested often happens with bureaucratic agencies. Yet powerful interests can dominate courts, as the work of Marc Galanter has shown. Galanter analyzes judicial implementation as a game in which the key variable is experience with the legal system. Repeat players—big corporations, government agencies, large organizations—are on the most experienced side of the continuum. One-shotters, as the name implies, arrive at a lawsuit with no experience. This gives repeat players huge advantages over one-shotters (Galanter 1974, 95–151; Kritzer and Silbey 2003).

Civil rights laws such as the ADA typically match a one-shotter plaintiff against a repeat-player defendant, a large corporate or governmental organization. There are repeat-player ADA plaintiffs—public-interest organizations and government agencies that bring disability rights cases strategically, just as the NAACP did in mobilizing civil rights law. But especially in employment, ADA lawsuits have principally been brought by lawyers hired only to advance the interests of one-shotter plaintiffs. In this circumstance—a battle between repeat-player defendants and one-shotter plaintiffs—Galanter's theory predicts that the law over time will benefit the interests of defendants. Because defendants have a long-term interest in building up precedents in their favor, Galanter argues, they will settle cases that make bad precedents, and take weak claims to court. Plaintiff one-shotters have no corresponding interest in building precedent and so will settle when it is to their advantage. Moreover, lacking the expertise of repeat players, they will frequently advance weak claims. The resulting body of precedent will consist overwhelmingly of plaintiff wins, Galanter argues, particularly in areas in which precedent is valuable to defendants, and so will over time tilt heavily to the defense side. Galanter's theory looks like a plausible explanation for what has happened with the ADA, one that does not depend much on the political composition of the judiciary or the difficulty of the transformative goals behind the statute.

If Galanter's theory is correct, judicial implementation is an excellent method of symbolic politics. Occasional symbolic victories like Casey Martin's Supreme Court triumph will be trumpeted, but the vast number of much more significant losses will be ignored. And these losses are predictable because of the stronger resources and position of the defendants. Far from a "backlash," or a turning away from the "original intent" of the ADA, in this story the experience of ADA implementation is a predictable exercise in regulatory symbolism.

STORY THREE: LAW OUTSIDE OF COURTS

The conjunction of stories one and two raise familiar concerns about legislatures and courts, and thus of principal–agent theory as applied to judicial implementation. They are about the ways in which formal institutions, courts and legislatures, deal with law, and the strategies by which plaintiffs, defendants, and other interested parties shape implementation. But this focus misses perhaps the most important aspects of judicial implementation of statutes, the mechanisms by which laws and litigation penetrate the larger society, the routines of nongovernmental organizations, and the everyday consciousness of citizens. Even in a book about the court–Congress relationship, then, we must venture beyond these formal institutions to understand the distinctive qualities of judicial implementation of statutes. Story three is about the generative quality of judicial implementation, its capacity to create new worlds.

One potentially important example from ADA case law is provided by *Olmstead v. LC*, 527 U.S. 581 (1999), a Supreme Court decision that seems to have led to a reexamination of the way states handle people with severe disabilities. In *Olmstead*, a 6–3 majority concluded that it is discriminatory under the ADA to institutionalize people with disabilities who could instead be placed in a community setting. The *Olmstead* decision, however, left a lot of room for argument about what exactly the ADA commanded. The decision delegated to lower courts the issue of whether the plaintiffs' demand for deinstitutionalization and community placement would be so disruptive and expensive for the defendant, the state of Georgia, that it would "fundamentally alter" state programs, a defense under the ADA. Justice Ruth Bader Ginsburg's majority opinion in *Olmstead* suggested that states could comply with the ADA by developing "a comprehensive, effectively working plan for placing qualified persons with mental disabilities in less restrictive settings" together with "a waiting list that moved at a reasonable pace" (527 U.S. 605–6).

Olmstead has generated a wave of follow-up lawsuits in roughly half the states (Fox-Grage, Folkemer, and Lewis 2003, 4). But as Ginsburg's opinion seemed to request, it has also catalyzed a nationwide review of institutional and community care programs. The federal Centers for Medicare and Medicaid Services have granted millions of dollars to states to develop reports on how they intend to comply with the *Olmstead* rules. Nearly all the states have created task forces to compile such reports, which identify barriers to deinstitutionalization and strategies for overcoming them. In some states, the effort has gone beyond mere planning. Massachusetts, for example, has closed a state hospital, moved hundreds of people into group or private homes, and created additional community services to facilitate closing more institutions (Dembner 2002, A1).

Olmstead seems to have stimulated a reexamination of institutions for people with disabilities that is mostly happening outside the courts. But because it began with a judicial ruling, *Olmstead* is still a conventional saga of judicial implementation of statutes. To move further beyond the formal institutions, we must consider enforcement and compliance that takes place entirely outside of courts. Sociolegal research suggests that the dispute that reaches trial is the exception; the vast majority of enforcement action takes place before disputes ever become court filings. In the standard metaphor of the "disputing pyramid," the base is all grievances that arise, cases in which people believe that they have been harmed by someone else's illegal conduct; the tip is trial and appellate cases, where the mechanisms of principal–agent theory become relevant. In a classic study of "middle-range" disputes the ratio between grievances and court filings was estimated at 20 to one. When the grievance involved discrimination, the ratio was even greater, 125 to one (Miller and Sarat 1980, figs. 1A and 1B, 544). Mostly people "lumped" their grievances, or negotiated an end to them outside the legal system.

If this study accurately represents disputing, analyzing judicial implementation through the lens of the court–Congress game misses most of the action. Indeed, a truly successful statute would never register in the court–Congress game. Few grievances would arise, because potential defendants would comply fully. Those disputes that did develop would be resolved before anyone contacted a lawyer, much less filed a lawsuit. The vision of lawsuit-free implementation of civil rights laws like the ADA is attractive to large organizations, which often employ sophisticated, elaborate strategies to ensure that disputes are smoothed out long before they reach the legal system, as Lauren Edelman and her colleagues have analyzed in a series of studies (see Edelman, Erlanger, and Lande 1993; Edelman 1990, 1999; see also Scheid and Suchman 2001). Edelman's research analyzes the techniques by which organizations "internalize" law, creating their own parallel processes for implementing workplace statutes such as the ADA. These typically feature dispute resolution systems that allow aggrieved individuals to bring their complaints "in-house."

In the process of internalization, Edelman concludes, the goals of civil rights laws are subtly reinterpreted. Complaint handlers within companies are typically not lawyers, and they do not worry about the niceties of the law. They read the law as requiring "fairness," by which they typically mean due process, consistency and respect (Edelman, Erlanger, and Lande 1993, 514–15). Concerns about institutionalized inequality and prejudice are deemphasized. Instead, complaint handlers tend to see disputes as arising from poor management and personal skills. Because the goal of the in-house process is dispute resolution, complaint handlers may provide a remedy even when they believe the complaint is ill-founded. Thus Edelman concludes, "the legal right to a nondiscriminatory workplace in effect becomes a 'right' to complaint resolution" (Edelman, Erlanger, and Lande 1993, 529). The radical social critique that informs the disability rights movement's reading of the ADA is turned into a matter of insensitive and inept management.

If organizations read the ADA in their own ways, so do individuals with disabilities. David Engel and Frank Munger have produced a study that beautifully illustrates this aspect of the ADA. Engel and Munger interviewed sixty people with disabilities about their life experiences. They did not ask about the Americans with Disabilities Act, or the disability rights movement, or even about law. Instead, the two researchers simply asked the interviewees to provide a life history, and then studied the extent to which the ADA entered into these autobiographical accounts. Not surprisingly, they found quite varying levels of engagement with the ADA. Some of the interviewees did not seem to know about the law; others had only a foggy sense of it. But for some the ADA was wrapped up in a process that transformed their identities and lives. Jill Golding, a nurse with learning disabilities, thought of herself as an unintelligent and uncooperative student when she was growing up, and thus accepted her exclusion from the mainstream educational system. But when as an adult she came to see herself as a person with a learning disability, she reconceived her treatment as illegitimate, a violation of her rights (Engel and Munger 2003, 33–34). Sara Lane, a newspaper editor who uses a wheelchair, hesitated to invoke the ADA in negotiating working conditions with her employer, but when the newspaper realized that the law applied to her, it became much more accommodating. "We treated you terribly. And we'll now try to make and try to do something" (Engel and Munger 2003, 26–27). Neither Lane nor Golding, nor any of the other fifty-eight interviewees in the study, ever made a formal complaint based on the ADA. Yet Engel and Munger fill an entire book describing the differences the ADA has made in their lives.

Engel and Munger's other purpose is to show how life experiences and beliefs frame reactions to the ADA and even understandings about what the law requires. Golding, the nurse, thinks of ADA rights as enforcing a "commitment to caring" that is the core of her value system. Her view is that employers, educators, and other organizations have duties of care to the individuals they come in contact with, and these duties involve accommodating differences like disability (Engel and Munger 2003, 35). Another interviewee, Raymond Militello, a hard-nosed businessman, mistakenly thinks the ADA creates affirmative action preferences for people with disabilities like himself. Although he believes the preferences illegitimate, and says he would vote against the ADA if he were a member of Congress, Militello also thinks it would be foolish not to take advantage of them (Engel and Munger 2003, 73–75). Sean O'Brien, a recent college graduate who is quadriplegic, interprets the "reasonable accommodation" standard in the ADA through his religious faith, considering for example whether an accommodation will benefit others as well as him—not a consideration in the law itself (Engel and Munger 2003, 157, 165). Political beliefs, life experiences, and religious faith shape the interviewees' understandings of the law. Their ADA is neither the drafter's, nor the Supreme Court's, but their own.

Engel and Munger do not dwell on the role of the media in framing understandings of the ADA, but especially for nondisabled Americans, this is likely a primary influence. In the news and entertainment media, the ADA's requirements are often portrayed as capricious and trivial. Thus ADA stories have become part of a larger frame about the overuse of courts and the litigiousness of Americans (see McCann, Haltom, and Bloom 2001; see also Burke 2002). One of the most common narratives in ADA journalism is the "litigation horror story," an amusingly outrageous claim. A story that was widely reported in the summer of 2002 concerned a wheelchair user who sued a strip club because its space for private lap dances was located up a flight of stairs; the story even reached the *New York Times*, one of nine occasions in which the *Times* reported on ADA lawsuits in 2002.[14] While *Olmstead*, the deinstitutionalization lawsuit, received little media attention, the case of Casey Martin, the professional golfer, loomed large.[15] His readily understandable, dramatic story fueled radio and television talk show debates over sportsmanship, fairness, and the nature of golf. The view of the ADA advanced in entertainment programs was predictably more one-sided. On *The Simpsons*, for example, Homer Simpson tries to gain 300 pounds so that he can become obese enough to be disabled under the ADA. The episode references other "disabilities" such as "achy breaky pelvis" and "juggler's despair" (LaCheen 2000, 228). Thus, while Engel and Munger's disabled interviewees struggle to make sense of the ADA, perhaps the most common media frame is that the law resists sense: It is simply absurd. If within the courtroom the ADA is understood in strikingly different ways, outside the courtroom the range of interpretations is even greater.

THREE (CONFLICTING?) STORIES

I have presented three stories about the ADA and, by extension, about judicial implementation of statutes. In one, the ADA is derailed by the federal courts because its revolutionary goals run up against powerful adversaries—and firmly entrenched conceptions about disability. In another, the ADA is a symbolic statute, enacted by Congress as a feel-good, low-cost law, and implemented by courts in just the way many of those who voted for it prefer. Yet another story looks beyond both the courts and Congress to see how government officials, the media, business, and people with disabilities themselves interpret the law and incorporate it into their lives.

We need not choose between the stories, for they all capture a truth about the judicial implementation process. The ADA *is* a revolutionary statute, and its handling in the federal courts *has* blunted a transformation in the way Americans understand disability. The ADA is also a symbolic statute, and there are doubtless congressional supporters, perhaps even a majority, who are perfectly happy with the way the law has been implemented by the courts. But beyond this, the ADA is also an extra-institutional statute, a law whose meaning cannot be fixed by either courts or Congress, that has a life, indeed many lives, outside both.

The great literary theorist Stanley Fish once titled a book of essays *Is There a Text in This Class?* The title comes from a question a somewhat clueless student put to Fish's colleague. The colleague, thinking the student had asked a mundane question about required books, answered that an anthology of literature would serve as the text. At this the student replied: "No, no, I mean in this class do we believe in poems and things, or is it just us?" (Fish 1980, 305). The student, having taken Fish's literature course the previous semester, and having learned a little about literary theory, was trying to ask whether the instructor would insist that texts have determinate meanings, so that there would be a single text for all students, or whether the instructor would, like Fish, insist on the indeterminancy of texts. The student's question gets Fish a little wrong, because he does not believe that it is "just us" who interpret texts: we make sense of communication, he says, by drawing on a "background of practices, purposes, and goals" that is social, not individual (Fish 1980, 318). Still the question, and the instructor's confusion about the question, nicely illustrates the openness of texts, the ability of humans to read them in strikingly different ways.

I draw on Fish's story not merely to note that legal texts are indeterminate, that statutes like the ADA will be read differently by different actors. That, after all, is a point that has been made in law at least since the rise of Realism in the early twentieth century. My chief point is to highlight how many readers of statutes there are—not just the judges, legislators, and bureaucrats who populate most studies of court–Congress interaction but also defendants, plaintiffs, lawyers, administrators, journalists, and even the mass public. Each of these actors starts from different contexts, different interests, and different interpretive frames, and so reads statutes differently. For a statute as wide-ranging as the ADA, that can create a surprising array of interpretations. Who would have thought the ADA was a statute about the conduct of professional golfing? Managerial skill? Affirmative action–like preferences? The process of implementing a big, complex statute like the ADA can generate hundreds and hundreds of surprising interpretations.

This is one of the ways in which statutes that are implemented by lawsuit seem different from bureaucratically administered laws. Because they are enforced by private individuals as well as governmental entities, judicially implemented laws are likely to penetrate more deeply into society. The ADA, because it is so wide-ranging and controversial, is a particularly powerful example. Many judicially implemented statutes regulate smaller spheres and so do not have the salience of civil rights statutes like the ADA. Still, by delegating enforcement to many actors rather than one agency, all judicially implemented statutes push the process of interpreting statutes outward into society. This creates an array of statute readers, and gives birth to an array of readings.

Inside the courtroom, the generativity of statutes, their life-giving capacity, is matched by an equally strong force: the murderousness of judges. Judges are, in the coinage of Cover, "jurispathic": "Confronting the luxuriant growth of a hundred legal traditions, they assert that *this one* is law and destroy or try to destroy the rest" (Cover 1995, 157). With every decision, a judge kills some interpretations in authorizing his own. And of course, judges have destroyed some interpretations of the ADA. *Sutton v. United Airlines*, for example, killed the idea that being nearsighted enough to need eyeglasses was a form of disability. In the principal–agent game between Congress and the courts, this is far from the last move. Congress, the nominal principal, can, if it passes a law, restore to life any interpretation. Moreover, Congress can itself act as killer, eliminating an interpretation a court has authorized. Yet judges, simply because they review statutes every day, have the greatest opportunity to impose their own readings.

But we miss a lot if we think only about courts and Congress in isolation. As the case of the ADA illustrates, the court–Congress game takes place in the context of readings of others—by the claims plaintiffs choose to advance, by the strategies of defense lawyers, by media stories about outrageous lawsuits, and by public opinion. ADA jurisprudence has become focused on who counts as disabled not because judges chose this issue, but because defendants raised it. Professional golfer Casey Martin became an ADA celebrity not because the Supreme Court promoted his story but because it proved to be easily digestible for the news media. (*Olmstead*, a much more significant but less entertaining case, was largely ignored.) It is at least plausible that the torrent of media stories about abuse of the ADA has persuaded some wavering members of the Supreme Court to adopt narrowed readings of the law—and may have contributed to the decision of disability rights activists not to seek a congressional override of the statute. The court–Congress game is played on a field that is contoured by other actors.

Moreover the court–Congress game hardly dominates legal interpretation. Out beyond the formal institutions, there are readings of statutes that are barely touched by court and Congress. Engel and Munger's subjects are blissfully ignorant of the intricacies of Supreme Court ADA jurisprudence; their reading of the law is shaped by their own frames and life experiences. Meanwhile, in the corporate human resources systems that Lauren Edelman and her colleagues study, the ADA is read through a managerial discourse of fairness that has little to do with what judges, members of Congress, or disability activists see as the essence of the statute. And in the popular culture, the ADA has yet another life, in which figures like Casey Martin take center stage. The most commonly recognized problem with principal–agent theory as applied to judicial implementation is that there are many principals. The case of the ADA suggests another problem: too many agents.

NOTES

1. One influential article argues that judges look to the committee reports and other bits of "legislative history" because it provides a signal of how likely Congress is to overturn a judicial ruling that goes against legislative intent (see Schwartz, Spiller, and Urbiztondo 1994).
2. Moreover, the agencies charged with enforcing the ADA can only act on a small percentage of the complaints that come into their offices, leaving much of the action to the judiciary (see Moss et al. 2001).
3. The five ADA cases decided during the 2001–2002 term were *Barnes v. Gorman*, 536 U.S. 181 (2002); *Chevron v. Echazabal*, 536 U.S. 73 (2002); *U.S. Airways v. Barnett*, 535 U.S. 391 (2002); *EEOC v. Waffle House Inc.*, 534 U.S. 279 (2002); and *Toyota Motor Mfg. v. Williams*, 534 U.S. 184 (2002).
4. Courts are divided over whether "interacting with others" counts as a disability. See, e.g., *Steele v. Thiokol*, 241 F.3d 1248, 1255 (10th Cir. 2001); *Soileau v. Guilford of Maine, Inc.*, 105 F.3d 12, 15 (1st Cir. 1997), with *McAlindin v. County of San Diego*, 192 F.3d 1226, 1234–35 (9th Cir. 1999); and on what counts as a "mitigating measure," *EEOC v. Sears*, 233 F.3d 432, 439 (7th Cir. 2000).

5. This definition was contained in a 1974 amendment to sections 501, 503, and 504 of the 1973 Rehabilitation Act; HR 17503, 93rd Cong., 2nd Sess. (1974).

6. Equal Employment Opportunity Commission, EEOC *Interpretive Guidance on Title I of the Americans with Disabilities Act*, 29 C.F.R. 1630.2(j)(1)(i)–(ii).

7. Feldblum notes that the EEOC regulations specify that "working" should be considered as a major life activity only in the rare case in which this is the only arena in which a person is substantially limited. She blames judges for focusing on "working" because of its close relationship to traditional notions about disability—an inability to work is in the eyes of many (and under some government programs) the very definition of disability (see Feldblum 2000, 140). Van Detta and Gallipeau focus more blame on plaintiffs, who they argue sometimes make a "fatal error" in relying on working as a major life activity (Van Detta and Gallipeau 2000, 522).

8. Another, even more fundamental, problem with "working" as a life activity is that the ADA plaintiff who is proving that he is substantially limited as a worker must then show that he is qualified to perform the "essential functions" of the job with "reasonable accommodation." If he is found to be too disabled, he may be deemed unqualified. Or if he is found to be too qualified, he may be deemed nondisabled.

9. The clearest victories are *Bragdon v. Abbott*, 524 U.S. 624 (1998) (dentist who refuses to treat HIV-positive patient violates the ADA); *Olmstead v. L.C. by Zimring*, 527 U.S. 581 (1999) (institutionalization of people with disabilities rather than community placement can be a form of discrimination prohibited by the ADA); *PGA Tour v. Martin*, 532 U.S. 661 (2001) (provision of a golf cart is "reasonable accommodation" for a professional golfer with a mobility disability); and *EEOC v. Waffle House*, 534 U.S. 279 (2002) (EEOC is not barred from suing in federal court by arbitration agreement signed by ADA complainant and employer).

10. In the 2002 case *U.S. Airways v. Barnett* (535 U.S. 391), the Court ruled that the ADA's requirement of "reasonable accommodation" of an employee with a disability did not normally require the employer to disregard seniority rules. But the Court left open the possibility that the plaintiff could prevail depending on the strength of an employer's seniority rule.

11. *Fussell v. Georgia Ports Authority*, 906 F. Supp. 1561, 1577 (S.D. Ga. 1994), quoting *Pedigo v. P.A.M. Transport, Inc.*, 891 F. Supp. 482, 485–86, as quoted in Van Detta and Gallipeau 2000, 512–13.

12. The problem is deepened by Kenneth Arrow's Impossibility Theorem, which demonstrates that in a system of majority rule, there is usually no single, stable preference that a majority will prefer, but instead a cycle of preferences. In other words, there can be no true majority outcome. According to this theorem, legislative outcomes, like the enactment of the ADA, are "structure-induced," in other words, a reflection of the fact that some in Congress have control over the process by which the law was debated and decided upon. The academics that have applied principal–agent theory to court–Congress interactions are, of course, aware of the fact that there is no true principal, and make simplifying assumptions to address this in their theories. For example, Schwartz, Spiller, and Urbitztondo assume there is a pivotal member of Congress whose preferences can stand in for the preferences of Congress (Schwartz, Spiller, and Urbitztondo 2000, 56–57, footnotes 16 and 17).

13. This reads: "findings enacted as part of the ADA require the conclusion that Congress did not intend to bring under the statute's protection all those whose uncorrected conditions amount to disabilities. Congress found that 'some 43,000,000 Americans have one or more physical or mental disabilities, and this number is increasing as the population as a whole is growing older.' This figure is inconsistent with the definition of disability pressed by petitioners" (*Sutton v. United Airlines*, 427 U.S., at 484).

14. Liptak 2002a. A LEXIS-NEXIS search for "Americans w/5 Disabilities" in the headline or first paragraph for the 2002 run of the *New York Times* turned up thirty-nine "hits,"

nine of which were news stories about ADA litigation. One of those involved a star football player's widely scorned claim that he had been discriminated against because of his depression (see Battista 2002).

15. A simple Lexis-Nexis search provides one modest measure of the difference in attention the two cases received. A search among "major papers" for the six months following the decision in *Olmstead* for any article with "Americans w/5 disabilities" and either "Olmstead," "Georgia," and "retarded," or "Georgia" and "institution," resulted in 26 unique articles. A similar search for "Americans w/5 disabilities" and "Casey Martin" found 159 articles.

8

The City of Boerne
Two Tales of One City

**STEPHEN G. BRAGAW
AND MARK C. MILLER**

IN A SMALL TEXAS CITY THAT IS QUICKLY TRANSFORMING IT-self into a reluctant suburb of San Antonio, a relatively mundane local dispute between a Catholic parish and the local historical preservation commission ultimately became a landmark U.S. Supreme Court decision that helped redefine the continuing struggle between the Supreme Court and the U.S. Congress over which institution has the final say on interpreting the Constitution. In *City of Boerne v. Archbishop Flores*, 117 S.Ct. 2157 (1997), known as the *City of Boerne* case, a 6–3 majority of the Court declared the federal Religious Freedom Restoration Act to be unconstitutional. The Court also decreed that Congress had no right to attempt to usurp the Court's asserted power to be the final arbiter of constitutional conflicts in the American political system. This chapter will explore one tale arising from this landmark Supreme Court decision, namely, this case's role in the epic struggle over the question of whether the Court or Congress can have the last word on determining what the Constitution means. Second, this chapter will explore another tale arising from this dispute, one dealing with the question of how interest groups exploit the inevitable conflicts between these two governmental institutions.

Before we can get to the lessons to be learned from the *City of Boerne* case, it is necessary to present some background information on how the Supreme Court has traditionally handled free exercise of religion cases. The First Amendment to the Constitution, of course, includes two clauses dealing with the question of freedom of religion in this country. The First Amendment prohibits Congress from interfering with the free exercise of religion, but it also prohibits it from contributing to the establishment of religion. Although the vast majority of Supreme Court decisions fall under the jurisprudence of the Establishment Clause, the *City of Boerne* case dealt instead with the Free Exercise Clause.

In order to understand the *City of Boerne* decision, we must first examine a few prior Free Exercise cases. In the 1963 case of *Sherbert v. Verner*, 374 U.S. 398 (1963), the Supreme Court ruled 7–2 that when the government enacts a law that burdens the free exercise of religion, the government violates the Free Exercise Clause unless it can show that it is protecting a compelling governmental interest and it is doing so in the least restrictive manner possible. This ruling gave a great deal of protection to members of generally minority religious groups who felt that the government was infringing on their free exercise rights. In 1990, however, in *Employment Division v. Smith*, 494 U.S. 872 (1990), a 6–3 majority explicitly rejected the Sherbert compelling interest standard. Instead, the Court majority ruled that the Free Exercise Clause does not relieve an individual from the obligation to comply with a valid and neutral law of general applicability on the ground that the law commands behavior inconsistent with a person's religious beliefs (see Epstein and Walker 2004, 137).

The Smith case concerned two members of the Native American Church who had been fired from their jobs as drug counselors working for a nonprofit organization because they had ingested peyote, a hallucinogenic drug, during a Native American sacramental religious ceremony. Their application for unemployment compensation benefits was denied by the State of Oregon under a state law that disqualifies employees from unemployment benefits if they were fired for work-related misconduct. The employer argued that remaining drug free was a critical condition of their employment as drug counselors (see Epps 2001). The Court ruled that the Free Exercise Clause permits a state to prohibit sacramental peyote use and to deny unemployment benefits to persons fired for violating a state law making peyote use illegal. The state may make the possession or use of a drug illegal even if it incidentally prohibits a religious practice (see Kahn 1999, 191). Four of the justices said the Sherbert compelling interest standard should still apply, although five of the justices abandoned that broad test (see Fisher 2003, 606–7).

Shocked by the Smith decision, interest groups representing mainstream religious organizations as well as minority religious groups lobbied very hard for Congress to overturn the Supreme Court ruling. In 1993, Congress enacted the Religious Freedom Restoration Act (RFRA), which attempted to require the use of the previous Sherbert compelling governmental interest standard for testing federal, state, and local laws that infringed on religious practices. Proponents of the new law worried that the Smith standard "threatened a number of religious practices, including the use of ceremonial wine, the practice of kosher slaughter, and the Hmong (Laotian) religious objection to autopsy" (Fisher 2003, 607).

All the major religious organizations in the United States strongly supported the passage of RFRA. In 1994, Congress went one step further and enacted legislation to legalize the use of peyote by Native Americans for ceremonial religious purposes. In 1997, in the *City of Boerne* case, the Supreme Court declared RFRA to be unconstitutional because it violated separation of powers and federalism principles. This chapter will explore two tales from the City of Boerne's experience.

A CITY ON A HILL

In his sermon at the founding of Boston, "A Model of Christian Charity," the first governor of Massachusetts Bay, John Winthrop, challenged, "We shall be a city set on a hill." To the Pilgrims, as radical dissenting Protestants, the notion of the "City on the Hill" as Zion—the New Jerusalem—that would be created on the shores of the "New World" represented the belief that model political communities could be created by acts of conscientious self-creation, based on guidance from scripture. The metaphor of the "City on the Hill" has been an enduring image of idealism as well as discontent since the advent of American political culture over three and a half centuries ago, in many ways encapsulating the paradoxical relationship of church and state in American constitutional politics. Ironically, the City of Boerne, Texas, is a city set on a hill.

Northwest from Corpus Christi, the lush low country of the Gulf coast gradually gives way to the terra cotta piedmont of the Texas hill country at San Antonio. Continuing northwest for another fifteen miles is a city set on a hill, the City of Boerne. Boerne [pronounced "Bernie," as the switchboard operators at City Hall kindly pointed out] is a small four-and-a-half-square-mile city of about 5,000 people, inexorably being brought into the expanding sprawl of metropolitan suburban San Antonio.

Occupying the high ground of Boerne's hill, with a commanding view of the old entry avenues to the city, sits Saint Peter the Apostle Roman Catholic Church. Built of locally dug fieldstone in 1923, the church is a rare surviving specimen of the historic mission revival style, with a particularly distinctive façade and bell tower spires. The original Saint Peter the Apostle Church in Boerne was built in 1867, and was replaced on the same spot in 1923 with a much larger 230-seat sanctuary. By the mid-1980s, the building was in need of significant repair work. By the late 1980s, the parish had grown to more than 1,200 families, representing a sizable portion of the population of the small city of 5,000. Because of overcrowding, the parish soon had to hold some masses and celebrations in a nearby senior center auditorium because the sanctuary was far too small to accommodate the worshipers.

Father Tony Cummins arrived at the parish in 1990, having come from his previous assignments with a solid track record as a "builder," of expanding parishes and of new sanctuaries. The parish and the archdiocese put together a plan for expanding Saint Peter's, and the final version approved by Archbishop Patrick Fernández Flores in late 1990 called for a much larger sanctuary with more than 800 seats in a modernistic design, which would have required taking down the old church building. According to its briefs in the case, the archdiocese did not consider "mission-revival" a distinct style, and did not consider the building in Boerne to be an historical landmark.

The same population growth that drove Saint Peter's pastor Father Tony Cummins to want to build a new sanctuary also drove the city leadership to create a Historic Landmark Commission (HLC) to preserve the charming character of downtown Boerne. In 1985, the city council approved the creation of the HLC. The HLC then proposed and the city council later approved the creation of a downtown historic district in Boerne, which became official in January 1992. Central to the plan was the preservation of what all agreed was the most distinct building in town, occupying the center of the city's hill: Saint Peter the Apostle Church. In December 1993, however, the archdiocese submitted the paperwork to build their vision of a new Saint Peter's. The HLC rejected the church's application, which was appealed to the City Council, which has final say over all HLC zoning issues. The council also rejected the petition but soon offered a counterproposal. The façade and roughly seventy percent of the existing exterior front perimeter wall of the church would be kept intact, and the "mission revival" style would remain with the whole complex. In return the diocese could tear down the rear of the church to build the 850-seat sanctuary, and the city would perform the public works necessary to move a side street to allow the new sanctuary to be built on the rear of the church's property. The archdiocese rejected the offer, however, because they felt it would be too expensive for the church.

The archdiocese then filed a lawsuit, claiming that the actions of the city represented an unconstitutional burden on their free exercise of religion—their ability to build a sanctuary to meet the worship space needs of their parishioners—as protected under the recently passed RFRA, whose advocates seized upon the dispute between Saint Peter's and the City of Boerne as a "slam-dunk" case to prove the Act's constitutionality. What issue, Father Cummins later asked, cut to the question of the free exercise of religion more than the state preventing the building of a church?[1] Ultimately, 109 groups and individuals signed on as amicus curiae in RFRA's defense. But by a vote of 6–3, the justices disagreed, allowing the City of Boerne the right to block the expansion of the Church sanctuary.

Much has been written and spoken about this case in the ensuing years. Yet, an important aspect of this case has been generally overlooked: *The new sanctuary was built anyway.* The diocese, the parish, the city, and the HLC brokered an agreement a month *after* the Supreme Court's decision that allowed the substantial renovation to be done after all. The diocese wound up taking the basic offer made to them by the city *three years earlier*, to keep the façade, spires, and exterior style while greatly expanding the rear of the building. The diocese got its new, expanded sanctuary, while the city got to preserve its zoning prerogatives and the architectural style of its downtown district. But the settling of this zoning dispute came at the price of the defeat of RFRA, and the cost of at least a half a million dollars in lawyer's fees on behalf of the city and the diocese alone[2]—not to mention the costs of the one hundred and thirty-three interest groups, individuals, and state governments which ultimately filed twenty-seven different amicus curiae briefs in the case.

THE GRAND FIGHT BETWEEN THE COURT AND CONGRESS

While the *City of Boerne* case started as a small local dispute between a church and a local historical preservation commission, it soon evolved into a bitter battle between the Supreme Court and Congress over which body had the stronger institutional will. The *Boerne* case became part of a larger struggle over whether the Supreme Court or Congress could have the last word on saying what various provisions in the Constitution actually mean. Thus, the *City of Boerne* case became another opportunity for the Court to strike back at Congress for enacting statutes that the Court felt infringed upon its judicial prerogatives.

By striking down RFRA and reemphasizing its ruling in the Smith case, the Supreme Court clearly told Congress that it viewed the judiciary as the final arbiter of all things constitutional. As the majority of the Court concluded in the *City of Boerne* case, "Our national experience teaches that the Constitution is preserved best when each part of the government respects both the Constitution and the proper actions and determinations of the other branches. When the Court has interpreted the Constitution, it has acted within the province of the Judicial Branch, which embraces the duty to say what the law is. . . . As the provisions of the federal statute here invoked are beyond congressional authority, it is this Court's precedent, not RFRA, which must control" (*Boerne v. Flores*, at 2172).

Many scholars have commented on the depth of the fight between Congress and the Court over RFRA (see, e.g., Franck 1998; Conkle 1998). RFRA passed *unanimously* in the House of Representatives, and with only three dissents in the Senate. The clear purpose of RFRA was explicitly and intentionally to overturn the Supreme Court's decision in Smith, a ruling many religious and social groups considered to be egregiously wrong (see O'Brien 2003, 363). But the Court refused to allow Congress to interfere with its precedent in the Smith case. Thus, the *Boerne* decision will be long known "for its stunning assertion of the Court's supremacy in settling all governmental disputes" (Bragaw and Perry 2002, 21).

Recently, the Supreme Court has been more emphatic in striking down legislation that it feels infringes on its judicial responsibilities. The *Boerne* case is just one example of this conflict between the Court and Congress. In *U.S. v. Lopez*, 514 U.S. 549 (1995), the Court struck down the Gun-Free School Zones Act because the majority of the justices felt that Congress had exceeded its constitutional authority to regulate interstate commerce when it prohibited the possession of guns near public schools. At the time, it was unclear whether the Lopez case would become a landmark decision, or whether "it may have been a case where Congress simply failed to present adequate findings to show an interstate commerce link with guns on school playgrounds" (Fisher 2003, 364). The Court clarified its Lopez ruling and at the same time substantially strengthened its power to interpret the Commerce Clause in *U.S. v. Morrison*, 529 U.S. 598 (2000). The Morrison decision declared unconstitutional portions of the federal Violence Against Women Act. In its Morrison opinion, a 5–4 majority of the Court very clearly stated that only the Supreme Court, and not Congress, could determine the limits of congressional authority under both the Commerce Clause and the Fourteenth Amendment. As the majority declared in Morrison, "whether particular operations affect interstate commerce sufficiently to come under the constitutional power of Congress to regulate them is ultimately a judicial rather than a legislative question, and can be settled finally only by this Court" (529 U.S., at 615). They also held that Congress exceeded its authority under the Fourteenth Amendment by enacting the Violence Against Women Act. The Morrison decision overturned over fifty years of Supreme Court precedent that had basically allowed Congress unlimited powers under the Commerce Clause.

This pattern of the Court restricting congressional powers has continued in other recent cases. In *Kimel v. Florida Board of Regents*, 528 U.S. 62 (2000), for example, the Supreme Court held that when Congress allowed state employees to sue under the Age Discrimination in Employment Act, the legislature had exceeded its constitutional authority because the Court had not yet declared that age discrimination violated the Fourteenth Amendment. Thus, the Court reasserted its power to determine what types of discrimination are prohibited by the Fourteenth Amendment (see O'Brien 2003, 364). In *Bush v. Gore*, 531 U.S. 98 (2000), when the Supreme Court determined that the recounts in Florida after the 2000 presidential election violated the Equal Protection Clause of the Fourteenth Amendment, the Court also clearly asserted its right to be the final arbiter of both intergovernmental and intragovernmental constitutional conflicts in the American political system (see Bragaw and Perry 2002). In *Dickerson v. U.S.*, 530 U.S. 428 (2000), the Court held that its previous ruling in *Miranda v. Arizona*, 384 U.S. 436 (1966), was a constitutionally based decision that Congress could not modify by statute. In Dickerson, the Court declared that "Congress may not legislatively supersede our decisions interpreting and applying the Constitution" (530 U.S., at 437). Thus, one tale from the City of Boerne case is the tale of the Supreme Court reasserting its institutional will to limit the powers of Congress.

THE ROLE OF INTEREST GROUPS

One aspect of the *City of Boerne* case that has not received much attention is the role of interest groups in the case. Thus, the second tale from this city deals with what this case indicates about the status of interest group litigation today. Two things stand out about the case that makes an inquiry of this kind relevant. First is the unusually high number of amicus curiae briefs filed from across the political and social spectrum in the case. States and territories, mainstream and fringe religious groups, conservative social and liberal political groups, members of Congress and state legislators, anti-takings and libertarian organizations, pro–historic preservationists, antiestablishmentarians, independent scholars, and prisoner rights advocates were all "represented" before the Justices. By contrast, *Employment Division v. Smith*—the case RFRA was designed to overturn—attracted only two amici curiae. Second is the unusual ultimate compromise settlement of the case after the Court's ruling, in which, according to Father Tony Cummins, "I think what happened was that some people got a little more sense."[3] Both these issues indicate a need to further examine the role of interest group litigation in the American judicial process in light of *Boerne v. Flores*.

Since the origins of the common law in early Norman England, groups have played an active and controversial role in litigation (see Yeazell 1987). Interest groups in America were active in the judicial process as early as the late nineteenth century, sparked by the maturation of the industrial revolution and the rise of the administrative state. David Truman's classic work in political science, *The Governmental Process*, discussed interest group litigation as an aspect of the influence of interest groups in American politics more broadly. Interest groups would not only be involved in trying to influence the selection of judges, Truman argued, but would need to participate effectively in litigation in order to protect their interests, even if this influence was much more indirect than in other forums. Lobbying the courts, to Truman, was as important—and as necessary—as lobbying the legislature, the executive, and the bureaucracy (Truman 1971, 498).

The *City of Boerne* case is not unusual because of the influence of interest groups in the litigation process but because of the unique combination of interest groups and subnational governments represented. A critical, yet often neglected, aspect of the study of interest group litigation is the role of state attorneys general, and municipal and district attorneys. A blind spot within the study of interest group litigation has been the tendency on the part of some scholars to romanticize the process, with interest group litigator "heroes" as "crusaders in court," (see, e.g., Greenberg 1994) and the "villains" representing the subnational governments (see Wilson 1996). The problem is that whatever the politics of midcentury, subnational officials have changed. Specifically, since the early 1980s subnational leadership organizations have taken significant steps to improve their representation before the Supreme Court, efforts which ultimately bore fruit in *Boerne v. Flores*.

In the early 1980s, there was a widely held anecdotal perception at the Supreme Court, in the Washington, D.C., bar, in the academy, and in the state capitals and big city halls, that the interests of state and local governments were inadequately being represented before the Supreme Court (see, e.g., Baker and Asperger 1982). The states and localities, it was felt, were many times losing cases they could win, often because of shoddy and inadequate preparation (see Howard 1982). Justice Lewis F. Powell went to the extreme of publicly chastising the states for poorly representing the public interest, asserting that the state and local lawyers were quite often "outgunned and overmatched" when before the Court (Powell 1974). The problem was exacerbated by the fact that an adverse ruling through one state's failure potentially harmed all the states: in a perverse reverse logic of *E Pluribus Unum*, from one, many were affected. State officials and federalism advocates were publicly declaring that it was time for the states to act on their own initiative to defend themselves through a coordinated strategy for the representation of their common interests (see Baker and Ausberger 1982, 368; Brennan 1980).

Among the regular litigators before the Supreme Court, it seemed as if the states were alone in leaving their prospects to chance. Others with just as much at stake in the actions of the Supreme Court had for years taken extensive steps to ensure their interests were adequately represented. Interest groups of every ideological stripe and hue were represented by legal defense organizations patterned on the mid-century successes of the NAACP Legal Defense and Education Fund. Spurred by the example of Ralph Nader, an entire "public interest bar" had arisen since the early 1970s dedicated to litigate "in the public interest." Corporations, trade associations, and labor unions, either through general counsel or through professional associations, were also represented. And, of course, the interests of the United States were represented by the Solicitor General's Office of the Department of Justice, through the decades always both the most frequent and most successful litigator before the high court. While the states were second only to the United States in appearance at the bar of the Supreme Court,[4] it was widely believed that they were not only the least successful but also the worst regular litigators (see, e.g., Ulmer 1985, 899; and Caldeira and McCrone 1983).[5]

Given these perceived weaknesses in the success of subnational governments at the Supreme Court, the National Association of Attorneys General (NAAG) created the Supreme Court Project in 1983. The creation of the Supreme Court Project by NAAG mirrored the actions taken by the National Governors Association, the U.S. Conference of Mayors, the National League of Cities, and the other four organizations representing state and local elected officials to create the State and Local Legal Center (see Bragaw 1999). Each group (the Supreme Court Project of NAAG and the State and Local Legal Center) was chartered to improve the representation of state and local interests before the Supreme Court by professional education, and the coordination of amicus curiae briefs. But where the State and Local Legal Center was to represent the "big seven" intergovernmental lobby groups in cases dealing with the capacity of subnational governments to govern—cases dealing with unfunded mandates, sovereign immunity, tax issues, regulatory preemption, and the general power distribution between states and the federal government—the mandate of the Supreme Court Project of the attorneys general was not so narrowly drawn. Instead of involving itself in specific policy areas, the Supreme Court Project was designed to be a "clearinghouse" to provide attorneys general and municipal attorneys the professional support to coordinate briefs and advocacy strategies.[6]

In the *City of Boerne* case, the Supreme Court Project became important right after the diocese sued the city. Susan Rocha, one of Boerne's lawyers who helped handle the suit in its early stages, was struck from the beginning with the participation of Douglas Laycock as a lawyer for the diocese.[7] Laycock is prominent in Texas as a noted University of Texas law professor, and as one of the most influential in lobbying Congress to pass RFRA. Others noted the impression of a good working relationship between Laycock and Archbishop Flores.

Saint Peter's had all the markings of a test case to prove RFRA's constitutionality. First, the fact that it involved a Roman Catholic congregation was perhaps a subtle pitch to the two Catholic archconservatives on the Court, Justices Antonin Scalia and Clarence Thomas. Substantively, the issue of historic landmarking of churches was a major issue for Catholic and mainline Protestant denominations as a clearly defined free exercise issue of, as Father Cummins put it, "the state telling us we can't build a church." Unlike other cases that were entering the pipeline—for example, the right of Sikh boys to wear the *kirpan* dagger in their turban without violating weapons in school ordinances—it was apparently felt by RFRA's interest group advocates that the Boerne dispute presented the best possible factual presentation of the law's necessity and legitimacy.

At this juncture the City of Boerne made a critical decision. The city's lawyers from the San Antonio firm of Denton, McKamie, and Navarro had much experience before the District and Fifth Circuit, but had no experience in the U.S. Supreme Court. Historically, this is where municipal attorneys have gotten themselves into the most trouble. For most lawyers, the chance to argue a case—let alone a major civil liberties case—before the Justices is a once in a lifetime professional opportunity, let alone a chance to garner a reputation in politics. Appellate lawyering, however, is a very specialized and highly nuanced business. One secret of interest group success in Supreme Court litigation was perhaps in taking advantage of the inexperience of state and municipal attorneys in that forum. Fully aware of that pitfall, the City retained Marci Hamilton, a professor at Cardozo Law School in New York, to represent Boerne at the Supreme Court. Professor Hamilton had clerked for Justice Sandra Day O'Connor during the term when *Employment Division v. Smith* had been decided, and had written a number of articles arguing against the constitutionality of RFRA, which Boerne's lawyers had found through Internet searches.[8] Hamilton directed the preparation of Boerne's brief, and subjected herself over the following months to the scrutiny of a number of moot courts with colleagues and former clerks at Cardozo and George Washington University Law School.

Attorneys for other subnational governments also took notice of the case. The acceptance of *City of Boerne v. Flores* by the Court for the October 1996 term caused initially a panic in the Columbus office of Todd Martie, the assistant attorney general of Ohio.[9] Martie directed the Corrections Litigation Section, which "fends off" lawsuits by prisoners against the state. Martie was also an active participant in the National Association of Attorneys General Supreme Court Project/ Prison Litigation Working Group, monitoring prisoner-rights–related litigation percolating in the federal court systems.

Martie and his colleagues were looking for a test case to "get rid of RFRA," which with its compelling state interest and least restrictive means tests was having a destructive effect on prison management in Ohio, as well as in other states. "We were getting buried in cases, it was very aggravating as most all were dismissed,"

Martie confided, describing in great detail many of the spurious claims made under RFRA by Ohio prisoners. They felt that they had a good test case to challenge RFRA in a lawsuit that involved prison regulations regarding hair length and grooming, and a prisoner who was a member of the Native American Church (ironically, the same group involved in *Employment Division v. Smith*). According to Martie, they contacted Boerne's lawyers to withdraw their case, as it was felt by many of their colleagues that the facts of the zoning case presented too clearly in favor of upholding RFRA.

Marci Hamilton's response was forceful and matter of fact: "They were flatly wrong—land use was just as good if not better an issue, and the facts of the case were much sounder." With the case going forward, Martie and Ohio Solicitor General Jeffrey Sutton contacted NAAG's Supreme Court Project to state their interest in preparing an amicus curiae brief in support of Boerne that would focus on the issues of RFRA and prison management. The Supreme Court Project's office faxed the memo to the amicus curiae coordinator in each of the attorneys general offices in the other forty-nine states and six territories, with the deadline for joining the brief. A week before the deadline, a copy of Sutton's brief for Ohio was faxed out to the coordinators, and a conference call was held in which different offices could make requests for changes to the brief in time for its submission to the Court.

In the end, fourteen states and three territories joined Sutton's Ohio brief, while five states (including Texas) joined two briefs in support of the diocese and RFRA. Ohio petitioned for and was granted the opportunity to argue its brief before the Justices, so that the oral argument was divided between Boerne and Marci Hamilton, Ohio and Jeff Sutton, the diocese and Douglas Laycock, and the United States and acting Solicitor General Dellinger. Sutton, a former clerk of Justices Powell and Scalia, also subjected himself to numerous moot courts to prepare for oral argument, both in Columbus, and in Washington with lawyers and former clerks from NAAG and the "clerk network."[10] But not just the attorneys general were paying attention to the case. A remarkable number of groups participated. However, upon reading the final decision of the case, one brief stands out in the prominence of its arguments echoed in Justice Kennedy's majority opinion: the Ohio brief of Jeff Sutton.

What conclusions can be drawn from this second tale of Boerne? First, scholars and commentators who observe courts and law need to pay greater attention to the role of subnational governmental litigation efforts to tell the full story of interest groups and legal change. In an age where interest group litigation has lost the gleam of the crusader's shield it had in an earlier generation, such an effort can help better demonstrate the effect such litigation has on the communities in which it takes place, when the conflict is not of clear moral absolutes but the clash of equally valued fundamental rights. By seeking the path of litigation rather than compromise, the archdiocese gained nothing, incurred a quite substantial bill, and lost RFRA, only to take the offer that the city had put on the table three years earlier.

While just a study of one case, the experience of the City of Boerne questions the effectiveness of interest group litigation as a strategy in the face of sophisticated and nuanced legal representation on the behalf of subnational governments. That a small city like Boerne recognized exactly when it was in over its head, and went out and found not only a high profile litigator but also the right one for the job, speaks volumes. That this lawyer was then able to work effectively with the state attorneys general network is a hallmark of this phenomenon not uncommon amid the Court's "federalism revolution" that began in 1992. This case also indicates that interest group litigants understood the broader context in which this case was set. The interest groups recognized and exploited the larger battle between the Supreme Court and Congress that played itself out in these two tales of a small city in Texas.

NOTES

1. Author interview with Fr. Tony Cummins, pastor of Saint Peter the Apostle Roman Catholic Church, Boerne, Tex., December 8, 1998.
2. As estimated by one of the city's attorneys. Author interview with Susan Rocha, municipal attorney for Boerne, Tex., December 4, 1998.
3. Author interview with Fr. Tony Cummins, December 8, 1998.
4. States appear as litigants on the Supreme Court's full decisional docket on average 37 percent of its total time. In the October 1986 term, the Supreme Court heard 156 hours of oral argument, 58 hours of which were by state and local governmental attorneys (Ross 1990, ix).
5. Some statistics are useful for comparison. Over the period of 1953 to 1990, the national government won 63 percent of the 1,237 cases it participated in as a direct party, whereas the states won 48 percent of the 1,338 cases they were involved with (Epstein et al. 2002, 569, 577). In cases specifically involving federalism issues (specifically defined as "conflicts between the federal and state governments, excluding those between state and federal courts, and those involving the priority of federal fiscal claims" (Epstein et al. 2002, 570, table 7.11, notes), the national government won 64.9 percent of its cases during the same period (with a success rate of 73.1 percent when the solicitor general appeared as amicus curiae), whereas, conversely, the states won only 35.4 percent of the time.
6. The Supreme Court Project was made possible by the Department of Justice loaning attorney Douglas Ross from the Office of Legislative and Intergovernmental Affairs to NAAG; the Supreme Court Project is now directed by Daniel Schweitzer (see Ross 1985; Ross 1990; Ross and Catalano 1988; Lempert 1982; Morris 1987; Clayton 1994).
7. Author interview with Susan Rocha, December 4, 1998.
8. Author interview with Marci Hamilton, December 7, 1998.
9. Author interview with Todd Martie, December 8, 1998.
10. Author interview with Jeffrey Sutton, December 14, 1998.

PART IV

Constitutional Interpretation: The Interbranch Perspective Applied

9

Judicial Finality or an Ongoing Colloquy?

LOUIS FISHER

ALTHOUGH THE SUPREME COURT PERIODICALLY ANNOUNCES that it has the "final word" on constitutional law, the reality has always been quite different. For reasons that stretch across political and institutional boundaries, the Court is not only adroit in sidestepping a number of constitutional issues, thereby shifting those disputes to others to resolve, but must acknowledge that even when it does act it can be reversed and substantially modified not only by Congress and the president, but also by the states operating under their own constitutions. Instead of a hierarchical system, with the Court sitting supremely at the top, the process of making constitutional law and shaping constitutional values is decidedly polyarchic.

There are many legitimate and authoritative participants in the shaping of constitutional law: some elected, some appointed, some in the status of citizens (such as those who serve on juries). Governmental acts are driven by powerful political pressures from the general public. Justices recognize that the most delicately crafted decision, backed by a rich array of prior precedents, has no chance of success in the face of broad public opposition. While the courts have some independence, they must step with caution and prudence to protect their institutional interests. In the best sense of the word, they must operate politically and deftly.

THE RISKS OF STEPPING OUT

Throughout its history, the Supreme Court has understood that its "independence" relies on an astute appreciation of how dependent the judiciary is on the political system for understanding, supporting, and implementing judicial rulings. The Court has an opportunity to exercise leadership and creativity, but the risk of a political backlash is always around the corner. Judicial efforts to shoehorn a "liberty of contract" into the U.S. Constitution, after meeting with some success from the 1890s to the 1930s, were finally abandoned because the doctrine was alien to political needs and economic conditions (Fisher 2003, 438–59). After the Court capitulated,

Justice Roberts remarked: "Looking back, it is difficult to see how the Court could have resisted the popular urge for uniform standards throughout the country—for what in effect was a unified economy" (Roberts 1951, 61).

This type of dialogue between the Court and Congress took place with legislative efforts to curb corrupt campaign practices. Legislation in 1907 prohibited any national bank or any corporation created by Congress from contributing money for political elections. Three years later, Congress passed the Federal Corrupt Practices Act, which limited the amount of money that congressional candidates could contribute to their own nomination or election (34 Stat. 864 [1907]; 36 Stat. 822 [1910]; see also 37 Stat. 25 [1911]). In *Newberry v. United States*, 256 U.S. 232 (1921), the Court held that the corrupt practices statute, to the extent that it covered primaries, was unconstitutional. Although Article I, Section 4, empowers Congress to alter state regulations concerning the "Manner of holding Elections" for U.S. senators and representatives, four justices held that elections in the constitutional sense meant "the final choice of an officer." Pushing original intent and strict construction to absurd lengths, the Court said that primaries "were then unknown" at the time of the Constitution, and that primaries were "in no sense elections for an office" (256 U.S. 250). As applied to primaries and nominating conventions, therefore, the statute usurped state power. Justice McKenna joined the four Justices in setting aside the conviction authorized by the statute, but offered no opinion on the constitutional distinction between primaries and elections.

In one of the dissents, Chief Justice White denounced the appeal to original intent as "suicidal" (256 U.S. 262). To underscore his point, he reviewed the Framers' expectation that members of the Electoral College would be free agents, capable of exercising discretion when choosing the president. In 1876, however, when James Russell Lowell was urged to exercise independence and vote for Samuel Tilden, he refused on the ground that "whatever the first intent of the Constitution was, usage had made the presidential electors strictly the instruments of the party which chose them." White concluded that whatever case could have been made for state autonomy in matters of national elections had evaporated in 1913 with the Seventeenth Amendment, which provided for the election of U.S. senators by the people rather than by state legislatures. Justice Pitney, joined by Justices Brandeis and Clarke, also repudiated the Court's foray into strict construction. Pitney wrote: "It is said primaries were unknown when the Constitution was adopted. So were the steam railway and the electric telegraph. But the authority of Congress to regulate commerce among the several States extended over these instrumentalities . . ." (256 U.S. 282).

Congress rewrote the Federal Corrupt Practices Act to conform to the Court's ruling, but it was only a matter of time before *Newberry* would be reversed. The Justice Department challenged the decision by insisting on political reality: "The relationship between a primary election and the ensuing general election is so intimate that the outcome of the former is often determinative of the latter."[1] The justice brief argued that congressional practice "has weight in determining the meaning of constitutional provisions."[2] In a subsequent case, the government argued that the right of voters in congressional primaries is secured by Article I, Section 2, calling for the choice of Representatives "by the People," as well as the Times, Places, and Manner Clause of Section 4 (Claude 1970, 33). Under these pressures and with a reconstituted membership, the Court in *United States v. Classic*, 313 U.S. 299 (1941), reversed *Newberry* and held that congressional power embraced not merely the final election but primaries as well. Even the three dissenters—Douglas, Black, and Murphy—rejected *Newberry's* conclusion that Congress had no power to control primary elections (313 U.S. 329–30).

In another state primary case, a unanimous Court in *Grovey v. Townsend*, 295 U.S. 45 (1935), held that a county clerk in Texas could refuse to give a ballot to a black who wanted to vote in the Democratic Party primary. The party convention, acting on its own without state legislation, had voted to restrict party membership to whites. The Court decided that the clerk was not a state officer, there was no "state action," and the conduct did not violate the federal constitution. However, the Court's decision in *Classic* undercut the 1935 ruling by holding that election officials in a Louisiana primary (conducted at public expense) acted "under color of" state law in altering and falsely counting ballots. Voters had a right under the U.S. Constitution to cast their ballots and have them counted. The Court finally overruled *Grovey* in 1944 when it declared (8 to 1) that Texas could not exclude blacks by limiting participation in state conventions to white citizens. This practice was held to be state action in violation of the Fifteenth Amendment (*Smith v. Allwright*, 321 U.S. 649 [1944]).

When Congress passed the Voting Rights Act of 1965, which represented the most comprehensive measure since 1870 to protect the voting rights of blacks, a number of states challenged the statute as an invasion of states' rights. However, an 8–1 Court upheld all challenged provisions of the act, giving broad recognition of the power of Congress to enforce the Fifteenth Amendment (*South Carolina v. Katzenbach*, 383 U.S. 301 [1966]). In another decision, upholding a congressional provision that waived the English language requirement for Puerto Rican voters, the Court acknowledged that fact-finding was a legislative, not a judicial, responsibility, and that it was for Congress "to assess and weigh the various conflicting considerations" (*Morgan v. Katzenbach*, 384 U.S. 641, 653 [1966]).

A judicial willingness to make policy in concert with other branches of government is evident in the Court's approach to state laws that prohibited miscegenation. Immediately after the Court had decided *Brown v. Board of Education*, 347 U.S. 483 (1954), it was faced with the constitutionality of a Virginia statute that banned mixed marriages. The Court's ruling on desegregation in 1954 had been criticized by opponents who predicted that integrated schools would produce "mongrelization" of the white race. A state court, in upholding the Virginia statute, said that natural law forbade interracial marriage: "the social amalgamation which leads to a corruption of races is as clearly divine as that which imparted to them different natures" (*Naim v. Naim*, 87 S.E.2d 749, 752 [Va. 1955]). State regulation of marriages was necessary, said the court, to prevent "a mongrel breed of citizens" (87 S.E. 2d 756).

Rather than decide this politically explosive issue, the Supreme Court returned the case to Virginia, giving time for its ruling on desegregation to build support across the nation (*Naim v. Naim*, 350 U.S. 891 [1955]). By 1967, with the Civil Rights Act of 1964 firmly in place, the Court was prepared to strike down miscegenation laws and did so unanimously. It pointed out that fourteen states in the previous fifteen years had repealed laws prohibiting interracial marriages. Contemporary public opinion, operating through legislatures, thus played an essential role (*Loving v. Virginia*, 388 U.S. 1 [1967]).

THE DEATH PENALTY

The meaning of the death penalty has been determined much more by broad social judgments than court decisions. Occasionally, the Supreme Court intervenes to prevent punishment it considers disproportionate,[3] but by and large it interprets the Eighth Amendment in light of the "evolving standards of decency that mark the progress of a maturing society" (*Trop v. Dulles*, 356 U.S. 86, 101 [1958]). The Court does not scrutinize the constitutional text or the Framers' intent to discover what constituted "cruel or unusual" punishment. Instead, it looks to "contemporary human knowledge" (*Robinson v. California*, 370 U.S. 660, 666 [1962]).

Only in the 1970s did the Court decide to wade deeply into issues of the death penalty. In 1971, it handed down the first of many long-winded, discursive explorations of the death penalty, deciding in this case that juries could be given absolute discretion to choose between life imprisonment and death, and that juries can decide both guilt and punishment in a single unitary proceeding. Due process did not require a bifurcated trial (*McGautha v. California*, 402 U.S. 183 [1971]). The next year, the Supreme Court of California declared the death penalty a violation of the state constitutional ban against cruel or unusual punishments. Within nine months, however, the California voters imposed their own view by amending the state constitution to reinstate the death penalty (*People v. Anderson*, 493 P.2d 880 [Cal. 1972], cert. denied, 406 U.S. 958 [1972]; Cal. Const. Art. I, § 27).

In 1972, the U.S. Supreme Court abruptly struck down death penalty statutes in Georgia and Texas as cruel and unusual because of the erratic nature of their application. A brief one-page per curiam—announcing the result—served as a preface for more than two hundred pages of concurrences and dissents. Only two Justices (Brennan and Marshall) regarded the death penalty unconstitutional in all cases (*Furman v. Georgia*, 408 U.S. 238 [1972]). The Court's decision confronted explicit language in the Constitution, which acknowledges the death penalty four times. The Fifth Amendment requires a presentment or indictment by grand jury for persons accused of a "capital, or otherwise infamous crime." The Double Jeopardy Clause refers to taking "life or limb." Also in the Fifth Amendment, no person shall be deprived of "life, liberty, or property" without due process of law. Under the Fourteenth Amendment, no state shall deprive any person of "life, liberty, or property" without due process of law. Of course, one could argue that *acknowledging* the death penalty in the Constitution does not mandate it or even favor it.

The Court's decision did not sit well in the country. The majority of states immediately reinstituted the death penalty for certain kinds of crime. In 1976, the Court reviewed the changes in Georgia's statute and upheld, 7–2, the new procedures (*Gregg v. Georgia*, 428 U.S. 153 [1976]). The majority noted that the positions of Justices Brennan and Marshall—that the Eighth Amendment prohibits the death penalty—had been "undercut substantially" by state actions from 1972 to 1976 to enact statutes calling for the death penalty (428 U.S. 179). The "evolving standards of decency" still favored executions.

What the Court has done since 1976 is to judge the propriety of the death penalty for certain classes of crimes, and it does this by looking to state practice. In

1977, it found the death penalty disproportionate for the crime of raping an adult woman. The gradual abandonment of that penalty by most states was accepted by the Court as persuasive evidence of contemporary public judgment (*Coker v. Georgia*, 433 U.S. 584, 593–96 [1977]) In deciding death penalty cases, the Court said that "attention must be given to the public attitudes concerning a particular sentence—history and precedent, legislative attitudes, and the response of juries reflected in their sentencing decisions" (433 U.S. 592).

At no time in the past fifty years had a majority of states authorized death as a punishment for rape. In 1925, eighteen states, the District of Columbia, and the federal government authorized capital punishment for the rape of an adult female. By 1971, that number had declined to sixteen states plus the federal government. When states had to rewrite their death penalty laws after the Court in 1972 invalidated existing laws on capital punishment, only three (Georgia, Louisiana, and North Carolina) decided to reinstate the death penalty for rape. Louisiana and North Carolina, responding to court challenges, reenacted the death penalty for murder but not for rape. This process of reconsideration by the states helped convince the Court that the penalty of death for rape was disproportionate.

In 1986, the Court held that the execution of prisoners who are insane violates the Eighth Amendment (*Ford v. Wainwright*, 477 U.S. 399 [1986]), but it hesitated three years later in striking down the death penalty for the retarded or mentally incapacitated. In holding that the Eighth Amendment does not categorically bar execution of the mentally retarded, a 5–4 Court cited a lack of "objective indicators" from society to prohibit such executions. The "clearest and most reliable objective evidence of contemporary values," it said, are the statutes passed by legislative bodies in the country. The Court also looked to data concerning the actions of sentencing jurors (*Penry v. Lynaugh*, 492 U.S. 302, 331 [1989]).

In 2002, the Court overturned its ruling on the retarded by noting changes in public attitudes as reflected in legislative judgments at the state level. In 1989, only two states (Georgia and Maryland) prohibited execution of the mentally retarded. Thirteen years later, the number of states exempting the mentally retarded from the death penalty had grown to eighteen, prompting the Court to remark: "it is fair to say that a national consensus has developed against it"(*Atkins v. Virginia*, 122 S.Ct. 2242, 2249 [2002]). The motor force for constitutional change is clearly the development of social judgment at the state level, not independent, free-ranging constitutional analysis by the Court.

ABORTION

The Court's decision in *Roe v. Wade*, 410 U.S. 113 (1973), is often cited as a leading example of judicial legislation. The Court attempted to steer a middle course by rejecting both abortion on demand and the absolute right to life, but in doing so it created a constitutional right of a woman to terminate her pregnancy in the early months, and devised a trimester framework to balance the woman's right against the interests of the state. After the fetus becomes viable (about seven months), the state may prohibit abortion except where necessary to preserve the life or health of the mother.

The Court had difficulty in identifying its source of authority. In discussing the right of privacy, the Court pointed to the First, Fourth, Fifth, and Ninth Amendments;

"the penumbras of the Bill of Rights;" and the "concept of liberty guaranteed by the first section of the Fourteenth Amendment." Precisely where to anchor the decision did not seem to matter: "This right of privacy, whether it be founded in the Fourteenth Amendment's concept of personal liberty and restrictions upon state action, as we feel it is, or, as the District Court determined, in the Ninth Amendment's reservation of rights to the people, is broad enough to encompass a woman's decision whether or not to terminate her pregnancy" (410 U.S. 153).

A close reading of *Roe* eliminates any chance that it could produce "finality" as constitutional analysis. The ruling is based largely on factual questions, such as "the light of present medical knowledge" (410 U.S. 163). The "compelling" point for state intervention, said the Court, is viability, a condition that is not fixed but varies with medical competence and techniques. As the Court noted in a subsequent case, viability is "a matter of medical judgment, skill, and technical ability, and we preserved the flexibility of the term" (*Planned Parenthood of Missouri v. Danforth*, 428 U.S. 52, 64 [1976]). As medical knowledge advanced, the Court's identification of trimester stages would provide increasingly less guidance.

In the decade after *Roe*, Congress and state legislatures debated whether to provide public funds for abortion. The Hyde Amendment, first passed by Congress in 1976, provided that no federal funds could be spent to perform abortions except to save the life of the mother or in cases of rape or incest. In 1980, a 5–4 Court upheld the Hyde Amendment. According to the Court, government may not place obstacles in the path of a woman's decision to choose abortion, but neither has it an obligation to remove obstacles it did not create (such as being poor) (*Harris v. McRae*, 448 U.S. 197 [1980]). A number of states handled public funding of abortion in a different manner. They reasoned that although the state has no constitutional obligation to provide medical care to the poor, once it does it bears a heavy burden of justifying a provision that withholds benefits from otherwise qualified individuals solely because they chose to exercise their constitutional right to have an abortion.[4]

In 1986, a 5–4 Court invalidated provisions in a Pennsylvania statute because they put pressure on women to continue their pregnancies (*Thornburgh v. American Coll. of Obst. & Gyn.*, 476 U.S. 747 [1986]). The dissent by Chief Justice Warren Burger was especially significant, because he formed part of the 7–2 majority in *Roe*. He agreed with the dissenters that "we should reexamine *Roe*." Three other dissenters (White, Rehnquist, and O'Connor) were much more emphatic in rejecting the premises of *Roe*. By 1989, four justices were on record as rejecting the trimester framework (*Webster v. Reproductive Health Services*, 492 U.S. 490 [1989]).

In 1992, the Court finally decided to jettison *Roe*'s trimester analysis and, in its place, announced an "undue burden" standard that would hold a law invalid if its purpose or effect is to place substantial obstacles in the path of a woman seeking an abortion before the fetus attains viability (*Planned Parenthood v. Casey*, 505 U.S. 833 [1992]). Instead of trying to rely on precise three-month stages to scrutinize statutory limitations, the Court clearly invited states to enact legislation that would withstand the more general strictures of the newly crafted undue-burden standard.

Following this decision, Congress began work on the Freedom of Choice Act (FOCA), intended to codify many of the protections originally announced in *Roe*. Just as the 1973 decision proved to be unacceptable judicially, so was it unworkable as a legislative product. FOCA was never enacted. During the Clinton administration, Congress passed legislation to prohibit late-term ("partial birth") abortions except to save the life of a woman. President Clinton, saying that he opposed late-term abortions but insisted on an exception to cover adverse health consequences, vetoed these bills and Congress was unable to override.

About thirty states passed legislation to prohibit late-term abortions, with a number of the statutes struck down by federal courts because they were vague and placed an undue burden on a woman's right to decide on an abortion. Nebraska's law, banning "partial birth abortions," was struck down by the Supreme Court in 2000. Divided 5 to 4, the Court split in many directions: an opinion written by Justice Breyer, separate concurrences by Stevens, O'Connor, and Ginsburg, and dissenting opinions by Rehnquist, Scalia, Kennedy, and Thomas (*Stenberg v. Carhart*, 530 U.S. 914 [2000]). States are now redrafting these bills to place prohibitions on partial-birth abortion in a manner that satisfies the standards announced by the Court.

Responding to the decision in 2000, Congress two years later passed the Born-Alive Infants Protection Act, which provides that the words "person," "human being," "child," and "individual" shall include every infant born alive at any stage of development. "Born alive" is defined as "the complete expulsion or extraction from his or her mother of that member, at any stage of development, who after such expulsion or extraction breathes or has a beating heart, pulsation of the umbilical cord, or definite movement of voluntary muscles, regardless of whether the umbilical cord has been cut, and regardless of whether the expulsion or extraction occurs as a result of natural or induced labor, cesarean section, or induced abortion." The purpose of the statute is to protect a child that emerges from the mother as a live baby. If a fetus were to survive an abortion procedure, it would be considered a person under federal law. The statute provides that it should not be constructed to affirm, deny, expand, or contract any legal right to abortion (116 Stat. 296 [2002]).

Although Congress has been as divided as the Court on abortion issues, the Born-Alive Infants Protection Act passed with broad support. The bill cleared the House Judiciary Committee on a roll-call vote of 25–2 and passed the House under suspension of the rules.[5] It passed the Senate in 2002 under a unanimous consent motion, after passing the Senate a year earlier, 98 to zero, as an amendment to the Patients' Bill of Rights legislation (148 *Cong. Rec.* S7084 [daily ed., July 18, 2002]).

THE RIGHT TO DIE

Having been singed (both internally and externally) by its decision in *Roe v. Wade*, the Court began to move more cautiously in discovering new rights within the Constitution. On the sensitive issue of the right to die for the elderly and for patients who survive solely because of life-support systems with no hope of recovery, the Court let the question percolate at the state level (*Matter of Quinlan*, 355 A.2d 647 [N.J. 1976]). The issue reached the Court in 1990, but a 5–4 Court decided that the federal constitution did not forbid Missouri from requiring "clear and convincing" evidence that an incompetent, permanently unconscious person wishes the withdrawal of life-support systems. At the same time, the Court held that a competent person has a constitutional right to refuse such systems (*Cruzan v. Director, Missouri Dept. of Health*, 497 U.S. 261 [1990]). The Court recognized that other states were at liberty to adopt more liberal laws than Missouri's, and that individuals may always protect their privacy rights to some extent by signing "living wills" that express their desire to reject life-support systems.

In response to the 1990 decision, Congress passed the Patient Self-Determination Act to require health care providers in Medicare and Medicaid programs to give patients information about living wills and to educate staff about rights and procedures under state law. For example, patients must be informed about their right to grant a power of attorney to someone else to make such a decision (104 Stat. 1388-117, § 4027 [1990]). One of the cosponsors of this legislation, Representative Sander Levin (D-Mich.), explained: "it is important to recognize what this bill does not do. It does not create any new rights. It only says that people should know what rights they already have" (136 *Cong. Rec.* 16588 [1990]).

At the state level, legal questions were raised about individuals who assist others to commit suicide. Jack Kevorkian, a retired pathologist, used a machine that allowed terminally ill patients to inhale carbon monoxide. By 1993 he had assisted nineteen people with such procedures. Murder charges brought by Michigan prosecutors were dropped because the state had no law against assisted suicide, but after the state passed legislation making assisted suicide a felony, he was sentenced to prison in 1999. His appeal to the Supreme Court was rejected in 2002, when the Court refused to hear his case (*Kevorkian v. Michigan*, 123 S.Ct. 90 [2002]).

Just as Congress passed the Hyde Amendment to limit federal funding of abortions, so did it in 1997 pass legislation to ban federal funding for assisted suicide. In this case, the statute had more of a preventative quality, because existing programs of the federal government did not provide any funds for assisted suicide. The bill passed the House 398 to 16, and cleared the Senate 99 to zero (143 *Cong. Rec.* H1397-1405 [daily ed., April 10, 1997], S3249-65 [daily ed., April 16, 1997]). As enacted, it banned the funding of assisted suicide, euthanasia, or mercy killing through Medicaid, Medicare, military and federal employee health plans, the veterans health care system, and other federally funded programs. Moreover, the statute prohibits the use of federal taxpayer funds to subsidize legal assistance or other forms of advocacy to support assisted suicide, euthanasia, or mercy killing (111 Stat. 23 [1997]).

In 1999, the Second Circuit struck down New York's law making it a crime for a physician to assist in a suicide. The court reasoned that if patients may ask physicians to withdraw life support systems, they also have a right for physicians to prescribe drugs to hasten death (*Quill v. Vacco*, 80 F.3d 716 [2d Cir. 1996]). The Second Circuit's ruling was similar to an earlier decision by the Ninth Circuit (*Compassion in Dying v. State of Wash.*, 79 F.3d 790 [9th Cir. 1996]). When those issues reached the Supreme Court, it decided not to follow the activist *Roe* model by discovering within the U.S. Constitution a right to assisted suicide. In so ruling, it allowed other states to permit physician-assisted suicide, shifting the matter from federal courts to state legislatures and popular judgment. The Court found a fundamental difference between patients refusing life-support systems (at issue in the 1976 Nancy Cruzan case) and doctors intervening with lethal medications (*Vacco v. Quill*, 521 U.S. 793 [1997]). Yet it clearly wanted the right-to-die issue transferred from the Court to the larger political process: "Throughout the Nation, Americans are engaged in an earnest and profound debate about the morality, legality, and practicality of physician-assisted suicide. Our holding permits this debate to continue, as it should in a democratic society" (*Washington v. Glucksberg*, 521 U.S. 702, 735 [1997]). In a concurrence, Justice O'Connor agreed that there "is no generalized right to 'commit suicide,'" but preferred to leave the policy choices to others: "There is no reason to think the democratic process will not strike the proper balance between the interests of terminally ill, mentally competent individuals who would seek to end their suffering and the State's interests in protecting those who might seek to end life mistakenly or under pressure" (521 U.S. 736–37).

The debate over assisted suicide was particularly intense in Oregon, which adopted the Death With Dignity Act in 1994 in a statewide referendum. Under the Oregon law, a mentally competent adult suffering from a terminal illness may receive a lethal dose of medication after consulting with two physicians and waiting fifteen days. When this issue reached the U.S. Supreme Court in 1997, it decided to deny certiorari rather than attempt to settle the case on the merits (*Lee v. Harcleroad*, 522 U.S. 927 [1997]).

Doctors who used the Oregon law to prescribe lethal drugs to terminally ill patients faced possible sanctions from the federal government, such as having their license to prescribe controlled substances suspended or revoked. That risk was removed in 1998, when Attorney General Janet Reno announced that states may enact and implement such laws without federal interference. Congress responded to her policy by drafting legislation to regulate the use of medication to hasten death. Part of the purpose of the bill, which states that the U.S. attorney "shall give no force and effect" to any state law authorizing or permitting assisted suicide or euthanasia, was to override Oregon's law. Although the bill permitted doctors to prescribe federally controlled substances to alleviate pain, even if the prescription "may increase the risk of death," it also prohibited doctors from assisting in suicide. Under this legislation, federal officers would have to decide whether the doctor's intent to ease suffering had passed an invisible threshold to hasten death. The bill passed the House on October 27, 1999, by a vote of 271 to 156, but the Senate did not act on the measure in 2000.[6]

With legislation this close to passage, one would have expected Congress in 2001, at the start of the 107th Congress, to complete action on the bill. However, Congress chose to let the matter be handled administratively by the new attorney general, John Ashcroft. On November 6, 2001, he reversed Reno by authorizing federal agents to prosecute doctors in Oregon who use lethal drugs to assist in the death of terminally ill patients (Verhovek 2001b, A1). After Oregon sued to prevent the federal government from implementing his order, a federal district judge issued a temporary restraining order within two days (Verhovek 2001a, A14).

In a final action on April 17, 2002 (*Oregon v. Ashcroft*, 192 F.Supp.2d 1077 [D. Ore. 2002]), the district court ruled that Ashcroft's directive exceeded his authority under the Controlled Substances Act (CSA) (Liptak 2002a, A16). The court held that the purpose of the CSA was to address problems of drug abuse and drug trafficking, not to restrict or proscribe prescriptions for controlled substances used under state law to assist suicide or hasten death (*Oregon v. Ashcroft*, 192 F.Supp.2d, at 1090). Nothing in the statute suggested that Congress "delegated to federal prosecutors the authority to define what constitutes legitimate *medical* practices" (192 F.Supp.2d 1090; emphasis in original). The determination of legitimate medical practices "has been left to the individual states. State statutes, state medical boards, and state regulations control the practice of medicine" (192 F. Supp. 2d 1092). The court noted that certain congressional leaders, having failed to pass the Pain Relief Promotion Act, "made a good faith effort to get through the administrative door that which they could not get through the congressional door, seeking refuge with the newly-appointed Attorney General whose ideology matched their views" (192 F.Supp.2d 1093).

GAY RIGHTS

In 1986, the Supreme Court narrowly sustained (5–4) the constitutionality of a Georgia statute that criminalized sodomy. Michael Hardwick was arrested for committing sodomy with another male adult in the bedroom of his home. After the district attorney decided not to present the matter to the grand jury, Hardwick challenged the statute as it applied to private, consensual sodomy. The majority held that the Constitution does not confer a fundamental right upon gays to engage in sodomy (*Bowers v. Hardwick*, 478 U.S. 186 [1986]).

Conscious of the reputation of *Roe v. Wade* as a case study in judicial activism, the Court was loath to discover within the four corners of the Constitution another right, particularly in the area of sodomy. Instead, it parceled that issue out to other branches and to the states. It emphasized that its decision "raises no question about the right or propriety of state legislative decisions to repeal their laws that criminalize homosexual sodomy, or of state-court decisions invalidating those laws on state constitutional grounds" (478 U.S. 190). A number of state courts have invalidated state statutes that criminalize consensual sodomy.[7] In addition, twenty-five state legislatures have recently repealed their sodomy laws, as has the District of Columbia. *Bowers* was eventually overturned by *Lawrence v. Texas*, 123 S.Ct. 2472 (2003), meaning that the Supreme Court has now declared all state antisodomy laws to be unconstitutional.

In the mid-1990s, the Court accepted and decided two cases involving the rights of gays, one involving free speech, the other civil rights. Neither case raised an issue nearly as sensitive as the question before the Court in the Georgia sodomy case. In the first case, in 1995, the justices reviewed the constitutionality of excluding gay marchers from a parade. A unanimous Court upheld the right of the organizers of Boston's Saint Patrick's Day parade to exclude gay marchers. To the Court, a parade is a "public drama" to make a collective point. The organizers had a right to exclude a group that would have altered the expressive content of the parade (*Hurley v. Irish-American Gay Group of Boston*, 515 U.S. 557 [1995]).

The following year, the Supreme Court struck down a provision of the Colorado Constitution that nullified existing civil rights protections for homosexuals in the state. The constitutional language prohibited all legislative, executive, or judicial action at any level of state or local government designed to protect the status of persons based on their "homosexual, lesbian or bisexual orientation, conduct, practices or relationships." Several cities in the states had adopted ordinances to prohibit discrimination against gays. The 6–3 decision stated that the constitutional provision, by placing the state's homosexuals "in a solitary class" and singling them out, had violated the U.S. Constitution's equal protection guarantee. The Colorado provision, said the Court, failed to show a rational relationship to a legitimate governmental purpose. The Court rejected the argument that the provision merely took away "special rights," not equal rights (*Romer v. Evans*, 517 U.S. 620 [1996]).

The Saint Patrick's Day parade case led to another gay rights decision in 2000. The case involved a conflict between a New Jersey law that prohibits discrimination against sexual orientation and the right of the Boy Scouts of America to expel an adult Scout who announced that he is gay. The Boy Scouts, a private organization engaged in instilling its system of values in young people, asserted that homosexual conduct is inconsistent with the values it seeks to promote. James Dale, whose membership was revoked, is a gay rights activist. Unlike the unanimous ruling in the Boston case, the Court split 5–4 in deciding that the New Jersey law violated the Boy Scout's First Amendment right of expressive association. Although the Scout Oath and Law do not mention sexuality or sexual orientation, the Court interpreted the terms "morally straight" and "clean" as opposition to homosexual conduct, a position the Boy Scouts have adopted ever since 1978. Dale's presence in the Boy Scouts would force the organization to send a message that it accepts homosexual conduct as a legitimate form of behavior (*Boy Scouts of America v. Dale*, 530 U.S. 640 [2000]).

How damaging this decision would be to the Boy Scouts organization depends on how public officials and the private sector respond. Initially, some cities—relying on nondiscrimination policies—told local Scout troops that they could no longer use parks, schools, and other municipal sites, while a number of charities and corporations reduced funding to the Scouts (Zernike 2000, A1). Breaking with this pattern, Attorney General Reno announced that the Clinton administration would not close the use of federal lands for Scout Jamborees (Taylor 2000, 2769).

Responding to these pressures, Congress passed legislation in 2002 called the "Boy Scouts of America Equal Access Act." It provides that public elementary and secondary schools, local educational agencies, and state educational agencies that receive federal funds shall not deny equal access or a fair opportunity to meet to any group officially affiliated with the Boy Scouts of America (115 Stat. 1981, § 9525 [2002]). The sponsor of the legislation explained: "This amendment is designed to stop this wasteful cycle in litigation and harassment. If one allows for an open forum for other groups to meet, it is only fair to allow equal access to the Boy Scouts" (147 *Cong. Rec.* H2618 [daily ed., May 23, 2001], statement by Rep. Hilleary). Earlier, a bill to repeal the federal charter for the Boy Scouts received a vote of only 12 to 362 (146 *Cong. Rec.* H7448–55, H7521–22 [daily ed., September 12–13, 2000]).

Litigation in Hawaii challenged a state marriage law that prohibited same-sex couples from obtaining marriage licenses. Reacting to this lawsuit, Congress passed the Defense of Marriage Act (DOMA) in 1996, which allows states to refuse to recognize such marriages performed in other states and also prohibits federal recognition of same-sex marriages. The latter provision prevents gay couples from filing joint tax returns or gaining access to spousal benefits under Social Security and other federal programs (110 Stat. 2419 [1996]). In passing this legislation, Congress acted under Section 1 of Article IV: "Full Faith and Credit shall be given in each State to the public Acts, Records, and judicial Proceedings of every other State. And the Congress may by general Laws prescribe the Manner in which such Acts, Records and Proceedings shall be proved, and the Effect thereof."

DOMA settled some national issues, but states remain free to adopt their own policies on same-sex marriages. In Vermont, a 1997 lawsuit challenging the state's prohibition of same-sex marriages led to legislation in 2000 that allowed gays to form a "civil union," giving them the same benefits, protections, and responsibilities granted to spouses in a marriage (See *Baker v. State*, 744 A.2d 864 [Vt. 1999]). However, more than thirty-five states have adopted explicit prohibitions on same-sex marriages. Because of these different state laws, gay couples united under Vermont law are finding that they cannot get other states to dissolve their legal partnerships (Ferdinand 2002, A3). In May 2004, Massachusetts became the first state to allow same-sex marriages, following the state supreme court's decision in *Goodridge v. Department of*

Public Health, 440 Mass. 309, 798 N.E. 2d 941 (2003). The Massachusetts ruling was similar to court decisions in the Canadian provinces of Ontario, British Columbia, and Québec, which also now recognize same-sex marriages.

IMPLEMENTING JUDICIAL DOCTRINES

Justice Frankfurter said it is "important to bear in mind that this Court can only hope to sets limits and point the way. It falls to the lot of legislative bodies and administrative officials to find practical solutions within the frame of our decisions" (*Niemotko v. Maryland*, 340 U.S. 268, 275–76 [1961]; concurring opinion). There is a good deal of truth in that. Much of what the Court does is to announce broad standards that must be fleshed out by others, whether it is "undue burden" for abortion, "all deliberative speed" for desegregation, or "prurient" for obscene material. It is up to elected officials and juries to translate those general principles and apply them to particular cases. The Court defines the edges; nonjudicial actors fill in the important middle. Yet it is equally true that the judiciary seeks practical solutions within the frame of congressional statutes, executive precedents, and public opinion.

It has long been the practice of jurors to rely on their own conscience to decide what is constitutional and proper. In their own way, jurors sense and articulate what is due process, equal protection, free speech, unreasonable searches and seizures, and cruel and unusual punishments. The concept of an independent juror, free under some circumstances to reject a judge's instruction of what the law is, has deep roots in America. Writing in 1771, John Adams noted that it was reasonable to expect the judge to instruct on the law and for juries to decide questions of fact. And yet Adams asked: "Is it not an absurdity to suppose that the law would oblige them to find a verdict according to the direction of the court, against their own opinion, judgment, and conscience?" It was not only a juror's "right, but his duty" to find a verdict "according to his own best understanding, judgment, and conscience, though in direct opposition to the direction of the court" (Adams 1850, 254–55).

In 1793, after President George Washington issued his neutrality proclamation and his administration began prosecuting citizens who violated his policy of remaining neutral in the war between France and England, jurors decided to acquit because they refused to convict someone for a crime established only by a proclamation. In their judgment, criminal law had to be based on a statute passed by the legislative body. With no statute to cite, the government was forced to drop prosecutions and come to Congress for a law that gave prosecutors the firm legal footing they needed (Wharton 1849, 84–85, 88; Marshall 1832, vol. 2, 273).

During the nineteenth century, jurors objected to legislation that mandated the death penalty not only for murder but for treason, piracy, arson, rape, robbery, burglary, and sodomy. Without the opportunity to vote for a lesser penalty, many jurors voted to acquit. Legislatures were then pressured to add sentencing discretion to the process, such as allowing juries to decide between the death penalty and life imprisonment (*Woodson v. North Carolina*, 428 U.S. 280, 289–91 [1976]; see also Bedau 1968, 27–28). Jurors can also oppose the underlying criminal law. In cases brought against individuals for violating laws regarding hunting, gambling, and liquor (during the Prohibition Era), jurors would typically acquit because they regarded the laws as unreasonable or too severe. No matter what evidence prosecutors offered or instructions the judge issued, jurors were likely to rebel (Kalven and

Zeisel 1966, 286–97). Legislators were then forced to rewrite or repeal the unpopular laws.

Juries may acquit when they decide that law enforcement officers have abused their powers and offended basic liberties. In some early cases, where defendants were not represented by counsel, jurors would acquit to protest fundamental unfairness. One juror told a judge: "Until the state provided a public defender, he would let everyone go free" (Kalven and Zeisel 1966, 319). The Supreme Court has devised many sophisticated (and often conflicting) standards to guide jurors on the meaning of entrapment.[8] However, if jurors decide that the government has used heavy-handed tactics to entrap an individual and help manufacture a crime that would not have happened without the government's manipulation, acquittal may be a signal to prosecutors that they have violated basic constitutional rights. Jurors help draw a line around permissible governmental behavior, no matter what legislators enact, prosecutors bring, or judges decide. Under such conditions, the last word on the meaning of entrapment (at least in a particular case) is with the juror.

Juror involvement in basic questions of constitutional law is evident in cases involving pornography and obscenity. The Court has issued general—if not incomprehensible—guidelines. Jurors are supposed to decide (1) whether the average person, applying contemporary standards, would find that the work, taken as a whole, appeals to the prurient interest; (2) whether the work depicts or describes, in a patently offensive way, sexual conduct specifically defined by the applicable state law; and (3) whether the work, taken as a whole, lacks "serious literary, artistic, political, or scientific value" (*Miller v. California*, 413 U.S. 15 [1973]; see also Fisher 2003, 559–67). Prurient means inclined to lascivious thought. Lascivious is associated with lust, wantonness, or lewdness. These words run in a circle. In the end, jurors will decide for themselves whether a book, movie, art exhibit, or music performance is harmful to their home community. In two highly controversial cases in 1990, juries in Cincinnati and Fort Lauderdale decided that an art gallery and the rap band 2 Live Crew were not guilty of obscenity charges. The constitutionality of obscenity depends more on the conscience, intuition, taste, and judgment of individual jurors than Supreme Court doctrines.

In 1983, the Supreme Court struck down the "legislative veto" that Congress had used for fifty years to monitor delegations of legislative authority to the executive branch (*INS v. Chadha*, 462 U.S. 919 [1983]). The decision far exceeded the Court's understanding of executive-legislative relations. Through an endless variety of formal and informal agreements, congressional committees will continue to exercise control over administrative decisions. Neither Congress nor the executive branch want the static model of government offered by the Court, which placed upon Congress the requirement of acting through both Houses and then presenting a bill or resolution to the president for his signature or veto. In one form or another, legislative vetoes will remain an important mechanism for reconciling legislative and executive interests. The accommodations fashioned by committees and agency officials will easily trump the doctrinaire and impractical rules announced by the Court (Fisher 1993).

INDIVIDUAL RIGHTS AND LIBERTIES

Studies in constitutional law generally recognize that many collisions between the executive and legislative branches are settled without recourse to the judiciary. Elected leaders devise various compromises to settle conflicts, with these structural disputes running the gamut from congressional access to information to the war power (see Fisher 1990, 2002a, 2002b, 2002c). However, scholars are less inclined to trust the political branches to settle disputes over individual rights and liberties. The judiciary is supposedly better structured than legislative bodies to protect minority rights. While it may seem logical that a majoritarian institution like Congress cannot be trusted to protect isolated and politically weak minorities, history does not follow logic. The record shows that for the past two centuries American legislatures have performed quite well in protecting minority rights, while courts during that period have been generally insensitive and unreliable.

The Supreme Court received great credit for issuing its desegregation decision in *Brown v. Board of Education* (1954). Overlooked in this praise is the general ineffectiveness of the 1954 ruling and the Court's exceedingly poor record over the previous century. From *Dred Scott v. Sandford* (1857) to *Plessy v. Ferguson* (1896), the Court upheld slavery and the "separate but equal" doctrine. Following the Civil War, it was the legislative branch—not the judiciary—that took action to improve the condition of blacks. Congress passed the Thirteenth Amendment, adopted in 1865, to abolish the institution of slavery. The Fourteenth Amendment, ratified in 1868, provided for the equality of whites and blacks before the law. The Fifteenth Amendment, ratified in 1870, gave blacks the right to vote.

The Fourteenth Amendment had been foreshadowed by the Civil Rights act of 1866. After passage of the Thirteenth Amendment, a number of Southern states enacted "Black Codes" to keep the newly freed slaves in a subordinate status economically, politically, and culturally. The 1866 statute made all persons born in the United States, excluding Indians not taxed, citizens of the United States. Such citizens, "of every race and color," had the same right in every state and territory "to make and enforce contracts, to sue, be parties, and give evidence, to inherit, purchase, lease, sell, hold, and convey real and personal property, and to full and equal benefit of all laws and proceedings for the security of person and property, as is enjoyed by white citizens . . ." (14 Stat. 27, § 1 [1866]).

Legislation in 1875 provided for equality of all races in using public accommodations: inns, "conveyances" (transportation), theaters, and other places of public amusement. This landmark legislation was struck down by the Court in the *Civil Rights Cases* of 1883 as a federal encroachment on the states and an interference with private relationships. Because of the Court's action, what could have been accomplished in 1875 had to await the Civil Rights act of 1964.

After the Court issued *Brown* in 1954, a year later it announced guidelines to implement the desegregation process. How quickly were states to make the transition? The answer: No great hurry. The Court largely deferred to local school authorities in determining the appropriate course, leaving to federal courts the duty of deciding whether school authorities were acting in good faith to comply with desegregation. Several phrases from the Court—including "practical flexibility," "as soon as practicable," "a prompt and reasonable start," and "all deliberate speed"— gave a green light to obstruction and procrastination (*Brown v. Board of Education*, 349 U.S. 294 [1955]). A decade later, the Court complained that there "has been entirely too much deliberation and not enough speed" in enforcing the 1954 decision (*Griffin v. School Bd.*, 377 U.S. 218, 229 [1964]). Reaching finality needed more than a court decision. Resolution required the concerted action of the elected branches: Congress and the president. A federal appellate court noted in 1966: "A national effort, bringing together Congress, the executive and the judiciary may be able to make meaningful the right of Negro children to equal educational opportunities. *The courts acting alone have failed"* (*United States v. Jefferson County Board of Education*, 372 F.2d 836, 847 [5th Cir. 1966]; emphasis in original).

The Civil Rights Act of 1964 represented the most far-reaching civil rights statute since the Reconstruction Era. The legislation passed by top-heavy majorities of 289–126 in the House and 73–27 in the Senate. Bipartisan support was solid. The House voted 153–91 Democratic and 136–35 Republican. The party split in the Senate: 46–21 for Democrats and 27–6 for Republicans. Major factions throughout the country had united to give the final word.

In 1988, the Court began to backtrack from its previous positions on civil rights. This pattern became pronounced during the spring of 1989, when the Court issued a series of stunning rulings. One decision shifted the burden to employees to prove that racial disparities in the work force resulted from employment practices and were not justified by business needs. Another decision limited the reach of the civil rights statute passed in 1866, which gave blacks the same right to "make and enforce contracts" as whites. A third decision gave white men new authority to challenge consent decrees that embody court-approved affirmative action plans. All these decisions represented judicial efforts to interpret congressional statutes, even though the statutory question was mixed with constitutional values. Congress passed the Civil Rights Act of 1991 to reverse or modify nine Court rulings dealing with employment discrimination (Fisher 2003, 841–43).

Just as Congress after the Civil War passed legislation to grant new legal rights to blacks, so did it protect the right of women to practice law. In 1873, the Court denied that the rejection of Myra Bradwell to practice law in Illinois (solely because she was a woman) represented a violation of the privileges and immunities of the Fourteenth Amendment (*Bradwell v. State*, 83 U.S. [16 Wall.] 130 [1873]). At that time, a rule adopted by the Court prohibited women from practicing there. In 1879, Congress passed legislation to authorize a woman who had been a member of the bar for three years and who qualified on moral character to practice before the U.S. Supreme Court (20 Stat. 292 [1879]). A few lawmakers argued that the Court's rule was an internal matter better left to the Justices, but the great majority of the House and the Senate felt strongly that what was at issue was a matter of national policy properly before Congress. In the words of Senator Aaron Sargent: "No man has a right to put a limit to the exertions or the sphere of women. That is a right which only can be possessed by that sex itself. . . . The enjoyment of liberty, the pursuit of happiness in her own way, is as much the birthright of woman as of man. In this land man has ceased to dominate his fellow—let him cease to dominate over his sister; for he has no higher right to do the latter than the former" (8 *Cong. Rec.* 1084 [1879]). Thus, an all-male legislative body provided impressive support for women's rights—rights unavailable from the Court.

Women later won some cases in the courts, but the victories were often premised on their inferiority, not their equality. Thus, in a case upholding a ten-hour day for women, Justice Brewer remarked: "Still again, history discloses the fact that woman has always been dependent upon man. He established his control at the outset by superior physical strength, and this control in various forms, with diminishing intensity, has continued to the present" (*Muller v. Oregon*, 208 U.S. 412, 421 [1908]). Judicial doctrines had not advanced very far by 1948, when the Court upheld a

Michigan law that prohibited female bartenders unless they were the wife or daughter of the male owner (*Goeseart v. Cleary*, 335 U.S. 464 [1948]; see also Fisher 2003, 862–63). Although the Court in 1960 rejected the "medieval view" that husband and wife are one person with a single will, and therefore legally incapable of entering into a criminal conspiracy (*United States v. Dege*, 364 U.S. 51 [1960]), medieval thinking triumphed the next year when a unanimous Court agreed that women could be largely exempted from jury service because they are "still regarded as the center of home and family life" (*Hoyt v. Florida*, 368 U.S. 57, 62 [1961]).

Not until 1971 did the Court issue a decision striking down sex discrimination. The judicial record up to that time was so deplorable that one study noted: "Our conclusion, independently reached, but completely shared, is that by and large the performance of American judges in the area of sex discrimination can be succinctly described as ranging from poor to abominable" (Johnston and Knapp 1971, 676). Progress for women came primarily from the legislative and executive branches, which showed a much greater capacity to recognize wrongs and right them.

These observations about the willingness of political branches to protect blacks and women apply equally well to the protection of other rights and liberties, such as religious freedom. Nonjudicial forces have safeguarded the religious freedom of minorities as well as—and often better than—the courts. Citizens, legislators, and executive officials act jointly to support minority rights left unsecured by the courts. Religious groups have turned to Congress for protection, often to challenge and countermand Supreme Court rulings (Fisher 2002b).

CONCLUSIONS

Congress and executive officials are constantly involved in constitutional interpretation through the passage of bills, agency implementation, and executive–legislative conflicts. Similar struggles take place at the state level. When constitutional disputes are brought before federal courts, there is no assurance that the controversy will be decided on the merits. The judiciary can avoid the constitutional issue by disposing of the case on statutory grounds or by invoking threshold questions of jurisdiction, standing, mootness, ripeness, political questions, and prudential considerations. If the constitutional question is directly addressed, more likely than not the courts will defer to the interpretation reached by the other branches. On those rare occasions where the courts invalidate a congressional action, usually it is only a matter of time before the statute is revised to initiate another dialogue with the judiciary. It is through this rich and dynamic political process that the Constitution is constantly adapted to seek a harmony between legal principles and the needs of a changing society.

NOTES

1. U.S. Department of Justice, "Statement as to Jurisdiction," *United States v. Classic*, 5; reprinted in Kurland and Casper 1975, vol. 38, 106.
2. U.S. Department of Justice, "Brief for the United States," *United States v. Classic*, 36; reprinted in Kurland and Casper 1975, vol. 38, 152.
3. *Weems v. United States*, 217 U.S. 349 (1910) (striking down the sentence of someone given fifteen years at hard labor and kept in chains day and night for falsifying a public document).

4. *Committee to Defend Reprod. Rights v. Myers*, 625 P.2d 779 (Cal. 1981). See also *Right to Choose v. Byrne*, 450 A.2d 925 (N.J. 1982); *Moe v. Secretary of Administration*, 417 N.E.2d 387 (Mass. 1981); *Planned Parenthood Ass'n v. Dept. of Human Res.*, 663 P.2d 1247 (Or. App. 1983); *Doe v. Maher*, 515 A.2d 134, 143 (Conn. Super. 1986).

5. H. Rept. No. 107-186, 107th Cong., 1st Sess. (2001), 15; 148 *Cong. Rec.* H792-96 (daily ed., March 12, 2002).

6. 145 *Cong. Rec.* H10868-903 (daily ed., October 27, 1999). See also H. Rept. No. 106-378 (Parts 1 and 2), 106th Cong., 1st Sess. (1999), and S. Rept. 106-299, 106th Cong., 2d Sess. (2000).

7. *People v. Onofre*, 415 N.E.2d 936 (N.Y. 1980); *Commonwealth v. Bonadio*, 415 A.2d 47 (Pa. 1980); *Commonwealth v. Wasson*, 842 S.W.2d 487 (Ky. 1992); *State v. Morales*, 826 S.W.2d 201 (Tex. App. 1992); *City of Dallas v. England*, 846 S.W.2d 957 (Tex. App. 1993); *Campbell v. Sundquist*, 926 S.W.2d 250 (Tenn. App. 1996) (the state supreme court denied appeal without an opinion); *Gryczan v. State*, 942 P.2d 112 (Mont. 1997); *Powell v. State*, 510 S.E.2d 18 (Ga. 1998).

8. E.g., *Jacobson v. United States*, 503 U.S. 540 (1992); *United States v. Russell*, 411 U.S. 423 (1973); *Sherman v. United States*, 356 U.S. 369 (1958); *Sorrells v. United States*, 287 U.S. 435 (1932).

10

Constitutional Interpretation from a Strategic Perspective

**LEE EPSTEIN,
JACK KNIGHT, AND
ANDREW D. MARTIN**

IN THE LATE 1950S, THE U.S. SUPREME COURT DECIDED TWO major constitutional cases that touched on a similar topic—the rights of witnesses to refuse to answer questions put to them by congressional committees investigating subversive activities in America. In the first, *Watkins v. United States*, 354 U.S. 178 (1957), the Court ruled in favor of the witness. But in the second, *Barenblatt v. United States*, 360 U.S. 109 (1959), it ruled against him. The majority in *Barenblatt* went to great lengths to indicate that the opinion amounted to nothing more than a clarification of *Watkins*. Many legal analysts (including the four justices who dissented in *Barenblatt*), however, have suggested that at minimum, the majority backed away from *Watkins* and, at maximum, the decision signaled a reversal from the earlier ruling.

If these analysts are right, how can we explain the shift, which occurred within a two-year period? One possibility is that *Barenblatt* constituted a "strategic" withdrawal (see Pritchett 1961). On this account, the majority sincerely preferred the policy it established in *Watkins* to that it articulated in *Barenblatt*. But, at the same time, it recognized that *Watkins* and other "liberal" decisions, such as *Brown v. Board of Education*, 347 U.S. 483 (1954), had made the Court the target of numerous congressional proposals. A few even sought to remove the Court's jurisdiction to hear cases involving subversive activities. Therefore, in *Barenblatt* the Court had every reason to misrepresent its true policy preferences to protect its legitimacy, and reach a result that would appease Congress. Which is precisely the course of action it took.

Certainly, other possible explanations for the seeming discrepancy between *Barenblatt* and *Watkins* exist (see, e.g., Murphy 1962). But scholars have told this "strategic" story for so many years that it is now a part of Court lore, even finding a comfortable home in contemporary constitutional law case and text books (see, e.g., Ducat 2000, 146; Epstein and Walker 2004, 171; Fisher 2003, 224; and Randall 2002, 385).

And, yet, we find the near-universal acceptance of this story quite puzzling. While we believe it to be an accurate account of the *Watkins-Barenblatt* shift, we are unsure why so many others find it plausible. That is because, for over a decade now, legal academics and social scientists alike have told one of two stories, neither of which leave room for the Court to take into account the preferences and likely actions of political actors (e.g., members of Congress and the president) when it is resolving a *constitutional* dispute (as it apparently did in *Barenblatt*). On the first story, justices simply pursue their jurisprudential or political goals in a vacuum; the views of external actors are entirely irrelevant. On the second, justices do take into account the views of external actors but only when they are *interpreting statutes*, not the *Constitution*. The rationale behind this latter claim is straightforward enough: It is within Congress's power to overturn the interpretations the Court gives to statutory law but, according to the justices themselves (see *City of Boerne v. Archbishop Flores*, 521 U.S. 507 [1997], and *Dickerson v. United States*, 530 U.S. 428 [2000]), it is not—at least not by simple majorities—within the legislature's power to overturn its constitutional decisions; that can only occur via a constitutional amendment.

Given the infrequency with which Congress passes amendments (at least relative to the frequency with which it disturbs the Court's statutory interpretation decisions),[1] we can understand why scholars argue that the justices need not be especially attentive (or, at the extreme, not attentive at all) to the desires of other government actors in constitutional disputes. But we disagree. Indeed, we believe it is entirely possible that justices feel equally (if not more) compelled in constitutional cases to take into account the preferences and likely actions of Congress, just as they do in those involving statutory interpretation.

We develop this argument in three steps. We begin by explaining the severe problems with any story holding that justices make decisions in a vacuum and by expressing our general sympathy with the second story—really, a strategic-institutional account of judicial decisions—which emphasizes the role institutional arrangements play in structuring choices made by strategic actors. Next, we attempt to make a theoretical case for applicability of this strategic account to constitutional decision making. Finally, we put our argument to a modest empirical test, assessing whether it can help account for decisions the Court reaches in constitutional disputes involving matters of civil rights.

A STRATEGIC-INSTITUTIONAL ACCOUNT OF JUDICIAL DECISION MAKING

When it comes to the question of how judges reach decisions, pockets of legal academics and political scientists offer fundamentally different responses. The former might say that judges are concerned with resolving disputes in the "right" or "correct" way—a way that conforms to their reading of existing precedent or their philosophical approaches; the latter might reply that judges are concerned with etching their politics into law.[2] When Chief Justice William Rehnquist reads a statute in a way that works adversely to a criminal defendant, law professors might argue that he does so because that reading is in line with his vision of how judges ought to interpret laws (perhaps in line with legislative intent), while social scientists may claim it is because the chief is "conservative" on matters of criminal law and desires to see his right-of-center views become the law of the land.

Our own views are closer to the political scientists', but we nonetheless believe that neither tells a particularly compelling story about Supreme Court decision making. That is so, at least in part, because both assume that justices advance their

FIGURE 10.1   Hypothetical Set of Preferences over Civil Rights Policy

Note: *X* is the Status Quo (intent of Enacting Congress); *C(M)* represents the *current* committees' indifference point (between their most preferred position and that desired by *M*); *M* denotes the most preferred position of the median member of Congress; *C* is the most preferred position of the key *current* committees (and other gatekeepers) in Congress that make the decision of whether or not to propose legislation to their respective houses. In denoting these most preferred points, we assume that the actors prefer an outcome that is nearer to that point than one that is further away. Or, to put it more technically, "beginning at [an actor's] ideal point, utility always declines monotonically in any direction. This . . . is known as single-peakedness of preferences" (Krehbiel 1988, 263). We also assume that the actors possess complete and perfect information about the preferences of all other actors and that the sequence of policymaking enfolds as follows: the Court interprets a law, the relevant congressional committees propose (or do not propose) legislation to override the Court's interpretation, Congress (if the committees propose legislation) enacts (or does not enact) an override bill, the president (if Congress acts) signs (or does not sign) the override bill, and Congress (if the president vetoes) overrides (or does not override) the veto. These are relatively common assumptions in the legal literature.

goals—whether philosophical or political—in a vacuum, that is, by behaving in accord with their sincerely held preferences without considering the preferences of others. To the legal academics, justices will base conclusions on principles or ideas about law (e.g., perhaps a particular mode of constitutional or statutory interpretation or precedent); to the political scientists, they will vote in ways that reflect their underlying political attitudes.

To see the implications of this assumption of purely sincere (or "naive") behavior, as well as why we find it troubling, consider figure 10.1. There we depict a hypothetical set of preferences over a particular policy, say, a civil rights statute (adapted from Ferejohn and Weingast 1992). The horizontal lines represent a (civil rights) policy space, here, ordered from left (most "liberal") to right (most "conservative"); the vertical lines show the preferences (the "most preferred positions") of the actors relevant in this example: the median member of the *current* Congress, *M*, and of the key *current* committees and other gatekeepers, *C*, in Congress that make the decision over whether to propose civil rights legislation to their respective houses. Note we also identify the current committees' indifference point, *C(M)*, "where the Supreme Court can set policy which the committee likes no more and no less than the opposite policy that could be chosen by the full chamber" (Eskridge 1991a, 381). To put it another way, because the indifference point and the median member of the current Congress are equidistant from the committees, the committees like the indifference point as much as they like the most preferred position of Congress; they are indifferent between the two. Finally, we locate the status quo, *X*, which represents the intent of the legislature that *enacted* the law.

Now suppose a justice has a case before her that requires interpretation of a civil rights law. Where would she place policy? If the justice believes she should interpret law in line with the preferences of the enacting legislature and if the story told by some legal academics holds, then the answer is obvious: She will place policy at *X*. If the justice votes in accord with her sincere political preferences, as some political scientists maintain, then the answer is that it depends on where her preferences lie.

If she is very liberal, she may too place policy at X; if she is very conservative, then she will vote C.

Notice, though, that neither the intent- nor policy-oriented justice takes into account the preferences and likely actions of the current Congress when they make decisions. And this is where our problems with these accounts begin, for they seem unable to address a natural, even obvious question: Why would justices who have clear preferences, whether jurisprudential or political, fail to realize that they will be unable to maximize those preferences without attending to other relevant actors? To put it in concrete terms, why would a justice whose goal is to see the law reflect the intent of enacting legislature place policy at X when she knows that Congress may very well override her position? (That would come about because the justice would be placing policy to the left of the indifference point of the relevant committees, giving them every incentive to introduce legislation lying at their preferred point. Congress would support such legislation because it would prefer the committees' preferred policy to the Court's.) We could raise the same question about our liberal justice: If she is truly "a single-minded seeker of legal policy," as some political scientists maintain, why would she take a position that Congress will overturn?[3]

We believe that she would not. For to claim that she would behave in this way—merely in line with her sincere preferences (whatever they may be)—is to argue the Court is full of myopic thinkers, who consider only the shape of the law in the short term. Such an argument does not square with important analyses of the Court or with the way an increasing number of contemporary scholars, in the legal academy and in social science departments alike, believe that political actors make decisions (see, e.g., Epstein and Knight 1998; Eskridge 1991a, 1991b; Maltman, Spriggs, and Wahlbeck 2000; and Murphy 1964).

Accordingly, we reject accounts suggesting that justices always act sincerely, and adopt a strategic one instead. The strategic approach, as we set it out,[4] starts off with the same premise as do traditional political science accounts: justices are "single-minded seekers of legal policy." But, from there, the two approaches veer dramatically. The strategic approach supposes that if justices truly care about the ultimate state of the law, then they must—as Fairman (1987) once put it—"keep [their] watch in the halls of Congress" and, occasionally, in the oval office of the White House, as well as paid heed to the various institutions structuring their interactions with these external actors. They cannot, as sincere approaches suggest, simply vote their own ideological preferences as if they are operating in a vacuum; they must instead be attentive to the preferences of the other institutions and the actions they expect them to take if they want to generate enduring policy.

This claim flows from the logic of an institution underlying the U.S. Constitution, the separation of powers system. That system, along with informal rules that have evolved over time (such as the power of judicial review), endows each branch of government with significant powers and authority over its sphere. At the same time, it provides explicit checks on the exercise of those powers such that each branch can impose limits on the primary functions of the others. So, for example, and as figure 10.2 shows, the judiciary may interpret the law and even strike down laws as being in violation of the Constitution, but Congress can pass new legislation, which the president may sign or veto.

Seen in this way, the rule of checks and balances inherent in the system of separation of powers provides justices (and all other governmental actors) with important

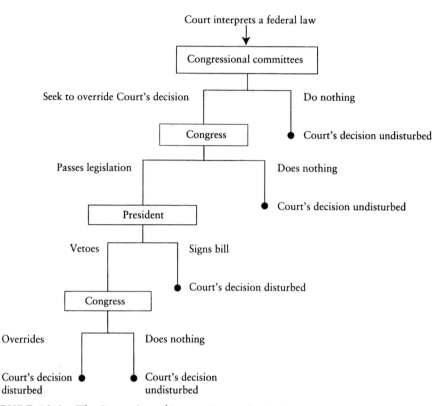

FIGURE 10.2   The Separation of Powers System in Action

Source: Adapted from Eskridge (1991b, 644).

information: *Policy in the United States emanates not from the separate actions of the branches of government but from the interaction among them.* Thus, it follows that for any set of actors to make authoritative policy—be they justices, legislators, or executives—they must take account of this institutional constraint by formulating expectations about the preferences of the other relevant actors and what they expect them to do when making their own choices.

IMPLICATIONS OF THE STRATEGIC-INSTITUTIONAL ACCOUNT

To see the implications of this argument, return to figure 10.1. Given the distribution of the most preferred positions of the actors in this figure, a strategic justice with liberal policy preferences—unlike a "naive" liberal policy seeker—would not be willing to take the risk and vote her sincere preference: She would see that Congress could easily override their position (the same holds for a justice whose preference is follow the intent of the enacting legislature). In fact, in this instance the rational course of action—the best choice for justices interested in maximizing their political preferences—is to place policy near the committees' indifference point. The reason is easy to see: Because the committees are indifferent between that point and the most preferred position of the median member of Congress, they would have no incentive to introduce legislation to overturn a policy set at the indifference point.

Thus, the Court would end up with a policy close to, but not exactly on, their ideal point without risking congressional reaction.

This does not mean, however, that justices can never vote their sincere preferences. Figure 10.1 shows how this could occur. Given the displayed distribution of preferences a conservative justice would be free to set policy in a way that reflects his raw preferences—as long as his preferences are within the $C(M)$–C interval, and not to the right of C. If he were to interpret laws within that interval, an override attempt would be unlikely. Even if his preferences fell on $C(M)$, the relevant congressional committees would have no incentive to waste precious legislative resources to overturn his decision. Because the committees' indifference point equals his most preferred position, they would be indifferent to his policy.

In short, the strategic model suggests that judicial decisions are not simply a function of the preferences of the Court but of the other relevant institutions as well. The Court—comprised of strategic single-minded seekers of legal policy—prefers to avoid reaching decisions considerably outside the range acceptable to the legislature (and the president). As strategic actors, the justices realize that by doing so the ultimate state of the law could end up farther away from their ideal points than is necessary.

CONSTITUTIONAL VS. STATUTORY INTERPRETATION

Thus far, we have focused attention on differences in the implications of various accounts for statutory interpretation. That we have done so is no accident. With only limited exceptions (e.g., Fisher 2003; Meernick and Ignagni 1997; Murphy 1964; and Rosenberg 1992), the existing literature exploring the constraint imposed on justices by the separation of powers system asserts that the constraint is far more—or, at the extreme, exclusively—operative in cases calling for the Court to interpret a law than on those asking the Court to assess a law's constitutionality.

The rationale behind this claim, as we noted at the onset, is simple: It is far more difficult for the elected branches of government to override a constitutional decision than a statutory one. Indeed, recent cases make quite clear that, as a matter of constitutional law, it is not—at least not by simple majorities—within the legislature's power to overturn its constitutional decisions (as it may with interpretations the Court gives to its laws); Congress must propose a constitutional amendment. In *Boerne v. Flores*, for example, the Supreme Court rejected Congress's attempt to dictate the level of scrutiny that the Court should apply to state laws that burden religious exercise. The Court had held in *Employment Division v. Smith*, 494 U.S. 872 (1990), that such laws do not receive heightened scrutiny. Congress then passed the Religious Freedom Restoration Act (RFRA), which mandated strict scrutiny review. The Court's decision to invalidate the statute included the following strong statement of judicial supremacy in constitutional matters:

> Our national experience teaches that the Constitution is preserved best when each part of the government respects both the Constitution and the proper actions and determinations of the other branches. When the Court has interpreted the Constitution, it has acted within the province of the Judicial Branch, which embraces the duty to say what the law is. *Marbury v. Madison*. When the political branches of the Government act against the background of a judicial interpretation of the Constitution already issued, it must

be understood that in later cases and controversies the Court will treat its precedents with the respect due them under settled principles, including *stare decisis*, and contrary expectations must be disappointed. RFRA was designed to control cases and controversies, such as the one before us; but as the provisions of the federal statute here invoked are beyond congressional authority, it is this Court's precedent, not RFRA, which must control.

Three years later, the Court reiterated this message in *Dickerson v. United States*, 530 U.S. 428 (2000). At issue was a law Congress enacted in 1968 that was designed to overturn the Court's decision in *Miranda v. Arizona*, 384 U.S. 4360 (1966). Once the justices held that *Miranda* announced a constitutional rule, they concluded that the 1968 congressional law was unconstitutional ("Congress may not legislatively supersede our decisions interpreting and applying the Constitution").

It is these sorts of decisions that give rise to the near-unanimous scholarly view that the justices need not be especially attentive (or, at the extreme, not attentive at all) to the preferences and likely actions of other government actors in constitutional disputes. After all, why should they? Congress apparently cannot overrule these decisions by passing simple legislation and it virtually never takes the alterative route of proposing constitutional amendments.

Is there thus any reason to suppose that the strategic institutional account, as developed here, applies to cases involving constitutional questions? Conventional wisdom, of course, suggests that there is not, that justices should feel free to ignore other relevant political actors in these disputes and vote in accord with their sincerely held preferences, because the risk of reversal is trivial. But we take issue with that wisdom. In fact, we might go so far as to argue that the justices feel more compelled in constitutional cases than in statutory ones to take into account the preferences and likely actions of the relevant actors. This argument—the contours of which we outline in table 10.1—follows from a consideration of the institutional costs and policy benefits of both types of decisions.

Let us begin with the benefits. Assuming that Congress does not (at least in the short term) respond adversely to a statutory interpretation decision, the Court accrues a policy benefit: It is able to read its preferences into law and, perhaps, fundamentally change the course of public policy. But that impact may be transitory because it is possible that future presidents and Congress will amend the statute in question to override the Court's interpretation. If Congress and the president respond in this manner, they may render the Court's decision (and its effect) meaningless. In contrast, owing to the difficulty of altering them both in the short and long terms, constitutional decisions (at least those that fail to generate a negative response from the relevant actors) are less permeable. Accordingly, they have greater policy value to the justices. They also have prescriptive benefits that statutory decisions do not. When the Court determines that a law is (or is not) constitutional, its decision does not merely hold for the particular law under analysis but is binding on all future action. Constitutional decisions set the parameters with which the contemporaneous Congress and president—as well as their successors—must comply.

What costs do the justices bear if the ruling regime has an adverse reaction to their decision? If the president and Congress are unsuccessful in their attempt to override an opinion interpreting a law, then no harm comes to the Court. If, however, they succeed (by overriding the Court's interpretation), the Court will certainly

TABLE 10.1.   A Comparison of the Costs and Benefits to the U.S. Supreme Court in Cases
Involving Statutory and Constitutional Interpretation

Court Action	Benefits[a]	Costs[b]	
		Cost of Unsuccessful Congressional Response	Cost of Successful Congressional Response
Court interprets a statute	Policy benefit (Court reads its policy preferences into existing law, though perhaps only a transitory one)	None	No policy benefit accrues; potential harm to the legitimacy of the Court
Court interprets the Constitution	Policy benefit (less transitory) and prescriptive benefit (Court prescribes standards for future government action)	Potential harm to the legitimacy of the Court	Infinite

Source: Adapted from Martin (1998).
[a]Assuming Congress or the president do not respond adversely to the Court's decision
[b]Assuming Congress or the president respond adversely to a statutory decision by passing a new law, and to a constitutional decision by attacking the Court

pay a policy price: its interpretation of the statute no longer stands, thereby robbing
it of the opportunity to affect public policy. It also may bear a cost in terms of its
legitimacy, at which every successful override chips if even marginally so. Given that
the justices' ability to achieve their policy goals hinges on their legitimacy—after all,
they lack the power to enforce their decisions—any erosion of it is of nontrivial concern to them.

Let us now consider constitutional cases, and begin with a simple fact: Though
Congress and the president may be unable to overturn these decisions with ease, they
have a number of weapons they can use to attack the Court. Rosenberg outlines a
few possibilities, all of which Congress, the president, or both have attempted to deploy (Rosenberg 1992, 377; Murphy 1962):

(1) using the Senate's confirmation power to select certain types of
    judges;
(2) enacting constitutional amendments to reverse decisions or change
    Court structure or procedure;
(3) impeachment;
(4) withdrawing Court jurisdiction over certain subjects;
(5) altering the selection and removal process;
(6) requiring extraordinary majorities for declarations of
    unconstitutionality;
(7) allowing appeal from the Supreme Court to a more 'representative'
    tribunal;
(8) removing the power of judicial review;
(9) slashing the budget; and
(10) altering the size of the Court.

In addition, and this is worthy of emphasis, however much the justices have stressed in recent cases they are the final arbiters of the Constitution, Congress has attempted to respond to constitutional decisions in the form of ordinary legislation. Fisher (2001, 28) makes this point when he writes, "If the Court decides that a government action is unconstitutional, it is usually more difficult for Congress and the president to contest the judiciary. . . . But even in this category, there are examples of effective legislative and executive actions in response to court rulings." Fisher goes on to provide a few illustrations, including an 1862 law prohibiting slavery in the territories that was designed to "repudiate the main tenets" of *Dred Scott v. Sandford*, 19 How. 393 (1857), and the Fair Labor Standards Act of 1938 outlawing child labor that the Supreme Court upheld in *United States v. Darby Lumber*, 312 U.S. 100 (1941), despite its earlier ruling in *Hammer v. Dagenhart*, 247 U.S. 251 (1918). More generally, as Meernik and Ignagni (1997, 458) assert:

> An examination of the frequency of reversal attempts and successes reveals that contrary to popular and scholarly opinion, the Congress can and does attempt to reverse Supreme Court rulings. Judicial review does not appear to be equivalent to judicial finality. . . . We find that the Congress repeatedly voted to reinterpret the Constitution after a High Court ruling of unconstitutionality. Although in 78% of the cases (444 out of 569) where the Supreme Court ruled some federal law, state law, or executive order constitutional, the Congress made no attempt to reverse its ruling; on 125 occasions, either the House or the Senate voted on legislation that would modify such a ruling. While many scholars have argued in the past that for all intents and purposes, judicial review is final, our results would seem to indicate that Congress is willing to challenge the power of the High Court. . . . We find that in 33% of the cases (41 out of 125) where the Congress did attempt to reverse the Court's decision, it was successful in passing legislation.

What does the ability of the ruling regime to attack—through overrides or other means—constitutional court decisions imply in terms of the costs the justices bear? If an attack succeeds (and the Court does not back down), it effectively removes the Court from the policy game and may seriously, or even irrevocably, harm its reputation, credibility, and legitimacy—thereby imposing a potentially infinite cost on the institution. But even if the attack attempt is unsuccessful, the integrity of the Court may be damaged, for the assault may compromise its ability to make future constitutional decisions and, thus, more long-lasting policy. We do not have to peer as far back as *Scott v. Sandford* to find examples; *Bush v. Gore*, 531 U.S. 98 (2000), may provide one. To be sure the new president and Congress did not attack it but other members of government did—unsuccessfully, of course, at least in terms of the ruling's impact. And yet there seems little doubt that the critics (not to mention the decision itself) caused some damage to the reputation of the Court, the effects of which the justices may eventually feel.[5]

Taken collectively, we are left with the following picture: The benefits to the Court of reaching a (successful) constitutional decision are roughly the same as (if not marginally greater than) those of reaching a successful statutory decision, but the costs of a challenge from members of the ruling regime, regardless of whether that challenge is successful or not, are far greater. Seen in this way, it seems to us quite reasonable to suppose that the strategic account is equally applicable (and, again, perhaps even more so) to cases involving constitutional and statutory questions. That is, if the justices pay heed to the preferences and likely actions of relevant external actors in statutory cases—as the weight of the literature suggests is the case—then they have good, if not better, reasons to do so in constitutional cases.

This leads us to the following testable propositions. If our account applies to constitutional cases, then we should expect to observe strategic behavior on the part of the justices. Specifically, (1) when the justices hold preferences close to relevant political actors, they will behave in a sincere fashion, that is, placing policy on their most preferred position but (2) when they hold preferences distant from the regime in power, they will behave in a sophisticated fashion, that is, placing policy not on their ideal point but rather on the point as close as possible to their most preferred position that will not unleash a congressional or presidential attack. If, however, more conventional accounts—whether those holding that justices behave in line with their sincere preferences regardless of the desires of other relevant actors or those suggesting that justices behave strategically but only in cases calling for the interpretation of statutes—then we should observe the justices always placing policy on their ideal point regardless of how far that point may be from the most preferred positions of Congress and the president.

ASSESSING THE PROPOSITIONS

To assess these propositions, we require data to animate the dependent variable— the vote of each justice in cases involving a particular type of policy—and measures of and data on the independent variables, the preferences of the Court, the president, and Congress with regard to that policy. We chose constitutional civil rights as the policy on which to focus our inquiry because that area of the law has (1) generated sufficient cases for meaningful analysis and (2) served as an empirical reference point for work concluding that the justices engage in sophisticated behavior with regard to other political actors when they interpret statutes (e.g., Eskridge 1991a, 1991b; Segal 1997). Whether this holds for constitutional interpretation is a question of extreme interest here.

We obtained data on the justices' votes and the direction of those votes (liberal or conservative) in civil rights cases involving constitutional issues from the U.S. Supreme Court Judicial Data Base for 1953 to 1992;[6] we measured the preferences of the median members of Congress and the president with, respectively, Poole and Rosenthal's (1997) NOMINATE Common Space Dimension One and their NOMINATE Common Space, which is estimated using announced presidential vote intentions. To assess the preferences of the justices, we relied on scores created by Segal and Cover (1989)—scores that many scholars have invoked. To derive them, the researchers content-analyzed newspaper editorials written between the time of justices' nomination to the U.S. Supreme Court and their confirmation. From this analysis, they created a scale of policy preferences, which ranges from -1 (unanimously conservative) to 0 (moderate) to $+1$ (unanimously liberal). For the purposes of presentation and analysis, we have rescaled the scores from 0 (most liberal) to 1 (most conservative). Table 10.2 displays the results.

With the data now in hand, we turn to assessing the propositions above. Let us begin with the one emanating from most existing accounts; namely, that justices

Table 10.2. Measuring the Policy Preferences of Supreme Court Justices Serving between 1953 and 1992: The Segal-Cover Scores

Justice	Segal-Cover Score	Justice	Segal-Cover Score
Brennan	0.000	Clark	0.500
Fortas	0.000	Whittaker	0.500
Jackson	0.000	O'Connor	0.585
Marshall	0.000	Kennedy	0.635
Harlan	0.125	Souter	0.670
Black	0.125	Burton	0.720
Goldberg	0.250	Stevens	0.750
Stewart	0.250	Powell	0.835
Warren	0.250	Thomas	0.840
Douglas	0.270	Blackmun	0.885
Reed	0.275	Burger	0.885
Minton	0.280	Rehnquist	0.955
Frankfurter	0.335	Scalia	1.000
White	0.500		

Note: The Segal and Cover (1989, 560) scores, as represented here, range from 0.000 (most liberal) to 1.000 (most conservative).

place policy (whether *always* as some political scientists suggest or *only in constitutional disputes,* as those who acknowledge strategic behavior in statutory cases suggest) on their ideal point regardless of how far that point may be from the most preferred positions of relevant members of the ruling regime.

To appraise this, we simply compare the preferences of the justices (as measured by the Segal-Cover scores) and their votes in constitutional civil rights cases—with figure 10.3 displaying the results. Note that if extant accounts are correct, we should see the justices (represented as circles in the figure) falling near the curve imposed on the data, meaning that their sincere preferences (again, as measured by the Segal-Cover scores) in fact explain their votes in the civil rights cases of interest. That many are quite close suggests that this argument seems to rest on solid ground; indeed, the most conservative justices vote conservatively 80 percent of the time; that figure for liberals is 20 percent.

STRATEGIC ANALYSIS

Although this simple test seems to lend support to the assumption of sincere behavior on the part of justices (again, whether always or only in constitutional disputes), the analysis cannot end there. That is because our account also acknowledges the possibility of sincere behavior. Recall that when a justice (say, the median member of the Court) holds preference close to contemporaneous elected actors, the account predicts that she will place policy on her ideal point; it is only when she holds a preference distant from the ruling regime that she will behave in a sophisticated fashion, that is, placing policy not on their ideal point but rather on the point as close as pos-

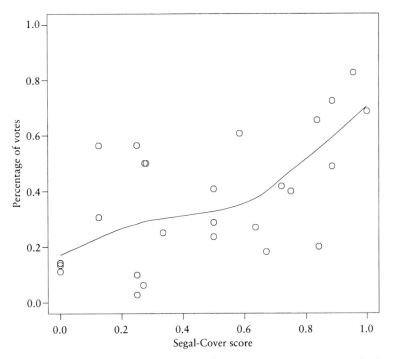

FIGURE 10.3 Scatterplot of the Percentage of Conservative Votes in Constitutional Civil Rights Cases on Justices' Preferences, 1953–92

Note: The Segal-Cover scores are rescaled from 0 to 1, with a high value representing a more conservative justice. A local regression (loess) curve is imposed to illustrate the relationship between the two variables.

sible to her most preferred position that will not unleash a congressional or presidential response.

To assess expectations generated by the strategic approach, we thus must disaggregate judicial behavior and study it over time, under periods of liberal and conservative regimes. We take two approaches to so doing. First, we consider the votes of several individual justices disaggregated by president. Second, we explore the behavior of the Court as a whole disaggregated by the president and Congress.

Let us begin with the individual justices, two of whom we have chosen for indepth analysis—Justices White and Black.[7] For both, we constructed figures (figures 10.4 and 10.5) displaying the relationship between their votes in constitutional civil rights cases by presidential administration. The points on each of these plots represent the percentage of conservative votes cast; and the error bars, the 95 percent confidence interval. If two error bars do not overlap, a statistically significant difference exists in voting between particular presidencies; if an overlap occurs, no significant difference exists. Our expectations are straightforward enough: (1) Under the strategic account, we should observe Black and White voting in a more conservative direction when a Republican is in the White House; (2) under strictly sincere voting models, we should observe no change in their behavior.

As figures 10.4 and 10.5 reveal, sophisticated strategic decision making characterizes the behavior of both justices. Note that Black was more conservative—

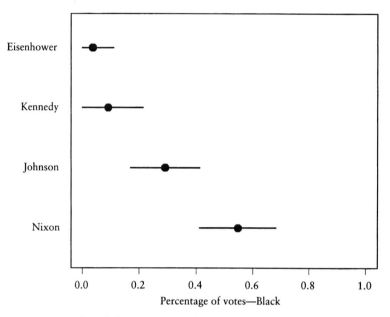

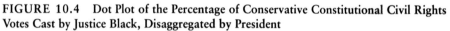

FIGURE 10.4 Dot Plot of the Percentage of Conservative Constitutional Civil Rights Votes Cast by Justice Black, Disaggregated by President

Note: In both figures 10.4 and 10.5, the error bars depict the 95 percent confidence intervals of the percentage.

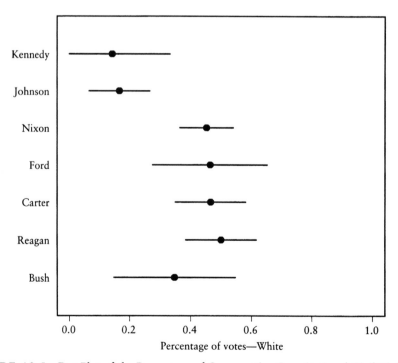

FIGURE 10.5 Dot Plot of the Percentage of Conservative Constitutional Civil Rights Votes Cast by Justice White, Disaggregated by President

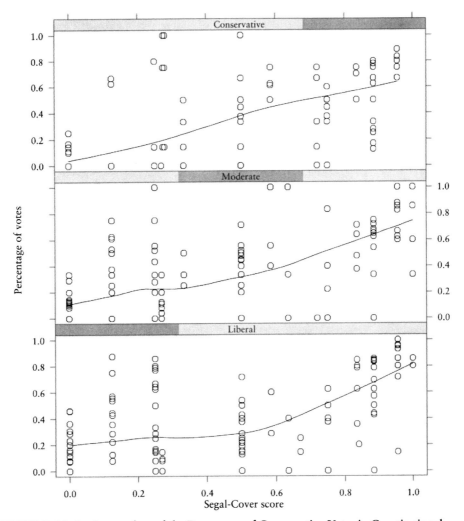

FIGURE 10.6 Scatterplots of the Percentage of Conservative Votes in Constitutional Civil Rights Cases on Justices' Preferences, Conditioned on the Preferences of the President

Note: The upper cell contains data from conservative presidents, as measured by common space NOMINATE scores, the middle cell from moderate presidents, and the lower cell from liberal presidents. In each cell, a local regression (loess) curve is imposed to illustrate the relationship between the variables.

significantly so—in his voting during the Nixon administration than he was during the more liberal Kennedy and Johnson presidencies. White was far more liberal when the two most liberal presidents (at least during his tenure on the bench) were in office than he was during the more conservative Nixon and Reagan eras. These patterns, we believe, suggest strategic adaptation, and precisely the sort of adaptation we would anticipate if justices are behaving in a sophisticated fashion with regard to the existing political regime: altering their decisions to reflect the preferences of that regime. What is more, it is precisely the adaptation we would not expect to observe if the assumption of sincere behavior rested on a firm empirical basis.

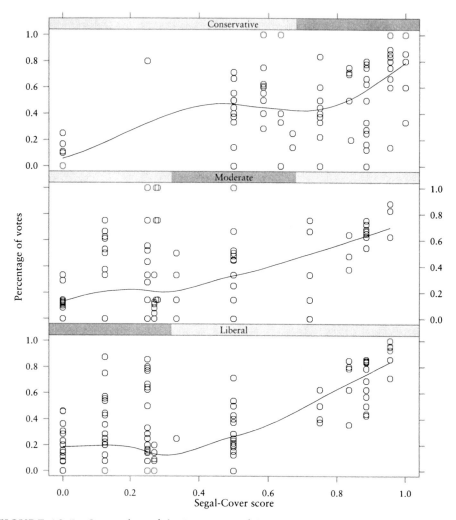

FIGURE 10.7 Scatterplots of the Percentage of Conservative Votes in Constitutional Civil Rights Cases on Justices' Preferences, Conditioned on the Median Member of the Senate

Note: The upper cell contains data from conservative senates, as measured by NOMINATE common space dimension one scores; the middle cell, from moderate senates; and the lower cell, from liberal senates. In each cell, a local regression (loess) curve is imposed to illustrate the relationship between the variables.

Do these same results hold at the Court level? To address this question, we constructed two plots (figures 10.6 and 10.7), both of which illustrate the relationship between voting in constitutional civil rights cases and preferences but which condition that relationship differentially. Figure 10.6 conditions it on presidential preferences, whether conservative, moderate, or liberal; and figure 10.7, on Senate preferences, again whether conservative, liberal, or moderate.

The plots differ, of course, but they tend to tell a similar story. First, strong ideologues on the Court (those with Segal-Cover scores close to 0 or 1) vote in accord with their preferences regardless of the preferences of the ruling regime. This lends support to an assumption of sincere voting. But—and this is a big but—moderate justices do not behave in this way. In figure 10.5, the loess curve shows that those with middle-range Segal-Cover scores are more likely to vote conservatively when there is a moderate or conservative president. The preferences of the Senate also seem to affect these justices, with voting taking a decisively more conservative turn when the Senate is right of center.

We interpret these tests to lend support both to sincere voting accounts and to our institutional approach. Both predict that justices will vote their sincere preferences when they hold preferences similar to those of the members of the other branches of government. And the empirical evidence is that they generally do so. But the empirical evidence also demonstrates sophisticated decision making in which the justices deviate from their personal preferences when those preferences are not shared by the members of the elected branches. Tests at both the individual and the aggregate levels support the proposition that justices adjust their decisions in anticipation of the potential responses of the other branches of government. This is behavior that is consistent with our institutional approach, but that accounts that predict sincere behavior in constitutional disputes (or in all disputes) cannot explain.

DISCUSSION

Let us end this chapter precisely where we begin it—with *Watkins* and *Barenblatt*, two cases decided in the 1950s that were similar in many important regards, except that one led to a ruling against the government and the other, to one in its favor. Recall that scholars explain this apparent shift with a strategic account—one that we now elaborate in figure 10.8, which depicts the ideal points of the key players. Notice that at the time the cases were decided the Court was to the left of (more liberal than) Congress, the president, and the relevant congressional committees. Given this configuration, the Court's holding in *Watkins*, which amounted to putting policy on its ideal point, provided the committees with every incentive to override, in one way or another, its decision. The reason is that the committees preferred any point on the line between *C(M)* and *M/P* to *J*. Congress and the president would have favored legislation to derail the decision because they too preferred *M/P* to *J*. In fact, responding to *Watkins* and other "liberal" rulings, members of Congress proposed numerous Court-curbing laws, including some that would have removed the Court's

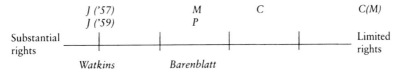
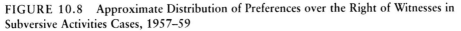

FIGURE 10.8   Approximate Distribution of Preferences over the Right of Witnesses in Subversive Activities Cases, 1957–59

Note: J ('57) is the most preferred position of the majority of the Court in 1957; *J ('59)* is the most preferred position of the majority of the Court in 1959; *M* denotes the most preferred position of the median legislator in Congress; *C* is the most preferred position of the relevant congressional committees; *P* is the most preferred position of the president; and *C(M)* is the indifference point of the congressional committees (between their most preferred position and that desired by *M*).

jurisdiction. It is hardly surprising thus that the Court, feeling the heat, acceded to congressional pressure—and acted in a sophisticated fashion in *Barenblatt*. Or at least this is the story scholars have told over and over again to explain the seeming discrepancy between the two cases.

What we have argued, and have attempted to demonstrate with data, is that *Barenblatt* is not the anomaly some suggest it is; that the Court is not the unconstrained actor in constitutional litigation existing accounts make it out to be. Rather, the justices understand they will be unable to generate efficacious decisions—decisions that other actors will respect and with which they will comply—unless they are attentive to the preferences of those other actors and the institutions that structure the Court's interactions with them.

The implications of this result for the study of constitutional interpretation are many. One that deserves particular mention is its bearing on questions raised by what has been called the "countermajoritiarian difficulty" (Bickel 1962, 16). In light of America's fundamental commitment to a representative form of government, why should its citizens allow a group of unelected officials—namely, federal judges—to override the wishes of the people, as expressed by their elected officials, and render legislation unconstitutional?

Scholars have offered a range of "solutions" to this "difficulty." Of particular interest to us is one that has been quite influential in political science circles—Dahl's (1957) "ruling regime" thesis. In Dahl's account, the "difficulty" is not especially problematic because justices will vote in accord with their sincerely held preferences, which, in many eras, coincide with the ruling regime's (Congress and the president).[8] Hence, the justices will rarely thwart the actions of the regime by striking down its acts, as those acts reflect not just the preferences of Congress and the president but the Court as well.

Under Dahl's logic, then, the Court almost never assumes an antimajoritarian role; rather, it typically will represent and therefore legitimize the interests of the ruling regime. To the extent that this logic discounts the seriousness of the "countermajoritarian difficulty" we believe that Dahl got it right; to the extent that it rests on a correspondence of preferences among the different branches of government, our account suggests otherwise. Indeed, an important implication of our study is that, given the institutional constraints imposed on the Court, justices cannot effectuate their own policy goals—whether they accord or collide with the ruling regime's (as occasionally occurs; e.g., *Barenblatt*)—without taking into account the goals and preferences of the other branches. Justices find the best way to have a long-term effect on the nature and content of the law is to adapt their decisions to the preferences of these others. In this sense, the resolution of the "difficulty" rests not on a coincidence of preferences, as Dahl suggests, but on an important effect of the separation of powers system: a strategic incentive to anticipate and then react to the desires of elected officials.

This at least is the primary lesson scholars have taken from the *Watkins-Barenblatt* decisions, and it is one that our data on constitutional civil rights cases reinforce. Whether it will hold as analysts explore other areas of the law is a question on which we can only speculate. But, taken together, the theory and data thus far point in the same direction: If justices care about the nature and content of the law—and it is difficult to believe that justices do not—then they will adopt the most effective means to influence it, whether that law is statutory or constitutional in nature.

NOTES

We are grateful to the National Science Foundation for supporting our work on strategic decision making (SBR-9320284, SBR-9614130, SES-0135855). We have adopted and adapted several passages in this chapter from some of that work (see especially Epstein and Knight 1998; Epstein, Knight, and Martin 2001; Epstein, Segal, and Victor 2002; and Epstein and Walker 2004). All the data used in this chapter are available via http://artsci.wustl.edu/~polisci/epstein/. We used STATA to manage the data and S-PLUS to create the figures.

1. Between 1967 and 1990, Congress overrode about 120 Court decisions. See Eskridge 1991a, 344.
2. Of course, this is a generalization. Not all legal academics neglected the role of politics and not all social scientists neglected the role of principles and law. Conversely, there are still plenty of legal academics and social scientists who continue to cling to these traditional answers.
3. As we explain later in the text, a sincerely behaving conservative justice would not be overridden if he placed policy on C. But that is only because his preferences coincide with Congress's, and not that he has made a strategic calculation.
4. In our version of the strategic account, we make the assumption that justices primarily pursue policy goals. We are not alone: Many strategic accounts of judicial decisions assume that the goal of most justices is to see the law reflect their most preferred policy positions (Epstein and Knight 1998; Eskridge 1991a, 1991b; Maltzman, Spriggs, and Wahlbeck 2000; Murphy 1964; Spiller and Gely 1992). But this need not be the case. Under the strategic account, actors—including justices—can be, in principle, motivated by many things. As long as the ability of a justice to achieve his or her goal, whatever that may be, is contingent on the actions of others (as the strategic account suggests), his or her decision is interdependent and strategic. To see this point, return to figure 10.1, and suppose a justice's goal is to interpret the law in line with the intent of the enacting legislature but, at the same time, to avoid an override attempt by the current Congress (as the strategic account would suggest). If she were so motivated (and assuming that the president and pivotal veto player in Congress were to the right of X), the Court would place policy at $C(M)$.
5. In a Gallup poll conducted on December 13, 2000, roughly a third of those surveyed said that *Bush v. Gore* led them to lose confidence in the Supreme Court. In surveys conducted several days later (December 15–17), 50 percent responded, "yes, influenced" to the following Gallup poll question: "Overall, do you think the Justices on the US Supreme Court were influenced by their personal political views when deciding this case, or don't you think so?" Gallup poll data available at: www.gallup.com/poll/releases/Pr001222bii.asp. For a different perspective, see Gillman 2001.
6. The U.S. Supreme Court Judicial Data Base is available at www.ssc.msu.edu/~pls/pljp/sctdata.html. We used the following selection commands to generate the data for analysis:

```
keep if ANALU==. | ANALU==1 (each docket number included)
keep if VALUE==2 (civil rights)
keep if DEC_TYPE==1 | DEC_TYPE==2 | DEC_TYPE==5 | DEC_TYPE==6
    |DEC_TYPE==7 (oral and signed opinion, per curiam, variant of formally
    decided cases, judgment of the court)
keep if TERM>52 & TERM<92 (53 to 91 terms)
keep if AUTHDEC1<3 (the primary authority for decision is constitutionality of
    federal or state action)
```

Given the selection, the data set was expanded from the case being the unit of analysis to the vote being the unit of analysis. Other measures were merged on to this new data set. These were matched by calendar year (e.g., the Congress and president measures from 1960 were matched to the 1959 term of the Court, etc.).

7. We constructed similar figures for all the justices who served under at least three presidents. For most of the justices, there is no statistically significant variation in their behavior, for some always voted their true preferences because they were extremist or did not cast pivotal votes. Moreover, because the number of constitutional civil rights cases is small, statistically significant differences are hard to come by. The key test of the mechanism is the conditional plots for the entire Court. See figures 10.6 and 10.7 above.

8. The reason for this, on Dahl's account (1957, 284–89), is that on average presidents have the opportunity to appoint two new justices during the course of a four-year term. Because presidents usually nominate justices with philosophies similar to their own and the Senate generally confirms only nominees who have views consistent with the contemporary political mainstream, regular turnover results in a Court majority rarely holding divergent political preferences from those held by Congress and the president.

11

Is Judicial Policymaking Countermajoritarian?

NEAL DEVINS

WHEN STRIKING DOWN FEDERAL AND STATE LEGISLATION, THE Supreme Court is often described as "countermajoritarian." Such decision making, as Bickel put it, "thwarts the will of representatives of the actual people of the here and now; [the Court] exercises control, not in behalf of the prevailing majority, but against it" (1962, 17). But is this classic view of interbranch relations an accurate characterization of the dialogue that takes place between the Court and elected government? More to the point, is it fair to measure the Court's countermajoritarian tendencies by simply looking to the frequency of judicial invalidations of legislation?

No doubt, elected officials represent the principal policymakers in American democracy. These officials, however, may signal to the Court that judicial invalidation of legislation is not especially problematic. Furthermore, Court decisions invalidating legislation may reflect public opinion or other populist trends. In other words, social and political forces—not judicial hubris—may explain supposedly countermajoritarian decision making.

In this chapter, I argue that judicial invalidation of statutes is often tied to majoritarian social and political forces. In part, I explain why it is that the Court cannot escape "the great tides and currents which engulf" the rest of us (Cardozo 1921, 168). Also, by focusing on 1995–2003 Rehnquist Court decisions striking down federal laws, this chapter details some of the ways that majoritarian forces have figured in these decisions.

THE NONMAJORITARIAN DIFFICULTY

When striking down legislation, the Supreme Court almost always takes its cues from elected officials, the public, or elites (academics, journalists, and other opinion leaders).[1] "Policy views dominant on the Court," as Dahl put it, "are never for long out of line with the policy views dominant among the lawmaking majorities of the United States" (1957, 285). The Court, in other words, cannot resist "a determined and persistent lawmaking majority;" it can only put its preferences in place against "a weak majority; e.g., a dead one, a transient one, a fragile one, or one weakly united against a policy of subordinate importance" (Dahl 1957, 286). This does not mean that the Court never falls out of step with lawmakers or the American people. During periods of political realignment, for example, the justices may embrace the constitutional views of the "old" majority, not the "newly dominant coalition" (Funston 1975, 806).

In the next section of the chapter, I will explain how Court decision making is inextricably linked to social and political forces. At this point, I think it useful to explain why decisions striking down legislation are not necessarily countermajoritarian. I will make use of examples linking judicial invalidations of legislation to public opinion and the preferences of elected officials.

PUBLIC OPINION

The American people often back judicial invalidations of federal and state legislation. Contrary to its image of "providing a 'haven of refuge' for minorities sufferings persecution from overreaching majorities," the Court "identifies and protects minority rights only when a majority or near majority of the community had come to deem those rights worthy of protection" (Klarman 1996, 17–18). Consider, for example, three of the Court's most countermajoritarian decisions: *Roe v. Wade*'s invalidation of state laws prohibiting abortion, *Brown v. Board of Education*'s repudiation of racial segregation, and *Lochner*-era decision making invalidating New Deal initiatives. In each instance, the justices were keenly aware of how their decisions would play with the American people.

At the time of *Roe*, public opinion polls favored abortion rights. These polls were fueled by two well-publicized episodes in which American women sought abortions to prevent the birth of severely deformed infants (see Garrow 1994). One incident involved Sherry Finkbine, a mother of four who had taken thalidomide during her pregnancy. After learning that the drug often caused severe birth defects, Finkbine sought an abortion at home, and ultimately was forced to travel to Sweden to obtain an abortion. The second episode was a 1962–65 outbreak of rubella, which resulted in 15,000 babies being born with birth defects. In the midst of this outbreak, two California physicians were charged with performing abortions. These arrests prompted a public outcry and, with it, the California legislature's approval of abortion reform legislation. By 1972, a Gallup poll revealed that 64 percent of Americans, including 56 percent of Roman Catholics, agreed that "the decision to have an abortion should be made solely by a woman and her physician" (Garrow 1994, 562). At the time of *Roe*, moreover, elite opinion strongly favored abortion rights. Against this backdrop, it is not especially surprising that the Supreme Court would recognize abortion rights in 1973. Indeed, opinion polls conducted in 1974 revealed that by a slim margin (47 to 44 percent) Americans favored *Roe* (Gallup 1987, 49).

When deciding *Roe*, the Supreme Court paid close attention to public opinion—especially the willingness of the American people to accept the decision. *Roe*'s author, Justice Harry Blackmun, proposed issuing a press statement to accompany the decision (something that had never been done before and ultimately was not done here) to keep the press from "going all the way off the deep end" in reporting news of the decision (quoted in Garrow 1994, 587). *Brown v. Board of Education* likewise underscores the powerful role of public opinion in Supreme Court decision making. In particular, the Court's willingness to strike down school segregation in

1954 is very much tied to changing populist attitudes about civil rights. At the time of *Brown*, opinion poll data revealed that half the country backed racial integration in the public schools (Klarman 1996, 8 n. 30). More striking, the great changes in race relations in the decades before *Brown* figured prominently in the Court's decision making. For example, Justice Felix Frankfurter noted that had *Brown* reached the Court a decade earlier he would have voted to uphold segregation because "public opinion had not then crystallized against it" (*Memorandum* of Justice Douglas, reprinted in Urofsky 1987, 169, quoting Justice Frankfurter). Consequently, even though Southern lawmakers (and their constituents) vigorously opposed *Brown*, the Court's decision reflected the nation's growing belief in desegregation.

Public opinion, finally, may have played an important role in both *Lochner* era invalidations of federal legislation and the Court's eventual repudiation of *Lochner*. With the important exceptions of minimum wage and child labor legislation, "it is not clear that much, if any change was required to bring *Lochner* era constitutional doctrine in line with public sentiment" (Cushman 2002, 59). Extensive polling of the American people in the 1930s revealed that either (1) the federal statutes struck down lacked popular support or (2) the Court seemed willing to uphold those portions of the bill that garnered public support (see Cushman 2002, 19–58). Perhaps more telling, after Roosevelt's landslide victory in 1936 (suggesting public support for centralized planning if not the individual statutes passed by the New Deal Congress), the Court moderated its decision making in order to uphold New Deal initiatives. In explaining this transformation, Justice Owen Roberts recognized the extraordinary importance of public opinion in undoing the *Lochner* era: "Looking back, it is difficult to see how the Court could have resisted the popular urge for uniform standards throughout the country—for what in effect was a unified economy"(Roberts 1951, 61).[2]

ELECTED OFFICIALS' PREFERENCES

Not only does the public sometimes support judicial invalidations of legislation, elected officials sometimes embrace countermajoritarian judicial review. This, of course, does not mean that elected officials are in lockstep with the public. As the New Deal makes clear, popular opposition to legislation is hardly a proxy for lawmaker opposition to legislation. By resisting reforms pushed by New Deal Democrats, *Lochner* Court invalidations of federal statutes placed the Court "squarely against the interests of the dominant political party of the period" (Whittington 2001b, 514).

It is often the case, however, that lawmakers are quite happy to leave a contentious social policy issue in the Court's hands. "Mainstream politicians," as Graber observed, "may facilitate judicial policymaking in part because they have good reason to believe that courts will announce those policies they privately favor but cannot openly endorse without endangering their political support" (Graber 1993, 43). For example, party leaders may prefer policies that their rank and file oppose. "In such cases, the aim of legislative deference to the judiciary is for courts to make controversial policies that political elites approve of but cannot publicly champion, and to do so in such a way that these elites are not held accountable by the general public, or at least not as accountable as they would be had they personally voted for that policy" (Graber 1993, 43).

Consider, for example, the Supreme Court's approval of the Voting Rights Acts of 1965 in *South Carolina v. Katzenbach*, 383 U.S. 301 (1966). Although Southern officials challenged the constitutionality of the act, the Court's decision gave cover to these very same officials. In particular, these officials were willing to comply with the policy but unwilling to alienate their white constituents by taking responsibility for it. For these officials, the Court served as a welcome "whipping boy . . . giv[ing] officials another institution to blame, even as they follow the new policy" (Murphy and Tanenhaus 1990, 1017).

Whether or not elected officials approve the Court's decision, policymakers may well prefer to have some external institution take the heat for settling an issue. Two of the Court's most controversial decisions, *Dred Scott v. Sandford* and *Roe v. Wade*, call attention to different ways that elected officials look to the Court to settle an issue. *Dred Scott* (striking down the Missouri Compromise as violating a slave-holder's rights to his "property") was undertaken only after Congress made clear that the Supreme Court should settle the slavery issue. The Kansas-Nebraska Act of 1854, for example, provided that "in all cases involving title to slaves . . . appeals shall be allowed and decided by the Supreme Court without regard to the value of the matter" (10 Statutes at Large 287). In enacting a "lawsuit" but "not a law," lawmakers thought it best to turn the "question between the North and the South into a constitutional and judicial question" (quoted in Graber 1993, 48). Along the same lines, James Buchanan (at his 1856 inauguration) assured the country that the divisive issue of slavery was before the Court where it would be "speedily and finally settled" (see Richardson 1897, 431).

Dred Scott, of course, did not settle the slavery issue; instead, it took a Civil War to resolve the divide separating pro slavery and antislavery interests. Likewise, *Roe* did little to convince prolife interests that a woman had a right to terminate her pregnancy. Between 1973 (the year *Roe* was decided) and 1989, forty-eight states passed 306 abortion measures. No doubt, there was significant resistance to *Roe*, especially its granting an unqualified right to abortion during the first trimester. On the other hand, many elected officials were quietly pleased by *Roe*. John Hart Ely, for example, speaks of the "sighs of relief as this particular albatross was cut from the legislative and executive necks" (Ely 1973, 947). That an avalanche of abortion restrictions were enacted may only mean that legislators saw no downside in responding to prolife interest groups because prochoice concerns were content to leave it to the courts to protect their interests. In a sense, federal and state efforts to limit abortion rights paid homage to a judiciary who would toe the line and provide whatever constitutional protections were appropriate. Indeed, prolife legislative initiatives were brought to a standstill following 1989 and 1992 Supreme Court decisions expanding state authority to regulate abortion. Knowing that prochoice forces were "going to take names and kick ankles," these decisions made right-to-life initiatives less likely to succeed.[3]

None of this is especially surprising. Lawmakers have little incentive to risk their political futures by staking out a position on a volatile political issue. For these lawmakers, it may well make sense to position themselves against the backdrop of a "definitive" Supreme Court decision. Moreover, the Court often hears cases in which elected officials are at loggerheads with each other. Federalism cases, for example, divide state and federal lawmakers; separation of powers cases pit the president against Congress. Here, the Court must choose between majoritarian institutions. In other words, the simple fact that the Court approves or invalidates a law does not tell us whether the Court's action is countermajoritarian. Instead, in sorting out whether a decision is truly countermajoritarian, one must also look to public and elite opinion, the preferences of elected officials, and possible divisions among the political parties and units of government.

HOW SOCIAL AND POLITICAL FORCES SHAPE COURT DECISION MAKING

It is hardly a coincidence that supposedly countermajoritarian judicial decision making is, upon closer examination, a reflection of popular opinion and/or elected government preferences. Just as the Supreme Court leaves its mark on American society, so are social forces part of the mix of constitutional law. As Lerner noted, judicial decisions "are not babies brought by constitutional storks, but are born out of the travail of economic circumstances" (Lerner 1937, 1290). True, the Justices work in a somewhat insulated atmosphere. But, as Chief Justice William Rehnquist reminded us, the "currents and tides of public opinion . . . lap at the courthouse door," for "judges go home at night and read the newspaper or watch the evening news on television; they talk to their family and friends about current events" (Rehnquist 1986, 768). As such, "judges, so long as they are relatively normal human beings, can no more escape being influenced by public opinion in the long run than can people working at other jobs."

Constitutional decision making, moreover, is a dynamic process that involves all parts of government and the people as well. In critical respects, the history of the Supreme Court has been a search for various techniques and methods that will permit the judiciary to limit and constrain its own power. Justices understand, by either instinct or experience, that the hazards are great when the Court attempts to settle political, social, and economic matters best left to the political process. Despite occasional utterances from the Court that it is the "ultimate interpreter" of the Constitution, Justices by necessity adhere to a philosophy that is much more modest, circumspect, and nuanced. Rather than settle transcendent values, Court decisions, at best, momentarily resolve the dispute immediately before the Court.

The strongest support for this proposition, ironically, comes from those cases in which the Court has defended its authority to bind government officials through its interpretation of the Constitution. *Marbury v. Madison*, 5 U.S. (1 Cranch) 137 (1803), the supposed foundation of judicial supremacy, nicely illustrates how political challenges to the Court's interpretive authority and claims of judicial supremacy are inextricably linked to each other. When *Marbury* was decided, the Supreme Court and its chief justice, John Marshall, were under attack. Court foe Thomas Jefferson had just been elected president and, at his urging, Secretary of State James Madison openly challenged the Court's authority to subject executive officers to judicial orders.[4] Further complicating matters, were the Court to rule against the Jeffersonians, Marshall believed that his political enemies would push for his impeachment. Unwilling to engage in a head-to-head confrontation with the Jeffersonians, the Court's supposed war cry in *Marbury*, that "[i]t is emphatically the province and duty of the judicial department to say what the law is" (5 U.S. [1 Cranch], at 177) is window dressing for the Court's reasoning in ultimately ducking the *Marbury* dispute on jurisdictional grounds.

Lacking the power to appropriate funds or command the military, the Court understands that it must act in a way that garners public acceptance. In other words, as the psychologists Tom Tyler and Gregory Mitchell observed, the Court seems to believe "that public acceptance of the Court's role as interpreter of the Constitution—that is, the public belief in the Court's institutional legitimacy—enhances public acceptance of controversial Court decisions" (Tyler and Mitchell 1994, 715). This emphasis on public acceptance of the judiciary seems to be conclusive proof that Court decision making cannot be divorced from a case's (sometimes explosive) social and political setting.

Education policymaking exemplifies the Court's willingness to take social and political forces into account in its decision making. Take the case of school desegregation. Beginning with *Brown v. Board of Education*, 349 U.S. 294 (1954), the Supreme Court allowed its perceptions of elected government preferences to shape its decision making in this area. In an effort to temper southern hostility to its decision, the Court did not issue a remedy in the first *Brown* decision. One year later, the Court issued a weak-kneed remedy, recognizing that "varied local school problems" were best solved by "[s]chool authorities" and that delays associated with "problems related to administration" were to be expected (349 U.S., at 299–300). By again taking into account potential resistance to its decision, the Court engaged in the type of interest balancing that has set political parameters on judicial participation in equal educational opportunity.

Social and political forces, especially federal government efforts to enforce Brown during the 1960s, also figured prominently in the Supreme Court's approval of mandatory busing remedies in *Swann v. Charlotte-Mecklenburg Board of Education*. *Swann*, however, went well beyond elected government preferences. During the Nixon and Reagan administrations, the Court and the elected branches of government fought a pitched battle over busing, a battle that has now abated (see Fisher and Devins 2001). In 1991, and again in 1992, the Supreme Court recognized greater state and local control over public schools and, in so doing, narrowed its controversial hard-line position on busing.[5]

A more telling manifestation of how public opinion affects Court decision making is evident when the Court reverses itself to conform its decision making to social and political forces beating against it. Witness, for example, the Court's reconsideration of decisions on sterilization and the eugenics movement (see Fisher 1987, 11–15), state-mandated flag salutes (see Manwaring 1962, 154–60; Hirsch 1981, 152–53), the *Roe v. Wade* trimester standard (see Devins 1996b, 56–77, 139–48), the death penalty (see Fisher 1988, 75–76), states' rights (see Tushnet 1996), and much more. It did not matter that some of these earlier decisions commanded an impressive majority of eight to one.[6] Without popular support, these decisions settled nothing. Justice Robert Jackson instructed us that, "the practical play of the forces of politics is such that judicial power has often delayed but never permanently defeated the persistent will of a substantial majority" (Jackson 1953, 761). As such, for a Court that wants to maximize its power and legitimacy, taking social and political forces into account is an act of necessity, not cowardice. Correspondingly, when the Court gives short shrift to populist values or concerns, its decision making is unworkable and destabilizing.

It is sometimes argued that courts operate on principle while the rest of government is satisfied with compromises. This argument is sheer folly. A multimember Court, like government, gropes incrementally towards consensus and decision through compromise, expediency, and ad hoc actions. "No good society," as Bickel observed, "can be unprincipled; and no viable society can be principle-ridden" (1961, 49).

During his service as a federal appellate judge, William Howard Taft commented on the interplay between judicial decisions and public opinion. He said that the right to publicly criticize judicial action is "of vastly more importance to the body politic than the immunity of courts and judges from unjust aspirations and attack." He added: "Nothing tends more to render judges careful in their decisions and anxiously solicitous to do exact justice than the consciousness that every act of theirs is to be subjected to the intelligent scrutiny of their fellow-men, and to their candid criticism" (Taft 1895, 642).

In other words, rather than definitively settling transcendent questions, courts must take account of social movements and public opinion. When the judiciary strays outside and opposes the policy of elected leaders, it does so at substantial risk. The Court maintains its strength by steering a course that fits within the permissible limits of public opinion. Correspondingly, "the Court's legitimacy—indeed, the Constitution's—must ultimately spring from public acceptance," for ours is a "political system ostensibly based on consent" (Murphy and Tanenhaus 1990, 992).

CONGRESS AS CULPRIT: HOW LAWMAKERS SPURRED ON THE REHNQUIST COURT'S ANTI-CONGRESS CRUSADE

What then of the Rehnquist Court? By invalidating all or parts of thirty-one federal statutes (from 1995 to 2003), the Court has been characterized as "arrogant, self-aggrandizing, and unduly activist" by "giving insufficient deference—or even a modicum of respect—to Congress" (Sherry 2002, 47). *But* is this characterization fair? I think not; in the pages that follow, I will explain how it is that the Rehnquist Court is paying close attention to signals sent it from Congress and the American people.

To start, I think it important to acknowledge that Rehnquist Court decision making can be divided into two periods.[7] During the second Rehnquist Court (1995–2003), the Court focused its efforts on constitutional federalism, generated several important doctrinal innovations, and invalidated scores of federal statutes. Before its turn to federalism, however, the Rehnquist Court was a Court in search of an agenda. From 1986 to 1994, the first Rehnquist Court, although investing much energy in social issues (abortion, race, religion), did little to change the law.[8] Social and political forces, especially Congress's support of civil and abortion rights, figure prominently in this story. In particular, the refusal of Justices Sandra Day O'Connor and Anthony Kennedy to sign onto the conservative social agenda may well be tied to the signals sent to the Court from Capitol Hill.

Consider, for example, *Planned Parenthood v. Casey*, 505 U.S. 833 (1992)—what may be the defining case of the first Rehnquist Court. Justices Kennedy and O'Connor's decision to reaffirm *Roe* seems inextricably linked to Senate Judiciary Committee efforts to "make clear to nominees that a willingness to profess belief in some threshold constitutional values is a prerequisite to the job" (Wermiel 1993, 121–22). Specifically, the Senate Judiciary Committee limited its sights on abortion and other social issues; for example, it rejected Robert Bork's nomination because Bork, if confirmed, almost certainly would have supplied the fifth vote needed to overturn *Roe*. Also, the committee's "severe hazing" of Clarence Thomas "served as a warning to the sitting Justices that if they persisted down the path of seeking to overturn *Roe* and securing other conservative objectives, they could expect equivalent retaliation of an unspecified nature" (Merrill 2003, 630–31). Against this backdrop, it seems certain that the Senate played an instrumental role in the defeat of the conservative social agenda. Not only did it keep Bork off the Court, it also sent a message to Justices O'Connor and Kennedy that the repudiation of Court decision making on abortion, school prayer, and the like would be seen as an act of political defiance.[9] Perhaps for this reason, the *Casey* plurality emphasized both the costs of "overrul[ing] under [political] fire" and explicitly linked the Court's "legitimacy" to "people's acceptance of the Judiciary" (505 U.S. at 867, 865).

Beyond the appointments process, Congress pressured the first Rehnquist Court in other important ways. On civil rights, Congress rejected Reagan- and Bush-era initiatives to limit proofs of discrimination grounded in disparate racial impact. Most telling, through the Civil Rights Act of 1991, Congress overturned thirteen Supreme Court decisions limiting the scope of civil rights laws. Finally, during its first three years, the Rehnquist Court was constrained by lawmaker rebukes to Reagan Justice Department efforts to grant tax breaks to racist schools, to disallow impact-based proofs of vote dilution, to put an end to forced busing, and to repudiate affirmative action.

The failure of the first Rehnquist Court to innovate doctrine and/or reach consensus on social issues is very much tied to social and political forces. In particular, efforts by social conservatives in the executive branch to remake the Court were vigorously opposed by lawmakers and interest groups. Rather than take sides in this culture war (by either rejecting or extending Warren and Burger Court decision making), the Court did not pursue doctrinal innovations. For quite similar reasons, second Rehnquist Court decision making invalidating federal statutes is also tied to social and political forces. This seems especially true of the Court's pursuit of doctrinal innovations on federalism-related issues, although the forces contributing to this federalism revival help explain the Court's willingness to strike down several other statutes.

First, unlike social issues, lawmakers barely mentioned federalism in the confirmation hearings, committee reports, or floor debates concerning any member of the Rehnquist Court. For example, the Senate Judiciary Committee never pressed Sandra Day O'Connor about states rights—even though O'Connor called attention to the fact that her "experience[s] as a State court judge and as a state legislator" gave her "a greater appreciation of the important role that States play in our federal system" (O'Connor 1981). Correspondingly, there are virtually no mentions of federalism in interest group testimony and written submissions.

Second, Congress is held in disrepute by both the public and members of Congress. Consider the following: As compared with 1964 (when 76 percent of those polled thought that the federal government could be trusted "just about always" or "most of the time"), 27 percent of those polled in 2001 think the government trustworthy. By a 74 to 17 percent margin, a 1997 poll revealed that Americans think that members of Congress care more about making themselves look better than making the country better. In 1992, 82 percent of those polled thought that people elected to Congress "lose touch with the people pretty quickly" (data from Schroeder 2001).

Making matters worse, when Republicans took over both houses of Congress in 1994 (the first year of the second Rehnquist Court), House Republicans ran on the so-called Contract with America. Premised on the belief that Congress is irresponsible and unworthy of trust, the Contract with America ostensibly sought to limit congressional power in several ways, including by imposing term limits, prohibiting unfunded mandates, and creating the line-item veto. On the line-item veto, for example, Senator Dan Coats (R-Ind.) and others argued: Congress "cannot discipline itself. . . . [It] is selfish and greedy and . . . cannot put the national interest ahead of parochial interests or special interests" (Coats 1995). And while the Contract with America has fizzled, Congress remains ready, willing, and eager to cede core powers—especially budgetary and war powers.[10] This pattern is likely to continue, for the declining public trust in government creates incentives for lawmakers to distance themselves from Congress by engaging in mutual self-flagellation.

Third, lawmakers sometimes signal the Court that—when it comes to interpreting the Constitution—Congress is not to be trusted. Sometimes, Congress treats the Constitution as the exclusive province of the Supreme Court; on other occasions, Congress simply seems indifferent to the constitutionality of its enactments, including whether the Supreme Court is likely to approve or disapprove of its decision making. In so doing, Congress signals the Court that it has little institutional stake in constitutional matters and, accordingly, that there is little, if any, institutional price the Court will pay when invalidating federal legislation. With little reason to think about how its decisions will play on Capitol Hill, the Rehnquist Court's willingness to strike down federal legislation of which it disapproves is anything but surprising.

One manifestation of this phenomenon is the growing use of "expedited Supreme Court review" provisions in cases for which Congress finds its handiwork constitutionally suspect. Specifically, rather than sorting out the constitutionality of the legislation it is considering, Congress sometimes enacts a fast-track provision enabling litigants both to bypass the federal courts of appeal and to secure automatic Supreme Court review. Over the past several years, Congress has included expedited review provisions on several high-profile enactments, including campaign finance legislation, flag burning legislation, the Gramm-Rudman Act, the Communications Decency Act, the Line Item Veto Act, and census reform legislation. When enacting such measures, lawmakers effectively delegate their power to interpret the Constitution to the Supreme Court. For example, Representative William Clinger (R-Pa.), chair of the House committee with jurisdiction over the item veto bill, declared that "it is not really our job to determine what is constitutional or what is not unconstitutional."[11]

There are other ways that Congress signals the Court that constitutional questions are the Court's domain. When deliberating about the Constitution's meaning, Congress often treats the Court's decisions as definitive and final. In other words, unlike Court-curbing periods (during which Congress has sought to limit the reach of Court decisions on, among other things, abortion, busing, and school prayer), the modern Congress hardly ever casts doubt on either the correctness of the Court's rulings or, more fundamentally, the Court's power to interpret the Constitution authoritatively.

Consider, for example, Congress's response to *Adarand Constructors, Inc. v. Pena*, 515 U.S. 200 (1995), a Supreme Court decision declaring that federal affirmative action programs must satisfy the Court's strictest standard of judicial review. In the immediate wake of the Court's decision, Senator Phil Gramm (R-Tex.) proposed eliminating set-asides for minorities and women in federal contracting. Gramm explained, "my amendment is written in total conformity with Adarand."[12] In sharp contrast, Senator Arlen Specter (R-Pa.) called attention to *Adarand*'s recognition that the government may act in response to "both the practice and the lingering effects of racial discrimination."[13] Along these lines, Senator Patty Murray (D-Wash.) countered Gramm's efforts by proposing that federal funds can be used only for "programs . . . completely consistent with the Supreme Court's recent decision in . . . Adarand."[14] In the end, the Murray amendment was approved by a lopsided 84–13 vote, and the Gramm amendment was soundly defeated by a bipartisan 61–36 vote (Merida 1995, A13).

It is little wonder that Supreme Court Justices feel empowered by such legislative deliberations. By seeing the Constitution as the Supreme Court's domain, Congress encourages the Court to strike down measures the justices dislike, to settle presidential elections, and so forth. And while the Justices may not know about the Gramm-Murray exchange, they certainly know that a legislative backlash has not followed in the wake of recent rulings limiting congressional power. There is no talk of packing the Court, of stripping it of jurisdiction, or of amending the Constitution in response to these rulings.

Indeed, there has been virtually no talk at all; the precedential effects of Court decisions limiting federal power are hardly ever mentioned in the *Congressional Record*. Moreover, with the exception of Court rulings invalidating the Violence Against Women Act and the Religious Freedom Restoration Act, no more than four comments exist about the wisdom of any of the Court's federalism-related decisions.[15] Furthermore, these decisions played no role in the 2000 or 2002 elections. Finally, Congress has shown relatively little interest in rewriting these statutes. And when Congress has revisited its handiwork, lawmakers have paid close attention to the Supreme Court's rulings, limiting their efforts to revisions the Court is likely to approve. Committee reports and sponsor statements of these statutes, for example, speak of Congress's "address[ing] the specific concerns raised by the Supreme Court" and "heed[ing] the Supreme Court's decision."[16]

Fourth, Congress has little incentive to take recent Supreme Court decisions into account and thereby slow down the pace of federalization because interest groups increasingly prefer national legislation to state and local measures (see, generally, Friedman 1997, 364–78; and Marshall 1998). As compared with lobbying fifty state legislatures, for example, there is a far lower transaction cost associated with national legislation. More significantly, the political culture has become increasingly nationalized. Changes in both media coverage and advertising have made all politics national—so that guns in schools, carjacking, and the like are considered national, not local, problems.

At the same time, Congress is not particularly disappointed with Court decision making. Unlike during Court-curbing periods, many members of Congress now are somewhat sympathetic to, say, Court efforts to protect state prerogatives. For this very reason, Representative Lee Hamilton (D-Ind.), after observing that lawmakers seemed "detached from the actual work of the federal judiciary, particularly as it relates to the exercise of congressional power," speculated that Congress "has become more conservative, and many members are comfortable with most of the Court's rulings."[17]

Fifth, it is also noteworthy that second Rehnquist Court federalism decision making has been incremental. Initially, the Court moved gingerly—striking down relatively few laws and striking them down on somewhat ambiguous grounds.

Today, however, the Court seems more aggressive, and with good reason. State governments and conservative interest groups have rallied behind the Court, filing briefs in support of federalism-based claims. For its part, Congress has not cast doubt on these decisions. Moreover, there is little reason to fear a populist backlash. The Court remains politically popular and somewhat middle-of-the-road on divisive social policy issues. And when the Court strikes down a law, it typically leaves Congress room to revisit the issue.

Sixth and finally, most of the measures struck down were "position taking" statutes, that is, laws in which legislators derive whatever political mileage they are going to get by casting a roll call vote in support of the law (Whittington 2001b, 512–14). For example, with state laws prohibiting both gun possession near schools and domestic violence, it was more important to members of Congress to make "a judgmental statement" than to see to it that the law, in fact, took effect. Correspondingly, Congress increasingly is concerned with "message politics," that is, using the legislative process to make a symbolic statement to voters and other constituents (see, generally, Evans 2000). Rather than look to committee leadership to define Congress's agenda, Republicans and Democrats alike see the lawmaking process as expressive, a way for the members of each party to coalesce behind their party's policy agenda. Likewise, by focusing its efforts on the message it is sending, Congress places less emphasis on what happens to legislation after it is enacted. Instead of negotiating with the president over the specifics of legislation (so as to stave off a possible veto), "Congress can, and routinely does, pass laws deliberately designed to provoke a presidential veto" (Gilmour 2002). Likewise, a Court decision striking down legislation is not especially problematic. Indeed, the Court's decision creates an occasion for Congress to revisit the issue and, in this way, facilitates lawmaker efforts to, once again, send a symbolic message to voters and other constituents.

CONCLUSION

Congress and the American people do not see Rehnquist Court decisions striking down federal legislation as especially problematic. The Court's reinvigoration of federalism, for example, reflects populist anti-Congress attitudes. And unlike judicial invalidations of New Deal legislation, Congress either approved or did not object to Rehnquist Court decision making. In particular, the changing face of lawmaking places less emphasis on securing judicial approval of legislation and more emphasis on doing what is politically popular (federalizing crime, for example).

Along the same lines, by reaffirming abortion rights, the ban on school prayer, and *Miranda* warnings, the Rehnquist Court paid close attention to social and political forces. None of this is surprising. The Supreme Court has good reason to listen to elected officials and the American people. Lacking the power of purse and sword, the Court's power is necessarily tied to public and lawmaker acceptance of its decisions.

And while the Court helps shape popular and elected government discourse, the Court must operate within parameters established by elected officials. For this very reason, decisions invalidating federal and state legislation are usually tied to signals sent to the Court by elected officials and the American people. It may be, for example, that the public no longer supports the law. Alternatively, instead of confronting the issue head-on, lawmakers may prefer to seek cover in a Court decision. Whatever the explanation, judicial policymaking is rarely countermajoritarian.

I do not mean to suggest that the courts are not making policy. It is rarely the case that elected officials and the American people demand that the Court strike down legislation (statutes, after all, can be repealed through the legislative process). My point, instead, is that court decisions striking down legislation can almost always be tied to social and political forces. That is the historical pattern. And the recent wave of Rehnquist Court decisions invalidating federal laws conforms to this historical pattern.

NOTES

Portions of this chapter first appeared in Devins and Fisher (1998) and in Devins (2001). In writing this chapter, I have greatly benefited from the scholarship and friendship of Louis Fisher and Mark Graber.

1. The heading for this section plays off of Graber's (1993) fine article; some of the examples mentioned in the section are also discussed by Graber.
2. For my views on whether public opinion, improved legislative drafting, or the FDR Court-packing plan was the impetus of this doctrinal shift, see Devins 1996a, 242–56.
3. 135 *Cong. Rec.*18, 170 (1989), statement of Rep. Les AuCoin (D-Ore.). For an extended treatment of this topic, see Devins 1996b.
4. Specifically, when William Marbury challenged Madison's failure to deliver him a judicial commission, Madison refused to present a defense, thereby forcing the Court to decide the case without the benefit of the executive's arguments. See Fisher and Devins 2001, at 26–27.
5. See *Freeman v. Pitts*, 503 U.S. 467, 485–92 (1992) (identifying several factors that supervising district courts should consider when relinquishing control over the implementation of a desegregation plan); and *Board of Education v. Dowell*, 498 U.S. 237, 250 (1991) (recognizing that once a school district complies with a desegregation decree, federal courts no longer retain control over regulatory policy and rules).
6. See, e.g., *Minersville School District v. Gobitis*, 310 U.S. 586 (1940) (upholding mandatory flag salute), overruled by *West Va. State Board of Education v. Barnette*, 319 U.S. 624 (1943).
7. For the definitive treatment of this topic, see Merrill 2003.
8. On abortion and school prayer, the Court reaffirmed decisions that had long been the bane of social conservatives; see *Planned Parenthood v. Casey*, 505 U.S. 833 (1992); and *Lee v. Weisman*, 505 U.S. 577 (1992). On affirmative action, the Court muddied that which was murky; through a string of fractured rulings, the justices did little more than reject Reagan administration efforts to undo all preferences; see Devins 1989. In 2003, however, the Court approved race-based admissions at colleges and universities; *Grutter v. Bollinger*, 123 S.Ct. 2325 (2003).
9. It is also noteworthy that the appointment of stealth nominee David Souter was made, in part, to avoid the controversy surrounding nominees—such as Bork—with a paper trail.
10. On the question of the congressional abdication of power, see, generally, Fisher 2000.
11. 142 *Cong. Rec.* 6912 (1996) (statement of Rep. Clinger).
12. 141 *Cong. Rec.* 19,670 (1995) (statement of Sen. Gramm).
13. 141 *Cong. Rec.* 19,671 (statement of Sen. Specter), quoting Justice O'Connor's opinion in *Adarand Constructors, Inc. v. Pena*, 515 U.S. 200, 237 (1995).
14. 141 *Cong. Rec.* 19,667 (statement of Sen. Murray).

15. Lexis database search, *Congressional Record*, ALL Congress Combined, for "Court" and either the name of the case or relevant law for the period of one month following the date of the decision.

16. H.R. Rep. No. 105-775, at 12 (1998) (legislation responding to Court invalidation of Communication Decency Act); 141 *Cong. Rec.* S7920 (daily ed., June 7, 1995) (statement of Sen. Herb Kohl, D-Wis., introducing legislation to respond to Supreme Court decision invalidating Gun Free School Zones Act).

17. 144 *Cong. Rec.* E48 (daily ed., January 28, 1998) (statement of Rep. Hamilton).

12

Governance as Dialogue

**JEB BARNES AND
MARK C. MILLER**

THIS CHAPTER WRAPS UP THE ANALYSIS, BRIEFLY LOOKING back at what we see as the main themes and lessons from the preceding chapters, and briefly looking forward to some of their implications for conceptualizing and evaluating contemporary American policymaking. The goal is not to review the chapters point-by-point, but to highlight how they challenge conventional views of contemporary American policymaking and force us to rethink standard approaches to studying the policymaking process. The main lesson is that the policymaking process is not simple and straightforward, but instead governance is a complex process of continuing dialogue.

LOOKING BACK: AMERICAN POLICYMAKING AS CONTINUING COLLOQUIES

The textbook account of federal lawmaking envisages the following: members of Congress and the president initiate the process, negotiating basic policy decisions that are written into laws. Experts in executive agencies then devise detailed regulations, which flesh out legislative bargains and govern the law's implementation. Federal judges serve as referees throughout the process, adjudicating disputes over the meaning of legal rules, protecting citizens against arbitrary governmental action, and safeguarding basic constitutional principles. This account is often summarized in terms of principal-agent theory, which holds that the elected members of Congress and the president represent the principals, who make statutes, and appointed bureaucrats and judges are the agents, who apply statutes as written provided that they are constitutional.

This volume fundamentally challenges this view. As a matter of constitutional design, the United States simply does not feature a hierarchy of lawmakers or compartmentalized niches for each branch of government (chapter 2 of this volume by Barnes). Instead, the U.S. Constitution creates a system of overlapping and diversely representative branches of government, which share and compete for power. Consider lawmaking power. As a formal matter, Congress does have the primary authority to draft laws. But this power can be checked by both the presidential veto and the courts' power of judicial review. More important, both the executive and judicial branches have considerable voice in the making of law. Specifically, the executive branch has the power to "take care" that the laws are faithfully executed, which includes the authority to write regulations that significantly shape the law. The courts can be intimately involved in the policymaking and lawmaking processes both because of their statutory interpretation opinions and because of their constitutionally based decisions. In matters of statutory interpretation, the courts' power to adjudicate disputes arising under the law includes substantial authority to "legislate interstitially" (Cardozo 1921; Shapiro 1966). Therefore, the courts fill gaps that inevitably appear when general rules are applied to particular cases. In constitutional matters, under the doctrine of judicial review, courts can strike down statutes under the Constitution and set formal parameters for any new legislation.

Equally important, each branch of government and chamber of Congress is designed to answer to different constituencies. Members of the U.S. House are elected by voters in congressional districts; U.S. senators were initially elected by state representatives and now are elected in statewide elections; the president is selected by the electors of the Electoral College, whose members represent all the states; and federal judges are insulated from electoral pressures as lifetime presidential appointees with guaranteed salaries. By combining these diverse modes of representation with branches of government that share power, the Constitution explicitly avoids creating an orderly division of labor among hierarchical branches with discrete policymaking roles; rather, it seeks to create a dynamic tension among politically distinct, nonhierarchical branches that have overlapping responsibilities. This tension promises to serve a number of important democratic and policy functions, such as (1) providing multiple points of access into the lawmaking process, which should encourage broad participation in policymaking; (2) reducing opportunities for unilateral action by any single branch of government or faction, which should protect individual liberty; and (3) fostering mutual supervision among the branches of government, which in turn should generate interbranch feedback, lead to revision of poorly drafted or outmoded laws, and, over time, promote policy consensus and hence legal certainty (Barnes, chapter 2 of this volume, and 2004; Peretti 1999; Sunstein 1993; Dahl 1956; and *Federalist Papers No. 10* and *No. 51*, 1788).

Of course, governing regimes are not written in legal stone; they are politically constructed over time. In the United States, waves of institutional reforms begun in the Progressive Era and greatly advanced during the New Deal Era of the 1930s and the Great Society Era of the 1960s created a distinctively American administrative state that further blurred the already blurry lines among the branches of government (in this volume, see chapters 1, by Kagan; 4, by Kassop; 5, by Melnick; and 8, by Bragaw and Miller). Of particular importance to this volume, reforms in the 1960s and 1970s changed the structure of legislative programs, which in turn unleashed a flood of policymaking by the courts.

To elaborate briefly, American reformers in the 1960s and 1970s sought to address widespread social issues, such as discrimination, environmental degradation, and consumer safety, but feared existing New Deal agencies had been captured by the very industries they were created to regulate. Accordingly, unlike their European counterparts who built on centralized bureaucracies to implement their ambitious social welfare agendas, American reformers added more and more agencies to the already fragmented structures of government, creating ever more bureaucratic entities that shared regulatory power with existing federal and state authorities. In addition, U.S. reformers created a series of new procedural mechanisms, such as public comment periods and citizen suits, which guarantee public interest groups a say in administrative decision making as well as giving them a means to challenge regulatory outcomes in court. At the same time, federal courts facilitated public interest group litigation by making changes in administrative law, such as easing standing requirements and creating new constitutional grounds for testing agency procedures. The net result is that American judges are far more central to policymaking than their counterparts abroad, serving not only as adjudicators of legal disputes but also as administrators of conflicts among contending regulatory authorities, overseers of public challenges to agency procedures and decisions, and arbiters of the practical problems and abstract principles of today's changing federalism.

According to Robert Kagan, these changes produced a surge of "adversarial legalism": a distinctively American mode of dispute resolution, policymaking, and implementation in which public interest groups frequently place core policy and regulatory issues before the courts, and politically selected, independent judges not infrequently make policy under the guise of resolving legal disputes. Or, to paraphrase Tocqueville, now more than ever, all legal disputes eventually become political disputes in the United States, and all political disputes eventually become legal ones. Meanwhile, the groups that lose in court often demand legislative or administrative relief from what they perceive to be unfavorable court decisions. As a result, the basic rules of the game are constantly litigated and politically revised; legislative, executive, and judicial functions are shared; and conventional roles are sometimes reversed, in that federal agencies and courts make basic policy and Congress resolves specific disputes among contending interests.

The bottom line? In contrast to textbook versions of federal lawmaking, this volume suggests that no dominant institution or even a roughly consistent pattern of relationships exists among the various players in the federal lawmaking process. Rather, under varying conditions and at critical points in the process, all governing institutions can have a clear role in making public policy as well as enforcing and legitimizing it. As Louis Fisher argues in chapter 9 of this volume, the common thread among these diverse patterns is an ongoing colloquy among roughly coequal actors in various branches and levels of government, who seek to promote a mix of strategic, institutional, and policy goals (in this volume, see also chapters 6, by Baum and Hausegger; and 10, by Epstein, Knight, and Martin). These colloquies are driven in the United States in part by its distinctive culture, which distrusts centralized authority, and in part by its constitutional design, which creates redundant lawmaking forums that face countervailing political pressures. And it occurs because of the distinctive evolution of adversarial legalism, which has given public interest groups tools to participate in—and second-guess—administrative decision making and challenge any momentary concentration of power in a given policy arena.

Despite their often maddening inefficiencies and unpredictability as a policy matter (see Kagan, this volume), the colloquies among institutions described in this volume often feature considerable democratic qualities, including responsiveness to shifts in the polity and openness to a large number and range of institutional inputs (in this volume, see chapters 7, by Burke; 8, by Bragaw and Miller; and 11, by

Devins). This finding of political responsiveness may seem surprising, because judicial policymaking is often assumed to be a recipe for decisions that run counter to majority preferences. After all, why should federal judges, who are appointed for life, respond to shifts in the electorate and the elected branches? The chapters suggest a straightforward answer: if judges want to affect policy in a system of separated institutions sharing power (as opposed to merely express their ideological views), they must anticipate the reactions of the other branches to avoid negative reactions, and preserve their institutional legitimacy, which in part rests on fitting their decisions within preexisting precedents and norms of judicial decision making (in this volume, see chapters 9, by Fisher; 10, by Epstein, Knight, and Martin; and 11, by Devins; but also see chapter 6, by Baum and Hausegger, who argue that these types of strategic assumptions must be qualified). In other words, unless federal judges only care about the purity of their ideological beliefs, they must consider the reactions of other political actors to their judicial decisions (see Epstein, Knight, Martin, this volume). Indeed, even when federal judges make decisions that seem to be based solely on legal reasoning and precedent, they are often anticipating how others will react to those legalistic decisions (see Baum and Hausegger, this volume).

The chapters also indicate that the American policymaking process is remarkably open, featuring inputs from the president, Congress, the courts, state and local governments, and a broad array of interest groups (see Kagan, Burke, and Bragaw and Miller, this volume). In his analysis of the Americans with Disabilities Act (ADA), Thomas Burke suggests that such openness stems from two deeply seated features: the indeterminate nature of legal texts and the fragmented structure of rule implementation in an era of heightened adversarial legalism. For example, the ADA requires employers to make a "*reasonable* accommodation" to workers with a "physical or mental impairment that *substantially* limits one or more of the *major* life activities of the individual." What is a "reasonable accommodation"? What does it mean to "substantially limit" one of the "major life activities"? Clearly, the text of the statute does not resolve these questions, because many of its operative terms are ambiguous.

As Burke implies, the structure of implementation of statutes greatly affects how these questions play out in practice. Thus, in European states that feature centralized bureaucracies, the answer to these questions would be straightforward, even though the texts are open-ended. Why? When a single governing authority is given a virtual monopoly over implementation, as is common in Europe, then it has greater capacity to set the definitive meaning of the law. As a result, although the law on the page is subject to a variety of interpretations, the law on the ground would be whatever the national government says it is. Thus the European approach to policymaking is often much more predictable and bounded than it is in the United States.

In the United States, implementation is rarely entrusted to a single entity. Instead, the power of implementation is shared among overlapping state and federal governmental agencies as well as with politically appointed federal judges. This decentralization of implementation power gives entrepreneurial lawyers and public interest groups enormous flexibility to push the limits of the laws at the federal and state levels (Bragaw and Miller, this volume), resulting in both broad participation in the shaping of the laws and continued uncertainty on the law's meaning. Of course, the added participation of nongovernmental actors as well as state and local entities only further contributes to the complexity and dynamism of the colloquies underlying the American lawmaking process, because these actors bring their own agendas, resources, and perspectives to the process and the colloquies often take on different shapes as they move from one level of government to another.

The point is not that American policymaking is a panacea. Clearly it is not. The point is that, in a system where all branches and levels of government participate in making, enforcing, and legitimizing policy, the key normative issues are not which branch of government is the principal or whether the branches adhere to assigned roles; there is no single principal in the process and the roles are extremely blurry. Instead, the key normative questions are whether the colloquies among different institutions serve important democratic values, such as openness and responsiveness, and whether promoting these types of values is worth the frequent inefficiency and unpredictability of such a decentralized system. It should be added that these types of judgments cannot be made across-the-board; rather, they must reflect careful case-by-case analyses because institutional competence is contingent, reflecting the enormous adaptability of institutions for laudable as well as objectionable ends (Williamson 1995; Komesar 1994; Rubin 1996).

LOOKING FORWARD: BROADER IMPLICATIONS AND TWO PATHS OF FUTURE INQUIRY

The main implication from this volume is that American policymaking is far more complex and protean than the standard textbook accounts describe. This finding brings the analysis full circle, presenting the question raised at the very outset: namely, how should we deal with this complexity as teachers and scholars? As noted in the Introduction, the dominant approaches have been to parse this complexity in the classroom and specialize in the field, concentrating on the role of particular actors, distinct points in the policymaking process, or particular methods of analysis.

While recognizing the value of teaching American policymaking piece-by-piece and the ongoing contributions of specialized studies, this volume suggests two additional paths for grappling with the inherent complexity of American policymaking, paths that focus on the process more holistically and encompass a wide range of methods. The first path is consistent with many of the major strands of the burgeoning new institutionalism literature, which typically retains the focus on particular institutions, but explicitly embeds actions of actors within a wider institutional and political context (in this volume, see Miller; Fisher; Baum and Hausegger; Epstein, Knight, and Martin; and Devins; see also Gillman and Clayton 1999; and Clayton and Gillman 1999). This also forces us to enlarge the types of causal factors we should consider when assessing the behavior of key actors. For example, in assessing Supreme Court decisions, this approach urges us to consider not only factors inside the courtroom, such as elements of the governing law and attributes of the deciding judges and participating litigants, but also factors outside the courtroom, such as shifts in public opinion and changes in the dominant ideology in Congress as well as changes in political culture.

The other path takes a different tack. Instead of using an interbranch perspective to enrich our understanding of individual actors or institutions, it focuses on important attributes of the colloquies themselves. Thus, instead of asking what motivates the actors in the colloquy, we might ask the following types of questions: (1) whether (and under what conditions) the colloquies are open and responsive, reflecting the inputs from a wide range of viewpoints, or narrow, reflecting the viewpoints of a relatively few, well-heeled interests; (2) whether (and under what conditions) the colloquies are contentious, reflecting a tug of war among the branches, or consensual, reflecting an agreed division of labor; (3) whether (and under what conditions) the colloquies are at equilibrium, and producing stable outcomes, or disequilibrium, and generating policy uncertainty; or (4) whether (and under what conditions) the colloquies enhance efficiency.

A variety of methods can be validly used to address these issues. Case studies of interbranch relations over specific issues can add to the useful store of knowledge, offering rich descriptions of the institutional, interest group, and issue contexts of interbranch relations. One can also create a typology of interbranch relations based on specific attributes, such as their openness and effectiveness in producing consensus, and explore the relative frequency of these types of interactions (see Barnes 2004). Game theory also offers a well-developed set of tools for studying conditions that produce strategic equilibrium among the branches, although as Baum and Hausegger argue, the assumptions of existing strategic models may need to be adjusted.

Of course, these paths and approaches are mutually reinforcing. Gaining a more integrated appreciation of how the continuing colloquies of American policymaking shape the actions of specific actors and institutions promises insights into the dynamics of the process. This in turn should help us build more general theories about the conditions that produce recurring patterns of interbranch discourse. Indeed, we encourage scholars to pursue both paths, recognizing that these paths share significant common ground: a conviction that American policy emanates from an ongoing colloquy among a bramble of lawmakers. These interactions are driven by processes of conflict and persuasion distinctive to specific policy arenas and are driven by the ideas, institutional realities, and interests in specific policy communities. Although complex, we believe that this view of American policymaking does not render it incomprehensible; rather, it pushes us to abandon the traditional notion of three separate branches performing distinct functions. Instead, this volume teaches us to see governance as a continuing dialogue.

References and Bibliography

Abraham, Henry J. 1985. *Justices and Presidents: A Political History of Appointments to the Supreme Court*, 2d ed. New York: Oxford University Press.

Ackerman, Bruce. 2000. The New Separation of Powers. *Harvard Law Review* 113: 633–729.

Adamany, David. 1980. The Supreme Court's Role in Critical Elections. In *Realignment in American Politics*, ed. B. Campbell and R. Trilling. Austin: University of Texas Press.

Adams, Charles Francis, ed. 1850. *The Works of John Adams*. Boston: Little, Brown.

Adler, David Gray. 1989. The President's Pardon Power. In *Inventing the American Presidency*, ed. Thomas E. Cronin. Lawrence: University Press of Kansas.

Arnold, Douglas R. 1990. *The Logic of Congressional Action*. New Haven, Conn.: Yale University Press.

Aronowitz, Stanley. 1988. Postmodernism in Politics. In *Universal Abandon? The Politics of Postmodernism*, ed. A. Ross. Minneapolis: University of Minnesota Press.

Arrow, Kenneth. 1963. *Social Choice and Individual Values*. New Haven, Conn.: Yale University Press.

Atiyah, P. S., and Robert S. Summers. 1987. *Form and Substance in Anglo-American Law: A Comparative Study of Legal Reasoning, Legal Theory, and Legal Institutions*. Oxford: Clarendon Press.

Atkinson, David N. 1974. Justice Sherman Minton and Behavior Patterns inside the Supreme Court. *Northwestern University Law Review* 69: 716–38.

Avila, Aaron. 2000. Application of the Chevron Doctrine in the D.C. Circuit. *New York University Environmental Law Journal* 8: 398–436.

Axline, Michael. 1996. Forest Health and the Politics of Expediency. *Environmental Law* 26: 613–40.

Badaracco, Joseph L. 1985. *Loading the Dice: A Five-Country Study of Vinyl Chloride Regulation*. Boston: Harvard Business School Press.

Baker, Nancy V. 1995. The Attorney General as a Legal Policy-Maker: Conflicting Loyalties. In *Government Lawyers: The Federal Legal Bureaucracy and Presidential Politics*, ed. Cornell W. Clayton. Lawrence: University Press of Kansas.

Baker, Stewart A., and James R. Asperger. 1982. Foreword: Toward a Center for State and Local Legal Advocacy. *Catholic University Law Review* 31: 367–73.

Barnes, Jeb. 1997. Bankrupt Bargain? Bankruptcy Reform and the Politics of Adversarial Legalism. 13 *Journal of Law & Politics* 13: 893–934.

———. 2004. *Overruled? Legislative Overrides, Pluralism, and Court–Congress Relations in an Age of Statutes*. Stanford, Calif.: Stanford University Press.

Battista, Judy. 2002. Glen Sues the League and Cites Depression. *New York Times*, January 31, D2.

Baum, Lawrence. 2001. *The Supreme Court*, 7th ed. Washington, D.C.: Congressional Quarterly Press.

Bedau, Hugh Adam, ed. 1968. *The Death Penalty in America*. Chicago: Aldine Publishing Co.

Berger, Raoul. 1969. *Congress v. the Supreme Court*. Cambridge, Mass.: Harvard University Press.

Berman, Larry, and Bruce Allen Murphy. 2003. *Approaching Democracy*, 4th ed. Upper Saddle River, N.J.: Prentice Hall.

Bernstein, Marver. 1955. *Regulating Industry by Independent Commission*. Princeton, N.J.: Princeton University Press.

Bickel, Alexander M. 1961. The Supreme Court, 1960 Term—Foreword: The Passive Virtues. *Harvard Law Review* 75: 40–79.

———. 1962. *The Least Dangerous Branch of Government: The Supreme Court at the Bar of Politics*. Indianapolis: Bobbs-Merrill.

Biskupic, Joan. 1999. Rehnquist Asks Congress to Clear Judiciary Funding. *Washington Post*, March 31, 1999, A27.

———. 2001. Supreme Court Limits ADA Suits. *USA Today*, February 22, 3A.

Borrelli, MaryAnne, Karen Hult, and Nancy Kassop. 2001. The White House Counsel's Office. *Presidential Studies Quarterly* 31: 570–71.

Bok, Derek. 1971. Reflecting on the Distinctive Character of American Labor Laws. *Harvard Law* Review 84: 1394–1463.

Brady, David W. 1988. *Critical Elections and Congressional Policy-Making*. Stanford, Calif.: Stanford University Press.

Bragaw, Stephen. 1999. Federalism's Legal Defense Fund: The Intergovernmental Lobby and the U.S. Supreme Court, 1983–1997. Paper presented at the Midwest Political Science Association Annual Meeting, Chicago, April.

Bragaw, Stephen G., and Barbara A. Perry. 2002. The "Brooding Omnipresence" in *Bush v. Gore*: Anthony Kennedy, the Equality Principle, and Judicial Supremacy. *Stanford Law and Policy Review* 13: 19–32.

Braithwaite, John. 1985. *To Punish or Persuade: Enforcement of Coal Mine Safety*. Albany: State University of New York Press.

Breckenridge, Adam Carlyle. 1970. *Congress against the Court*. Lincoln: University of Nebraska Press.

Brennan, Joseph. 1980. Foreword to *I'll See You in Court: The States and the Supreme Court*, by A. E. Dick Howard. Washington, D.C.: National Governors Association Center for Policy Research.

Breyer, Stephen. 1992. On the Uses of Legislative History in Interpreting Statutes, *Southern California Law Review* 65: 845–74.

Brickman, Ronald, Sheila Jasanoff, and Thomas Ilgen. 1985. *Controlling Chemicals: The Politics of Regulation in Europe and the United States*. Ithaca, N.Y.: Cornell University Press.

Brigham, John. 1987. *The Cult of the Court*. Philadelphia: Temple University Press.

Brudney, James. 1994. Congressional Commentary on Judicial Interpretations of Statutes: Idle Chatter or Telling Response? *Michigan Law Review* 93: 2–106.

Bruni, Frank. 1999. Bush Explains His Opposition to Abortion. *New York Times*, November 22, A24.

Burke, Thomas F. 2002. *Lawyers, Lawsuits, and Legal Rights*. Berkeley: University of California Press.

Bussel, Daniel. 2000. Textualism's Failures: A Study of Overruled Bankruptcy Decisions. *Vanderbilt Law Review* 53: 887–943.

Calabresi, Steven, and Kevin H. Rhodes. 1992. The Structural Constitution: Unitary Executive, Plural Judiciary. *Harvard Law Review* 105: 1155–1216.

Caldeira, Gregory, and Donald McCrone. 1983. Of Time and Judicial Activism: A Study of the U.S. Supreme Court, 1870–1973. In *Supreme Court Activism and Restraint*, ed. Stephen Halpern and Charles Lamb. Lexington, Mass.: Lexington Books.

Campbell, Colton C., and John F. Stack, Jr., eds. 2001. *Congress Confronts the Court: The Struggle for Legitimacy and Authority in Lawmaking*. Lanham, Md.: Rowman & Littlefield.

Canon, Bradley C., and Charles A. Johnson. 1999. *Judicial Policies: Implementation and Impact*, 2d ed. Washington, D.C.: CQ Press.

Cardozo, Benjamin. 1921. *The Nature of the Judicial Process.* New Haven, Conn.: Yale University Press.

Carelli, Richard. 1999. Rehnquist Lobbies Congress for Money. *Associated Press Newswire,* August 10.

Carney, Dan. 1998. Indicting the Courts: Congress' Feud with Judges. *Congressional Quarterly Weekly Report,* June 20, 1660–66.

Casper, Jonathan. 1976. The Supreme Court and National Policy-Making. *American Political Science Review* 70: 50–63.

Ceaser, James. 1986. In Defense of Separation of Powers. In *Separation of Powers—Does It Still Work?* ed. R. Goldwin and A. Kaufman. Washington, D.C.: American Enterprise Institute.

Chemerinski, Erwin. 1987. A Paradox without a Principle: A Comment on the Burger Court's Jurisprudence in Separation of Powers Cases. *Southern California Law Review* 60: 1083–1111.

Church, Thomas W., and Robert Nakamura. 1994. Beyond Superfund: Hazardous Waste Cleanup in Europe and the United States. *Georgetown International Environmental Law Review* 7: 15–57.

Clark, John A., and Kevin T. McGuire. 1996. Congress, the Supreme Court, and the Flag. *Political Research Quarterly* 49: 771–81.

Claude, Richard. 1970. *The Supreme Court and the Electoral Process.* Baltimore: Johns Hopkins University Press.

Clayton, Cornell W. 1992. *The Politics of Justice: The Attorney General and the Making of Legal Policy.* Armonk, N.Y.: M. E. Sharpe, Inc.

———. 1994. Law, Politics and the New Federalism: State Attorneys General as Policymakers. *Review of Politics:* 56: 525–53.

———, ed. 1995. *Government Lawyers: The Federal Legal Bureaucracy and Presidential Politics.* Lawrence: University Press of Kansas.

Clayton, Cornell W., and Howard Gillman, eds. 1999. *Supreme Court Decision-Making: New Institutionalist Approaches.* Chicago: University of Chicago Press.

Coats, Dan. 1995. Line-Item Veto: Joint Hearing before the House Comm. on Government Reform and Oversight and the S. Comm. on Governmental Affairs, 104th Cong. 22.

Coffee, John C., Jr. 1995. Class Wars: The Dilemma of the Mass Tort Class Action. *Columbia Law Review* 95: 1343–1465.

Coglianese, Cary. 1997. Assessing Consensus: The Promise and Performance of Negotiated Rulemaking. *Duke Law Journal* 46: 1255–1349.

Colker, Ruth. 1999. The Americans with Disabilities Act: A Windfall for Defendants. *Harvard Civil Rights–Civil Liberties Law Review* 34: 99–162.

Conkle, David O. 1998. Congressional Alternatives in the Wake of *City of Boerne v. Flores:* The (Limited) Role of Congress in Protecting Religious Freedom from State and Local Infringement. *University of Arkansas at Little Rock Law Journal* 20: 633–88.

Coombs, Clyde H. 1964. *A Theory of Data.* New York: John Wiley and Sons.

Cooper, Charles. 1986. The President's Compliance with the "Timely Notification" Requirement of Section 501 (B) of the National Security Act. *Opinion of the Office of Legal Counsel,* vol. 10, December 10, 159.

Cooper, Joseph. 1985. The Legislative Veto in the 1980s. In *Congress Reconsidered,* 3d edition, ed. Lawrence C. Dodd and Bruce I. Oppenheimer. Washington, D.C.: Congressional Quarterly Press.

Cooper, Phillip. 1988. *Hard Judicial Choices: Federal District Court Judges and State and Local Officials.* New York: Oxford University Press.

Cooter, Robert, and Tom Ginsburg. 1996. Comparative Judicial Discretion: An Empirical Test of Economic Models. *International Review of Law and Economics* 16: 295–313.

Cover, Robert. 1995. Nomos and Narrative. In *Narrative, Violence and the Law,* ed. Martha Minow, Michael Ryan, and Austin Sarat. Ann Arbor: University of Michigan Press.

Cross, Frank, and Emerson Tiller. 1998. Judicial Partisanship and Obedience to Legal Doctrine: Whistleblowing on the Federal Courts of Appeals. *Yale Law Journal* 107: 2155–176.

Currie, David. 1990. Lochner Abroad: Substantive Due Process and Equal Protection in the Federal Republic of Germany. *Supreme Court Review* 1989: 333–72.

Cushman, Barry. 1998. *Rethinking the New Deal Court: The Structure of a Constitutional Revolution.* New York: Oxford University Press.

———. 2002. Mr. Dooley and Mr. Gallup: Public Opinion and Constitutional Change in the 1930s. *Buffalo Law Review* 50: 7–101.

Dahl, Robert A. 1956. *A Preface to Democratic Theory.* Chicago: University of Chicago Press.

———. 1957. Decision-Making in a Democracy: The Supreme Court as a National Policy-Maker. *Journal of Public Law* 6: 279–95.

———. 2001. *How Democratic Is the American Constitution?* New Haven, Conn.: Yale University Press.

Davidson, Roger H., and Walter J. Oleszek. 2002. *Congress and Its Members*, 8th ed. Washington, D.C.: Congressional Quarterly Press.

Davis, Martha F. 1993. *Brutal Need: Lawyers and the Welfare Rights Movement.* New Haven, Conn.: Yale University Press.

Day, Patricia, and Rudolf Klein. 1987. The Regulation of Nursing Homes: A Comparative Perspective. *Milbank Quarterly* 65: 303–47.

Deering, Christopher J., and Steven S. Smith. 1997. *Committees in Congress*, 3d ed. Washington, D.C.: CQ Press.

Dellinger, Walter. 1993. The Legal Significance of Presidential Signing Statements. *Opinion of the Office of Legal Counsel*, U.S. Department of Justice, vol. 17, November 3, 131–41.

———. 1994. Presidential Authority to Decline to Execute Unconstitutional Statutes. *Opinion of the Office of Legal Counsel*, U.S. Department of Justice, vol. 18, November 2, 199–211.

Dembner, Alice. 2002. Mass. Plans New Push to Home Care for Disabled: U.S. Court Rulings Drive Move from Institutions. *Boston Globe*, August 21, A1.

Denniston, Lyle. 2003. US Appeals Court Eases Pledge Ruling. *Boston Globe*, March 1, A3.

Derthick, Martha. 1990. *Agency under Stress.* Washington, D.C.: Brookings Institution Press.

———. 2002. *Up in Smoke: From Legislation to Litigation in Tobacco Politics.* Washington, D.C.: CQ Press.

Detlefsen, Robert. 1995. Government Consent Decrees and the Paradox of "Consent": A Critical Case Study. *Justice System Journal* 18: 13–27.

Devins, Neal. 1989. Affirmative Action after Reagan. *Texas Law Review* 68: 353–79.

———. 1996a. Government Lawyers and the New Deal. *Columbia Law Review* 96: 237–67.

———. 1996b. *Shaping Constitutional Values: Elected Government, the Supreme Court, and the Abortion Debate.* Baltimore: Johns Hopkins University Press.

———. 2001. Congress as Culprit: How Lawmakers Spurred on the Court's Anti-Congress Crusade. *Duke Law Journal* 51: 435–64.

Devins, Neal, and Louis Fisher. 1998. Judicial Exclusivity and Political Instability. *Virginia Law Review* 84: 83–106.

Dewar, Helen. 2003. Bush, Daschle Trade Charges: Senate's Talkathon on Judicial Nominees Exceeds 30 Hours. *Washington Post*, November 14, A6.

Dewees, Donald, Michael Trebilcock, and Peter Coyte. 1991. The Medical Malpractice Crisis: A Comparative Empirical Perspective. *Law and Contemporary Problems* 54: 217–51.

DiIulio, John. 1987. Prison Discipline and Prison Reform. *The Public Interest*, fall, 73.

———. 1990a. Introduction: Enhancing Judicial Capacity. In *Courts, Corrections, and the Constitution: The Impact of Judicial Intervention on Prisons and Jails*, ed. John DiIulio. New York: Oxford University Press.

———. 1990b. The Old Regime and the Ruiz Revolution: The Impact of Judicial Intervention on Texas Prisons. In *Courts, Corrections, and the Constitution: The Impact of Judicial Intervention on Prisons and Jails*, ed. John DiIulio. New York: Oxford University Press.

Diller, Matthew. 2000. Judicial Backlash, the ADA and the Civil Rights Model. *Berkeley Journal of Employment and Labor Law* 21: 19–52.

Dlouhy, Jennifer A. 2002. Parties Use Judicial Standoff to Play to Core Constituents. *Congressional Quarterly Weekly Report*, October 19, 2722–27.

———. 2003a. Bush Nominee for Appeals Court Faces Senate Democrats Poised to Play the Filibuster Card Again. *Congressional Quarterly Weekly Report*, April 12, 869.

———. 2003b. Estrada Battle Just Part of the War over Who Controls U.S. Judiciary. *Congressional Quarterly Weekly Report*, February 15, 394–95.

Dodd, Lawrence C. 1981. Congress, the Constitution, and the Crisis of Legitimation. In *Congress Reconsidered*, 2d edition, ed. Lawrence C. Dodd and Bruce I. Oppenheimer. Washington, D.C.: Congressional Quarterly Press.

Dodd, Lawrence C., and Calvin Jillson. 1994. Conversations on the Study of American Politics: An Introduction. In *The Dynamics of American Politics: Approaches and Interpretations*, ed. Lawrence C. Dodd and Calvin Jillson. Boulder, Colo.: Westview Press.

Dodd, Lawrence C., and Bruce I. Oppenheimer, eds. 2000. *Congress Reconsidered*, 7th ed. Washington, D.C.: CQ Press.

Douglas, Mary, and Aaron Wildavsky. 1982. *Risk and Culture: An Essay on the Selection of Technological and Environmental Dangers*. Berkeley: University of California Press.

Downs, Anthony. 1957. *An Economic Theory of Democracy*. New York: Harper Collins.

Dror, Yehezkel. 1964. Muddling Through—Science or Inertia? *Public Administration Review* 24: 153–75.

Ducat, Craig R. 2000. *Constitutional Interpretation*. Belmont, Calif.: Wadsworth.

Dudziak, Mary. 1988. Desegregation as a Cold War Imperative. *Stanford Law Review* 41: 61–120.

Dwyer, John. 1990. The Pathology of Symbolic Legislation. *Ecology Law Quarterly* 17: 233–316.

Eastland, Terry. 1992. *Energy in the Executive: The Case for the Strong Presidency*. New York: Free Press.

The Economist. 1990. The Forest Service: Time for a Little Perestroika. March 10, 28.

Edelman, Lauren B. 1990. Legal Environments and Organizational Governance: The Expansion of Due Process in the American Workplace. *American Journal of Sociology* 95: 1401–40.

———. 1999. When the "Haves" Hold Court: Speculations on the Organizational Internalization of Law. *Law and Society Review* 33: 941–91.

Edelman, Lauren B., Howard S. Erlanger, and John Lande. 1993. Internal Dispute Resolution: The Transformation of Civil Rights in the Workplace. *Law and Society Review* 27: 497–534.

Edelman, Murray. 1974. *The Political Uses of Symbolism*. Champaign: University of Illinois Press.

Edmonds, Curtis D. 2002. Snakes and Ladders: Expanding the Definition of "Major Life Activity" in the Americans with Disabilities Act. *Texas Tech Law Review* 33: 321–76.

Edwards, Harry. 1998. Collegiality and Decision Making on the D.C. Circuit. *Virginia Law Review* 84: 1335–70.

Ehrlichman, John. 1982. *Witness to Power: The Nixon Years*. New York: Simon & Schuster.

Elliott, E. Donald. 1989. Why Our Separation of Powers Jurisprudence Is So Abysmal. *George Washington Law Review* 57: 506–32.

Ely, John H. 1973. The Wages of Crying Wolf: A Comment on *Roe v. Wade. Yale Law Journal* 82: 920–49.

Engel, David M., and Frank W. Munger. 2003. *Rights of Inclusion: Law and Identity in the Life Stories of Americans with Disabilities*. Chicago: University of Chicago Press.

Environmental Law Institute, and Environmental and Energy Study Institute. 1985. *Statutory Deadlines in Environmental Legislation: Necessary but Need Improvement*. Washington, D.C.: Environmental Law Institute, and Environmental and Energy Study Institute.

Epp, Charles R. 1998. *The Rights Revolution*. Chicago: University of Chicago Press.

Epps, Garrett. 2001. *To an Unknown God: Religious Freedom on Trial*. New York: St. Martin's Press.

Epstein, Lee, ed. 1995. *Contemplating Courts*. Washington, D.C.: CQ Press.

Epstein, Lee, and Jack Knight. 1998. *The Choices Justices Make*. Washington, D.C.: CQ Press.

Epstein, Lee, Jack Knight, and Andrew D. Martin. 2001. The Supreme Court as a Strategic National Policy Maker. *Emory Law Journal* 50: 583–611.

Epstein, Lee, Jack Knight, and Olga Shvetsova. 2001. The Role of Constitutional Courts in the Establishment and Maintenance of Democratic Systems of Government. *Law and Society Review* 35: 117–63.

Epstein, Lee, Jeffrey A. Segal, and Jennifer Nicoll Victor. 2002. Dynamic Agenda Setting on the U.S. Supreme Court: An Empirical Assessment. *Harvard Journal on Legislation* 39: 395–433.

Epstein, Lee, and Thomas G. Walker. 1995. The Role of the Supreme Court in American Society: Playing the Reconstruction Game. In *Contemplating Courts*, ed. Lee Epstein. Washington, D.C.: CQ Press.

———. 2004. *Constitutional Law for a Changing America: Rights, Liberties, and Justice*, 5th ed. Washington, D.C.: CQ Press.

Epstein, Lee, Thomas G. Walker, and William J. Dixon. 1989. The Supreme Court and Criminal Justice Disputes: A Neo-Institutional Perspective. *American Journal of Political Science* 33: 825–41.

Epstein, Lee, Thomas G. Walker, Jeffrey A. Segal, and Harold J. Spaeth. 2002. *The Supreme Court Compendium*, 3d ed. Washington, D.C.: CQ Press.

Eskridge, William N. 1991a. Overriding Supreme Court Statutory Interpretation Decisions. *Yale Law Journal* 101: 331–417.

———. 1991b. Reneging on History? Playing the Court/Congress/President Civil Rights Game. *California Law Review* 79: 613–84.

Evans, C. Lawrence. 2000. Message Politics: Party Campaigning and Legislative Strategy in Congress. Paper presented at the Annual Meeting of the American Political Science Association, Washington, D.C., August 31–September 3.

Fairman, Charles. 1987. *Reconstruction and Reunion, 1864–88; Volume 7, History of the Supreme Court of the United States*. New York: Macmillan.

Farber, Daniel A. 1989. Democracy and Disgust: Reflection on Public Choice. *Chicago-Kent Law Review* 65: 161–76.

Farrar-Myers, Victoria. 2002. Presidential Use of Executive Agreements in the Post-Case World. Paper delivered at the 2002 Annual Meeting of the American Political Science Association, Boston, August 29.

Feeley, Malcolm M., and Edward L. Rubin. 1998. *Judicial Policy Making and the Modern State: How the Courts Reformed America's Prisons*. Cambridge: Cambridge University Press.

Feldblum, Chai R. 2000. Definition of Disability under Federal Anti-Discrimination Law: What Happened? Why? And What Can We Do about It? *Berkeley Journal of Employment and Labor Law* 21: 91–165.

Fenno, Richard F. 1973. *Congressmen in Commmittees*. Boston: Little, Brown.

———. 1978. *Home Style: House Members in Their Districts*. Boston: Little, Brown.

Ferdinand, Pamela. 2002. For Gay Couples, Civil Unions Tougher to Undo Than Create. *Washington Post*, November 28, A3.

Ferejohn, John. 2003. Madisonian Separation of Powers. In *James Madison: The Theory and Practice of Republican Government*, ed. Samuel Kernell. Stanford, Calif.: Stanford University Press.

Ferejohn, John, and Barry Weingast. 1992. A Positive Theory of Statutory Interpretation. *International Review of Law and Economics* 12: 263–79.

Fiorina, Morris. 1996. *Divided Government*, 2d ed. Boston: Allyn & Bacon.

Fish, Stanley. 1980. *Is There a Text in This Class?* Cambridge, Mass.: Harvard University Press.

Fisher, Louis. 1987. Social Influences on Constitutional Law. *Journal of Political Science* 15: 7–19.

———. 1988. *Constitutional Dialogues*, Princeton, N.J.: Princeton University Press.

———. 1990. Separation of Powers: Interpretation Outside the Courts. *Pepperdine Law Review*, 18: 57–93.

———. 1993. The Legislative Veto: Invalidated, It Survives. *Law and Contemporary Problems* 56: 273–92.

———. 1997. *Constitutional Conflicts between Congress and the President*, 4th ed. rev. Lawrence: University Press of Kansas.

———. 2000. *Congressional Abdication on War and Spending*. College Station: Texas A&M University Press.

———. 2001. Congressional Checks on the Judiciary. In *Congress Confronts the Court: The Struggle for Legitimacy and Authority*, ed. Colton C. Campbell and John F. Stack. Lanham, Md.: Rowman & Littlefield.

———. 2002a. Congressional Access to Information: Using Legislative Will and Leverage. *Duke Law Journal* 52: 323–402.

———. 2002b. *Religious Liberty in America: Political Safeguards*. Lawrence: University Press of Kansas.

———. 2002c. When Presidential Power Backfires: Clinton's Use of Clemency. *Presidential Studies Quarterly* 32: 586–99.

———. 2003. *American Constitutional Law*, 5th ed. Durham, N.C.: Carolina Academic Press.

Fisher, Louis, and Neal Devins. 2001. *Political Dynamics of Constitutional Law*, 3d ed. Saint Paul: West Group.

Fiss, Owen. 1972. *Injunctions*. New York: Foundation Press.

Fitzgerald, John. 1986. *Congress and the Separation of Powers*. New York: Praeger Publishers.

Fox-Grage, Wendy, Donna Folkemer, and Jordan Lewis. 2003. *The States' Response to the Olmstead Decision: How Are States Complying?* National Conference of State Legislatures; www.ncsl.org/programs/health/forum/olmsreport2003.pdf.

Franck, Matthew J. 1998. Support and Defend: How Congress Can Save the Constitution from the Supreme Court. *Texas Review of Law and Politics* 2: 315–33.

Franklin, Kurt A., and David A. Weldy. 1993. Dark of the Night Legislation Takes Aim at Forum Selection Clauses: Statutory Revisions in Reaction to *Carnival Cruise Lines, Inc. v. Shute. U.S.F. Maritime Law Journal* 6: 259–71.

Frieden, Bernard J. 1979. The New Regulation Comes to Suburbia. *The Public Interest* 55: 15–27.

Friedman, Barry. 1993. Dialogue and Judicial Review. *Michigan Law Review* 91: 577–682.

———. 1997. Valuing Federalism. *Minnesota Law Review* 82: 317–412.

———. 2001. The History of the Countermajoritarian Difficulty: The Lesson of Lochner. *New York University Law Review* 76: 1383–1455.

Friedman, Lawrence M. 1973. *A History of American Law*. New York: Simon & Schuster.

———. 1985. *Total Justice*. New York: Russell Sage Foundation.

Frug, Gerald. 1978. Judicial Power of the Purse. *Pennsylvania Law Review* 126: 715–94.

Fuller, Lon. 1978. The Forms and Limits of Adjudication. *Harvard Law Review* 92: 353–409.

Funk, Robert. 1986. Disability Rights: From Caste to Class in the Context of Civil Rights. In *Images of the Disabled, Disabling Images*, ed. Alan Gartner and Tom Joe. New York: Praeger Publishers.

Funston, Richard. 1975. The Supreme Court and Critical Elections. *American Political Science Review* 69: 795–811.

Galanter, Marc. 1974. Why the "Haves" Come Out Ahead: Speculations on the Limits of Legal Change. *Law and Society Review* 9: 95–151.

Gallup, George. 1987. *The Gallup Poll: Public Opinion, 1986*. Wilmington, Del.: Scholarly Resources.

Garber, Marc N., and Kurt A. Wimmer. 1987. Presidential Signing Statements as Interpretations of Legislative Intent: An Executive Aggrandizement of Power. *Harvard Journal on Legislation* 24: 363–95.

Garrow, David J. 1994. *Liberty and Sexuality: The Right to Privacy and the Making of Roe v. Wade*. New York: Macmillan.

Gely, Rafael, and Pablo T. Spiller. 1990. A Rational Choice Theory of Supreme Court Statutory Decisions with Applications to the *State Farm* and *Grove City* Cases. *Journal of Law, Economics, and Organization* 6: 263–300.

———. 1992. The Political Economy of Supreme Court Constitutional Decisions: The Case of Roosevelt's Court-Packing Plan. *International Review of Law and Economics* 12: 45–67.

Gillman, Howard. 1999. The Court as an Idea, Not a Building (or a Game): Interpretive Institutionalism and the Analysis of Supreme Court Decision-Making. In *Supreme Court Decision-Making: New Institutionalist Approaches* ed. Cornell W. Clayton and Howard Gillman. Chicago: University of Chicago Press.

———. 2001. *The Votes That Counted*. Chicago: University of Chicago Press.

———. 2002. How Political Parties Can Use the Courts to Advance Their Agendas: Federal Courts in the United States, 1875–1891. *American Political Science Review* 96: 511–24.

Gillman, Howard, and Cornell Clayton, eds. 1999. *The Supreme Court in American Politics: New Institutionalist Interpretations*. Lawrence: University Press of Kansas.

Gilmour, John B. 2002. Institutional and Individual Influences on the President's Veto. *Journal of Politics* 64: 198–218.

Ginsberg, Benjamin, Theodore Lowi, and Margaret Weir. 2003. *We the People: An Introduction to American Politics*, 4th ed. New York: W. W. Norton.

Ginsburg, Ruth Bader, and Peter W. Huber. 1987. Commentary: The Intercircuit Committee. *Harvard Law Review* 100: 1417–21.

Ginsburg, Tom. 2003. *Judicial Review in New Democracies*. New York: Cambridge University Press.

Glazer, Nathan. 1975. Toward an Imperial Judiciary? *The Public Interest* 41: 104–23.

Glendon, Mary Ann. 1987. *Abortion and Divorce in Western Law*. Cambridge, Mass.: Harvard University Press.

Goldman, Sheldon. 1967. Judicial Appointments to the U.S. Courts of Appeal. *Wisconsin Law Reveiw* 1967: 186–214.

———. 1997. *Picking Federal Judges: Lower Court Selection from Roosevelt through Reagan*. New Haven, Conn.: Yale University Press.

Goldman, Sheldon, and Elliot Slotnick. 1997. Clinton's First Term Judiciary: Many Bridges to Cross. *Judicature* 80: 254–73.

Goldstein, Robert Justin. 1996. *Burning the Flag: The Great 1989–1990 American Flag Desecration Controversy*. Kent, Ohio: Kent State University Press.

Goodnough, Abby. 1997. Court Rejects New Jersey School Plan. *New York Times*, May 15, A18.

Goodwyn, Lawrence. 1978. *The Populist Moment: A Short History of the Agrarian Revolt in America*. New York: Oxford University Press.

Graber, Mark. 1993. The Nonmajoritarian Difficulty: Legislative Deference to the Judiciary. *Studies in American Political Development* 7: 35–73.

———. 1995. The Passive-Aggressive Virtues: *Cohens v. Virginia* and the Problematic Establishment of Judicial Power. *Constitutional Commentary* 12: 67–92.

Graham, Hugh Davis. 1999. Since 1964: The Paradox of American Civil Rights Regulation. In *Taking Stock: American Government in the Twentieth Century*, ed. Morton Keller and R. Shep Melnick. Cambridge: Cambridge University Press.

Greenawalt, Kent. 1999. *Legislation: Statutory Interpretation 20 Questions.* New York: Foundation Press.

Greenberg, Jack. 1994. *Crusaders in Court.* New York: Basic Books.

Greenhouse, Linda. 2000. Women Lose Right to Sue Attackers in Federal Court. *New York Times*, May 16, A1, A14.

Greve, Michael S. 1989a. Environmentalism and Bounty Hunting, *The Public Interest* 97: 15–29.

———. 1989b. The Non-Reformation of Administrative Law: Standing to Sue and Public Interest Litigation in West German Environmental Law. *Cornell International Law Journal* 22: 197–208.

Griffin, Stephen. 1991. Bringing the State into Constitutional Theory. *Law and Social Inquiry* 16: 659–711.

———. 1996. *American Constitutionalism: From Theory to Politics.* Princeton, N.J.: Princeton University Press.

Grofman, Bernard, and Timothy J. Brazill. 2002. Identifying the Median Justice on the Supreme Court through Multidimensional Scaling: Analysis of "Natural Courts" 1953–1991. *Public Choice* 112: 55–79.

Gwyn, William. 1989. The Interdeterminancy of the Separation of Powers and the Federal Courts. *George Washington Law Review* 57: 474–505.

Hall, Peter A., and Rosemary C. R. Taylor. 1996. Political Science and the Three New Institutionalisms. *Political Studies* 94: 936–57.

Halpern, Stephen. 1995. *On the Limits of the Law: The Ironic Legacy of Title VI of the 1964 Civil Rights Act.* Baltimore: Johns Hopkins University Press.

Hamilton, Alexander, James Madison, and John Jay. 1961. *The Federalist Papers.* New York: New American Library.

Harris, Lis. 1995. Banana Kelly's Toughest Fight. *New Yorker*, July 24, 32–40.

Hartz, Louis. 1955. *The Liberal Tradition in America: An Interpretation of American Political Thought since the Revolution.* New York: Harcourt, Brace & World.

Hausegger, Lori, and Lawrence Baum. 1998. Behind the Scenes: The Supreme Court and Congress in Statutory Interpretation. In *Great Theatre: The American Congress in the 1990s*, ed. Herbert F. Weisberg and Samuel C. Patterson. New York: Cambridge University Press.

———. 1999. Inviting Congressional Action: A Study of Supreme Court Motivations in Statutory Interpretation. *American Journal of Political Science* 43: 162–85.

———. 2001. The Motivations of Supreme Court Justices: Invitations to Congress in Majority and Dissenting Opinions. Paper presented at the annual meeting of the American Political Science Association, San Francisco, August 30–September 2.

Havemen, Judith. 1989. Rehnquist Urges Raise for Judges. *Washington Post*, May 4, A4.

Hayes, Michael T. 1992. *Incrementalism and Public Policy.* New York: Longman.

Heclo, Hugh. 1994. Ideas, Interests, and Institutions. In *The Dynamics of American Politics*, ed. Lawrence C. Dodd and Calvin Jillson. Boulder, Colo.: Westview Press.

Heise, Michael. 1998. Schoolhouses, Courthouses, and Statehouses: Educational Finance, Constitutional Structure, and the Separation of Powers Doctrine. *Land and Water Law Review* 33: 282–327.

Henschen, Beth M. 1983. Congressional Response to the Statutory Interpretations of the Supreme Court. *American Politics Quarterly* 11: 441–59.

Henschen, Beth M., and Edward I. Sidlow. 1988. The Supreme Court and the Congressional Agenda-Setting Process. Paper presented at the annual meeting of the Midwest Political Science Association, Chicago, April.

Hettinger, Virginia A. 2001. Inviting Trouble: Supreme Court Signals and Congressional Responses. Paper presented at the Conference on Institutional Games and the U.S. Supreme Court, Texas A&M University, College Station, November 1–4.

Hettinger, Virginia A., and Christopher J. W. Zorn. 2004. Explaining the Incidence and Timing of Congressional Responses to the U.S. Supreme Court. *Legislative Studies Quarterly* (forthcoming).

Heymann, P., and L. Liebman. 1988. No Fault, No Fee: The Legal Profession and Federal No-Fault Insurance Legislation. In *The Social Responsibilities of Lawyers*, ed. P. Heymann and L. Liebman. Westbury, N.Y.: Foundation Press.

Hirsch, H. N. 1981. *The Enigma of Felix Frankfurter*. New York: Basic Books.

Holland, Gina. 2004. Justice Raps Sentencing Rules. *Boston Globe*, March 18, A2.

Hoogenboom, Ari, and Olive Hoogenboom. 1976. *A History of the ICC: From Panacea to Palliative*. New York: W. W. Norton.

Horowitz, David. 1977. *The Courts and Social Policy*. Washington, D.C.: Brookings Institution Press.

Horwitz, Morton. 1977. *The Transformation of American Law, 1780–1860*. Cambridge, Mass.: Harvard University Press.

Howard, A. E. Dick. 1982. The States and the Supreme Court. *Catholic University Law Review* 31: 375–438.

Hoyer, Steny H. 2002. Not Exactly What We Intended, Justice O'Connor. *Washington Post*, January 20, B1.

Huber, John D., and Charles R. Shipan. 2002. *Deliberate Discretion? The Institutional Foundations of Bureaucratic Autonomy*. New York: Cambridge University Press.

Hurst, J. Willard. 1956. *Law and the Conditions of Freedom in the Nineteenth-Century United States*. Madison: University of Wisconsin Press.

Ignagni, Joseph, and James Meernik. 1994. Explaining Congressional Attempts to Reverse Supreme Court Decisions. *Political Research Quarterly* 47: 353–71.

Jackson, Robert H. 1953. Maintaining Our Freedoms: The Role of the Judiciary. *Vital Speeches of the Day* 19: 759–62.

Jackson, Vicki C. 2001. Federalism and the Court: Congress as the Audience? *Annals of the American Academy of Political and Social Science* 574: 145–57.

Jacobson, Gary C. 1996. The 1994 House Election in Perspective. *Political Science Quarterly* 111: 203–23.

———. 1997. *The Politics of Congressional Elections*. New York: Longman.

Johnson, Mark. 1999. Congress, Justices at Odds over Funds; Legislators Slash Millions from Budget. *Richmond Times Dispatch*, September 8, A2.

Johnston, John D., Jr., and Charles L. Knapp. 1971. Sex Discrimination by Law: A Study in Judicial Perspective. *New York University Law Review*. 46: 675–747.

Kagan, Robert A. 1988. What Makes Uncle Sammy Sue? *Law and Society Review* 21: 717–42.

———. 1991. The Dredging Dilemma: Economic Development and Environmental Protection in Oakland Harbor. *Coastal Management* 19: 313–41.

———. 1994. Do Lawyers Cause Adversarial Legalism? *Law and Social Inquiry* 19: 1–62.

———. 1997. Should Europe Worry about Adversarial Legalism? *Oxford Journal of Legal Studies* 17: 167–83.

———. 1999. Adversarial Legalism: Tamed or Still Wild? *New York University Journal of Legislation* 2: 217–45.

———. 2001. *Adversarial Legalism: The American Way of Law*. Cambridge, Mass.: Harvard University Press.

————. 2002. Constitutional Litigation in the United States. In *Constitutional Courts in Comparison: The U.S. Supreme Court and the German Federal Constitutional Court*, ed. Ralph Rogowski and Thomas Gawron. NewYork: Berghahn Books.

Kagan, Robert A., and Lee Axelrad, eds. 2000. *Regulatory Encounters: Multinational Corporations and American Adversarial Legalism*. Berkeley: University of California Press.

Kagan, Robert A., Robert Detlefsen, and Bobby Infelise. 1984. American State Supreme Court Justices, 1900–1970. *American Bar Foundation Research Journal* 1984: 371–408.

Kahn, Ronald. 1999. Institutional Norms and Supreme Court Decision-Making: The Rehnquist Court on Privacy and Religion. In *Supreme Court Decision-Making: New Institutional Approaches*, ed. Cornell W. Clayton and Howard Gillman. Chicago: University of Chicago Press.

Kalven, Harry, Jr., and Hans Zeisel. 1966. *The American Jury*. Boston: Little, Brown.

Kasindorf, Martin. 2003. The Court Conservatives Hate. *USA Today*, February 7, 3A.

Kassop, Nancy. 2002. Expansion and Contraction: Clinton's Impact on the Scope of Presidential Power. In *The Presidency and the Law: The Clinton Legacy*, ed. David Gray Adler and Michael A. Genovese. Lawrence: University Press of Kansas.

Katzmann, Robert A. 1986. *Institutional Disability: The Saga of Transportation Policy for the Disabled*. Washington, D.C.: Brookings Institution Press.

————, ed. 1988. *Judges and Legislators: Toward Institutional Comity*. Washington, D.C.: Brookings Institution Press.

————. 1997. *Courts and Congress*. Washington, D.C.: Brookings Institution Press.

Kay, Richard. 1988. Adherence to Original Intentions in Constitutional Adjudication: Three Objections and Responses. *Northwestern Law Review* 82: 226–92.

Kelley, Christopher S. 2002. "Faithfully Executing" and "Taking Care": The Unitary Executive and the Presidential Signing Statement. Paper delivered at the 2002 Annual Meeting of the American Political Science Association, Boston, August 29.

Kemp, Evan, Jr. 1981. Aiding the Disabled: No Pity, Please. *New York Times*, September 3, A19.

Kernell, Samuel. 2003. "The True Principles of Republican Government": Reassessing James Madison's Political Science. In *James Madison: The Theory and Practice of Republican Government*, ed. Samuel Kernell. Stanford, Calif.: Stanford University Press.

Kirp, David L. 1979. *Doing Good by Doing Little: Race and Schooling in Britain*. Berkeley: University of California Press.

————. 1982. Professionalization as a Policy Choice: British Special Education in Comparative Perspective. *World Politics* 34: 137–74.

Kirp, David, John Dwyer, and Larry Rosenthal. 1995. *Our Town: Race, Housing and the Soul of Suburbia*. New Brunswick, N.J.: Rutgers University Press.

Klarman, Michael. 1996. Rethinking the Civil Rights and Civil Liberties Revolution. *Virginia Law Review* 82: 1–67.

Komesar, Neil. 1994. *Imperfect Alternatives*. Chicago: University of Chicago Press.

Krehbiel, Keith. 1988. Spatial Models of Legislative Choice. *Legislative Studies Quarterly* 13: 259–319.

Krent, Harold. 1988. Separating Strands of Separation of Powers Doctrine. *Virginia Law Review* 74: 1253–1323.

Krieger, Linda Hamilton. 2000a. Afterword: Socio-Legal Backlash. *Berkeley Journal of Employment and Labor Law* 21: 476–520.

————. 2000b. Foreword: Backlash against the ADA: Interdisciplinary Perspectives and Implications for Social Justice Strategies. *Berkeley Journal of Employment and Labor Law* 21: 1–18.

Kritzer, Herbert, and Susan Silbey, eds. 2003. *In Litigation: Do the Haves Still Come Out Ahead?* Stanford, Calif.: Stanford University Press.

Kurland, Philip B., and Gerhard Casper. 1975. *Landmark Briefs and Arguments of the Supreme Court of the United States: Constitutional Law.* Arlington, Va.: University Publications of America.

Kutler, Stanley. 1990. *The Wars of Watergate.* New York: Alfred A. Knopf.

LaCheen, Cary. 2000. Achy Breaky Pelvis, Lumber Lung and Juggler's Despair: The Portrayal of the Americans with Disabilities Act on Television and Radio. *Berkeley Journal of Employment and Labor Law* 21: 223–45.

Lane, Charles. 2002. O'Connor Criticizes Disabilities Law as Too Vague. *Washington Post,* March 15, A2.

———. 2003. Pledge of Allegiance Ruling Is Upheld. *Washington Post,* March 1, A1.

Lasser, William. 2000. *Perspectives on American Government,* 3d ed. Boston: Houghton Mifflin.

Lieberman, Lee S. 1989. *Morrison v. Olson:* A Formalist Perspective on Why the Court Was Wrong. *American University Law Review* 38: 313–58.

Leiter, Brian. 1996. Heidegger and the Theory of Adjudication. *Yale Law Journal* 106: 253–82.

Lempert, Larry. 1982. DOJ Loans Lawyer to NAAG to Follow High Court. *Legal Times,* August 30, 2.

Lerner, Max. 1937. Constitution and Courts as Symbols. *Yale Law Journal* 46: 1290–1319.

Lester, Charles. 1992. The Search for Dialogue in the Administrative State: The Politics, Policy, and Law of Offshore Oil Development. Ph.D. dissertation, Jurisprudence and Social Policy Program, University of California, Berkeley.

Leventhal, Harold. 1974. Environmental Decisionmaking and the Role of the Courts. *University of Pennsylvania Law Review* 122: 509–55.

Lewis, Neil A. 2003. Senate Fails to End Filibuster on Bush Judicial Nominee. *New York Times,* March 7, A18.

Lindblom, Charles E. 1959. The Science of "Muddling Through." *Public Administration Review* 19: 79–88.

———. 1979. Still Muddling, Not Yet Through. *Public Administration Review* 39: 517–26.

Lindgren, Janet. 1983. Beyond Cases: Reconsidering Judicial Review. *Wisconsin Law Review* 1983: 591–638.

Liptak, Adam. 2002a. Disabled Man Sues Club over Privacy of Lap Dance. *New York Times,* July 18, A10.

———. 2002b. Judge Blocks U.S. Bid to Ban Suicide Law. *New York Times,* April 18, A16.

Lockhart, William, Yale Kamisar, Jesse Choper, and Steven Shifrin. 1991. *The American Constitution,* 7th ed. Saint Paul: West Publishing Co.

Long, Carolyn N. 2000. *Religious Freedom and Indian Rights: The Case of Oregon v. Smith.* Lawrence: University Press of Kansas.

Lovell, George I. 2003. *Legislative Deferrals: Statutory Ambiguity, Judicial Power, and American Democracy.* New York: Cambridge University Press.

Lund, Nelson. 1995. Guardians of the Presidency: The Office of the Counsel to the President and the Office of Legal Counsel. In *Government Lawyers: The Federal Legal Bureaucracy and Presidential Politics,* ed. Cornell W. Clayton. Lawrence: University Press of Kansas.

Lundqvist, Lennart J. 1980. *The Hare and The Tortoise: Clean Air Policies in the United States and Sweden.* Ann Arbor: University of Michigan Press.

Madison, James. 1987 (1788). *The Federalist Papers.* New York: Penguin Books.

Maltese, John Anthony. 1998. *The Selling of Supreme Court Nominees.* Baltimore: Johns Hopkins University Press.

Maltzman, Forrest, James F. Spriggs II, and Paul J. Wahlbeck. 2000. *Crafting Law on the Supreme Court: The Collegial Game.* New York: Cambridge University Press.

Mann, Thomas. 1981. Elections and Change in Congress. In *The New Congress,* ed. Thomas Mann and Norm Ornstein. Washington, D.C.: American Enterprise Institute.

Manwaring, David R. 1962. *Render unto Caesar: The Flag-Salute Controversy*. Chicago: University of Chicago Press.

March, James G., and Johan P. Olsen. 1984. The New Institutionalism: Organizational Factors in Political Life, *American Political Science Review* 78: 734–49.

———. 1989. *Rediscovering Institutions: The Organizational Basis of Politics*. New York: Free Press.

Marshall, John. 1832. *The Life of George Washington*. Philadelphia: J. Crissy.

Marshall, Thomas R. 1989. *Public Opinion and the Supreme Court*. Boston: Unwin Hyman.

Marshall, William P. 1998. American Political Culture and the Failures of Process Federalism. *Harvard Journal of Law and Public Policy* 22: 139–55.

Martin, Andrew D. 1998. Strategic Decision Making and the Separation of Powers. Ph.D. dissertation, Washington University of Saint Louis.

———. 2001. Statutory Battles and Constitutional Wars: Congress and the Supreme Court. Paper presented at the Conference on Institutional Games and the U.S. Supreme Court, Texas A&M University, College Station, November 1–4.

Mashaw, Jerry. 1989. The Economics of Politics and the Understanding of Public Law. *Chicago-Kent Law Review* 65:123–160.

Mashaw, Jerry L., and Daniel Harfst. 1991. *The Struggle for Auto Safety*. Cambridge, Mass.: Harvard University Press.

Mauro, Tony. 2000a. Little Deference to Congress as the Court Curbs Federal Power. *Legal Times*, May 22, 8.

———. 2000b. Split Branches. *Legal Times*, May 22, 1.

Mayer, Kenneth R. 2001. *With the Stroke of a Pen: Executive Orders and Presidential Power*. Princeton, N.J.: Princeton University Press.

Mayhew, David. 1974. Congressional Elections: The Case of the Vanishing Marginals. *Polity* 6: 295–317.

———. 1991. *Divided We Govern: Party Control, Lawmaking, and Investigations, 1946–1990*. New Haven, Conn.: Yale University Press.

McAdam, Doug. 1982. *Political Process and the Development of Black Insurgency, 1930–1970*. Chicago: University of Chicago Press.

McCann, Michael. 1986. *Taking Reform Seriously: Perspectives on Public Interest Liberalism*. Ithaca, N.Y.: Cornell University Press.

———. 1999. How the Supreme Court Matters in American Politics: New Institutionalist Perspectives. In *The Supreme Court in American Politics*, ed. Howard Gillman and Cornell Clayton. Lawrence: University of Kansas Press.

McCann, Michael, William Haltom, and Anne Bloom. 2001. Java Jive: Genealogy of a Juridical Icon. *University of Miami Law Review* 56: 113–78.

McCarthy, Cathy A., and Tara Treacy, eds. 2000. *The History of the Administrative Office of the United States Courts: Sixty Years of Service to the Federal Judiciary*. Washington, D.C.: Administrative Office of the United States Courts.

McCreary, Scott T. 1989. Resolving Science-Intensive Public Policy Disputes: Lessons from the New York Bight Initiative. Ph.D. dissertation, Massachusetts Institute of Technology.

McCurdy, Howard E. 1990. *The Space Station Decision: Incremental Politics and Technological Choice*. Baltimore: Johns Hopkins University Press.

McDowell, Gary L. 1988. *Curbing the Court: The Constitution and the Limits of Judicial Power*. Baton Rouge: Louisiana State University Press.

McKelvey, Richard. 1976. Intransitivities in Multidimensional Voting Models and Some Implications for Agenda Control. *Journal of Economic Theory* 12: 472–82.

Meernik, James, and Joseph Ignagni. 1995. Congressional Attacks on Supreme Court Rulings Involving Unconstitutional State Laws. *Political Research Quarterly* 48: 43–59.

———. 1997. Judicial Review and Coordinate Construction of the Constitution. *American Journal of Political Science* 41: 447–67.

Melady, Mark. 2004. U.S. Constitution Changes Not Easy. *Worcester Telegram & Gazette*, March 14, A1.

Melnick, R. Shep. 1983. *Regulation and the Courts: The Case of the Clean Air Act*. Washington, D.C.: Brookings Institution Press.

———. 1985. The Politics of Partnership. *Public Administration Review* 45: 653–60.

———. 1992. Administrative Law and Bureaucratic Reality. *Administrative Law Review* 44: 245–59.

———. 1994. *Between the Lines: Interpreting Welfare Rights*. Washington, D.C.: Brookings Institution Press.

———. 1995. Separation of Powers and the Strategy of Rights: The Expansion of Special Education. In *The New Politics of Public Policy*, ed. Marc Landy and Martin Levin. Baltimore: Johns Hopkins University Press.

———. 1996. Federalism and the New Rights. *Yale Law and Policy Review* 14: 325–54.

———. 1999a. Governing More but Enjoying It Less. In *Taking Stock: American Government in the Twentieth Century*, ed. Morton Keller and R. Shep Melnick. Cambridge: Cambridge University Press.

———. 1999b. Risky Business: Government and the Environment after Earth Day. In *Taking Stock: American Government in the Twentieth Century*, ed. Morton Keller and R. Shep Melnick. Cambridge: Cambridge University Press.

Mendeloff, John. 1987. *The Dilemma of Rulemaking for Toxic Substances*. Cambridge, Mass.: MIT Press.

Merida, Kevin. 1995. Senate Rejects Gramm Bid to Bar Affirmative Action Set-Asides. *Washington Post*, July 21, A13.

Merrill, Thomas W. 1992. Judicial Deference to Executive Precedent. *Yale Law Journal* 101: 969–1034.

———. 2003. The Making of the Second Rehnquist Court: A Preliminary Analysis. *Saint Louis University Law Journal* 47: 569–658.

Miller, Mark C. 1992. Congressional Committees and the Federal Courts: A Neo-Institutional Perspective. *Western Political Quarterly* 45: 949–70.

———. 1993. Courts, Agencies, and Congressional Committees: A Neo-Institutional Perspective. *Review of Politics* 55: 471–89.

———. 1995. *The High Priests of American Politics: The Role of Lawyers in American Political Institutions*. Knoxville: University of Tennessee Press.

Miller, Richard E., and Austin Sarat. 1980. Grievances, Claims and Disputes: Assessing the Adversary Culture. *Law and Society Review* 15: 525–66.

Mishler, William, and Reginald Sheehan. 1993. The Supreme Court as Countermajoritarian Institution? The Impact of Public Opinion on the Court. *American Political Science Review* 87: 87–101.

Moe, Terry M. 1989. The Politics of the Bureaucratic State. In *Can the Government Govern?* ed. J. Chubb and P. Peterson. Washington, D.C.: Brookings Institution Press.

Moynihan, Daniel Patrick. 1988. *Came the Revolution: Argument in the Reagan Era*. New York: Harcourt Brace Jovanovich.

Morris, Thomas. 1987. States before the United States Supreme Court: State Attorneys General as Amicus Curiae. *Judicature* 70: 298–305.

Moss, Kathryn, Scot Burris, Michael Ullman, Matthew Johnsen, and Jeffrey Swanson. 2001. Unfunded Mandates: An Empirical Study of the Implementation of the Americans with Disabilities Act by the Equal Employment Opportunity Commission. *Kansas Law Review* 50: 1–110.

Murphy, Walter F. 1962. *Congress and the Court: A Case Study in the American Political Process*. Chicago: University of Chicago Press.

———. 1964. *Elements of Judicial Strategy*. Chicago: University of Chicago Press.

Murphy, Walter F., and C. Herman Pritchett. 1961. *Courts, Judges, and Politics: An Introduction to the Judicial Process*. New York: Random House.

Murphy, Walter F., C. Herman Pritchett, and Lee Epstein, eds. 2002. *Courts, Judges, and Politics*, 5th ed. New York: McGraw-Hill.

Murphy, Walter F., and Joseph Tanenhaus. 1990. Publicity, Public Opinion, and the Court. *Northwestern University Law Review* 84: 985–1023.

Nagel, Stuart S. 1965. Court-Curbing Periods in American History. *Vanderbilt Law Review* 18: 925–44.

———. 1969. *The Legal Process from a Behavioral Perspective*. Homewood, Ill.: Dorsey Press.

National Research Council. 1986. *Dredging Coastal Ports*. Washington, D.C.: National Academy Press.

Neal, David, and David Kirp. 1986. The Allure of Legalization Reconsidered: The Case of Special Education. In *School Days, Rule Days: The Legalization and Regulation of Education*, ed. D. Kirp and D. Jensen. New York: Falmer Press.

Nelson, Michael, ed. 2000. *The Presidency and the Political System*, 6th ed. Washington, D.C.: CQ Press.

Neustadt, Richard E. 1960. *Presidential Power: The Politics of Leadership*. New York: John Wiley and Sons.

———. 1964. *Presidential Power: The Politics of Leadership*. New York: John Wiley and Sons.

———. 1980. *Presidential Power: The Politics of Leadership from FDR to Carter*. New York: Macmillan.

———. 1990. *Presidential Power and the Modern Presidents: The Politics of Leadership from Roosevelt to Reagan*. New York: Free Press.

Nivola, Peitros, and David Rosenbloom, eds. 1990. *Classic Readings in American Politics*. New York: St. Martin's Press.

Note. 1958. Congressional Reversal of Supreme Court Decisions: 1945–1957. *Harvard Law Review* 71: 1324–37.

Note. 1975. The Wyatt Case: Implementation of a Judicial Decree Ordering institutional Change. *Yale Law Journal* 84: 1338–79.

Nourse, Victoria. 1996. Toward a "Due Foundation" for the Separation of Powers: The *Federalist Papers* as Political Narrative. *Texas Law Review* 74: 447–521.

Novak, William. 2002. The Legal Origins of the Modern American State. In *Looking Back at Law's Century*, ed. Austin Sarat, Bryant Garth, and Robert A. Kagan. Ithaca, N.Y.: Cornell University Press.

Nutter, Franklin, and Keith Bateman. 1989. *The U.S. Tort System in the Era of the Global Economy*. Schaumberg, Ill.: Alliance of American Insurers.

O'Brien, David M. 2003. *Storm Center: The Supreme Court in American Politics*, 6th ed. New York: W. W. Norton.

O'Brien, Ruth. 2002. *Crippled Justice: The History of Modern Disability Policy in the Workplace*. Chicago: University of Chicago Press.

O'Connor, Karen, and Lee Epstein. 1985. Bridging the Gap between Congress and the Supreme Court: Interest Groups and the Erosion of the American Rule Governing Awards of Attorneys' Fees. *Western Politics Quarterly* 28: 238–49.

O'Connor, Sandra Day. 1981. The Nomination of Judge Sandra Day O'Connor of Arizona to Serve as an Associate Justice of the Supreme Court of the United States: Hearings before the Senate Comm. on the Judiciary, 97th Cong. 59, serial no. j-97-51, September 9–11.

O'Hare, Michael, and Lawrence Bacow. 1983. *Facility Siting and Public Opposition*. New York: Van Nostrand.

Olsen, Mancur. 1971. *The Logic of Collective Action*. Cambridge, Mass.: Harvard University Press.

Ordeshook, Peter. 1986. *Game Theory and Political Theory*. New York: Cambridge University Press.

Osoba, Wayne L. 1985. The Legislative Response to *Anti-Monopoly*: A Missed Opportunity to Clarify the Genericness Doctrine. *University of Illinois Law Review* 1985: 197–218.

Palmer, Elizabeth A. 2000. High Court Further Circumscribes Congress' Power in Ruling on Violence Against Women Act. *Congressional Quarterly Weekly Report*, May 20, 1188.

Palmer, Thomas. 1994. Commitments to Foes Raise Artery Price Tag. *Boston Globe*, September 14, 1, 6.

Panning, William H. 1985. Formal Models of Legislative Processes. In *Handbook of Legislative Research*, ed. Gerhard Loewenberg, Samuel C. Patterson, and Malcolm Jewell. Cambridge, Mass.: Harvard University Press.

Patterson, Bradley H., Jr. 2000. *The White House Staff: Inside the West Wing and Beyond.* Washington, D.C.: Brookings Institution Press.

Peretti, Terri Jennings. 1999. *In Defense of a Political Court.* Princeton, N.J.: Princeton University Press.

Perine, Keith. 2003a. AMBER Child Crimes Bill Clears, Propelled by News and Strategy. *Congressional Quarterly Weekly Report*, April 12, 879–81.

———. 2003b. Both Parties Find Political Benefit from Battle over Judicial Nominees. *Congressional Quarterly Weekly Report*, October 4, 2431.

———. 2004a. Another Recess Appointment by Bush Sets William Pryor as Two-Year Judge. *Congressional Quarterly Weekly Report*, February 21, 456.

———. 2004b. Congress Shows Little Enthusiasm for Bush's Marriage Amendment. *Congressional Quarterly Weekly Report*, February 28, 532–34.

Perry, Barbara A. 1999. *The Priestly Tribe: The Supreme Court's Image in the American Mind.* Westport, Conn.: Praeger.

Peterson, Mark A. 1990. *Legislating Together: The White House and Capitol Hill from Eisenhower to Reagan.* Cambridge, Mass.: Harvard University Press.

Pfiffner, James P. 1995. *Governance and American Politics: Classic and Current Perspectives.* Forth Worth: Harcourt Brace.

Pierce, Richard. 1988. Two Problems in Administrative Law: Political Polarity on the District of Columbia Circuit and Judicial Deterrence of Agency Rulemaking. *Duke Law Journal* 1988: 300–28.

———. 1989. The Role of the Judiciary in Implementing an Agency Theory of Government. *New York University Law Review* 64: 1239–85.

———. 1991. The Unintended Effects of Judicial Review of Agency Rules: How Federal Courts Have Contributed to the Electricity Crisis of the 1990s. *Administrative Law Review* 43: 7–29.

Pierson, Paul, and Theda Skocpol. 2002. Historical Institutionalism in Contemporary Political Science. In *Political Science: State of the Discipline*, ed. Ira Katznelson and Helen V. Milner. New York: W. W. Norton.

Pika, Joseph A., John Anthony Maltese, and Norman C. Thomas. 2002. *The Politics of the Presidency*, 5th ed. Washington, D.C.: CQ Press.

Polsby, Nelson. 1983. *The Consequences of Party Reform.* New York: Oxford University Press.

Poole, Keith T., and Howard Rosenthal. 1997. *A Political-Economic History of Roll Call Voting.* New York: Oxford University Press.

Potter, Edward, and Ann Reesman. 1992. *Compensatory and Punitive Damages under Title VII: A Foreign Perspective.* Washington, D.C: Employment Policy Foundation.

Powell, Lewis F. 1974. Address before the Fifth Circuit Judicial Conference, New Orleans, May 27.

Pressman, Jeffrey L., and Aaron Wildavsky. 1984. *Implementation: How Great Expectations in Washington Are Dashed in Oakland; Or, Why It's Amazing That Federal Programs Work at All, This Being a Saga of the Economic Development Administration as Told by Two Sympathetic Observers Who Seek to Build Morals on a Foundation of Ruined Hopes*, 3d ed. Berkeley: University of California Press.

Priest, George L. 1985. The Invention of Enterprise Liability: A Critical History of the Intellectual Foundations of Modern Tort Law. *Journal of Legal Studies* 14: 461–527.

Pritchett, C. Herman. 1961. *Congress versus the Supreme Court, 1957–60.* Minneapolis: University of Minnesota Press.

Quam, Lois, Robert Dingwall, and Paul Fenn. 1987. Medical Malpractice in Perspective I: The American Experience. *British Medical Journal* 294: 1529–97.

Rabkin, Jeremy. 1989. *Judicial Compulsions: How Public Law Distorts Public Policy.* New York: Basic Books.

Randall, Richard S. 2002. *American Constitutional Development,* vol. 1. New York: Longman.

Ranney, Austin. 1983. The President and His Party. In *Both Ends of the Avenue: The Presidency, the Executive Branch and Congress in the 1980s,* ed. Anthony King. Washington, D.C.: American Enterprise Institute.

Rawls, John. 1971. *A Theory of Justice.* Cambridge, Mass.: Harvard University Press.

Reed, Douglas. 1998. Twenty-Five Years after *Rodriguez:* School Finance Litigation and the Impact of the New Judicial Federalism. *Law and Society Review* 32: 175–220.

Rehnquist, William H. 1986. Constitutional Law and Public Opinion. *Suffolk University Law Review* 20: 751–69.

———. 2000. *2000 Year-End Report on the Federal Judiciary.* Washington, D.C.: Supreme Court of the United States.

———. 2002. *2002 Year-End Report on the Federal Judiciary.* Washington, D.C.: Supreme Court of the United States.

———. 2003. *2003 Year-End Report on the Federal Judiciary.* Washington, D.C.: Supreme Court of the United States.

Reich, Charles. 1964. The New Property. *Yale Law Journal* 73: 733–87.

Reich, Robert. 1985. Bailout: A Comparative Study in Law and Industrial Structure. *Yale Journal of Regulation* 2: 163–224.

Resnik, Judith. 2000. Trial as Error, Jurisdiction as Injury: Transforming the Meaning of Article III. *Harvard Law Review* 113: 924–1037.

Resnik, Judith, Danny J. Boggs, and Howard Berman. 2004. The Independence of the Federal Judiciary. *Bulletin of the American Academy of Arts and Sciences,* winter: 17–28.

Revesz, Richard. 1997. Environmental Regulation, Ideology, and the D.C. Circuit. *Virginia Law Review* 83: 1717–72.

Richardson, James D., ed. 1897. *A Compilation of the Messages and Papers of the Presidents (1789–1897).* Washington, D.C.: U.S. Government Printing Office.

Riker, William. 1986. *The Art of Political Manipulation.* New Haven, Conn.: Yale University Press.

Rishikof, Harvey, and Barbara A. Perry. 1995. Separateness but Interdependence, Autonomy but Reciprocity: A First Look at Federal Judges' Appearances before Legislative Committees. *Mercer Law Review* 46: 667–76.

Roberts, Owen. 1951. *The Court and the Constitution.* Cambridge, Mass.: Harvard University Press.

Rosenbaum, David E. 2001. Ruling on Disability Rights Called a Blow by Advocates. *New York Times,* February 22, A20.

Rosenberg, Gerald. 1992. Judicial Independence and the Reality of Political Power. *Review of Politics* 54: 369–98.

Ross, Douglas. 1985. Safeguarding Our Federalism: Lessons for the States from the Supreme Court. *Public Administration Review* 45: 723–31.

Ross, Douglas, and Michael Catalano. 1988. How State and Local Governments Fared in the United States Supreme Court for the Past Five Years. *Urban Lawyer* 20: 341–52.

Ross, Lynne. 1990. *State Attorneys General: Powers and Responsibilities.* Washington, D.C.: Bureau of National Affairs.

Rubin, Edward L. 1991. Legislative Methodology: Some Lessons from the Truth-in-Lending Act. *Georgetown Law Journal* 80: 233–307.

———. 1996. The New Legal Process, The Synthesis of Discourse, and the Microanalysis of Institutions. *Harvard Law Review* 109: 1393–1438.

Ryden, David K., ed. 2000. *The U.S. Supreme Court and the Electoral Process*. Washington, D.C.: Georgetown University Press.

Salokar, Rebecca Mae. 1992. *The Solicitor General: The Politics of Law*. Philadelphia: Temple University Press.

———. 1995. Politics, Law and the Office of the Solicitor General. In *Government Lawyers: The Federal Legal Bureaucracy and Presidential Politics*, ed. Cornell W. Clayton. Lawrence: University Press of Kansas.

Sander, R., and E. D. Williams. 1989. Why Are There So Many Lawyers? Perspectives on a Turbulent Market. *Law and Social Inquiry* 14: 431–79.

Sanders, Joseph, and Craig Joyce. 1990. "Off to the Races": The 1980s Tort Crisis and the Law Reform Process. *Houston Law Review* 27: 207–95.

Sandler, Ross, and David Shoenbrod. 2003. *Democracy by Decree: What Happens When Courts Run Government*. New Haven, Conn.: Yale University Press.

Scalia, Antonin. 1978. Vermont Yankee: The APA, the D.C. Circuit, and the Supreme Court. *Supreme Court Review* 1978: 345–409.

———. 1997. *A Matter of Interpretation: Federal Courts and the Law*. Princeton, N.J.: Princeton University Press.

Scheid, Teresa L., and Mark C. Suchman. 2001. Ritual Conformity to the Americans with Disabilities Act: Coercive and Normative Isomorphism. *Research in Social Problems and Public Policy* 9: 101–36.

Scheingold, Stuart. 1974. *The Politics of Rights: Lawyers, Public Policy, and Political Change*. New Haven, Conn.: Yale University Press.

Schmidhauser, John R., and Larry L. Berg. 1972. *The Supreme Court and Congress: Conflict and Interaction 1945–1968*. New York: Free Press.

Schmidt, Peter. 2003. Hundreds of Groups Back U. of Michigan on Affirmative Action. *Chronicle of Higher Education*, February 28, A24–A25.

Schroeder, Christopher H. 2001. Causes of the Recent Turn in Constitutional Interpretation. *Duke Law Journal* 51: 307–62.

Schubert, Glendon A. 1960. *Constitutional Politics: The Political Behavior of Supreme Court Justices and the Constitutional Policies They Make*. New York: Holt, Rinehard, and Winston.

———. 1965. *The Judicial Mind: Attitudes and Ideologies of Supreme Court Justices 1946–1963*. Evanston, Ill.: Northwestern University Press.

Schuck, Peter. 1983. *Suing Government: Citizen Remedies for Official Wrongs*. New Haven, Conn.: Yale University Press.

———. 1992. Legal Complexity: Some Causes, Consequences, and Cures. *Duke Law Journal* 42: 1–52.

Schuck, Peter, and E. Donald Elliott. 1990. To the Chevron Station: An Empirical Study of Federal Administrative Law. *Duke Law Journal* (November): 984–1077.

Schwartz, Edward P., Pablo T. Spiller, and Santiago Urbiztondo. 1994. A Positive Theory of Legislative Intent. *Law and Contemporary Problems* 57: 51–74.

Schwartz, Gary. 1991. Product Liability and Medical Malpractice in Comparative Context. In *The Liability Maze*, ed. Peter Huber and Robert Litan. Washington, D.C.: Brookings Institution Press.

Schwartz, Herman, ed. 2002. *The Rehnquist Court: Judicial Activism on the Right*. New York: Hill and Wang.

Scott, W. Richard. 1992. *Organizations: Rational, Natural, and Open Systems*. Upper Saddle River, N.J.: Prentice Hall.

Seager, Susan. 1991. Saving the Earth. *California Lawyer*, April, 39–43.

Segal, Jeffrey A. 1991. Courts, Executives, and Legislatures. In *The American Courts: A Critical Assessment*, ed. John B. Gates and Charles A. Johnson. Washington, D.C.: CQ Press.

———. 1997. Separation-of-Powers Games in the Positive Theory of Law and Courts. *American Political Science Review* 91: 28–44.

Segal, Jeffrey A., and Albert D. Cover. 1989. Ideological Values and the Votes of U.S. Supreme Court Justices. *American Political Science Review* 83: 557–65.

Segal, Jeffrey A., and Harold J. Spaeth. 1993. *The Supreme Court and the Attitudinal Model.* New York: Cambridge University Press.

———. 2002. *The Supreme Court and the Attitudinal Model Revisited.* New York: Cambridge University Press.

Selznick, Philip. 1976. The Ethos of American Law. In *The Americans: 1976*, ed. Irving Kristol and Paul Weaver. Lexington, Mass.: Lexington Books.

Shapiro, Martin. 1964. *Law and Politics in the Supreme Court.* New York: Free Press.

———. 1966. *Freedom of Speech.* Saddle River, N.J.: Prentice Hall.

———. 1988. *Who Guards the Guardians: Judicial Control of Administration.* Athens: University of Georgia Press.

Shapiro, Martin, and Alec Stone. 1994. The New Constitutional Politics of Europe. *Comparative Political Studies* 26: 397–420.

Shefter, Martin. 1994. *Political Parties and the State: The American Historical Experience.* Princeton, N.J.: Princeton University Press.

Shepsle, Kenneth. 1992. Congress Is a "They" Not an "It": Legislative Intent as Oxymoron. *International Review of Law and Economics* 12: 239–56.

Sherry, Suzanna. 2002. Irresponsibility Breeds Contempt. *Green Bag 2d* 6: 47–56.

Silverstein, Gordon. 1994. Statutory Interpretation and the Balance of Institutional Power. *Review of Politics* 56: 475–501.

Simon, Richard. 2004. The Nation: Bush, Frustrated by Democrats, Again Bypasses Senate on Judge. *Los Angeles Times*, February 21, A1.

Skowronek, Stephen. 1982. *Building a New American State: The Expansion of National Administrative Capacities, 1877–1920.* New York: Cambridge University Press.

Smith, Neal. 1996. *Mr. Smith Went to Washington: From Eisenhower to Clinton.* Ames: Iowa State University Press.

Smith, Rogers M. 1988. Political Jurisprudence, the "New Institutionalism," and the Future of Public Law. *American Political Science Review* 82: 89–108.

———. 1993. Beyond Tocqueville, Myrdal, and Hartz: The Multiple Traditions in America. *American Political Science Review* 87: 549–66.

Smith, Stephen. 1989. *Call to Order: Floor Politics in the House and Senate.* Washington, D.C.: Brookings Institution Press.

Solimine, Michael E., and James L. Walker. 1992. The Next Word: Congressional Response to Supreme Court Statutory Decisions. *Temple Law Review* 65: 425–58.

Spaeth, Harold, and Jeffrey Segal. 1999. *Majority Rule or Majority Will: Adherence to Precedent on the U.S. Supreme Court.* New York: Cambridge University Press.

Spiller, Pablo T., and Rafael Gely. 1992. Congressional Control or Judicial Independence: The Determinants of U.S. Supreme Court Labor-Relations Decisions, 1949–1988. *RAND Journal of Economics* 23: 463–92.

Spiller, Pablo T., and Emerson H. Tiller. 1996. Invitations to Override: Congressional Reversals of Supreme Court Decisions. *International Review of Law and Economics* 16: 503–21.

Stewart, Richard. 1975. Reformation of American Administrative Law. *Harvard Law Review* 88: 1667–1813.

Stewart, Richard B., and Cass Sunstein. 1982. Public Programs and Private Rights. *Harvard Law Review* 95: 1193–1322.

Stigler, George. 1971. The Theory of Economic Regulation. *Bell Journal of Economics and Management Science* 2: 3–21.

Stone, Alec. 1994. *The Birth of Judicial Politics in France.* Oxford: Oxford University Press.

Strauss, Peter L. 1987. Formal and Functional Approaches to Separation-of-Powers Questions: A Foolish Inconsistency? *Cornell Law Review* 72: 488–526.

Stumpf, Harry F. 1965. Congressional Response to Supreme Court Rulings: The Interaction of Law and Politics. *Journal of Public Law* 14: 377–95.

Suchman, Mark, and Mia Cahill. 1996. The Hired Gun as Facilitator: Lawyers and the Suppression of Business Disputes in Silicon Valley. *Law and Social Inquiry* 21: 679–712.

Successful Job Accommodations Strategies. 1999. Recent Supreme Court Rulings Prompt Possible ADA Amendments. 5 (August 24): 5.

Summers, Robert, and Michele Taruffo. 1991. Interpretation and Comparative Analysis. In *Interpreting Statutes: A Comparative Study,* ed. D. N. McCormick and R. Summers. Aldershot, U.K.: Dartmouth Publishing.

Sunstein, Cass. 1990. *After the Rights Revolution.* Cambridge, Mass.: Harvard University Press.

———. 1993. *The Partial Constitution.* Cambridge, Mass.: Harvard University Press.

———. 1996. *Legal Reasoning and Political Conflict.* Oxford: Oxford University Press.

Swedlow, Brendon. 2003. Scientists, Judges, and Spotted Owls: Policymakers in the Pacific Northwest. *Duke Environmental Law and Policy Forum* 13: 187–278.

Taft, William Howard. 1895. Criticisms of the Federal Judiciary. *American Law Review* 29: 641–74.

Taylor, Serge. 1984. *Making Bureaucracies Think: The Environmental Impact Strategy of Administrative Reform.* Stanford, Calif.: Stanford University Press.

Taylor, Stuart, Jr. 2000. Boy Scouts vs. Gays: The System Is Working Just Fine. *National Journal,* September 9, 2769.

Teff, Harvey. 1987. Drug Approval in England and the United States. *American Journal of Comparative Law* 33: 567–610.

Teubner, Gunther, and Alberto Febbrajo, eds. 1992. State, Law and Economy as Autopoietic Systems. *European Yearbook of the Sociology of Law.* Milan: Dott. A. Giuufre.

Thompson, James, and Arthur Tuden. 1959. Strategies, Structures, and Processes of Organizational Decision. In *Comparative Studies in Administration,* ed. Staff of Administrative Science Center. Pittsburgh: University of Pittsburgh Press.

Thurber, James. 1991. Representation, Accountability, and Efficiency in Divided Party Control of Government. *PS: Political Science and Government,* December, 653.

Tort Policy Working Group. 1986. *Report of the Tort Policy Working Group on the Causes, Extent and Policy Implications of the Current Crisis in Insurance Availability and Affordability.* Washington, D.C.: U.S. Government Printing Office.

Truman, David. 1971. *The Governmental Process: Political Interests and Public Opinion.* New York: Alfred A. Knopf.

Tushnet, Mark. 1996. Living in a Constitutional Moment? Lopez and Constitutional Theory. *Case Western Reserve Law Review* 46: 845–75.

Tyack, David, and Aaron Benavot. 1985. Courts and Public Schools: Education Litigation in Historical Perspective. *Law and Society Review* 19: 339–80.

Tyler, Tom R., and Gregory Mitchell. 1994. Legitimacy and the Empowerment of Discretionary Legal Authority: The United States Supreme Court and Abortion Rights. *Duke Law Journal* 43: 703–88.

Ulmer, S. Sidney. 1985. Governmental Litigants, Underdogs, and Civil Liberties in the Supreme Court: 1903–1968 Terms. *Journal of Politics* 47: 899–909.

Urofsky, Melvin I, ed. 1987. *The Douglas Letters: Selections from the Private Papers of Justice William O. Douglas.* Bethesda, Md.: Adler & Adler.

Ursin, Edmund. 1981. Judicial Creativity and Tort Law. *George Washington Law Review* 49: 229–308.

U.S. Bureau of Justice Statistics. 1991. *Jail Inmates, 1990.* Washington, D.C.: U.S. Department of Justice.

U.S. Courts Office of Public Affairs, Administrative Office. 2003. Judiciary Under Attack. *The Third Branch,* August.

U.S. Department of Justice, Office of Legal Policy. [n.d.]. Nominations. Available at http://www.usdoj.gov/olp/nominations.htm (accessed March 29, 2004).

U.S. House of Representatives. 1974. Hearings on the Pardon of Richard M. Nixon and Related Matters, Committee on the Judiciary, U.S. House of Representatives, 93d Cong., 2d Sess.

Van Detta, Jeffrey A., and Dan Gallipeau. 2000. Judges and Juries: Why Are So Many ADA Plaintiffs Losing Summary Judgment Motions, and Would They Fare Better before a Jury? A Response to Professor Colker. *Review of Litigation* 19: 505–77.

Verhovek, Sam Howe. 2001a. Federal Judge Stops Effort to Overturn Suicide Law. *New York Times*, November 9, A14.

———. 2001b. U.S. Acts to Stop Assisted Suicides. *New York Times*, November 7, A1.

Verweij, Marco. 2000. Why Is the River Rhine Cleaner Than the Great Lakes (Despite Looser Regulation)? *Law and Society Review* 34: 1007–54.

Vinke, Harriet, and Ton Wilthagen. 1992. *The Non-Mobilization of Law by Asbestos Victims in the Netherlands: Social Insurance versus Tort-Based Compensation.* Amsterdam: Hugo Sinzheimer Institute, University of Amsterdam.

Vogel, David. 1986. *National Styles of Regulation: Environmental Policy in Great Britain and the United States.* Ithaca, N.Y.: Cornell University Press.

Volcansek, Mary L. 2001. Separation of Powers and Judicial Impeachment. In *Congress Confronts the Court: The Struggle for Legitimacy and Authority in Lawmaking*, ed. Colton C. Campbell and John F. Stack Jr. Lanham, Md.: Rowman & Littlefield.

Warren, Earl. 1969. Chief Justice Earl Warren's Address to the Bar Association of the District of Columbia. *Washington Post*, March 16, A1, A4.

Warren, Susan. 2003a. Asbestos Quagmire. *Wall Street Journal*, January 27, B1, B3.

———. 2003b. Swamped Courts Practice Plaintiff Triage. *Wall Street Journal*, January 27, B1, B3.

Warshaw, Shirley Anne. 2000. *The Keys to Power: Managing the Presidency.* New York: Addison Wesley Longman.

Washington Post. 2000. A Shot From Justice Scalia (editorial). May 5, A22.

Weingast, Barry R. 2002. Rational-Choice Institutionalism. In *Political Science: State of the Discipline*, ed. Ira Katznelson and Helen V. Milner. New York: W. W. Norton.

Weinstein, Henry. 2003. Controversial Ruling on Pledge Reaffirmed. *Los Angeles Times*, March 1, 1.

Weiss, Andrew, and Edward Woodhouse. 1992. Reframing Incrementalism: A Constructive Response to the Critics. *Policy Sciences* 25: 255–73.

Welles, Holly, and Kirsten Engel. 2000. A Comparative Study of Solid Waste Landfill Regulation: Case Studies from the United States, the United Kingdom, and the Netherlands. In *Regulatory Encounters: Multinational Corporations and American Adversarial Legalism*, ed. Robert A. Kagan and Lee Axelrad. Berkeley: University of California Press.

Wermiel, Stephen J. 1993. Confirming the Constitution: The Role of the Senate Judiciary Committee. *Law and Contemporary Problems* 56: 121–44.

West, Jane. 1994. *Federal Implementation of the Americans with Disabilities Act, 1991–94.* New York: Milbank Memorial Fund.

Wharton, Francis. 1849. *State Trials of the United States during the Administrations of Washington and Adams.* Philadelphia: Carey and Hart.

Whittington, Keith E. 2001a. Constitutional Theory and the Faces of Power. Draft paper prepared for a State University of New York book project.

———. 2001b. Taking What They Give Us: Explaining the Court's Federalism Offensive. *Duke Law Journal* 51: 477–520.

Wilensky, Harold. 2002. *Rich Democracies.* Berkeley: University of California Press.

Williamson, Oliver. 1995. Transaction Cost Economics and Organization Theory. In *Organization Theory: From Chester Barnard and Beyond*, ed. O. Williamson. New York: Oxford University Press.

Wilson, James Q. 1989. *Bureaucracy: What Government Agencies Do and Why They Do It.* New York: Basic Books.

Wilson, James Q., and John DiIulio. 1995. *American Government.* Lexington, Mass.: D. C. & Heath.

Wilson, Paul. 1996. *A Time to Lose: Representing Kansas in Brown v. Board of Education.* Lawrence: University of Kansas Press.

Wise, Charles R., and Rosemary O'Leary. 2003. Breaking Up Is Hard to Do: The Dissolution of Judicial Supervision of Public Services. *Public Administration Review* 63: 177–91.

Wood, Robert, ed. 1990. *Remedial Law: When Courts Become Administrators.* Amherst: University of Massachusetts Press.

Yarbrough, Tinsley. 1981. *Judge Frank Johnson and Human Rights in Alabama.* Tuscaloosa: University of Alabama Press.

Yeazell, Stephen C. 1987. *From Medieval Group Litigation to the Modern Class Action.* New Haven, Conn.: Yale University Press.

Yudof, Mark. 1991. School Finance Reform in Texas: The Edgewood Saga. *Harvard Journal on Legislation* 28: 499–505.

Zernike, Kate. 2000. Scouts' Successful Ban on Gays Is Followed by Loss in Support. *New York Times*, August 29, A1.

Court Cases

Abercrombie & Fitch Co. v. Hunting World, Inc., 537 F.2d 4 (2d Cir. 1976).
Abington School District v. Schempp, 374 U.S. 203 (1963).
Adams v. Richardson, 358 F.Supp. 97 (D.D.C. 1973).
Adarand Constructors, Inc. v. Pena, 515 U.S. 200 (1995).
Albertson's v. Kiringburg, 527 U.S. 555 (1999).
Alexander v. Sandoval, 532 U.S. 275 (2001).
Altman and Co. v. U.S., 224 U.S. 583 (1912).
American Civil Liberties Union v. Ashcroft, 322 F.3d 240 (3d Cir. 2003).
Anti-Monopoly, Inc. v. General Mills Fun Group, Inc., 611 F.2d 296 (9th Cir. 1979).
Anti-Monopoly, Inc. v. General Mills Fun Group, Inc., 684 F.2d 1316 (9th Cir. 1982) cert.
    den'd 459 U.S. 1227 (1983).
Ashcroft v. American Civil Liberties Union, 535 U.S. 564 (2002).
Atkins v. Virginia, 122 S.Ct. 2242 (2002).
Baker v. State, 744 A.2d 864 (Vt. 1999).
Barenblatt v. United States, 360 U.S. 109 (1959).
Barnes v. Gorman, 536 U.S. 181 (2002).
Bas v. Tingy, 4 U.S. 37 (1800).
Bayer Drug Co. v. United Drug Co., 272 F. 505 (S.D.N.Y. 1921).
Bell v. Wolfish, 441 U.S. 520 (1979).
Bivens v. Six Unknown Agents of the Federal Narcotics Bureau, 403 U.S. 388 (1971).
Blessing v. Freestone, 520 U.S. 329 (1997).
Board of Education v. Dowell, 498 U.S. 237 (1991).
Board of Trustees of the University of Alabama v. Garrett, 531 U.S. 356 (2001).
Bob Jones University v. United States, 461 U.S. 595 (1983).
Bowers v. Hardwick, 478 U.S. 186 (1986).
Bowsher v. Synar, 478 U.S. 714 (1986).
Boy Scouts of America v. Dale, 530 U.S. 640 (2000).
Bradwell v. State, 83 U.S. (16 Wall.) 130 (1873).
Bragdon v. Abbott, 524 U.S. 624 (1998).
Brown v. Board of Education of Topeka, 347 U.S. 483 (1954).
Buckley v. Valeo, 424 U.S.1 (1976).
Bush v. Gore, 531 U.S. 98 (2000).
Calvert Cliffs Coordinating Committee v. AEC, 449 F.2d 1109 (D.C. Circuit, 1971).
Campbell v. Sundquist, 926 S.W.2d 250 (Tenn. App. 1996).
Carleson v. Remillard, 406 U.S. 598 (1972).
Chevron v. Echazabal, 536 U.S. 73 (2002).
Chevron v. NRDC, 467 U.S. 837 (1984).
Chisholm v. Georgia, 2 U.S. 419 (1793).
Christensen v. Harris County, 529 U.S. 576 (2000).
City of Boerne v. Archbishop Flores, 521 U.S. 507 (1997).
City of Dallas v. England, 846 S.W.2d 957 (Tex. App. 1993).

City of Mobile v. Bolden, 446 U.S. 55 (1980).
Civil Rights Cases, 109 U.S. 3 (1883).
Coker v. Georgia, 433 U.S. 584 (1977).
Committee to Defend Reproductive Rights v. Myers, 625 P.2d 779 (Cal. 1981).
Commonwealth v. Bonadio, 415 A.2d 47 (Pa. 1980).
Commonwealth v. Wasson, 842 S.W.2d 487 (Ky. 1992).
Compassion in Dying v. State of Washington, 79 F.3d 790 (9th Cir. 1996).
Cruzan v. Director, Missouri Dept. of Health, 497 U.S. 261 (1990).
Dellmuth v. Muth, 491 U.S. 223 (1989).
Dickerson v. United States, 530 U.S. 428 (2000).
Doe v. Maher, 515 A.2d 134 (Conn. Super. 1986).
Douglas County v. Lujan, 810 F. Supp 1470 (D. Ore., 1992).
Dred Scott v. Sandford, 60 U.S. 393 (1857).
EDF v. Ruckelshaus, 439 F.2d 584 (D.C. Circuit, 1971).
EEOC v. Sears, 233 F.3d 432 (7th Cir. 2000).
EEOC v. Waffle House Inc., 534 U.S. 279 (2002).
Employment Division v. Smith, 494 U.S. 872 (1990).
Estelle v. Gamble, 429 U.S. 97 (1976).
Ex parte Garland, 71 U.S. 333 (1866).
Ex parte Grossman, 267 U.S. 107 (1925).
Ex Parte McCardle, 74 U.S. 506 (1869).
Ex parte Milligan, 71 U.S. 2 (1866).
Finney v. Hutto, 410 F.Supp. 251 (E.D. Ark. 1975).
Ford v. Wainwright, 477 U.S. 399 (1986).
Freeman v. Pitts, 503 U.S. 467 (1992).
Furman v. Georgia, 408 U.S. 238 (1972).
Fussell v. Georgia Ports Authority, 906 F. Supp. 1561 (S.D. Ga. 1994).
Gebser v. Lago Vista Independent School District, 524 U.S. 274 (1998).
Gitlitz v. Commissioner, 531 U.S. 206 (2001).
Goeseart v. Cleary, 335 U.S. 464 (1948).
Goldberg v. Kelly, 397 U.S. 254 (1970).
Goldwater v. Carter, 444 U.S. 996 (1979).
Gonzaga University v. Doe, 536 U.S. 273 (2002).
Goodridge v. Department of Public Health, 440 Mass. 309, 798 N.E. 2d 941 (2003).
Greater Boston Television Corp. v. FCC, 444 F.2d 841 (D.C. Cir. 1970).
Gregg v. Georgia, 428 U.S. 153 (1976).
Gregory v. Ashcroft, 501 U.S. 452 (1991).
Griffin v. School Bd., 377 U.S. 218 (1964).
Grovey v. Townsend, 295 U.S. 45 (1935).
Grutter v. Bollinger, 123 S.Ct. 2325 (2003).
Gryczan v. State, 942 P.2d 112 (Mont. 1997).
Gutierrez de Martinez v. Lamagno, 515 U.S. 417 (1995).
Hammer v. Dagenhart, 247 U.S. 251 (1918).
Harris v. McRae, 448 U.S. 197 (1980).
Harrison v. PPG Industries, 446 U.S. 578 (1980).
Holt v. Hutto, 363 F.Supp. 194 (E.D. Ark. 1973).
Holt v. Sarver, 300 F. Supp. 825 (E.D. Ark. 1969).
Holt v. Sarver, 309 F. Supp. 362 (E.D. Ark. 1970).
Hoyt v. Florida, 368 U.S. 57 (1961).
Humphrey's Executor v. U.S., 295 U.S. 602 (1935).
Hurley v. Irish-American Gay Group of Boston, 515 U.S. 557 (1995).
Immigration and Naturalization Service v. Cardozo-Fonseca, 480 U.S. 421 (1987).

Immigration and Naturalization Service v. Chahda, 462 U.S. 919 (1983).

In re Debs, 158 U.S. 564 (1895).

In re Neagle, 135 U.S. 1 (1890).

Jacobson v. United States, 503 U.S. 540 (1992).

Johnson v. United States, 529 U.S. 694 (2000).

Kellog Co. v. National Biscuit Co., 305 U.S. 111 (1938).

Kevorkian v. Michigan, 123 S.Ct. 90 (2002).

Kimel v. Florida Board of Regents, 528 U.S. 62 (2000).

King v. Smith, 392 U.S. 309 (1968).

K-Mart v. Cartier, 486 U.S. 281 (1988).

Lawrence v. Texas, 123 S. Ct. 2472 (2003).

Lear Siegler, Inc. v. Lehman, 842 F. 2d 1102 (9th Cir. 1988).

Lee v. Harcleroad, 522 U.S. 927 (1997).

Lee v. Weisman, 505 U.S. 577 (1992).

Little v. Barreme, 6 U.S. 170 (1804).

Lochner v. New York, 198 U.S. 45 (1905).

Loving v. Virginia, 388 U.S. 1 (1967).

Mansell v. Mansell, 490 U.S. 581 (1989).

Marbury v. Madison, 5 U.S. (1 Cranch) 137 (1803).

Mathews v. Eldridge, 425 U.S. 319 (1976).

Matter of Quinlan, 355 A.2d 647 (N.J. 1976).

McAlindin v. County of San Diego, 192 F.3d 1226 (9th Cir. 1999).

McConnell v. Federal Election Commission, 124 S. Ct. 619 (2003).

McGautha v. California, 402 U.S. 183 (1971).

Miller v. California, 413 U.S. 15 (1973).

Minersville School District v. Gobitis, 310 U.S. 586 (1940).

Miranda v. Arizona, 384 U.S. 436 (1966).

Mistretta v. U.S., 488 U.S. 361 (1989).

Moe v. Secretary of Administration, 417 N.E.2d 387 (Mass. 1981).

Monnell v. New York City Department of Social Services, 436 U.S. 658 (1978).

Monroe v. Pape, 365 U.S. 167 (1961).

Morgan v. Katzenbach, 384 U.S. 641 (1966).

Morrison v. Olson, 487 U.S. 654 (1988).

Motor Vehicle Mfg. Association v. State Farm Mutual Auto Insurance Co., 463 U.S. 29 (1983).

Muller v. Oregon, 208 U.S. 412 (1908).

Murphy v. UPS, 527 U.S. 516 (1999).

Myers v. U.S., 272 U.S. 52 (1926).

Naim v. Naim, 87 S.E.2d 749 (Va. 1955).

Naim v. Naim, 350 U.S. 891 (1955).

Newberry v. United States, 256 U.S. 232(1921).

Newdow v. U.S. Congress, 292 F.3d 597 (2002).

New York Times v. U.S., 403 U.S. 713 (1971).

Niemotko v. Maryland, 340 U.S. 268 (1961).

Northern Pipeline Construction Co. v. Marathon Pipe Line Co., 458 U.S. 50 (1982).

Northern Spotted Owl v. Hodel, 716 F. Supp. 479 (W.D. Wash, 1988).

Office of Communications, United Church of Christ v. FCC, 359 F2d 994 (D.C. Circuit, 1966).

Olmstead v. L.C. by Zimring, 527 U.S. 581 (1999).

Oregon v. Ashcroft, 192 F.Supp.2d 1077 (D. Ore. 2002).

Oregon v. Mitchell, 400 U.S. 112 (1970).

Pedigo v. P.A.M. Transport, Inc., 891 F. Supp. 482 (W. D. Ark. 1994).

Pell v. Procunier, 417 U.S. 817 (1974).

Pennhurst State School and Hospital v. Halderman, 451 U.S. 1 (1981).

Penry v. Lynaugh, 492 U.S. 302 (1989).

People v. Anderson, 493 P.2d 880 (Cal. 1972), cert. denied, 406 U.S. 958 (1972).

People v. Onofre, 415 N.E. 2d 936 (N.Y. 1980).

PGA Tour v. Martin, 532 U.S. 661 (2001).

Planned Parenthood Ass'n v. Dept. of Human Res., 663 P.2d 1247 (Ore. App. 1983).

Planned Parenthood v. Casey, 505 U.S. 833 (1992).

Planned Parenthood of Missouri v. Danforth, 428 U.S. 52, (1976).

Plessy v. Ferguson, 163 U.S. 537 (1896).

Pollock v. Farmers' Loan & Trust Co., 158 U.S. 601 (1895).

Portland Audubon Society v. Hodel, 866 F.2d 302, (9th Cir. 1989).

Portland Cement Association v. Ruckelshaus, 486 F. 2d 375 (D.C. Cir. 1973).

Powell v. State, 510 S.E.2d 18 (Ga. 1998).

The Prize Cases, 67 U.S. 635 (1863).

Quill v. Vacco, 80 F.3d 716 (2d Cir. 1996).

Reno v. American Civil Liberties Union, 521 U.S. 844 (1997).

Reynolds v. Sims, 377 U.S. 533 (1964).

Right to Choose v. Byrne, 450 A.2d 925 (N.J. 1982).

Robinson v. California, 370 U.S. 660 (1962).

Roe v. Wade, 410 U.S. 113 (1973).

Romer v. Evans, 517 U.S. 620 (1996).

Scenic Hudson Preservation Conference v. FPC, 354 F.2d 608 (2d Circuit, 1965).

School Board of Nassau v. Arline, 480 U.S. 273 (1987).

State v. Morales, 826 S.W.2d 201 (Tex. App. 1992).

Scott v. Sandford, 60 U.S. 393 (1857).

Sherbert v. Verner, 374 U.S. 398 (1963).

Sherman v. United States, 356 U.S. 369 (1958).

Shick v. Reed, 419 U.S. 256 (1974).

Smith v. Allwright, 321 U.S. 649 (1944).

Soileau v. Guilford of Maine, Inc., 105 F.3d 12 (1st Cir. 1997).

Sorrells v. United States, 287 U.S. 435 (1932).

South Carolina v. Katzenbach, 383 U.S. 301 (1966).

State v. Morales, 826 S.W.2d 201 (Tex. App. 1992).

Steele v. Thiokol, 241 F.3d 1248 (10th Cir. 2001).

Stenberg v. Carhart, 530 U.S. 914 (2000).

Surgicenters of America, Inc. v. Medical Dental Surgeries Co., 601 F.2d 1011 (9th Cir. 1979).

Sutton v. United Air Lines, 527 U.S. 471 (1999).

Swann v. Charlotte-Mecklenburg, 402 U.S. 1 (1971).

Talbot v. Seeman, 5 U.S. 1 (1801).

Texas v. Johnson, 491 U.S. 397 (1989).

Thornburgh v. American College of Obst. & Gyn., 476 U.S. 747 (1986).

Toyota Motor Mfg. v. Williams, 534 U.S. 184 (2002).

Trop v. Dulles, 356 U.S. 86 (1958).

United States v. Belmont, 301 U.S. 324 (1937).

United States v. Classic, 313 U.S. 299 (1941).

United States v. Curtiss-Wright Export Corporation, 299 U.S. 304 (1936).

United States v. Darby Lumber, 312 U.S. 100 (1941).

United States v. Dege, 364 U.S. 51 (1960).

United States v. Eichman, 496 U.S. 310 (1990).

United States v. Jefferson County Board of Education, 372 F.2d 836 (5th Cir. 1966).

United States v. Klein, 80 U.S. 128 (1872).

United States v. Lopez, 514 U.S. 549 (1995).

United States v. Mead Corp., 533 U.S. 218 (2001).

United States v. Morrison, 529 U.S. 598 (2000).

United States v. National Treasury Employees Union, 513 U.S. 454 (1995).

United States v. Nixon, 418 U.S. 683 (1974).

United States v. Pink, 315 U.S. 203 (1941).

United States v. Russell, 411 U.S. 423 (1973).

U.S. Airways v. Barnett, 535 U.S. 391 (2002).

Vacco v. Quill, 521 U.S. 793 (1997).

Vermont Yankee Nuclear Power Corp. v. NRDC, 435 U.S. 519 (1978).

Washington v. Glucksberg, 521 U.S. 702 (1997).

Watkins v. United States, 354 U.S. 178 (1957).

Webster v. Reproductive Health Services, 492 U.S. 490 (1989).

Weems v. United States, 217 U.S. 349 (1910).

Welch v. Texas Highways and Public Transportation Departments, 483 U.S. 468 (1987).

Wesberry v. Sanders, 376 U.S. 1 (1964).

West Coast Hotel v. Parrish, 300 U.S. 379 (1937).

Westfall v. Irwin, 484 U.S. 292 (1988).

West Va. State Board of Education v. Barnette, 319 U.S. 624 (1943).

Wolfe v. McDonnell, 418 U.S. 539 (1974).

Woodson v. North Carolina, 428 U.S. 280 (1976).

Wyatt v. Stickney, 325 F.Supp. 582 (M.D. Ala 1972).

Wyatt v. Stickney, 344 F.Supp. 373 (M.D. Ala 1972).

Youngberg v. Romeo, 457 U.S. 307 (1982).

Youngstown Sheet and Tube Company v. Sawyer, 343 U.S. 579 (1952).

INDEX

Abington School District v. Schempp (1963), 22–23
abortion decisions, 157–59. *See also Roe v. Wade* (1973)
Adams, John, 164
Adams v. Richardson (D.D.C. 1973), 102
Adarand Constructors, Inc. v. Pena (1995), 197–98
administrative law, 6, 13, 19, 22, 35–36, 90–97, 101–4, 204
Administrative Procedures Act (1946), 91–92, 104n1
adversarial legalism, 6, 13–34, 204; and British common law tradition, 19–21; and Congress, 19, 28–30, 34n9; and constitutional adjudication/judicial review, 21–24, 28; Courts of Appeals and, 15–16, 18, 26; explaining prominence of, 24–32; fragmented government and the politics of rights, 28–30; the hallmarks of, 17–19; the intensification of, 26–28; lawyers, legal culture, and, 31–32; Northwest forests and the spotted owl controversy, 14–19, 33nn2–3; and political conservatives, 30–31; the roots of, 25–26; and state courts, 19–21, 34n5, 49n3; and Supreme Court, 19, 21–23, 26–28; and tort law, 20–21, 31, 32, 34n6; "total justice" and constitutional adjudication, 28. *See also* judicial policymaking/decision making; lawyers as agents of political change
adversarial legalism and separation-of-powers doctrine, 6, 35–50; and alternative conception of separation of powers, 47–49; and Congress, 35, 39, 41, 42–46, 50n10; critiquing the standard view of the separation of powers, 38–47; and due process, 21, 36; and formal rationale of standard view, 38–40; Framers and constitutional separation of powers, 38–40, 46–47, 50n10; and functional rationale of the standard view, 40–42; and normative rationale of the standard view, 42–43; and policymaking processes, 37–38, 49n4; and questions about majority rule and decision making, 43–47; and rise of judicial policymaking, 35–37; and social choice theory, 43, 45–46; Supreme Court and separation of powers, 36–37
Age Discrimination in Employment Act (1967), 144
Aid for Dependent Children (AFDC), 18–19
Albertson's v. Kiringburg (1999), 128
Amendments to the Constitution: and congressional resolutions, 119–20; First, 140–41, 157–58; Fourth, 98, 157–58; Eighth, 156, 157; Ninth, 157–58; Eleventh, 63, 70n5; Thirteenth, 166; Fifteenth, 155, 166; Sixteenth, 63, 70n5; Seventeenth, 154. *See also* Fourteenth Amendment
American Bar Association (ABA), 79, 91
Americans with Disabilities Act (ADA), 58, 125–37, 205; and backlash against plaintiffs, 127–30; enforcement of, 125–27, 137n2; and intentions of Congress/drafters, 130–32, 138n13; and judicial implementation of statutes, 125–37, 205; and Martin victory, 128–29, 132, 135, 137; in the media, 135, 138n14, 139n15; and soci-
etal reexamination of disabilities, 132–35; and strained Court–Congress relations, 58. *See also* judicial implementation of statutes and the Americans with Disabilities Act
American Trial Lawyers Association, 31
amicus curiae briefs, 60, 114, 145, 146
Anti-Monopoly, Inc. v. General Mills Fun Group, Inc. (9th Cir. 1979, 1982), 41, 49n8
"Anti-Monopoly" case, 41
antitrust law, 110
appropriations, congressional, 53, 57, 64–65, 67, 177
Armacost, Michael H., 56
Arrow, Kenneth, 45, 138n12
Ashcroft, John, 161
Atiyah, P. S., 24, 32
Atomic Energy Commission (AEC), 89
Attorney General, U.S., 78, 82–83
attorneys general, state, 146, 148
Australia, 19

Babbitt, Bruce, 17
Baker v. State (Vt. 1999), 163
Bankruptcy Reform Act (1978), 36
Barenblatt v. U.S. (1959), 170–71, 185–86
Barnes, Jeb, 6, 11, 19, 124. *See also* adversarial legalism
Bas v. Tingy (1800), 86
Baum, Lawrence, 8, 63, 207. *See also* Supreme Court–Congress interaction and standard strategic model
Bazelon, Judge David, 93–94
behavioralist approach to study of politics, 4, 55
behavioral revolution in political science, 3–4
Bell, Griffin, 83

Berg, Larry L., 64, 68
Bickel, Alexander, 42–43, 189, 194
Biddle, Francis, 82–83
Biden, Sen. Joseph, 59
Bill of Rights, 23, 25, 28, 89
Black, Justice Hugo, 72, 155, 181–84
Black Caucus, 59
Blackmun, Justice Harry, 80, 190
Board of Education v. Dowell (1991), 200n5
Board of Trustees of the Univ. of Alabama v. Garrett (2001), 58
Bob Jones Univ. v. U.S. (1983), 81
Boerne case. *See City of Boerne v. Archbishop Flores* (1997) and Court–Congress interactions
Bork, Robert, 79, 195–96
Born-Alive Infants Protection Act (2000), 159
Bowers v. Hardwick (1986), 162
Bowsher v. Synar (1986), 36
Boy Scouts of America Equal Access Act (2002), 163
Boy Scouts of America v. Dale (2000), 162–63
Bradwell, Myra, 167
Bragaw, Stephen, 9. *See also City of Boerne v. Archbishop Flores* (1997) and Court–Congress interactions
Bragdon v. Abbott (1998), 138n9
Brandeis, Justice Louis, 154
Brennan, Justice William J., 32, 80, 156
Brewer, Justice David, 167
Breyer, Justice Stephen, 57
Brigham, John, 55
Brown, Janice Rogers, 80
Brownlow, Louis, 85
Brown v. Board of Education (1954), 22, 65; and constitutional interpretation, 22, 89, 97–98, 155, 166, 170; and judicial activism, 89, 97–98; social and political forces in decision making, 190–91, 194
Buchanan, James, 192
Buchen, Philip, 83
Buckley v. Valeo (1976), 36–37, 108
Bureau of Land Management (BLM), 14–16
Burger, Chief Justice Warren, 38, 61, 93, 158
Burke, Thomas, 8–9, 205. *See also* judicial implementation of

statutes and the Americans with Disabilities Act
Bush, George H. W., and Bush administration: and the ADA, 131; and adversarial legalism, 16, 31; judicial nominees, 61; and Northwest forests–spotted owl controversy, 16; and Office of Legal Counsel, 84, 85; and office of White House counsel, 83, 84, 85; pardons by, 74; and president's lawmaking role, 74, 77, 88n1; and Supreme Court civil rights decisions, 113
Bush, George W., and Bush administration: and *Bush v. Gore* decision, 87; and constitutional amendment prohibiting abortion, 122n8; and court-stripping, 71n6; judicial nominees, 61–62, 79, 80; and liberal activist judges, 60; and office of solicitor general, 82; and office of White House counsel, 85; and president's lawmaking role, 77; recess appointments, 61–62, 80
Bush v. Gore (2000), 82, 87, 144, 178, 187n5

campaign finance reform, 108, 154
Canada, 19, 24, 164
Carter, Jimmy, 78, 80, 83
Case-Zablocki Act (1972), 75
Chase, Samuel, 65
checks and balances, 53, 66, 173
Chevron v. NRDC (1984), 96
Chisholm v. Georgia (1793), 70n5
City of Boerne v. Archbishop Flores (1997) and Court–Congress interactions, 9, 140–49, 175; the *Boerne* case, 141–43; and Court–Congress fights over constitutional interpretations, 143–45; Court rulings restricting congressional powers, 144–45; and interest group litigation, 145–49, 149nn4–5; and other free exercise of religion cases, 116, 140–41; and RFRA declared unconstitutional, 63, 116, 140, 141, 143, 175–76; and RFRA enactment, 116, 140, 141, 175; RFRA interest groups and *Boerne* as test case, 147–49
City of Mobile v. Bolden (1980), 116
Civil Rights Act (1866), 166
Civil Rights Act (1875), 22

Civil Rights Act (1964), 34n9, 155–56, 166–67; Title VI, 101–2
Civil Rights Act (1991), 113–14, 167, 196
Civil Rights Cases (1883), 22, 166
Civil Rights of Institutionalized Persons Act (1980), 101
Clarke, Justice John H., 154
Clayton, Cornell, 5
Clean Air Act (1970), 34n9
Clean Air Act (1990), 30
Clinger, Rep. William, 197
Clinton, Bill, and Clinton administration: and abortion legislation, 158–59; and gay rights decisions, 163; and independent counsel appointments, 87; judicial appointments, 61, 78, 79, 80; and Northwest forests–spotted owl controversy, 16, 17; and office of White House counsel, 83, 85; pardons by, 74; and president's lawmaking role, 74, 77, 88n1
Coats, Sen. Dan, 197
Colker, Ruth, 129
Commerce Clause, 144
committees in Congress, 7, 29–30, 59, 62, 64–65, 67, 73–74, 159, 170, 195, 196; lawyers on, 62; reports as legislative history, 57, 70n2, 198
Common Law tradition, 19–21, 35, 145
Compassion in Dying v. State of Wa. (9th Cir. 1996), 160
Competition in Contracting Act (1984), 77
Congress: and abortion legislation, 158–59; and adversarial legalism, 19, 28–30, 34n9, 35, 39, 41, 42–46; and federal agencies, 90–93, 94–95, 101–3; ideology in, 117–18; judiciary's dependence on, 153–56; and lawyers as agents of political change, 7, 32, 62, 68; overrides by, 109, 113–20, 121n2; and the president, 75–77; and right-to-die legislation, 159–62; and separation of powers, 35, 39, 41, 42–46, 50n10. *See also City of Boerne v. Archbishop Flores* (1997) and Court–Congress interactions; committees in Congress; constitutional interpretation and interbranch relations;

Congress (*continued*): constitutional interpretation and strategic model of Court–Congress relations; federal court–Congress relations, from neoinstitutional perspective; judicial policymaking/decision making

Congressional Quarterly Weekly Report, 58–59

conservatives and adversarial legalism, 30–31

Constitution, U.S.: Article I, 76; Article I (Section 2), 154; Article I (Section 4), 154; Article I (Section 6), 39; Article II, 73, 76, 77, 87–88; Article IV (Section 1), 163. *See also* Amendments to the Constitution; Framers of Constitution

constitutional interpretation and interbranch relations, 9–10, 153–69; abortion decisions and legislation, 157–59; civil rights and desegregation decisions, 166–67; Court–Congress fights, 143–45; death penalty decisions and state level statutes, 156–57; and federal review of state and local agencies, 90, 97–101; gay rights decisions, 162–64; implementing judicial doctrines, 164–65; and individual rights and liberties, 165–68; and the judiciary's dependence on Congress, 153–56; and jurors' roles, 164–65; and legislation on campaign corruption and voting rights, 154–55; and legislative vetoes, 165; miscegenation law decisions, 155–56; right-to-die decisions and legislation, 159–62; women's rights and sex discrimination rulings, 167–68. *See also City of Boerne v. Archbishop Flores* (1997) and Court–Congress interactions

constitutional interpretation and strategic model of Court–Congress relations, 10, 170–88; applicability of strategic account, 179–80; constitutional vs. statutory interpretation, 175–79; explaining the *Watkins-Barenblatt* shift, 170–71, 185–86; implications of the strategic-institutional account, 174–75; strategic analysis and accounting

for decisions, 180–85, 188n7; strategic-institutional account of judicial decision making, 171–79, 187n4

Consumer Product Safety Commission, 92

Contract with America, 196–97

Controlled Substances Act (CSA), 161

Conyers, Rep. John, Jr., 59

Cooper, Charles, 85

Corps of Engineers, 18, 89

countermajoritarian decision making. *See* judicial policymaking/decision making

Court–Congress relations. *See City of Boerne v. Archbishop Flores* (1997) and Court–Congress interactions; constitutional interpretation and strategic model of Court–Congress relations; federal court–Congress relations, from neoinstitutional perspective; judicial policymaking/decision making

court-packing, 65, 80, 108

Courts of Appeals: and ADA cases, 129; and adversarial legalism, 15–16, 18, 26, 35; Bush's nominees to, 80; and federal oversight of federal agencies, 93–95, 96. *See also individual courts*

"court-stripping," 66–68, 71n6

Cover, Robert, 136, 179

Crime Control and Safe Streets Act (1968), 63

criminal sentencing issues, 66–68

Cruzan v. Director, Mo. Dept. of Health (1990), 159

Cummings, Homer, 84

Cummins, Tony, 142, 143, 145, 147

Cutler, Lloyd, 84

Dahl, Robert A., 111, 186, 188n8, 189

Dale, James, 163

Davidson, Roger H., 53, 70n3

D.C. Circuit Court of Appeals, 61, 80, 93–95, 96

Dean, John, 84

death penalty decisions, 156–57

Death With Dignity Act (Oregon) (1994), 161

Defense of Marriage Act (DOMA) (1996), 163

DeLay, Rep. Tom, 59, 60, 66

Dellinger, Walter E., 148

Democratic Party, 29, 31; in Congress, 59–61, 79, 199; judges as members of, 14, 96

democratic theory, 13, 44, 48

Developmentally Disabled Assistance and Bill of Rights Act (1975), 101

Devins, Neal, 10, 56, 58. *See also* judicial policymaking/decision making

Dickerson v. U.S. (2000), 63, 144–45, 171, 176

Dodd, Lawrence, 5

Douglas, Justice William O., 65–66, 155

Dred Scott v. Sandford (1857), 25, 70n5, 166, 178, 192

"due process" clause, 21, 100

Dwyer, Judge William, 16, 17

economists, 11, 40–41

Edelman, Lauren, 133–34, 137

Edelman, Murray, 131

EDF v. Ruckelshaus (D.C. Circuit, 1971), 93–94

Education Amendments (1972), Title IX, 102

Education for All Handicapped Children Act (1975), 101

EEOC v. Waffle House Inc. (2002), 138n9

Eighth Amendment, 156, 157

Eisenhower, Dwight D., 76, 80

Electoral College, 47, 154, 203

Eleventh Amendment, 63, 70n5

Eleventh Circuit Court of Appeals, 80

Ely, John Hart, 192

empirical research, 6, 54, 171

Employee Retirement Income Security Act (1974), 30

Employment Division v. Smith (1990), 116, 141, 143–44, 145, 147, 175

Endangered Species Act (ESA), 14–16, 17

Endangered Species Commission, 16

Engel, David, 134–35, 137

England, Norman, 145

Environmental Protection Agency (EPA), 18, 89, 92, 93–94, 95

Epstein, Lee, 5, 10. *See also* constitutional interpretation and strategic model of Court–Congress relations

Equal Employment Opportunity Act (1972), 34n9

Equal Employment Opportunity Commission (EEOC), 31, 89, 92, 126, 128, 138n7
Equal Protection Clause, 22, 28, 144
Eskridge, William N., 63, 111, 113, 114
Establishment Clause, 140–41
Estrada, Miguel A., 61, 80
Ethics in Government Act (1978), 86
Europe and adversarial legalism, 24, 27, 28
executive agreements, 74–75
executive orders, 74–75
Ex parte Garland (1866), 73
Ex parte Grossman (1925), 73
Ex parte McCardle (1869), 66
Ex parte Milligan (1866), 86

Fair Labor Standards Act (1938), 178
Fairman, Charles, 173
federal agencies and federal courts, 7–8, 89–104; and Administrative Procedures Act, 91–92, 104n1; Congress and federal agencies, 90–93, 94–95, 101–3; consequences of judicial demands, 95–96; and constitutional interpretations, 90, 97–101; court review of federal agencies/administrative law, 90–97; court review of state and local agencies, 90, 97–104; and Courts of Appeals, 93–95, 96; and institutional reform cases, 99–101; judicial activism, 89, 97–101; and New Deal agencies, 89–91; and readings of federal laws and regulations, 90, 101–4; and school desegregation cases, 89, 97–98; and "social regulation" agencies, 92; and state/local police behavior, 98–99; and Supreme Court, 90–91, 96
Federal Bureau of Investigation (FBI), 79, 82
Federal Communications Commission (FCC), 89
Federal Corrupt Practices Act (1910), 154
federal court–Congress relations, from neoinstitutional perspective, 7, 53–71, 206; and assumption of reverence for the courts, 68–69; and congressional committees, 62; and congres-

sional funding for the judiciary, 64–65; and individual attacks on the courts, 57–60; and institutional attacks on the courts, 65–68; and institutional wills, 62–64; and judicial activism, 58–60; and liberal activist court decisions, 59–60; and neoinstitutionalism, 54–56; party caucuses and judicial nominations, 60–62; and strained institutional perspectives, 56–59, 70nn2–4; Supreme Court and strained relations, 56–59, 64–65, 70nn2–4
Federal Election Campaign Act (1972), 37, 108
Federal Highway Administration, 89
Federalist Papers, 39–40, 49n5, 50n10, 72
Federal Land Policy and Management Act, 14
Federal Power Commission (FPC), 93
Federal Sentencing Commission, 66
Federal Trade Commission, 91
Feeley, Malcolm, 42
Feeney, Rep. Tom, 60, 66, 67
Feeney Amendment (2003), 66–68
Feldblum, Chai, 125, 130–31, 138n7
Fifteenth Amendment, 155, 166
Fifth Amendment, 98, 156, 157–58
Fifth Circuit Court of Appeals, 80
filibusters, 61–62, 79–80
Finkbine, Sherry, 190
First Amendment, 140–41, 157–58
Fish, Stanley, 136
Fisher, Louis, 9–10, 53, 56, 58, 63, 178, 204. *See also* constitutional interpretation and interbranch relations
flag burning, 62, 63, 108, 116, 119, 197
Flag Protection Act (1989), 63
Flores, Patrick Fernández, 142, 147
Ford, Gerald, 73–74, 83
Fortas, Justice Abe, 61
Foster, Vince, 85
Fourteenth Amendment, 63, 70n5; and civil rights, 166; due process clause, 21, 100; Equal Protection Clause, 22, 28, 144; and federal court review of agencies, 89, 98; and liberty and right of privacy, 158; and religious freedom, 116; and rights of women, 167; and

rulings restricting congressional powers, 144
Fourth Amendment, 98, 157–58
Framers of Constitution: and power of presidency, 87; and separation of powers, 38–40, 46–47, 50n10
France, 24, 28
Frankfurter, Justice Felix, 164, 191
Freedom of Choice Act (FOCA), 158–59
Freeman v. Pitts (1992), 200n5
Friedman, Lawrence, 27
Frye, Judge Helen, 15–16
Fuller, Lon, 40
Funk, Bob, 126
Furman v. Georgia (1972), 118

Galanter, Marc, 131–32
game theory, 11, 124, 207
gay rights decisions, 162–64
General Accounting Office (GAO), 33n2
Gephardt, Rep. Richard, 60
Germany, 24, 32
Gillman, Howard, 5
Ginsburg, Justice Ruth Bader, 57, 133, 159
Gitlitz v. Commissioner (2001), 107, 114
Goesart v. Cleary (1948), 168
Goldberg v. Kelly (1970), 36
Golding, Jill, 134
Goldman, Sheldon, 79
Goldwater v. Carter (1979), 86
Gonzales, Alberto, 85
Goodlatte, Rep. Bob, 60
Goodridge v. Department of Public Health (2003), 60, 163–64
Gore, Al, 17
governance as dialogue, 10–11, 17–19, 21–24, 53, 69, 154, 168, 202–7
Graber, Mark, 4, 46, 68, 191
Graham, Hugh Davis, 102
Gramm, Sen. Phil, 197–98
Gramm-Rudman Act (1985), 36, 197
Gray, C. Boyden, 83, 84, 85
Grovey v. Townsend (1935), 155
Grutter v. Bollinger (2003), 60
Gun-Free School Zones Act, 144
Gutierrez de Martinez v. Lamagno (1995), 116

Hall, Peter A., 54, 55
Hamilton, Alexander, 87–88
Hamilton, Rep. Lee, 198

Hamilton, Marci, 147, 148
Hammer v. Dagenhart (1918), 178
Hand, Judge Learned, 49n7
Hardwick, Michael, 162
Harkin, Sen. Tom, 58
Hartz, Louis, 34n7
Hatch, Sen. Orrin, 59
Hausegger, Lori, 8, 207. *See also* Supreme Court–Congress interaction and standard strategic model
Henley, Judge J. Smith, 99
House Appropriations Committee, 64–65, 67
House Commerce Committee, 62
House Government Reform Committee, 74
House Judiciary Committee, 59, 62, 73–74, 159
House Working Group on Judicial Accountability, 60
Hoyer, Rep. Steny, 125
Hoyt v. Florida (1961), 168
Hughes, Chief Justice Charles Evan, 21, 22
Humphrey's Executor v. U.S. (1935), 86
Hurley v. Irish-American Gay Group of Boston (1995), 162
Hyde Amendment, 158

Ignagni, Joseph, 111, 121n4, 178
Immigration and Naturalization Service (INS), 82
impeachment of judges, 65–66, 177
implementation of policy, 6, 7, 9, 27, 29–30, 37–38, 123–37, 153, 164–65, 202, 205. *See also* judicial implementation of statutes and the Americans with Disabilities Act
incrementalism, 41–42, 198–99
In re Debs (1895), 86
In re Neagle (1890), 74, 86
institutional culture, 7, 9, 53, 54–55, 56–59, 64–65, 70nn2–4. *See also* federal court–Congress relations, from neoinstitutional perspective
institutional wills, 7, 53, 55–57, 62–64, 69
INS v. Chadha (1983), 36, 38, 63, 165
interbranch perspectives on policymaking: and continuing colloquies, 202–7; and four lessons about contemporary policymaking, 11; and limitations of

behavioralist perspectives, 4; value of, 3–6. *See also* constitutional interpretation and interbranch relations; federal agencies and federal courts; judicial policymaking/decision making
interest groups, 113–14, 145–49, 149nn4–5; and lawyers as agents of political change, 19, 32, 132, 145–49
Interstate Commerce Commission (ICC), 91
Issa, Rep. Darrell, 59

Jackson, Andrew, 77
Jackson, Justice Robert, 194
Japan, 19
Jillison, Calvin, 5
Job Creation and Worker Assistance Act (2002), 107
Johnson, Judge Frank, 99–100, 104n7
Johnson, Lyndon, 61
Johnson v. U.S. (2000), 70n2
Jones, Judge Robert, 16
judicial activism: and Court–Congress relations, 58–60; and federal agencies, 89, 97–101; in institutional reform cases, 99–101; and "Lochnerism," 97, 104n6, 190, 191; and school desegregation cases, 89, 97–98; and state/local police behavior, 98–99. *See also* judicial policymaking/decision making
judicial implementation of statutes and the Americans with Disabilities Act, 8–9, 123–39, 205; and ADA enforcement, 125–27, 137n2; and ADA plaintiff victories, 128–29, 132, 135, 137; appellate ADA decisions, 129; backlash against ADA plaintiffs, 127–30; Court–Congress relations and statute implementation, 123–24, 136–37, 137n1; and disability definitions, 127–28, 129, 130, 138n13, 138nn7–8; and individuals' engagement with the ADA, 134–35, 137; and law outside the courts (generative quality of implementation), 132–35; and *Olmstead* decision, 132–33, 135, 137; and organizational techniques for dispute resolution, 133–34; and principle-agent theory, 123, 130, 135–37, 138n12; Supreme Court

ADA decisions, 125, 127–30, 132–33, 135, 138nn9–10; and symbolic politics, 130–32, 138n13
judicial nominations/appointments, 60–62, 77, 78–80
judicial policymaking/decision making, 10, 189–201; and common view of Court as countermajoritarian, 189; Congress's role in, 195–200; and elected officials' preferences, 191–93; in federalism-related decisions, 195, 196–99; and growing use of judicial review, 197; and public opinion, 190–91, 193–95, 199–200; Rehnquist Court, 195–200, 200nn8–9; social and political forces on, 190–200, 200nn8–9; strategic-institutional account of, 171–79, 187n4. *See also* adversarial legalism; constitutional interpretation and strategic model of Court– Congress relations; judicial activism
judicial review: constitutional adjudication and policy dialogue, 21–24; and constitutional interpretations, 21–24, 90, 97–101; of federal agencies and administrative law, 90–97; and readings of federal laws and regulations, 90, 101–4; and Rehnquist Court's federalism decisions, 197; by state courts, 104n1
Judiciary Act (1789), 82
judiciary and adversarial legalism. *See* adversarial legalism
judiciary and constitutional interpretation. *See* constitutional interpretation and interbranch relations; constitutional interpretation and strategic model of Court–Congress relations
judiciary and federal agencies. *See* federal agencies and federal courts
juries, 33, 153, 164–65
"Jurisdiction-Stripping Proposals in Congress," 66
Justice Department, U.S., 79, 82, 83–85, 146, 154
Justice Department Act (1870), 81

Kagan, Robert A., 6, 35, 204. *See also* adversarial legalism
Kansas City (Mo.) school desegregation case, 100

Kansas-Nebraska Act (1854), 192
Kassop, Nancy, 7, 50n10. *See also*
    presidency
Kastenmeier, Rep. Robert, 70n3
Katzmann, Judge Robert A., 53,
    54, 69
Kelley, Christopher S., 88n1
Kellog Co. v. National Biscuit Co.
    (1938), 49n7
Kemp, Evan, 126
Kennedy, Justice Anthony, 67, 148,
    159, 195–96
Kennedy, John F., 83
Kennedy, Robert, 83
Kernell, Samuel, 49n5
Kevorkian, Jack, 160
Kimel v. Florida Board of Regents
    (2000), 144
King v. Smith (1968), 33n4
Knight, Jack, 10. *See also* constitu-
    tional interpretation and strategic
    model of Court–Congress rela-
    tions
Kuhl, Carolyn, 80

LaFollette, Sen. Robert M., 58
Lane, Sarah, 134
Lawrence v. Texas (2003), 60, 162
law schools, 24, 31–32
lawyers as agents of political
    change, 9, 20–21, 25–26, 29,
    31–32, 33, 93, 136, 145–49; and
    civil rights, 28, 132, 167; in
    Congress, 7, 32, 62, 68; in federal
    government, 32; in interest
    groups, 19, 32, 132, 145–49; in
    state government, 9, 145–46; trial
    lawyers, 31; women, 167. *See
    also* adversarial legalism
Laycock, Douglas, 147, 148
Leahy, Sen. Patrick, 58
Least Dangerous Branch, The
    (Bickel), 42
legislative history, 57, 69n1,
    70nn2–3, 77, 130–31, 137n1,
    198
Lerner, Max, 193
Leventhal, Judge Harold, 49n2, 92,
    94
Levi, Edward, 83
Levin, Rep. Sander, 160
Lincoln, Abraham, 86
Linder, Rep. John, 59
Little v. Barreme (1804), 86
lobbying and lobbyists, 43, 145,
    198
Lochner-era decision making, 97,
    104n6, 190, 191

Lochner v. New York (1905),
    104n6
Lott, Sen. Trent, 65
Lowell, James Russell, 154

Madison, James, 39–40, 49n5, 72,
    85–86, 87–88, 193, 200n4
Maltese, John Anthony, 76
Marbury v. Madison (1803), 86,
    193
Marshall, Chief Justice John, 193
Marshall, Justice Thurgood, 112,
    156
Martie, Todd, 147–48
Martin, Andrew D., 10. *See also*
    constitutional interpretation and
    strategic model of
    Court–Congress relations
Martin, Casey, 128–29, 132, 135,
    137
Matter of Quinlan (1976), 158
Mauro, Tony, 58
Mayhew, David, 44
McCain-Feingold law (2002), 108
McCann, Michael, 29
McClellan, Sen. John L., 58
McGovern, Rep. Jim, 59
McKenna, Justice Joseph, 154
Meernik, James, 111, 121n4, 178
Meese, Edwin, 38, 77, 81, 83, 85
Melnick, R. Shep, 7–8, 114, 124.
    See also federal agencies and
    federal courts
Militello, Raymond, 134
Miller, Mark C., 7, 9, 68. *See also*
    *City of Boerne v. Archbishop
    Flores* (1997) and
    Court–Congress interactions;
    federal court–Congress relations
Miranda v. Arizona (1966), 115,
    144, 176
Mistretta v. U.S. (1989), 66
Mitchell, Gregory, 193–94
Mitchell, John, 83
Monroe v. Pape (1961), 98
Moorhead, Rep. Carlos, 70n3
Morrison v. Olson (1988), 86
Muller v. Oregon (1908), 167
Munger, Frank, 134–35, 137
Murphy, Justice Frank, 155
Murphy, Walter F., 68, 69, 120
Murphy v. UPS (1999), 128
Murray, Sen. Patty, 198
Myers v. U.S. (1926), 86

NAACP Legal Defense and Educa-
    tion Fund, 146
Nader, Ralph, 146

Nagel, Stuart S., 68
National Association of Attorneys
    General (NAAG), 146, 148
National Environmental Policy Act
    (1969), 15, 92
National Environmental Protection
    Act (1969), 14, 17, 34n9
National Forest Management Act
    (NFMA), 14, 16, 17
National Highway Traffic and
    Motor Safety Act (1966), 34n9
National Highway Traffic Safety
    Administration, 18, 92
National Labor Relations Board, 91
National Security Act, 85
National Security Council (NSC),
    82
Native American Church, 141, 148
Nelson, Michael, 5
neoinstitutionalism, 54–56, 206.
    See also federal court–Congress
    relations, from neoinstitutional
    perspective
Neustadt, Richard E., 69
Newberry v. U.S. (1921), 154–55
New Deal: and Court–Congress
    relations, 56, 58, 65, 108; and
    courts–agencies relations, 89–91;
    legislation, 22, 56, 58, 65, 108,
    190, 191; and *Lochner*-era deci-
    sion making, 190, 191
Newdow v. U.S. Congress (2002),
    59
New York Times, 135, 138n14
New York Times v. U.S. (1971), 87
Ninth Amendment, 157–58
Ninth Circuit Court of Appeals:
    "Anti-Monopoly case," 41; and
    Northwest forests–spotted owl
    controversy, 14, 15–16; Pledge
    decision, 59–60; and right-to-die
    decisions, 160
Nixon, Richard, and Nixon admin-
    istration: and Douglas
    impeachment, 65–66; executive
    orders by, 75; judicial nomi-
    nees/appointments, 61, 78, 80;
    pardoning of, 73–74; and school
    busing/desegregation battles, 194
*Northern Pipeline Construction
    Co. v. Marathon Pipe Line Co.*
    (1982), 36
Nuclear Regulatory Commission,
    96
Nussbaum, Bernard, 83

O'Brien, David M., 66
O'Brien, Sean, 134–35

Occupational Safety and Health Act (1974), 34n9
Occupational Safety and Health Administration (OSHA), 18, 89, 92
Oceans Act (1992), 114, 115
O'Connor, Justice Sandra Day: abortion decisions, 158, 159, 195–96; ADA decisions, 125, 130; *Boerne* decision, 147; confirmation process, 196; right-to-die decisions, 160–61
Office of Civil Rights, 102
Office of Congressional Relations (OCR), 76
Office of Counsel to the President, 83–85
Office of Legal Counsel (OLC), 83–85
Office of Management and Budget (OMB), 76, 95–96
O'Leary, Rosemary, 100
Oleszek, Walter J., 53, 70n3
Olmstead v. L.C. by Zimring (1999), 132–33, 135, 137, 138n9
Olson, Theodore, 82
Omnibus Judgeship Act (1978), 78
Oppenheimer, Bruce, 5
Oregon v. Ashcroft (D. Ore. 2002), 161
Oregon v. Mitchell (1970), 70n5, 107–8
organizational theory, 11
Owen, Priscilla, 80

Pacific Northwest forests–spotted owl controversy, 14–19, 33nn2–3
Paez, Richard, 79
pardons, executive, 73–74
parliamentary systems, 6, 19, 24, 39, 48
Patient Self-Determination Act (1990), 160
Patterson, Bradley, 76
Pedigo v. P.A.M. Transport, Inc. (W.D. Ark. 1994), 129
Peterson, Mark A., 76
PGA Tour v. Martin (2001), 128–29, 132, 135, 137, 138n9
Pickering, Charles, Jr., 80
Pierce, Richard, 95
Pierson, Paul, 55, 69
Pika, Joseph A., 76
Pitney, Justice Mahlon, 154
Planned Parenthood of Missouri v. Danforth (1976), 158

Planned Parenthood v. Casey (1992), 158, 195–96
Plessy v. Ferguson (1896), 166
political liberalism and judicial policymaking, 25, 34n7
political parties, 3, 13, 24, 28, 30, 35, 60–62
Pollock v. Farmers' Loan & Trust Co. (1895), 22, 70n5
Poole, Keith T., 179
Portland Audubon Society v. Hodel (9th Cr. 1989), 15
postmodernism, 44
Powell, Justice Lewis F., 86, 146
Pratt, Judge John, 102
presidency, 7, 72–88; and the attorney general, 82–83; and Congress, 75–77; and the courts, 77–87; executive orders/executive agreements, 74–75; executive pardons, 73–74; expanded powers of, 72; and judicial selection/appointments, 77, 78–80; Office of Legal Counsel and Office of Counsel to the President, 83–85; and presidential "signing statements," 77, 88n1; and the solicitor general, 78, 80–82; Supreme Court review of, 73, 74, 85–87; unilateral lawmaking by, 73–75
Presidential Records Act, 84
Pressman, Jeffrey, 123
principle-agent theory, 9, 123, 130, 135–37, 138n12, 202. *See also* judicial implementation of statutes and the Americans with Disabilities Act
Pritchett, C. Herman, 68, 69
Prize Cases (1863), 86
PROTECT Act (2003), 67
Pryor, William, Jr., 80
public opinion, 43, 187n5, 190–91, 193–95, 199–200

qualitative research, 5, 11
quantitative research, 5, 10, 11, 179–86
Quill v. Vacco (2d Cir. 1996), 160

Radical Republicans (Reconstruction period), 56, 58
Randolph, Edmund, 82
rational choice research, 8–9, 43, 54, 55, 108, 121
Rawls, John, 55
Reagan, Ronald, and Reagan administration: and

Court–Congress relations, 56, 58, 61, 196; judicial nominees/appointments, 61, 78, 80; and liberal activist judges, 56, 58; and Office of Counsel to the President, 85; and Office of Legal Counsel, 85; and office of solicitor general, 81; and presidential lawmaking role, 77, 88n1; and school busing/desegregation battles, 194; and spotted owl controversy, 33n2
Reconstruction Acts, 56, 66
Rehabilitation Act (1973), Section 504, 127
Rehnquist, Chief Justice William: abortion decisions, 158, 159; appointment of, 80; and cases reviewing presidential power, 86; and Court–Congress relations, 56–57, 64, 65, 67; and federal-sentencing guidelines, 67; and social/political forces in decision making, 171, 193
Religious Freedom Restoration Act (RFRA) (1993): and *City of Boerne*, 63, 116, 140, 141, 143, 175–76; declared unconstitutional, 63, 116, 140, 141, 143, 175–76, 198; enactment of, 116, 140, 141, 175
Reno, Janet, 161, 163
repeat players in courts, 131–32
Republican Party, 29, 30–31, 92; in Congress, 59–61, 196–97, 199; judges as members of, 14, 96
Resnik, Judith, 53, 71n6
reverence for courts, 68–69
Reynolds v. Sims (1964), 23
right-to-die/assisted suicide decisions, 159–62
Roberts, Justice Owen, 65, 80, 154, 191
Rocha, Susan, 147
Roe v. Wade (1973), 23, 119, 157–58, 190, 192, 194
Romer v. Evans (1996), 162
Roosevelt, Franklin D., and Roosevelt administration: appointment of attorney general, 82–83; and Congress–president relationship, 75; and court–federal agencies relationship, 90–91; court-packing plan, 65, 80, 108; judicial nominees, 22, 78, 80; and New Deal, 22, 56, 58, 65, 89–90, 108, 191; and Office of Legal Counsel and

Office of Counsel to the President, 84
Roosevelt, Theodore, 75
Rosenberg, Gerald, 177
Rosenman, Samuel, 84
Rosenthal, Howard, 179
Rubin, Edward, 42
Ruff, Charles, 85
Ryden, David, 5

Sargent, Sen. Aaron, 167
Sawyer, Charles S., 75
Scalia, Justice Antonin: abortion
  decisions, 159; *Boerne* decision,
  147; and Court–Congress relations, 57, 70n2; on
  courts–federal agencies relationship, 96
Schmidhauser, John R., 64, 68
School Board of Nassau v. Arline
  (1987), 127
school desegregation cases, 22, 89,
  97–98, 100, 166–67, 190–91,
  194, 200n5
Schubert, Glendon A., 68
Schumer, Sen. Charles E., 58–59
Scott v. Sandford (1857), 178
Second Circuit Court of Appeals,
  93, 160
Segal, Jeffrey A., 179
Senate judicial confirmations,
  61–62, 77, 79–80, 195–96
Senate Judiciary Committee, 59,
  195, 196
Sensenbrenner, Rep. James, Jr., 59
Sentencing Reform Act (1984), 66
separation institutions sharing
  power, 9, 11, 39–40, 48–49, 69,
  202–3, 205
separation-of-powers doctrine,
  standard view of: and adversarial legalism, 35–50; critiquing,
  38–47; formal rationale of,
  38–40; and Framers, 38–40,
  46–47, 50n10; functional
  rationale of, 40–42; normative
  rationale of, 42–43; and policymaking process, 37–38, 49n4;
  rethinking, 47–49; and Supreme
  Court, 36–37. *See also* adversarial legalism and
  separation-of-powers doctrine
Seventeenth Amendment, 154
Shapiro, Martin, 94
Sherbert v. Verner (1963), 140–41
Shick v. Reed (1974), 73
Sierra Club Legal Defense Fund
  (SCLDF), 14–17

Sixteenth Amendment, 63, 70n5
Skocpol, Theda, 55, 69
Skowronek, Stephen, 35
Slotnick, Elliot, 79
Smith, Neal, 64–65
Smith, Rogers M., 54, 55
Smith, William French, 83
social choice theory, 43, 45–46
Social Security Act, 33n4
solicitor general, 78, 80–82, 146
Solimine, Michael E., 62
Souter, Justice David, 70n2, 200n9
South Carolina v. Katzenbach
  (1966), 192
Specter, Sen. Arlen, 198
spotted owl controversy, 14–19,
  33nn2–3
state agencies, federal court review
  of, 90, 97–104
State and Local Legal Center, 146
state courts: and adversarial
  legalism, 19–21, 34n5, 49n3;
  and judicial review, 104n1
state governments and interest
  groups, 146, 149nn4–5
statutory interpretation. *See City of
  Boerne v. Archbishop Flores*
  (1997) and Court–Congress
  interactions; constitutional interpretation and interbranch
  relations; judicial implementation of statutes and the
  Americans with Disabilities Act
Stevens, Justice John Paul, 159
Stewart, Richard, 94
strategic model. *See* constitutional
  interpretation and strategic
  model of Court–Congress relations; Supreme Court–Congress
  interaction and standard
  strategic model
Stumpf, Harry, 68
Summers, Robert S., 24, 32
Supreme Court: ADA decisions,
  125, 127–30, 132–33, 135,
  138nn9–10; and adversarial
  legalism, 19, 21–23, 26–28;
  Burger Court, 80; confirmation
  processes, 61, 79–80, 195–96;
  and congressional funding for
  the judiciary, 64–65; and court-
  stripping, 66; and federal
  agencies, 89, 93, 97–98; and free
  exercise of religion cases, 116,
  140–41; and judicial review,
  21–23; and the presidency, 73,
  74, 86–87; Rehnquist Court,
  113, 195–200, 200nn8–9; and

the RFRA, 63, 116, 140, 141,
  143, 175–76; and separation of
  powers, 36–37; social and political forces in decision making,
  190–200, 200nn8–9; and
  strained institutional perspectives, 56–59, 64–65, 70nn2–4;
  Warren Court, 89, 93, 97–98.
  *See also City of Boerne v. Arch-
  bishop Flores* (1997) and
  Court–Congress interactions;
  constitutional interpretation and
  interbranch relations
Supreme Court–Congress interaction and standard strategic
  model, 8, 107–22; assumptions
  and actual reality, 110–17;
  assumptions of standard model,
  109–10; basics of
  Court–Congress interaction,
  107–9; congressional overrides,
  109, 113–20, 121n2; congressional reversals, 111, 112–13,
  121n4; constitutional amendments, 119–20; and frequency of
  congressional action, 111–12;
  and ideological factors, 109–10,
  113–15, 117–18, 121n3; implications of assumptions-reality
  deviations, 117–20; and interest-
  group pressures, 113–14; and
  judicial indifference to congressional action, 112–13, 120; and
  long-term strategizing, 118–19;
  and symbiotic relationships,
  119–20. *See also* constitutional
  interpretation and strategic
  model of Court–Congress relations
Supreme Court Project, NAAG's,
  146–47, 148, 149n6
Surface Mining and Reclamation
  Act (1977), 34n9
Sutton, Jeffrey, 148
Sutton v. United Airlines (1999),
  128, 130, 136–37, 138n13
Swann v. Charlotte-Mecklenburg
  (1971), 194

Taft, William Howard, 195
Talbot v. Seeman (1801), 86
Taylor, Rosemary C. R., 54, 55
Texas v. Johnson (1989), 116, 119
Thirteenth Amendment, 166
Thomas, Justice Clarence: abortion
  decisions, 159, 195; *Boerne* deci-
  sion, 147; confirmation process,
  61, 79, 195

Thomas, Norman C., 76
Thornburgh v. American Coll. of Obst. & Gyn. (1986), 158
Tocqueville, Alexis de, 25, 35
tort law and adversarial legalism, 20–21, 31, 32, 34n6
Traynor, Judge Roger, 32
Truman, David, 145
Truman, Harry, 22, 75, 76
Truth-in-Lending Act (1968), 31
Twenty-Sixth Amendment, 63, 70n5, 108
Tyler, Tom, 193–94

United Kingdom, 24, 28, 32, 90
U.S. Airways v. Barnett (2002), 138n10
U.S. Code Congressional and Administrative News (USSCAN), 77
U.S. Fish and Wildlife Service (USFWS), 14–16, 33nn2–3
U.S. Forest Service (USFS), 14–17, 18, 89
U.S. v. Belmont (1937), 86
U.S. v. Classic (1941), 155
U.S. v. Curtiss-Wright Export Corporation (1936), 86

U.S. v. Darby Lumber (1941), 178
U.S. v. Dege (1960), 168
U.S. v. Eichman (1990), 63
U.S. v. Klein (1872), 66
U.S. v. Lopez (1995), 144
U.S. v. Morrison (2000), 58, 144
U.S. v. National Treasury Employees Union (1995), 112
U.S. v. Nixon (1974), 87

veto, legislative, 63–64, 165
veto, presidential, 3, 39, 46, 203
Violence Against Women Act, 58, 144, 198
Voting Rights Act (1965), 34n9, 155, 192

Wald, Judge Patricia, 57, 70n4
Walker, James L., 62
Wallace, Lawrence, 81
Warren, Chief Justice Earl, 23, 32, 64, 65, 80
Washington, George, 82, 164
Washington v. Glucksberg (1997), 160
Watkins v. U.S. (1957), 170–71, 185–86

Webster v. Reproductive Health Services (1989), 158
Wesberry v. Sanders (1964), 23
West Coast Hotel v. Parrish (1937), 80
Western Europe, 19, 21, 25–26, 32, 34n6, 36, 203–4, 205
Westfall v. Irwin (1988), 116
White, Justice Byron, 158, 181–84
White, Chief Justice Edward D., 154
Wildafsky, Aaron, 123
Wilson, James Q., 98
Wilson, Woodrow, 75
Winthrop, John, 141–42
Wise, Charles R., 100
women's movement, 27, 167–68
Wright, Judge Skelly, 94
Wyatt v. Stickney (M.D. Ala. 1972), 99–100, 101

Youngstown Sheet and Tube Co. v. Sawyer (1952), 72, 75, 87

Zilly, Thomas, 15
zoning laws, 9, 26, 143